France
— AND THE —
AMERICAN CIVIL WAR

CIVIL WAR AMERICA

Peter S. Carmichael, Caroline E. Janney,
and Aaron Sheehan-Dean, editors

This landmark series interprets broadly the history and culture
of the Civil War era through the long nineteenth century and
beyond. Drawing on diverse approaches and methods, the
series publishes historical works that explore all aspects of
the war, biographies of leading commanders, and tactical and
campaign studies, along with select editions of primary sources.
Together, these books shed new light on an era that remains
central to our understanding of American and world history.

France

AND THE

AMERICAN CIVIL WAR

A DIPLOMATIC HISTORY

STÈVE SAINLAUDE

Translated by Jessica Edwards * *Foreword by Don H. Doyle*

THE UNIVERSITY OF NORTH CAROLINA PRESS *Chapel Hill*

Publication of this book was supported in part by a generous
gift from Anne Faircloth and Fred Bejeu-DuFour.

Translation of this book was supported by a grant from the Anonymous Trust.

Designed by Jamison Cockerham
Set in Arno, Dear Sarah, Brothers, Cutright, and Scala Sans
by Tseng Information Systems, Inc.

Manufactured in the United States of America

The University of North Carolina Press has been a member
of the Green Press Initiative since 2003.

Cover illustration: Édouard Manet, *The Battle of the USS "Kearsarge" and
the USS "Alabama,"* 1864, courtesy of the Philadelphia Museum of Art,
John G. Johnson Collection, Cat. 1027. (Also appears on pages i, iii, xvi–xvii.)

LIBRARY OF CONGRESS CATALOGING-IN-PUBLICATION DATA
Names: Sainlaude, Stève, author. | Edwards, Jessica, translator. | Doyle, Don Harrison,
1946–, writer of introduction. | Sainlaude, Stève. Gouvernement impérial et la guerre de
sécession (1861–1865) English. | Sainlaude, Stève. France et la Confédération sudiste,
1861–1865. English.
Title: France and the American Civil War : a diplomatic history / Stève Sainlaude ;
translated by Jessica Edwards ; foreword by Don H. Doyle.
Other titles: Civil War America (Series)
Description: First edition. | Chapel Hill : The University of North Carolina Press, [2019] |
Series: Civil War America | Includes bibliographical references and index.
Identifiers: LCCN 2018040232| ISBN 9781469649948 (cloth : alk. paper) |
ISBN 9781469649955 (ebook)
Subjects: LCSH: France — Foreign relations — United States — History — 19th
century. | France — Foreign relations — Confederate States of America. | United
States — Foreign relations — France — History — 19th century. | Confederate States of
America — Foreign relations — France. | United States — Foreign relations — 1861–1865. |
France — Foreign relations — 1852–1870.
Classification: LCC DC59.8.U6 S25513 2019 | DDC 973.7/20944 — dc23
LC record available at https://lccn.loc.gov/2018040232

A variation of this work originally appeared in French in two books by Stève
Sainlaude, *Le gouvernement impérial et la guerre de Sécession (1861–1865)* and
La France et la Confédération sudiste (1861–1865) © Editions l'Harmattan.
Both books were awarded the Prix Napoléon III prize in 2013.

To my parents

who never forgot what the United States did for France

that morning in June 1944

How great and holy is the mission, and how worthy of inspiring man's ambition, that consists in mitigating evil passions, in healing wounds, in calming the sufferings of humanity, in uniting the citizens of one country in a common cause, and in hastening a project which civilization must sooner or later accomplish.

LOUIS NAPOLÉON BONAPARTE,
Extinction of Pauperism, 1844

Contents

Illustrations

Foreword

America's Civil War was much more than a military conflict between the North and South. From the outset the American Question, as foreign powers called it, involved multiple European empires and the young nations of Latin America in matters of diplomacy, commerce, and geopolitical strategy. It soon became apparent to foreign observers that the insurrection of Southern slaveholders was not going to be easily put down and would become a protracted conflict. Though they remained officially neutral, most of the European powers were betting on the South to win, not by military prowess so much as sheer determination to outlast the North.

The aristocratic European governing classes despised America's brand of democracy and were delighted to see the so-called Great Republic tearing itself apart, and they instantly recognized the Civil War as an unexpected opportunity for European empires to reclaim lost American colonies or otherwise project their power in the New World. From its stronghold in Cuba, Spain swept into its former colony the Dominican Republic even before the attack on Fort Sumter. Later, Spain's navy provoked wars with Peru and Chile, part of a strategy to reassert Spanish power in South America. Britain nearly went to war with the United States in December 1861 after a U.S. Navy ship apprehended a British mail packet, the RMS *Trent*, which was carrying two Confederate envoys to Europe. While war fever reached its peak, Britain took the opportunity to send 10,000 troops to Canada and fortify its navy in the Caribbean.

In October 1861, Spain, Britain, and France sent delegates to London to create the Tripartite Alliance, a military pact whose mission was to invade and occupy Mexico, supposedly to recover debts. The Mexican republic was recovering from its own civil war, the Guerra de Reforma (1857–60), and was forced to suspend interest payments to creditors for two years. Napoléon III, the mercurial emperor of France, had more in mind than recovering debts. He saw in Mexico the key to his Grand Design, which would have France leading the "Latin race" in the New World and Europe, countering the influence of Anglo-Saxons in both spheres. The Latin temperament, according to French imperial thought on this matter, was wholly unsuited to republicanism and could only be governed by a monarch sustained by the moral authority of the Catholic Church.

Mexico had been through some fifty changes of government since breaking with Spain in 1821 and had endured a long civil war in which the Conservative Party (also known as the Church Party) rebelled against the Liberal Party and its program of reform that vastly reduced the power of the church. After the conservatives lost, they sought help from Europe, which led to Napoléon III's fateful decision to install the Austrian Habsburg Archduke Maximilian as monarch of the Mexican Empire. Napoléon would never have considered such a venture were the United States not consumed by civil war. The United States feared that to oppose French intervention in Mexico might throw Napoléon III into the arms of the Confederacy.

In many respects, Napoléon's Grand Design depended on the success of the Confederacy. John Slidell, the Confederate envoy in Paris, invited the French emperor to make war against their "common enemy," the United States. Having realized that antislavery sentiment in Britain spoiled chances of an alliance, the Confederacy shifted its attention to France in 1863. Its envoys and propagandists in Europe flattered the French with the idea that the South, with its Louisiana Creole, South Carolina Huguenot, and Anglo-Norman heritage shared a natural Latin antipathy toward the fanatical Puritan zealots to their North. To sweeten the deal, the Confederacy authorized Slidell to offer a lucrative "cotton bribe" exclusively to France, if it would break the Union blockade and ally with the South against the United States.

Why the French did not make common cause with the Confederacy is the central question Stève Sainlaude analyzes in this remarkable book. Stève Sainlaude is the author of two important scholarly works that came out of his doctoral studies at the Sorbonne in Paris, where he now teaches. The first, *Le gouvernement impérial et la guerre de Sécession (1861–1865): L'action diplomatique* (2011), is an overview of French policy during America's Civil War. The second, *La France et la Confédération sudiste: La question de la reconnaissance diplomatique pendant la guerre de Sécession* (2011), focuses narrowly on French policy involving the Confederacy. Both books won the prestigious Prix Napoléon III in 2013.

In his review for the *American Historical Review* (February 2014), David Wetzel, professor of European history at the University of California, Berkeley, wrote, "These two books are, to come to the point, blockbusters — path-breaking, fascinating analyses of French policy during the time of the American Civil War.... Each overflows with important revisionist theses. The mastery of many of the materials treated, the boldness of statement, the freshness and directness of style, and the subtle undertone of much of the argument — all these are the hallmarks of Stève Sainlaude's scholarship."

Other Anglophone scholars, including Warren Spencer, Lynn Case, and Alfred and Kathryn Hanna, have dealt expertly with French diplomacy during the Civil War era, but none have revealed so effectively as Stève Sainlaude just how French foreign policy was made. He moves beyond the diplomatic correspondence between the Quai d'Orsay (the French Ministry of Foreign Affairs) and the French embassy in Washington to pay close attention to French consular dispatches. Most notable among the French consuls was Alfred Paul, whose post in Richmond provided a unique perspective on the war and lent authority to his warnings against taking sides with the Confederacy. Sainlaude also reveals important policy differences between the impulsive Napoléon III and his successive foreign ministers, Edouard Thouvenel and Edouard Drouyn de Lhuys. Their savvy understanding of French global strategy and their ability to rein in the emperor, in Sainlaude's telling, explain why the Confederacy's "Latin strategy" failed.

There were early signs that Britain might recognize the Confederacy and bring an end to the war. But Confederate diplomats soon came to realize that the British government faced a voting public steeped in antislavery sentiment and increasingly unsympathetic to the South's aristocratic affinities, such that Confederate hopes for British intervention dimmed by 1863 when the United Kingdom recalled its envoy, James Mason. France, the high command in Richmond realized, was the Confederacy's best hope. France's ambitions to revive Bonapartism and resume its role as the leading power on the European Continent, its competition with Britain, and its self-appointed mission to regenerate the "Latin race" in the Americas all augured well for the Confederacy. So too did Napoléon III's "Grand Design" to establish a model monarchy in Mexico, for its success seemed to require a weakened United States hemmed in by an independent Confederacy that would serve as a buffer between the

United States and Mexico. Why the Confederate mission in Paris failed, and why, therefore, the South's ambition to join the world of nations ended in defeat, is told with compelling savoir-faire in this book.

Readers will find in this book a penetrating view of America's Civil War through the foreign eye of French diplomats at the time but also through the refreshing perspective of a historian writing from outside the nation-bound debates that preoccupy most American historians of "our Civil War." Among the more important revelations Sainlaude offers readers is that, despite decided sympathy in the court of Napoléon III for the Confederate cause and the apparent affinity between its pursuit of independence and France's need for a buffer state between the United States and the Mexican Empire, French diplomats, familiar with the lengthy history of Southern ambition in Latin America, were gravely concerned with the dangers of an independent South and understood that its ambitions would be contained within an intact Union controlled by antislavery Republicans. We also learn more about the failings of "King Cotton Diplomacy" in France. The Confederate "cotton bribe" that was intended to induce French intervention to secure the lucrative cotton trade was thwarted by the sober understanding that Northern commerce, especially the import of grains, was even more vital to France's economic health and social stability. Nor do the usual assumptions about popular antislavery sentiment in France appear to play a decisive role in the making of French foreign policy, according to Sainlaude's vigilant investigation of the archival evidence. These and other insights show us that French diplomats and political leaders, far from simply complying with Britain's policy on the American Question, were devising a distinctly French foreign policy based on independent calculations of French national interest and guided by the sagacious advice of Consul Alfred Paul from his uniquely advantageous perch in Richmond.

Stève and I first met in Paris in the summer of 2013. I was putting together an international conference that would involve a dozen historians specializing in various parts of the Atlantic world that had been involved in an interconnected set of crises that had seized the Euro-American Atlantic world during and after the American Civil War. I had heard about Stève's work from one of the conference participants, and we made arrangements to meet when I came to Paris for research that summer. We met near his home south of Paris and, with my wife, Marjorie, took a long evening walk in the Parc de Sceaux. I was in the thick of writing *The Cause of All Nations*, a book about public diplomacy and foreign affairs surrounding the Civil War and had immersed myself in the prolific writings of John Bigelow, the very capable U.S. consul in Paris. Bigelow ran public diplomacy operations in France and backed up William Dayton, a genial politico from New Jersey whom Lincoln had appointed as minister to France. I came away from that evening with Stève having learned far more than I had from numerous other published accounts of French thinking about America's civil war. A few days later, Marjorie and I joined Stève and his wife, Mylane, for a Civil War tour through the streets of Paris. We visited the site where John Slidell lived, the apartment building where William Dayton died of a stroke in the arms of a femme fatale; rue Lincoln, a small street off the Champs Elysées, and from there on to a bistro for another evening of conversation on France, America, and the Civil War that spanned the Atlantic Ocean.

Stève's parents, he told us, had named him after Steve McQueen, the Hollywood movie star. But there was more to this story, we learned. His parents had been teenagers living in Paris and had never forgotten that day in August 1944 when American GIs liberated the city after four years of Nazi occupation. He came by his interest in *la question américaine* naturally, it appeared.

Stève took part in the conference I organized at the University of South Carolina in 2014, and the volume that came out of the conference, *American Civil Wars: The United States, Latin America, Europe, and the Crisis of the 1860s*, was published by the University of North Carolina Press in 2017. His essay gave American and other Anglophone readers their first glimpse of Stève Sainlaude's research. Shortly before the conference took place, David Wetzel's enthusiastic review appeared in the *American Historical Review*, and it gave me the idea that something more might be done to make Stève's important achievement more widely known to American readers.

All of this reminded me of John Bigelow and his favorite French intellectual, Edouard Laboulaye, a historian at the Collège de France who was the leading expert on American history and constitutional law in the 1860s. Laboulaye greatly admired America's experiment in republican self-rule, and Bigelow encouraged him to explain to the French all that was at stake for them in the distant contest in America. Bigelow also saw to it that Laboulaye's best work on the subject was translated and made available to the English-speaking world in America and Britain. Stève and I joked that if I could play Bigelow to his Laboulaye, perhaps his work might also find the wider audience it deserved. Thanks to Mark Simpson-Vos and the University of North Carolina Press, this wish has now been realized. American readers of this book will discover extraordinary insights of a kind only the foreign eye can reveal.

Don H. Doyle

France
— AND THE —
AMERICAN CIVIL WAR

INTRODUCTION

At the same time that the American Civil War, dubbed the "War of Secession" by the French, was tearing the Union apart, French diplomacy also had to deal with European troubles. As events in Italy, Poland, and Denmark caused turbulence across the Continent, the fratricidal drama unfolding in the New World captivated not only Napoléon III and his government but also many other European observers. They stayed abreast of events with information from multiple sources, transmitted to Western capitals through several channels of communication.[1] The Parisian elite, engrossed by the tragedy, scrutinized the fits and starts of this heroic duel and analyzed it in the light of their own worldview.

One reason for France's interest in the American conflict lay in the historic ties that bound the two nations. Eighty years earlier, France had contributed to the American settlers' struggle for independence. Now the Union they had helped form risked being swept away. French spectators were dismayed to see such a paroxysm of violence bloodying the great nation France had helped at its birth.

Next, those interested in the conflict understood that the weakening of the United States was likely to have a profound impact on the geopolitical balance. France held a powerful position on the world stage, second only to the United Kingdom. From the Tuileries Palace France's emperor, Napoléon III, saw the American war as an opportunity to further his designs on the New

World. The breakup of the Union could offer France a chance to regain international influence in the world. For the conflict coincided with a turning point in the French regime in which distant expeditions fueled Napoléon's expanding imperial ambitions. His global plan stretched from a strong purchase on the islands of the Pacific and Indian Oceans to the edges of Asia and Africa. Other French observers worried about the risks that such a crisis could pose to the European economies, an apprehension heightened by the growing interdependence of trade relations within the Western world. Finally, many Europeans saw the war as a test for democracy and the values of freedom of which the imperial regime had deprived France.

After the First French Empire collapsed in 1814 and was dismantled by a dozen allied European powers, Napoléon I's reign ended the following year with an irrevocable defeat. In 1852, against all odds, France revived the empire. The new emperor, Napoléon III, took advantage of his election four years earlier to the French presidency to organize a coup d'état and style himself emperor. Despite his prestigious ancestry—he was the son of Louis Bonaparte (brother of Napoléon I) and Hortense de Beauharnais, daughter of Josephine, wife of the founder of the dynasty—the emperor was long the victim of a "black legend," which Victor Hugo had helped cultivate.[2] It was not difficult to find arguments to discredit Napoléon III. His seizure of power by force, the dictatorial police regime he imposed during much of his reign, and the military disaster that triggered his downfall nearly twenty years later tarnished his reputation. Both the statesman and his policies have probably been underestimated. In spite of his mistakes—particularly in conducting foreign policy—the emperor certainly was not lacking in intelligence, and his ideas were not without interest; indeed, his visionary mind put him ahead of his time. Bonapartism had until then been simply an authoritarian mode of government combining hereditary power and popular consent, but he turned it into a body of doctrine. He helped the French people domesticate the universal suffrage newly granted to men in 1848. In response to the economic upheavals of the Industrial Revolution, he sought to modernize his country, develop the territory, and facilitate capital investment, without losing sight of social issues. He raised Paris to the rank of world metropolis, conscious that a nation's influence also depends on its culture and urbanism. All in all, we must recognize that his record was considerable.[3] The country changed more than at any other time. A new France was born with the Second Empire.

Napoléon III felt confined on the domestic stage. Thinking himself born to a unique destiny, he nurtured ambitions for an active foreign policy. Moreover, involvement in international affairs was a necessity for him, since national glory was the hallmark and source of his power. He felt obliged by his exceptional lineage to inspire France with awe. Moreover, with external affairs even less subject to parliamentary control than domestic politics, he had a free hand.

Internationally, Napoléon III wanted to break the shackles that had been holding France back since 1815. To restore his country's freedom of action, he aimed to overturn the treaties that had sanctioned his uncle's defeat four decades earlier. He wanted to undo the territorial and political order instituted by the Congress of Vienna, which continued to defend absolutism and suppressed national movements. To this end, he sought to organize the European entente by ensuring the success of conferences. In 1856, the Congress of Paris crowned his efforts to determine the settlement of the Crimean War. Nevertheless the borders of the old continent were not enough for him. With Napoléon III, Bonapartism trained its sights beyond the European and Mediterranean theaters. Unlike Napoléon I, the nephew's ambitions were universal. If the word was not anachronistic, it could be said that this polyglot was the first to have perceived the stakes of globalization.[4] He did not fear it; on the contrary, he intended to use it to his advantage.

In this new world order to which he aspired, the United States figured prominently in his concerns but low in his affections. Napoléon III forgot the special ties binding America to France, its ally during the American Revolution. On the domestic level, he saw only two asymmetrical political constructs; certainly, the American republic and the imperial regime were at variance in every respect. "Democratic Caesarism" emerged from a coup and was backed by plebiscites, while the heart of American democracy beat from Washington in time to the electoral rhythm. Napoléon believed in a providential man chosen by destiny, while the United States preferred a leader designated by the ballot box. He saw the assemblies as not a counterweight but an instrument of government, while the occupant of the White House had to deal with the two chambers of Congress. The emperor alone could propose legislation, while in the United States this was the prerogative of Congress. He established a direct link with the people, but on the other side of the Atlantic, universal suffrage passed through the filter of the Electoral College. Napoléon's power was centralized, whereas presidential power found its limits in federalism.

If Napoléon III looked down on the political system of the United States, he was even more critical of its foreign policy. He was not the only one. Since 1848, the U.S. image had deteriorated considerably in the eyes of his contemporaries. The integration of Texas into the Union and the war against Mexico more particularly had altered their judgment of the former ally. The brutality of "Polk's War" had not escaped them. They felt it had undermined the essential principles of state sovereignty and law. Many French observers now perceived the United States as a dangerous nation that had taken advantage of its neighbor's weakness. The moderation of American democracy once praised by Alexis de Tocqueville seemed remote. From then on, many thought, U.S. behavior had become impetuous, its language extreme, and force its only means of action.

The place the United States held on the American continent worried the emperor greatly. This concern was not new. François Guizot, King Louis-Philippe's foreign minister from 1840 to 1848, already feared the ascendancy of the United States in his day and had spearheaded France's new American policy.[5] Napoléon III made this policy his own and, like Guizot, took a critical view of the Union's development. In 1848, the United States suddenly acceded to the rank of continental power. Its dramatic rise overturned all existing geopolitical representations. Napoléon integrated this new state of affairs into his overall reflection.

He was not content, however, just to think about the new situation created by the Mexican defeat. He aspired to alter the new order and apply the principle of balance of powers to the whole American continent. Napoléon III believed that the war against Mexico foreshadowed another conflict. He was aware that the new borders of the United States were not natural but delimited by men and capable of varying according to the strength of U.S. "imperialist" ambition. Mexico's impotence was likely to tempt its neighbor's seemingly inexhaustible appetite. Mexican apathy was a call for expansion. In the knowledge that journalist John O'Sullivan's famous pronouncement, "It is our manifest destiny to overspread the continent allotted by Providence," had set no limit on expansionist designs, the emperor had every right to believe that the 1848 Treaty of Guadalupe Hidalgo was only a pause in the progressive takeover of the hemisphere. Far from sanctioning a completed conquest, the treaty enshrined the threat of future expansion over the rest of the Americas. While France, like England, endeavored to curb Russian appetites in Europe and Asia, it seemed crucial to the emperor to contain the U.S. energy in the New World.

The emperor felt it all the more pressing to stem U.S. expansion because he believed himself endowed with a mission in America. He wanted to protect monarchical and imperial regimes. Besides fearing the Americans' takeover of new territories, Napoléon III judged that their territorial ambitions reflected their determination to destroy the institutions of monarchy. He was anxious that the United States, as it seized new lands, would export its republican model and end up placing the entire continent under a single political system.

There was also a cultural issue at stake in Latin America: Napoléon III wanted to preserve Catholicism and the Latin world. Again, he saw a contrast between two spheres, a civilizational clash between two "races" in the sense of cultural families. The "Latin race" must fear being submerged by the Anglo-Saxons. The emperor advocated using the community of Latin and Catholic culture to prevent the whole American continent from succumbing to the values, knowledge, and thought of Washington.

The emperor objected to the Monroe Doctrine for this reason. He did not see on what grounds the New World should be made into a sanctuary by a federal decision. He disputed the right of the United States to prohibit Europeans from interfering in the affairs of the continent. France had concluded all kinds of treaties with nations across the Atlantic and, consequently, Napoléon III felt his country had the right to maintain and strengthen these ties while seeking to establish relations with other American partners.

It would have been preferable had Napoléon III confined his belief in his lucky star to matters of national development. Whereas his uncle — who was at the *end* of his reign at the age the nephew began his own — stood out for his extraordinary skill in all domains, his self-proclaimed successor had not inherited such genius. That explains why the results of his foreign policy were very mixed. His diplomatic abilities were limited. First, he lacked analytical depth, so his audacious ideas were often confused and impracticable. This former Carbonaro, twice imprisoned for his coup attempts, often let his fanciful ideas — if not daydreams — shape his policy. Far from gathering concrete facts to inform his strategy, the self-taught politician was often guided more by his imagination than a firm grasp of political reality.[6] Second, he procrastinated constantly and could not sustain a course of action. While he displayed a certain taste for risk in his decisions, he was also extremely indecisive in their execution.[7] Only through constant hesitations did he manage to contain his overactive imagination. His idealism was limited by his uncertainty. Napoléon III's frequent changes of mind made it tricky to get a clear idea of his final intentions.

Third, his policies lacked not only consistency but also coherence. The emperor wanted to return France to its former rank and see it play the role of civilizing power. To restore his country's freedom of action, the emperor sought to overturn the treaty of 1815, but the United Kingdom was very hostile to the idea. Keen as he was to cultivate a special relationship with the British, he had to reckon with his neighbor's reluctance. Similarly, as a cosmopolitan who had spent much time outside his country, he imagined remodeling the old continent by giving "the great nationalities" their due. However, since such nation-states would threaten his empire, he wanted to unify them only partially. He defended the freedom of peoples but paradoxically hoped to annex Belgium. He dreamed of a European confederation that would counterbalance the two giants in the making, Russia and the United States. To this end, he aspired to build a peaceful Europe that would settle disputes at conferences. This desire for peace within Europe did not mean he balked at military action or pushing back borders to secure French interests. He championed an altruistic foreign policy but readily accepted territorial compensation in payment for his interventions. His foreign policy thus resembled a perpetual balancing act.

Fortunately, to formulate his policy, the emperor could rely on men of experience based in a brand-new diplomatic headquarters. In 1853, after eight years of construction work, the Ministry of Foreign Affairs moved into its new home on the south bank of the Seine, on the Quai d'Orsay, property ceded by the Hôtel de Lassay, the seat of the legislature. A showcase of the art of the Second Empire, the prestigious building afforded the French government and its representatives new diplomatic standing. The choice of the Quai d'Orsay was more than just a change of address; it was the first time a ministry had been set up in purpose-built premises.[8] The building symbolized the transition from "external relations" to a genuine foreign policy that could now be conducted with the proper tools in the proper setting.

Since January 1860, the Quai d'Orsay (as the French still refer to the Ministry of Foreign Affairs) had been headed by Edouard Thouvenel, a gifted forty-two-year-old with vast experience and tireless energy. This former political director's legal knowledge, skill at argumentation, and subtle reasoning were universally acknowledged. In 1854 the British secretary of state George Villiers, fourth Earl of Clarendon, referred to him as the "ablest writer in European diplomacy."[9] The doors of the Quai d'Orsay were opened to him by Italian affairs; and it would be Italian affairs that led to his removal from the ministry in October 1862.[10] Napoléon III, on the advice of his half-brother Charles de Morny and the empress, sought a successor for Thouvenel capable of reconciling the regime with French Catholics. They were displeased with the decline of the Papal States following Italy's 1859 War of Independence, in which France had taken part. To the great satisfaction of the clerics and conservatives, Napoléon chose Edouard Drouyn de Lhuys as the new head of foreign affairs.[11] Although he lacked Thouvenel's naturally keen mind, Drouyn de Lhuys, fifty-seven, was a skillful and experienced minister. The embodiment of the ideal, classic diplomat, Drouyn de Lhuys found in diplomacy the "unity of his life."[12] This veteran agent, who had climbed through the ranks from embassy to embassy, obtained his fourth and final appointment as foreign minister.[13] He was a talented writer raised on the classics, and his dispatches were models of precision and elegance.

Both men had an ambiguous relationship with the emperor. Though obviously accepting to serve him, they often regarded him with irreverence. For Thouvenel, deciphering Napoléon III's goals amounted to consulting an oracle. Though a brilliant diplomat, he was often baffled by what he saw as the emperor's inscrutable thinking.[14] Drouyn de Lhuys, who knew Napoléon well and was on excellent terms with his wife, was no more impressed by the emperor than his predecessor. He once scathingly commented that "the Emperor has immense desires and limited abilities. He wants to do extraordinary things but is only capable of extravagances."[15] Napoléon's diplomatic conduct often offended these men of experience. The former conspirator conducted his foreign policy through two different channels. Alongside the official line he decided upon with the Foreign Ministry, he took more secretive action through all sorts of unofficial emissaries.

American affairs came under one of four political subdepartments, "America and Indochina," and one of the three trade subdepartments, the "South and America." The political department of the North—which included Europe, not America—was considered the most important. At the time, France regarded the United States as a secondary power. Diplomats often scoffed at U.S. attempts to meddle in international affairs and at the blundering of U.S. civil servants, unfamiliar with the codes of the old continent. The ranks of the diplomatic missions reflected this hierarchy. French affairs in Washington were conducted by not an embassy but a legation headed by a minister plenipotentiary.[16] No one was in a hurry to assume this post. It was seen as unglamorous, far from the theater where history was written, and of interest only to specialists.[17] It did not attract young diplomats, who preferred junior positions in Europe. For them, the Old World offered the only field of action where their merits could be recognized and rewarded.

After being accredited, the minister plenipotentiary represented his government in negotiations with the local government and protected his country's nationals and interests. To pass on instructions and keep his government informed, he had the support of eight consulates. New York was a consulate general, that is, a post headed by a high-ranking diplomat and generally located in the country's second city in terms of economic importance or population. The other consulates were in Boston, Philadelphia, Richmond, Charleston, New Orleans, San Francisco, and Los Angeles (honorary consulate). Added to these were nine vice-consulates (such as Chicago) and sixteen consular agencies (such as Galveston), which were run by honorary consuls, who were not professional diplomats and continued to earn their living in other occupations.

The consuls began their mission after receiving their exequatur from the U.S. government, a procedure comparable to the signing of an ambassador's letter of credence.[18] They were covered by a diplomatic immunity clarified by the Franco-American Consular Convention of 1853. Thus the consul was immune, his staff was exempt from military service, and its correspondences, carried by the "diplomatic pouch," could not be seized. Consuls performed the functions of mayor and notary for expatriates. They were also responsible for protecting and assisting their country's nationals, in compliance with the laws of the host state. It might therefore fall to them to organize the evacuation of their fellow French nationals. This was made easier by the presence of eleven French warships sailing along the American coast beginning in summer 1861. But it was the business and political information these agents collected for their government, over the legation, or the nationals concerning developments in the country's situation that were of prime importance. The foreign minister repeatedly reminded the diplomats and consuls to keep him fully informed of all matters relating to the crisis in the United States.[19] Indeed, there was a desperate lack of information when consulates were deprived of incumbents or when dispatches could not be sent.[20] So because, of the secession, the consuls in the South were isolated from their hierarchy.

In the context of U.S. events, the highly codified drafting of dispatches occupied much of the agents' time. Given the distance, their replies were slow to reach the Foreign Ministry. Every two weeks French or English warships carried consular dispatches from New York. The correspondence of the consulates located in the Confederate states were gathered in Richmond and shipped from Norfolk to New York, which collected correspondence from consulates in the other states. We must constantly bear in mind that, not counting the time required to unload and dispatch the mail to its destination, the round trip between the two continents ordinarily took up to a month. It was not until after the Civil War, in July 1866, that the transatlantic cable would link the United Kingdom to the United States. The long delivery time for dispatches was not conducive to responsiveness, as one piece of news sometimes canceled out another. For the Quai d'Orsay, however, this time lag was less a handicap than an advantage, as there was no need to make immediate decisions. It allowed time to reflect and establish a comprehensive view. Other matters could be dealt with while waiting for the return post.

At the outbreak of war, the French government's first concern was to find legal responses to various situations, beginning with the status to grant the two governments and the combatants. Next, without neglecting the navigation rules to apply to neutral vessels, it had to reflect on how the belligerents' ships were to be received in French ports and on the conditions under which the Federal government's blockade of Southern ports was put into effect. As the hostilities wore on, Napoléon III determined to get involved in the conflict and attempted to bring Great Britain in with him. He offered his mediation to try and bring the enemies to some sort of agreement and leaned more and more overtly toward the South, whose government he wanted to recognize.

This diplomatic recognition, which the insurgents' supporters sought actively to obtain, was indeed the central question for France's American policy. Recognition would give the Confederacy the rights of a sovereign state among the family of nations, and its agents an accreditation abroad. Apart from their mission to defend their nationals, it would give them the power to negotiate treaties, sign defense agreements, and contract loans. However, while the South's "heroic struggle" gained the sympathies of many in France despite its practice of slavery, acknowledging Confederate independence posed a number of problems for diplomats and consuls. They had to consider the intrinsic nature of the new republic, its viability, its compatibility with the French agenda in Mexico, its trade arrangements, the disappearance of the Union, and French relations with Washington. Granting legitimacy to a government hostile to the one thus far considered legal, and with which France had no dispute, would look like intervention—if not interference—in American affairs. Such recognition could therefore turn the Civil War into a tripartite international conflict involving France, Mexico, and the divided Union.

Whereas Anglo-American relations during the Civil War have been well documented, up until now there were few books works dealing specifically with Franco-American relations in the same period. The only studies that existed were over forty years old. They provided an overview of the subject (Blumenthal), were outdated (Donaldson), constituted the chapter of a book (Pinkney), or were very focused (Carroll). It is true that the publication of a major study in 1970 discouraged many researchers from continuing their investigations. *The United States and France: Civil War Diplomacy*, by Lynn Marshall Case and Warren F. Spencer, quickly established itself as a standard reference work on the subject. Extremely impressive in scope, the analysis of these historians draws on many sources collected in both the United States and Europe. All in all, it is a remarkable book whose reputation is well deserved. However, it is important to note the point of view of Case and Spencer. They do not look to explain the foreign policy of the imperial government toward

America at war; rather they explore American diplomacy toward France during the conflict. Understandably therefore, Case and Spencer do not go into the reasons why Napoléon III did not recognize the South.

France and the American Civil War results from the rewriting of two works published in French in 2011, *Le gouvernement impérial et la guerre de Sécession* and *La France et la Confédération sudiste*, which were based on a doctoral dissertation that took nine years to research and produce. The subject was French foreign policy toward the United States from 1839 to 1867.[21] Although the Civil War occupies less than 15 percent of the study period, it accounts for half the volume of the dissertation, which shows the abundance of French diplomatic sources. To address this period, although the correspondence of the Washington legation had already been studied by historians such as those mentioned above, it seemed wise to begin again from these primary sources to make sure they had not suffered any unintentional distortion.

This book's originality lies in its use of the previously unexplored correspondence of the French consuls. Their political dispatches are gathered into fifteen volumes of 600 to 700 pages on average, added to which are ten volumes of trade correspondence. As review of the archival material challenged older interpretations, it was essential, in addition to the dispatches from the agents in the United States, to examine and compare the political correspondence of diplomats posted in the United Kingdom and Mexico. The archives collected under "Mémoires et Documents," "Affaires Diverses et Politiques," "Livres Jaunes," and diplomatic collections were a valuable complement to the core research, while the "Papiers du Personnel" (or staff papers) provided useful details on the careers of the diplomats and consuls concerned. This biographical information is recorded in the notes.

In the interest of clarity, as much as to conduct an original historical inquiry, the book favors an analytical approach over chronology. Given this entirely argument-based structure, I hope that readers will accept the primacy given to ideas over the order of events in time and will not be overly troubled by the backtracking that inevitably occurs in each chapter. I examine the motivations for imperial France's policy toward the United States in great detail. At the same time, readers will glimpse how agents selected from the information they collected. They will also perceive how the minister defined the general framework of his policy using the information and comments with which he was provided. Note, however, that the perceptions of these players and the view that historians today have of this deadly conflict do not always coincide — proof, perhaps, of the discrepancy between diplomatic truth and historical truth.

Part One

THE FRENCH POSITION

Edouard Thouvenel, 1854. Courtesy of the Pera Müzesi.

» 1 «

THE IMPLEMENTATION
OF NEUTRALITY

Though an internal conflict, the American crisis took on an international dimension very early. Alerted by the first signs of discord, European governments closely monitored the violent antagonism that erupted in the wake of Lincoln's election. They had in mind the crises that had shaken the Union in the previous decade and were not surprised by the tensions that were arising over the slavery issue. They deliberated over which position to adopt. From the Quai d'Orsay, until the spring of 1861, Foreign Minister Edouard Thouvenel observed the splintering of the American federation with caution. He warned his agents not to make any move that could be interpreted as favoring either camp.[1] As he wrote to Henri Mercier, his minister in Washington, he hoped that reason would triumph. He still believed that the dispute would result in a new compromise, which France might help to obtain by "supporting the reestablishment of an understanding."[2] However, when news of the fall of Fort Sumter reached Paris on April 27, followed by the blockade of the rebel states' ports, France was abruptly forced to adopt a position. The imperial government was well aware that France could be drawn into the conflict: French ships cruised U.S. territorial waters, and it was possible that belligerent ships would put in at French ports.

The burgeoning civil war raised several fundamental questions for the French government. Should it consider France a nonbelligerent, in other words simply pledge not to intervene militarily while reserving the option of providing weapons to the belligerents? Or should it go further and maintain strict neutrality, which would entail not only a commitment to abstention — providing no military support to the belligerents — but also a duty of impartiality, giving both belligerents the same treatment? Was it possible to treat both parties equally when the conflict was not between two states but between a legal government and an insurgency? How should the French government treat the diplomatic agents sent by the rebels? How should it condition belligerent vessels' use of French ports and regulate trade between Europe and America? It was urgent to define a legal framework because both the blockade decreed by the North and any naval operations in which the two enemies might clash were liable to affect the U.S. market.

NEUTRALITY AND THE RIGHT OF BELLIGERENCY

What stance should France have taken? Opinions wavered. On the one hand, France had not forgotten that in 1778 the thirteen colonies in revolt against George III's government had received the backing of the Bourbon monarchy. Had that revolution itself not been a form of secession?[3] On the other hand, this precedent could also be used to promote favoring the Union because France's engagement had contributed to the birth of the United States, whose breakup the French therefore could not view with indifference. This historic bond did not mean Paris shared the Federal government's view that no state had the right to leave the federation. The French did not see why a state should be prevented from breaking with a union that it had joined voluntarily. This did not exempt the rebels from criticism, however. Thouvenel was shocked that they would contest the results of a democratic election. How could legitimacy be granted to a power hostile to the government that had until then been considered legal? As we can see, the diplomatic choice was anything but easy.

On May 13, 1861, in response to the state of war, the British cabinet published a proclamation of neutrality accompanied by recognition of Southern belligerency.[4] In France, the Foreign Ministry mandated a committee of experts to determine how to respond to the crisis. The committee submitted its conclusions in early May, and the ensuing memorandum defined French policy toward the United and Confederate States of America throughout the war.[5]

On May 11, 1861, Thouvenel wrote to his minister in Washington to inform him of the panel's conclusions. He stressed first that the empire was not indifferent to the rebellion within the Union.[6] Although Napoléon III's government had hoped that the crisis could be resolved peacefully, it could no longer deny that civil war was inevitable. Thouvenel thus advocated a change in diplomatic position. Instead of taking a stance on the central problem, the French sought to anticipate the conflict's damage to French interests in the United States. As would be the case in any war, his first concern was how best to safeguard the interests of French nationals — there were about 110,000 in the United States — and to define the rules they must respect with regard to the conflict, in both France and the divided Union.[7] He considered that France must maintain a strict neutrality. In his dispatch, Thouvenel crossed out the word "government" first used to refer to the new Confederate power and replaced it with "separate authority," a term less likely to offend the Federal government.[8]

Although the proclamation of neutrality had been ready for almost a month, it was not made public until June 10, 1861.[9] It employed the same cautious language to describe the Southern authority, stating that Napoléon III had "resolved to maintain a strict neutrality in the current struggle between the government of the Union and the states which claim to form a separate confederation." From then on, any military engagement on the part of French nationals could lead to loss of their French nationality. Article 21 of the Napoleonic Code explicitly recalled this injunction.

One may wonder why a whole month went by between the publication of the British proclamation and the French one, as both were ready at the same time. Richard Lyons, the British minister to Washington, suspected the French government of a ploy, allowing this time to pass so that its British counterpart would endure the wrath of the Lincoln administration alone.[10] Though possible, it is equally conceivable that the imperial cabinet simply wanted to avoid being hasty. The French ministers were aware that their decision would displease the Lincoln administration. Indeed, by keeping an equal distance from both belligerents, France and England immediately set themselves in opposition to the Federal government, which denied that its enemy had any legitimacy to fight. Moreover, France was in a more paradoxical situation than England. Though instrumental in the birth of the United States, France chose *not* to act when it saw the Union splitting apart. The French decision may have been legally sound, but it lacked historical consistency. Most observers would have expected the imperial government to side at once with the guarantors of the Union that France had helped to build.

What especially drew the ire of the Lincoln administration was the pairing of the proclamation of neutrality with recognition of Confederate belligerency. For the Federal government there could be no Southern right to belligerency because there was no official war.[11] Certainly, France's granting of belligerent status gave the claim of neutrality an ambiguous tone. First, such status bestowed important rights on the Confederacy. According to international law, being recognized as belligerents allowed them to contract loans and buy arms in neutral countries. Recognized belligerents could also sail cruisers on the high seas that were authorized to search and seize enemy ships.[12] Second, the proclamation showed that France and England viewed the secession not as a mere rebellion but as a war within the federal country. Like its British counterpart, the French imperial government considered it indisputable that the insurgents controlled parts of the country, were supported by a significant share of the population, and fought with an organized army boasting a modicum of symmetry with the Union forces. Consequently, it saw no difference in the rights to which the two sides were entitled as military combatants.[13]

However, this does not mean that France regarded the opponents in the same way. By obtaining recognition of belligerency, the insurgent party certainly acquired a status, but this was temporary as limited to the duration of the conflict, and partial because it was restricted to the application of the law of war.[14] The legal government remained the one in Washington because the French did not recognize the Confederacy as a state. France acknowledged that the Confederacy existed, but only as a combatant. Furthermore, it was not the Civil War that brought about the recognition of belligerency but the fact that France considered the definition of its relationship with the two enemies essential to protect French interests. Thouvenel wrote to Mercier, his minister in Washington, that the proclamations of neutrality by France and England were made solely to contain the dangers that a maritime dispute between the two parties of the Union could entail for the trade of third parties.[15] The decision, therefore, seems to have been a measure of expediency.

Notwithstanding, granting belligerent status to combatants was no small matter, for recognition of belligerency could pave the way to diplomatic recognition of the Confederacy. In fact, this status gave a moral authority to the Confederacy, which could lead to future diplomatic recognition if military events became favorable to Washington's enemies.[16] However, the Quai d'Orsay stressed that there was no automatic relationship between these measures. To the contrary, both of Napoléon III's foreign ministers made every effort to distinguish between the two.[17] Moreover, the longer the conflict wore on, the clearer it became that the gap between the Confederacy's status on paper and its situation on the ground was widening. While the blockade limited the Southerners' movements, their territory suffered repeated assaults by Union troops and was liable to be invaded at any moment. The Confederate government's survival was dependent on the military situation. While in the early days of hostilities it seemed that the recognition of Confederate belligerency would soon be followed by diplomatic recognition, this became less true the longer the war continued.

If the imperial government thought it could escape the wrath of the Lincoln administration, it was mistaken.[18] Washington considered the position taken by the European powers a direct intervention in U.S. affairs. Through his minister in Paris, William L. Dayton, Secretary of State William Seward expressed his firm disapproval of the Confederate states' recognition as a belligerent power by nations friendly to the United States.[19] Over the following months, Seward regularly encouraged Dayton to attempt to compel the imperial government to backtrack.[20] In Seward's view, the South was driven to resist not by Confederate army victories but by the recognition of the South's belligerent status, which gave the Confederacy hope of one day receiving support from the European powers.[21] Apparently, the Federal government was looking to external causes to explain its difficulties in subduing its opponent.

On March 25, 1862, Dayton met with Napoléon III. When the emperor bemoaned the crisis that the continuation of the war had inflicted on the French economy, Dayton echoed the words of his secretary of state: the only way to stop the war was to revoke the rebels' belligerent status; in his opinion, the insurgency would then immediately collapse.[22] He said the same thing to Thouvenel.[23] Belligerency was to prove a nagging issue and would sour relations between France and the Union government throughout the conflict.

The French government was not overly concerned by these reprimands. First, France was not alone in its choice, which powers such as the Netherlands and Spain had made as well.[24] Second, Paris attributed the Federal government's conduct to domestic political considerations. It considered the message of disapproval to be intended for U.S. public opinion, to counteract any overtures that might be addressed to the South. Finally, the French saw Washington as in no position to criticize. Were the United States not, as Thouvenel stressed, born out of a revolution?[25] As his British counterpart pointed out, at the time of the revolt of the Spanish colonies had not the Americans argued that the existence of civil war entitled the respective parties to the rights of war?[26] In 1836, during the war against Mexico, did they not grant belligerent status to Texas?[27] The French foreign minister criticized Seward for opposing recognition of the South's belligerent status when his own government observed toward the South the customs that govern hostilities between enemy governments. For instance, the North was willing to exchange prisoners. If the Union dealt with the Confederate government in the interests of its soldiers it could not also dispute neutral countries' desire to act in the interests of their nationals. Moreover, what of the proclamation of the blockade on April 19, 1861, which presupposed the application of the law of naval warfare? From that point, third-party countries were simply acknowledging the existing state of war.[28] Four years later, Thouvenel's successor would use the same argument to justify the French decision.[29]

Nevertheless, the U.S. secretary of state's immoderate remarks, while they could be explained by a specific political context, showed the French that Washington could adopt an uncompromising stance toward relations the European powers maintained with the Confederacy.

The proclamation of neutrality was favorably received in the French press. Even *Le Temps*, an organ close to Republican circles and very pro-American, was satisfied.[30] Newspapers closest to the North, however, were divided on the question of belligerent rights. The editor of *Le Temps* was shocked that a government should be subjected to the same treatment as seditionaries.[31] His counterpart at *Le Journal des Débats* argued to the contrary that there would be a breach of neutrality if the South's belligerent rights were not recognized, because Southern privateers would then be considered pirates.[32] Finally, *La Revue des Deux Mondes* took a moral stance. To speak of belligerents' rights without mentioning their responsibilities struck the editor as asymmetrical.[33]

Overall, apart from certain newspapers such as *Le Temps*, the French press mainly concurred with the diplomatic choices of June 1861. While it is no surprise that the most conservative papers shared the views of the imperial government, approval from their liberal counterparts was not a given. The explanation lies in the Federal government's past choices. The editorialists agreed that it was difficult to contest France's granting belligerent rights to the South when, in times past, the United States had extended those very rights to rebels. The Federal government's past position therefore justified the French decision.[34]

DIPLOMATIC MISSION AND NEUTRALITY

Because the Lincoln administration remained the legal government, diplomatic relations between the Union and Napoléon III's government continued as usual. However, there seemed to be a curse on the U.S. legation in Paris. When the representative of the Buchanan administration, John Mason, died suddenly in October 1859, a member of the House of Representatives, Charles James Faulkner, was appointed in January 1860 to succeed him. Later Faulkner felt obliged by his loyalty to the Confederate cause to ask that the United States recall him. The U.S. minister to Belgium, Henry Shelton Sanford, oversaw the legation in Paris—not without difficulty—pending the arrival of Faulkner's replacement.[35] Sanford was perhaps the best diplomat that Washington had in Europe at the time. He knew France well because in 1849 he had been secretary of the U.S. legation in Paris, then chargé d'affaires. He was also covertly the head of the Union's secret services in Europe.[36] He played a decisive role at the start of the conflict by setting up contacts with the imperial government.[37]

The new U.S. minister, William Dayton, arrived in France in May 1861. This former lawyer, a fifty-four-year-old Princeton graduate, had been a Republican candidate for vice president on the unsuccessful Fremont ticket in the 1856 election. He set up his office at 25 rue Circulaire, which has since become 6 rue de Presbourg, a street encircling the Place de l'Etoile. Dayton had plenty of political experience but was a novice in diplomatic matters. He was unfamiliar with Europe and did not speak a word of French. Fortunately, he was ably assisted by the consul general of the legation, John Bigelow, who battled Confederate propaganda through the articles he arranged to have published in opposition newspapers.[38] Bigelow took over as minister plenipotentiary after Dayton's death, on December 1, 1864, under rather remarkable circumstances. He was struck with apoplexy at the Hôtel du Louvre, in the apartment occupied by Lizzie St. John Eckel. There was a risk of scandal as the lady had the reputation of a seductress.[39] To safeguard the deceased's good name, Dayton's secretary moved his body to the premises of the legation.[40]

On the other side of the Atlantic, the imperial government had chosen Henri Mercier to represent France. Mercier was born in Baltimore, where his father ran the French consulate. His career took off in 1851 after Bonaparte's coup.[41] The new ruler offered him the top post in several legations, including Washington, where he replaced the comte de Sartiges in 1860. In contrast to his outstandingly gifted predecessor, Mercier proved a very poor diplomat, further hindered by his appalling English. The emperor's cousin Prince Napoléon met the minister plenipotentiary in 1861 during his stay in the United States and judged him "a bit lightweight."[42] During the Civil War, Mercier met up again in Washington with his British colleague Richard Lyons, whom he had first encountered in Dresden.[43] Unlike Lyons, who would remain in Washington until the end of the Civil War, Mercier's mission ended prematurely in December 1863.[44]

Because France did not recognize the Confederate government, neither power accredited a representative to the other. When the consuls of France and the United Kingdom based in Charleston wished to contact the new president, Jefferson Davis, they were instructed by their governments to choose an intermediary.[45] However, this restriction did not apply to all diplomatic agents; for instance, the consul in Richmond, Alfred Paul, spoke directly with the Southern authorities.[46]

Pierre Rost was the Confederacy's first envoy to France. He was a Frenchman, educated at the Ecole Polytechnique, who had moved to Louisiana to practice law after the Bourbon restoration in 1815. Chosen in 1861 by Jefferson Davis to enter into contact with Napoléon III's government, he was given only the title of "Emissary." In 1862, John Slidell, who had also lived in Louisiana, where he had held political office,[47] replaced Rost as the "Confederate States of America's commissioner to France." In the capital, he moved into 16 rue de Marignan and quickly found supporters at the highest levels of the imperial government. He and his family were even invited to the court balls.[48] He also had an informant in the Quai d'Orsay who kept him privy to the slightest details. This was a well-known figure of the Ministry of Foreign Affairs and close colleague of Thouvenel's, Pierre Cintrat, director of the archives and of the chancellery. Slidell and Cintrat met discreetly on a regular basis. Cintrat's betrayal of the French government was no doubt financially motivated.[49] Slidell left France after the fall of the empire but, like Judah P. Benjamin, the Confederacy's secretary of state, he was buried in France.[50]

On April 24, 1861, Sanford, the U.S. minister to Belgium, obtained an interview with Thouvenel. Sanford gave Thouvenel a letter from Seward requesting that he not to receive the Confederate envoys who had just arrived in Europe. Thouvenel ignored the request and replied that he intended to grant Pierre Rost an unofficial interview.[51] Seward was furious and a month later sent a new letter in the care of Mercier. This time, Seward warned that a break in diplomatic relations might result.[52] In June, following Thouvenel's meeting with Rost, Dayton was received at the Quai d'Orsay. The Union's new agent repeated to the French foreign minister his government's opposition to these meetings, but Thouvenel stuck to his guns. He did not consider himself to be violating neutrality because the visit was in no way official. The meeting would serve only to inquire about the situation in America, to comment on the consequences of the conflict for Europe, and to restate the rights of neutrals. Rost did not come as a Confederate envoy, because if he had he would not have been received.[53] Thouvenel argued that he could not ignore the Confederacy's emissary while agreeing to speak with the representative of the Union. To do so, in his view, would constitute a breach of neutrality.[54] The same precaution was observed when it came to French agents wanting to make contact with the Davis government. For instance, when Mercier went to Richmond in April 1862, it was with the express agreement of Secretary of State Seward. Seward was only too glad for a chance to sound out the views of his Confederate counterpart and arranged for Mercier to cross the lines.[55] To avoid controversy, Mercier tried to have himself accompanied by a diplomat considered pro-North.[56] In the end, the Quai d'Orsay affirmed that this meeting was organized without its approval. The French ministry held that it was a personal initiative designed to "impress upon the Confederate government the reasons why it should decide to return to the Union and persuade it of the impossibility of prolonging its resistance."[57] No greater caution could be exercised.

INTERNATIONAL LAW AND MARITIME AFFAIRS

Maritime affairs represented another problem for neutrality. To maintain its neutral position in French ports, the imperial government drew on an edict from 1681. Reference to such a long-standing law conferred a moral advantage.[58] The updated clause appearing in the final declaration of June 10, 1861, stated that, except in cases of force majeure (bad weather, damage, exhaustion of supplies), no Northern or Southern warship could put into a French port for more than twenty-four hours. During that time, they would not be permitted to sell their captured prize. The authorities could provide nothing but supplies and means of repair. It was prohibited for French nationals to contribute in any way to the equipping or arming of belligerent vessels, or to enlist. Violations would be rigorously punished.[59]

Sometime later, an additional clause was added to avoid any risk of confrontation off the coasts of France and Great Britain. Two clashes had, in fact, occurred at a year's interval in Martinique, and the French authorities feared a repeat episode in their territorial waters.[60] On February 5, 1864, a circular addressed to the maritime prefects by the minister of the navy confirmed the following: if two enemy belligerents were to find themselves in a French port, twenty-four hours must pass after the departure of the first before the other could cast off.[61] The French fears were not unfounded. On June 19, 1864, off the coast of Cherbourg, before 15,000 onlookers gathered at the hillside cemetery of Querqueville—some who had made the trip from Paris—the USS *Kearsarge* put an end to the exploits of the CSS *Alabama* in little over an hour. Edouard Manet later immortalized the duel in a famous painting.[62]

While some members of the Federal government wanted France simply to close its ports to ships from the South, overall, compared to the State Department's reactions to the other elements of neutrality, the circular was fairly well received in Washington.[63] It doubtless found favor because the edict of 1681 was prejudicial to the South. While the Union's commerce continued—the North had every right to sell its merchandise in France—the South, for which the use of privateers was vital, was forbidden to sell prizes in neutral ports. This would have been a means for the Confederacy to procure weapons and basic necessities, things the North had in abundance. The South was even refused the right to return any captured prize.[64]

London and Paris were well aware of this imbalance between the two sides.[65] In his speeches to the Confederate congress in December 1862 and January 1863, Jefferson Davis denounced what he saw as a feigned neutrality.[66] Benjamin, the Confederate secretary of state, also expressed his indignation on several occasions.[67] Throughout the conflict, the Confederate government repeatedly called for a relaxation of the rules governing the use of French ports by belligerents.[68]

To resolve the matter of commerce between Europe and America, the powers disposed of the rules set out in the Declaration of Paris of April 16, 1856, which forty-three countries had ratified. The declaration, which introduced significant changes to international maritime law, was seen as a major advance. There was now a framework governing commerce in wartime and protecting those who practiced it. The first article prohibited privateering. It therefore marked the end of the traditional distinction between legal capture, under the authority of a state, and illegal capture, a matter of private initiative. The second article, "the neutral flag covers enemy's goods," meant that nonbelligerent vessels carrying enemy goods that were not contraband of war were exempt from confiscation. This principle had been recognized since the eighteenth century, unlike the following article, which stated that, conversely, neutral goods onboard an enemy ship could not be captured. This rule was unprecedented because it abolished the confusion still common at the time between the property of states and that of private individuals.

The fourth and final article concerned blockades. In order to be binding, blockades had to be effective, that is, maintained by a force strong enough to prevent access to the enemy coast. This provision came in response to the efforts of Great Britain, during the Seven Years' War (1756–53), to impose a paper blockade that neutrals had to respect, a decision that sparked violent protest in Europe.

Of the maritime powers, the United States alone had refused to adhere to the Declaration of Paris. The text was only binding on contracting parties, so the United States was not obliged to comply.

With the Civil War came the question of how the North and South would behave toward neutrals. Certainly, the state of belligerency recognized by France and Britain obliged combatants to respect the laws of war regarding neutral goods conveyed onboard neutral ships. But this was not enough. England wanted to persuade the United States to adopt articles 2 and 3 of the 1856 declaration. Thouvenel was in total agreement with this proposal.[69] The two powers seemed to have gotten their wish when Seward said he was prepared to adhere to all articles of the Declaration of Paris.[70] However, Thouvenel was wary of this sudden about-turn. He suspected Seward of wanting to adopt the full text to prohibit Southerners from privateering, which was the only way they could make up for their naval inferiority. By adhering to article 1, the North would put its enemy outside the law; Confederate privateers would, therefore, be considered pirates and could be hanged upon capture.[71] Consequently, Thouvenel favored acceptance of articles 2 and 3 by both the North and the South, and his British counterpart eventually came around to this opinion.[72] For his part, Confederate secretary of state Benjamin, besides wanting to maintain privateering, demanded that England and France allow Southern vessels to sell their prizes in British and French ports, a possibility that the edict of 1681 denied them.[73] Under these circumstances, it was difficult to come to an arrangement. After the summer of 1861 and the first engagement between the North and South, Thouvenel judged that the time to open negotiations had passed and put an end to all discussion.[74] Seward bemoaned Thouvenel's stance, which prevented France and England from regarding Southern privateers as pirates.[75]

With regard to the blockade, Lincoln's proclamation of April 19, 1861, to close the ports from South Carolina to Texas, "in pursuance of the laws of the United States, and of the law of Nations, in such case provided." This language signaled Washington's accession to the principle set by article 4 of the Declaration of Paris;[76] namely, that to be binding, blockades must be "effective," that is, maintained by a sufficient force. Unlike the Anglo-Saxon conception, the French took article 4 to the letter. They called for a physical occupation such that neutral ships could not pass between the blockading vessels without being hit by their projectiles. On August 1, 1861, Napoléon III forcefully recalled this to Union general James W. Webb: "See to it that your blockade is effective! I hope it is not true that you will neglect it. That would not do; it would put me in an awkward position."[77]

The emperor was referring to the Federal government's decision to order some ports closed to foreign trade not by ships but by law. The measure elicited strong opposition from Britain, and France followed suit.[78] The French government could not condone the decision to blockade the Confederate coast in a spurious manner. That would be to reverse a position it seemed to advocate most firmly, for it was France that had pushed the other powers to ban such methods five years earlier. The Union blockade was the first test of the new international rules. For political as much as legal reasons, tolerating the closure of the Southern coast by a simple proclamation would set a dangerous precedent.

To compel the Federal authorities to renounce the idea, London and Paris brandished the threat of naval intervention.[79] The warning to the Federals was lent weight by the rumor circulating in the summer of 1861 that France, England, and Spain intended to land troops in Mexico. If this were true, the European powers could take advantage of having a fleet of warships at hand to pressure the Lincoln administration. The threat came at a difficult time for the Union — the first battle with the South had ended in defeat — and so the North preferred to back down. The Federal government's abandonment of the "paper blockade" can, therefore, be attributed to intimidation by the two allies. However, the episode had a definite impact on the image of effectiveness that the Union hoped to give the blockade.

There is no need to debate the blockade's effectiveness. What counts are the impressions of those involved. Did they see the blockade as effective? This question is important because, as we have seen, it concerns a point of international law that legitimizes the maritime powers' recognition of the blockade and also helps explain the scarcity of cotton (see chapter 2).[80]

One fact was inescapable: there was simply too much coastline to watch over. The consuls' skepticism was supported by the conclusions of French commanders such as Rear Admiral Aimé Reynaud, who ran the Caribbean squadron of eleven warships. Since July 1861 he had cruised back and forth along the supposedly blocked coasts. His conclusion was clear: it would be very difficult to enforce the blockade by effectively patrolling all the ports on the coast.[81] The consuls pointed out that the Federal navy had too few ships to do so.[82] They also recalled that the time of day, or the season, could interrupt patrols, whereas the Southern blockade runners had learned to sail at night or in fog.[83] The consuls regularly passed on to their government the statistics on blockade runners that the Richmond authorities eagerly provided them.[84] The figures suggested that only slow craft had any chance of being captured.[85]

In the spring of 1862, the conclusion of these agents was clear. In their view, the ships that had attempted to run the blockade had done so with great ease.[86] An analysis covering the first three years of war substantiated claims of the blockade's porousness. The acting chargé d'affaires of the Charleston consulate estimated that from November 1861 to March 1864, "of about four hundred and twenty-five attempts by steamers to run the blockade, three hundred and sixty-three were successful." He added that "each vessel has made five journeys on average."[87] In fact, by the spring of 1862 the imperial government was fully aware that compliance with article 4 of the Declaration of Paris could at best be theoretical. It did not need the lists of blockade runners so conscientiously supplied by Southern supporters to question the strength of the blockade put in place by the North.[88]

What, then, can explain France's stubborn insistence on continuing to recognize a blockade that a legal assessment based on plain evidence had shown to be unlawful—a contradiction that the Confederates were quick to highlight?[89] To understand the constancy of the French position we must look to Franco-British relations. As Napoléon III confided to his pro-South acquaintances, he was repeatedly tempted to intervene but did not want to act without England.[90] Yet London did not observe as strict a definition of the blockade as the French did. British foreign minister Lord Russell considered that a few ships' managing to get past patrols and thereby enter or exit ports did not mean that a blockade must be considered ineffective.[91] In his view, what counted was the presence of warships, even if they were not necessarily anchored in front of each port.[92] He therefore considered the blockade legal because the law's intention was to counter paper blockades unsupported by any naval forces.[93]

The French, who read the Declaration of Paris in the most unconditional manner, were forced to reconsider their point of view. The credit indisputably goes to Thouvenel for having been able to dissuade Napoléon III, as attached as he was to strict application of the declaration, from risking a conflict for a point of law. Doubtless in this renunciation lay not only a concession to Britain but also the realization of a fact: article 4 was unenforceable. The French government well remembered the relative failure of the continental blockade in 1806–7, when Napoléon I had tried in vain to make England yield by sealing off Europe completely. This historic precedent had left its mark and, given the extent of coast concerned by the blockade, the minister of foreign affairs had to accept the obvious.

———

It may be argued that France strove to respect the declaration of neutrality as closely as possible, but this position nonetheless proved detrimental to the South. The imperial government maintained diplomatic relations with the Lincoln administration, while French relations with the authorities in Richmond remained unofficial. This was no small disadvantage for Southerners, who could not make contacts without the utmost precaution. While their right of belligerency had been recognized, it was more out of concern for protecting neutrals from any aggression at sea, on the one hand, and in keeping with the blockade, on the other, for the blockade presupposed the existence of a state of

Edouard Drouyn de Lhuys. Courtesy of the Bibliothèque de Bordeaux.

war. Finally, the edict of 1681 deprived them of precious income because their privateer's prizes could not be sold. Moreover, England took more liberties with neutrality than did France (see chapter 2).

We can also see that both Thouvenel and his successor Edouard Drouyn de Lhuys found it easier to depart from a strict reading of the Declaration of Paris because the text did not clearly specify any practical arrangements for certifying a blockade's effectiveness. Furthermore, given that the United States was exempted from articles 2 and 3 concerning neutrals and their goods, it was hard not to do the same with article 4. Such complacency also came from the advantages that France could derive from the situation. As Thouvenel admitted to the comte de Flahaut, his ambassador to the United Kingdom, the blockade's flaws could be a boon to French trade. The Federal navy would not be able to demand customs duties, and neutral ships would enter ports without paying a cent.[94] In any case, apart from the legal aspect, the blockade's effectiveness was chiefly of concern in relation to the scarcity of imported cotton in Europe (see chapter 2). Once a solution was found for this shortage, the lists of blockade runners gradually disappeared from the consuls' correspondence.

» 2 «

THE EMPEROR GETS INVOLVED IN THE WAR

Napoléon III had always been fascinated by the New World. He was better informed about American life and affairs than most of his contemporaries. Along with King Louis-Philippe, he was one of the few French leaders of the nineteenth century to have visited the United States. However, Napoléon's knowledge of the country had not endeared it to him. He considered the Americans to be amoral. He scorned their mercantile spirit and mocked the nation's immaturity. He was particularly worried about their "manifest destiny" and suspected them of constantly wanting to push back their border by maintaining the idea that their continent offered unlimited possibilities for expansion. After the West, he believed, the United States would eventually covet the territory south of the Rio Grande. The Civil War weakened the Union at just the right moment. Although not displeased to see the United States so tormented, the emperor was not content to revel in its new vulnerability. He wanted to be more than a mere spectator because by the summer of 1861, he had chosen his camp. It was the South. In defiance of neutrality, he pursued a policy openly favorable to the Confederate government. He tried to gain the Confederates a respite from the war they were so fiercely waging; he twice sought a way to recognize their government; and he wanted to buy them maritime weapons. Although he used every means possible to achieve his ends, all his attempts failed. Why?

In 1837, at age twenty-nine, the future emperor spent two and a half months in the United States. It was too short a stay for him to grasp the realities of the country in any depth, but it was enough to give him an idea. He stayed a while in New York, where he was very well received.[1] He met several of the leading families — the Hamiltons, Livingstones, and Dewitt-Roosevelts — and was introduced to the writer Washington Irving.[2] He planned a trip through the country but never made it.[3] A few years later, he learned more about American affairs by reading the accounts of travelers in North America and copies of the American press. He eventually gained a good understanding of the debates in Congress and kept himself regularly informed.[4]

So his disenchantment with the country did not come from ignorance. The United States, in general, and Americans, in particular, simply had failed to appeal to him.[5] On May 8, 1837, he wrote to his mother, Queen Hortense, from New York that a European in the United States could not help feeling "shocked, hurt, offended, mortified, disoriented, materialized, petrified, stalactized, gilded, silvered, channeled, and vaporized, and all this ten times a day."[6] Several things tarnished the memory of this trip, not least the reason for it in the first place. Louis-Napoléon Bonaparte did not choose to go to America. It was the government of Louis-Philippe, against which he had fomented a plot in Strasbourg the year before, in October 1836, that decided to send him there.[7] To add to the humiliation, he had to accept a subsidy from the government to pay for his passage, as he was ruined. He reached his destination after a difficult, four-month crossing.[8]

The context also played a role in forming his opinion of the United States. When Louis-Napoléon landed on American soil, the reparations crisis had only just come to an end.[9] This disruption of relations between the two countries shaped contemporary views of the young republic. It demonstrated that the naive vision of an eternal "Franco-American friendship" was far removed from the substance of diplomatic reality. Finally, the news that his mother had cancer persuaded him to cut his stay short.[10] Then, just before Louis-Napoléon left the continent, the American banker with whom he had deposited funds refused to return them to him, claiming he was under threat of bankruptcy.[11]

It is surprising that the future emperor retained only the inconveniences he suffered and turned them into a wholesale generalization. One might have thought that as a supporter of the Saint-Simonians, who sought to promote industrial development for the benefit of society, he would have been enthused by American modernity.[12] He was certainly not blind to these develop-

Napoléon III, 1869. Courtesy of the Library of Congress,
Prints and Photographs Division.

ments, speaking of "the transition of a caterpillar who emerges from its cocoon and unfolds its wings to fly even higher than a beautiful butterfly."[13] However, that was not what marked him most. First, he found the Americans' obsession with money repulsive, as had his cousin a few years earlier.[14] He regarded them as the servile subjects of King Dollar. Their appetite for profit struck him more than their taste for progress. Second, far from recognizing the Americans as ahead of their time, he considered them a people in their infancy, a nation still at the stage of an "independent colony" whose future was fraught with peril, as it contained the seeds of disunity.[15] For Louis-Napoléon Bonaparte, the future of the United States was compromised. The country, therefore, could not be a model.

In 1840 Louis-Napoléon Bonaparte led another coup attempt, and this time the king was less indulgent, incarcerating him. Behind bars he formed ambitious plans for the New World, redrawing the interior of the continent in his fertile imagination. He pondered the fate of Central America, for which he dreamed of economic development and prosperity. Imagining a canal linking the two oceans across Nicaragua, he saw a bridge connecting Europe to Asia from which a commercial hub would emerge, offering attractive rewards to the local people. As his study progressed, he developed a broader vision that took in Latin America in general and Mexico in particular, which he thought it possible to save from decline or even downfall. So while thinking about the future of America, he did not lose sight of the Latin world he hoped to see regenerated and able to hold its own against an expanding Anglo-Saxon counterpart. This Latin world he defended connected the two hemispheres, with its Mexican section in North America and a Caribbean section further south.

This grand plan explains why the U.S. success against Mexico greatly concerned Louis-Napoléon, who became president of the French republic the year that the Treaty of Guadalupe Hidalgo was signed. Like many of his contemporaries, he was convinced that the conquests by the United States, though substantial, had not satisfied the victor's appetite. He was obsessed with the idea of stemming the new power's southern expansion to preserve the Latin world he held dear. When President Louis-Napoléon Bonaparte became Emperor Napoléon III in 1852, he did not abandon his designs. In fact, his hostility to the United States only grew, especially as during the Crimean War, the Federal government favored Russia over the Franco-British alliance. The American representatives in France, such as John Young Mason in the 1850s, took note of Napoléon's dislike for their country.[16]

In the spring of 1861, Napoléon III in his heart of hearts could only welcome the news of the American crisis that was weakening the Union. Word of Virginia's secession reached France a little after news of the bombing of Fort Sumter, yet while both events heralded serious difficulty for the Federal government, the emperor did not want to rush his response. Playing down the adversaries' determination despite their having taken up arms, he felt that an agreement could still be reached. Had a peace conference not been held in February, before the bombing of Fort Sumter?[17] The emperor thought that in the search for a rapprochement, France would have a part to play in bringing the two sides together. Behind this desire for intercession lay his eagerness to take on a role that delighted him: the intermediary required to find a solution to the crisis.[18] However, Napoléon was cautious. He did not want to appear to be taking advantage of the outbreak of violence, which might not last. In any case, a month and a half after hostilities began, the French minister in Washington, Henri Mercier, dampened the emperor's enthusiasm. He considered any mediation premature and guaranteed it would fail.[19]

Nevertheless, this did not stop Mercier from testing the waters. On the eve of his meeting with Secretary of State Seward in June, Mercier wrote to the consul in Charleston asking him to sound out the Southern authorities.[20] While on June 6, 1861, Seward had resolutely rejected Mercier's mediation, in September after the Confederate victory at Bull Run, the French agent thought there could yet be an opportunity to persuade the Lincoln government to make concessions.[21] However, the rumor of possible negotiations between Washington and Richmond—which was also reported by Flahaut, France's ambassador to the United Kingdom—sapped any interest in the French offer, because direct contact between the two sides rendered French involvement useless.[22]

In early 1862 the press buzzed with rumors of an initiative, but Napoléon III contented himself with expressing the wish that the dispute would soon come to an end.[23] In fact, he was holding back.[24] This time, the emperor's moderation reflected his doubts over whether the Union forces had the military capacity to put down their enemy. He was waiting for the result of the attack the Federals were about to lead against Confederate forces. Sartiges, the former French minister in Washington whose opinion was much heeded, thought it possible that the North would accept mediation if there was a strain on Federal finances and the South was able to resist in the Potomac.[25] In a letter to the French ambassador to the United Kingdom, Foreign Minister

Thouvenel repeated the same analysis.[26] The time for mediation would come if and when the North was ready to give up the fight. However, after the series of Union successes in February, there could be no question of diplomatic mediation. Thouvenel merely encouraged the North to open discussions.[27] This caution was all the more justified by the fact that in Washington, the rumors of French intervention were perceived as interference.[28]

However, in April 1862, following the costly Union victory at Shiloh, Mercier judged that the time was right to offer his services. Of his own free will, with the secretary of state's approval, he wanted to go to Richmond. Seward asked him to convince the Confederates they could not win and to inform them that if they agreed to return to the Union, they would not suffer any reprisals for the act they had just committed. For his part, Mercier sought to prepare an appeal to the neutral powers' good offices to facilitate a peaceful settlement between the two belligerents.[29] As we can see, their goals for the mission differed. Mercier was pursuing the idea of bringing both sides to accept an Anglo-French mediation to put an end to their duel, which assumed concessions from both sides, while in the secretary of state's mind there was nothing to negotiate but surrender.

Without waiting for a response from the minister, Mercier left for Richmond, arriving on April 16, 1862. There he met with the Confederate secretary of state, Judah P. Benjamin. Benjamin refused all compromise and showed no reluctance to see the war through to the end. He recalled the example of the Revolutionary War where, on paper, British victory had seemed a foregone conclusion. He counted on the North's running out of money.[30] Mercier's mission ended, predictably, in failure.

This journey was met with skepticism by the liberal press. Few newspapers believed that Mercier had acted on his own initiative to ascertain the standpoint of the government in Richmond.[31] The trip was all the more suspect because it coincided with the launch of a campaign by *Le Constitutionnel*, a semiofficial daily newspaper, against those who hoped to see the Union restored.[32] Had it not been for censorship, some editors would have openly speculated that Napoléon III had mandated Mercier to carry out the mission.[33] Its failure was blamed on inflexible leaders in Richmond and the North's refusal to accept the idea of an armistice.[34]

Should we suspect Napoléon III of being behind all this as Slidell did?[35] It must be acknowledged that Mercier frequently acted without orders, as he had the previous June. As such, it is difficult to see this trip as an underhanded maneuver by the emperor. Furthermore, if this were the case, it is highly likely that the emperor would have gone through another, less visible intermediary than Mercier. Moreover, on May 2, 1862, Thouvenel, in a letter to the French ambassador to the United Kingdom, mentioned Mercier's visit to the Southern capital and stressed the embarrassment that this personal initiative had caused the emperor.[36] The minister of foreign affairs was very surprised by Mercier's efforts and urged his agent to refrain from taking any initiative in the future.[37] The way Mercier presented his intentions is highly significant. To shield himself from any possible reproach by Thouvenel—who wanted to appeal to Washington, not Richmond, to stop the war—he said his trip had been encouraged by Seward, compelling evidence that he had lacked instructions from Paris. His trip to Richmond became a mission entrusted to him by the U.S. secretary of state.

Following the Union's conquest of New Orleans in April 1862 and the attack being prepared against the Southern capital, Thouvenel thought that for the Federals, who were readying themselves to deal their rival the final blow, brutal domination would not be enough.[38] On June 12, he suggested that Paris propose its good offices, this time not to stop the war but to facilitate negotiations to prepare for the postwar period. He made this intention known both to the Federal government representative in France and to his minister in Washington, who informed Secretary of State Seward.[39] The conservative press reported this position, thus preparing public opinion for the idea of mediation: if the North wanted to convince millions of hostile subjects to return to the Union, it would have to negotiate with the enemy.[40]

Of course, the newspapers hostile to the regime had their doubts about this initiative. For *Le Journal des Débats*, the offer had little chance of being accepted when the Federals had been scoring points for the last year.[41] Above all, France's arbitration would be taken as interference. *Le Temps* suspected a ruse, with France hoping for a predictable rejection by the North in order to recognize the Confederate States.[42] It pointed out that London had been careful not to make such a proposal, perhaps so as to let France sink into this quagmire alone.[43] Only *Le Siècle* sounded a dissenting voice. It called for mediation but on terms that would mandate the abolition of slavery.[44]

Then the unthinkable happened. By the end of the Seven Days' Battles, Confederate Gen. Robert E. Lee had driven U.S. Maj. Gen. George B. McClellan's troops into a retreat. On Wednesday, July 16, 1862, Slidell went to see Napoléon III in Vichy. The emperor was taking his second cure in the spa town 230 miles south of Paris. He had arrived by train five days earlier and was lodging at the Villa Strauss. He was very fond of "spa diplomacy." This meeting was the first of four between the two men. The conversation was recounted only by the Southern envoy, who did not take notes during the interview and wrote from memory. Napoléon began their conversation in French, with the German accent that had never left him, then switched to English. The meeting lasted an hour and ten minutes. Slidell's account presents a surprisingly eloquent Napoléon, far from the "Sphinx" to which many of his contemporaries compared him because of his impassive attitude and the long silences into which he would retreat.[45] With Slidell he appeared unusually loquacious.

The emperor, who had news of the Confederate successes, suggested the idea of mediation but feared that the North would refuse. He mentioned Lincoln's decree to raise 300,000 men, which Napoléon saw as proof that the struggle was hopeless. Slidell affirmed that the South, in any case, would accept his good offices. He advised Napoléon to take action on the eve of the congressional elections, which were to be held in November. The proposal of mediation might in this way "awaken" the peace party. The emperor thought, too, that the doves now enjoyed a greater audience in the North. Slidell suggested terms for the mediation: peace would be preceded by an armistice during which Southern ports would be open to international commerce.[46]

Thouvenel, like Mercier, agreed the overture should be timed to coincide with the elections.[47] But the foreign minister wished to proceed with caution and determine which partners France might find for such an undertaking. After hearing of England's reluctance, he wanted to ascertain the position of Russia, the Union's strongest European ally.[48] On July 23, 1862, he wrote to the chargé d'affaires of the French embassy in St. Petersburg, asking him to find out if the Russian government would be willing to join France and England in an attempt "to have Washington hear the voice of reason and to arrive at the means to end, through a conciliatory action, a war so disastrous for humanity."[49] Russia balked at being associated with England, making the French diplomats' task far more difficult.[50]

In September 1862, news of the Union's new setback at Bull Run reached Paris. It did not change the foreign minister's way of thinking. Thouvenel confirmed that he counted on the result of the congressional elections to assess how events had influenced the real mood of the country before making a final decision.[51] He attached little importance to Pope's defeat, except for its potential impact on Northern opinion. The public might wish for a return to peace and make it known by their vote, which would facilitate the mediation proposal.[52] However, news of McClellan's pyrrhic victory at Antietam on September 17 reinforced Thouvenel's wish not to undertake anything before November.[53] Alfred Paul, the French consul in Richmond, agreed with Thouvenel that no action should be taken yet.[54]

The events of the summer generated new supporters for the idea of media-

tion. The newspapers aligned with the regime continued to defend this solution, especially after the Second Battle of Bull Run. One such advocate, *Le
Pays*, published a series of three letters by Southern sympathizers attempting
to show that their rights had been violated by the North, that the Confederates
were supported by a strong government, and that they had proven they could
defeat the Union armies.[55] However, among newspapers at odds with the imperial authorities, the consensus broke down. *Le Journal des Débats* said it was
now in favor of mediation on the condition that it not lead to recognition of
the Confederacy, while *Le Temps* stood its ground, as it equated this proposal
to a dangerous intervention in favor of the South and was certain the North
would reject it.[56] Where most newspapers converged, however, was in the dis-
connection of their position from the military context; whether the situation
favored the North or not, their opinion remained unchanged.

On October 26, 1862, Slidell met Drouyn de Lhuys, who had just replaced
Thouvenel at the Quai d'Orsay. The new minister of foreign affairs admitted
that he had yet to give the American question any attention and therefore
could not offer an opinion. However, when the emperor received Slidell for
an hour two days later, this time at Saint-Cloud, the emperor submitted a proposal to him. He asked whether, in order to end the bloodshed, both parties
would accept the joint mediation of France and England. Napoléon III then
repeated Slidell's proposition from the previous summer: he suggested a six-
month truce with Southern ports open to international trade. If the North
rejected the overture, the emperor acknowledged that this would provide a
good reason for more active intervention. Slidell thought the North might
now consent to mediation, but he could not say whether the same was true
of the South. The Confederate commissioner did not conceal the fact that obtaining an agreement with England would be difficult. The emperor replied
that he had received a letter from the king of Belgium, dated October 15, pressing him to take the lead in this initiative. He added that Leopold had written
this letter during a visit to Brussels by Queen Victoria, who was his cousin and
over whom he had great influence. Napoléon wondered about the upcoming
U.S. congressional elections and how the Democratic Party could benefit from
them. Slidell said it appeared likely that the Democrats would win in two or
three states but that this partial success would exert little influence on the Lincoln administration.[57]

The emperor's offer no doubt owed much to the position of England. Leopold's letter, which Napoléon III suspected to have been written jointly with
Victoria, had convinced him that London would adhere to his plan. The previous month, following news of the second Union defeat at Bull Run, the British

cabinet had also considered proposing mediation on the basis of separation, followed, if this failed, by recognition of the Confederate government (see chapter 3).[58] One could be forgiven for wondering about the emperor's timing; why did he not simply take advantage of the fact Earl Russell and Lord Palmerston were well disposed toward an offer of mediation in September and convince them to join his endeavor? A plausible response is that Thouvenel's replacement by Drouyn de Lhuys on October 15, 1862, facilitated the emperor's task. While the former minister of foreign affairs did start to lay the groundwork for mediation, he had never advocated a truce. More important, Thouvenel had always wanted to see the results of the congressional elections before taking action. Napoléon, however, wanted to act without delay. Consuls such as Charles de Montholon in New York predicted electoral success for the Democrats, who would take advantage of hostility to the declaration of martial law and to the Emancipation Proclamation, and to the "general discouragement" ensuing from the lack of decisive Union victories.[59] The emperor also predicted a Democratic victory. Being a little hasty in anticipating the Northern electorate's pacifist inclinations, he judged that Washington would take up his proposal in order to facilitate reconciliation.

While Napoléon III could hope for more flexibility and fewer objections from Drouyn de Lhuys, who was new to the question, than from his predecessor, the new minister nonetheless laid down his own conditions for a mediation proposal. He insisted that no option be predetermined. He recalled that it was for the Americans, not the European powers, to decide the future of the Union and the basis on which the talks could take place. In his mind, it was simply a question of facilitating discussions.[60] Like his predecessor, he wanted to associate the cabinet in St. Petersburg with the Franco-British initiative, given its traditional alliance with the government in Washington. He was aware that as the difficulty would come from the North, "the support of Russia can only help to overcome it."[61]

As various rumors were circulating about the French proposal, it was made public, wrote Drouyn de Lhuys, in order to cut short "any conjecture."[62] The plan was published in *Le Moniteur* on November 13. It received a mixed reaction from the press, which divided along political lines. The more conservative papers such as *Le Constitutionnel* supported mediation while, unsurprisingly, the liberal and Republican papers were much more reserved.[63] Their main criticism was that it favored the South by raising the blockade.[64] *Le Journal des Débats* denounced the mediation for treating both sides equally despite the divergence in their military situations and diplomatic status.[65] Acceptance of this proposal would amount to the North's "recognizing the fact of the Confederacy's existence and the final dismemberment of the republic."[66] *Le Journal des Débats* viewed such an overture as unacceptable. Publication of the proposal in *Le Moniteur* aimed only to exonerate the French government of any bias against the North.[67] However, hardly was the mediation offer disclosed than it was rumored likely to fail. *Le Temps* had understood that the British prime minister did not think the moment right for mediation.[68]

Mediation failed primarily because the North never wanted it. The Federal representative, William Dayton, told Drouyn de Lhuys that his government could not accept a truce just as the huge effort being made was beginning to bear fruit. He plotted the Union armies' progress on a map.[69] Conversely, as one might expect, the South approved the proposal of mediation. The Confederate government was obviously eager for an armistice that would give it some respite.[70] The initiative was also not carried through because Russia and England declined the French proposal. On November 8, 1862, the tsar's government informed the French ambassador, the duc de Montebello, that as Russia refused to offend the United States, it would not join Britain and France in proposing an armistice. On November 11, the French ambassador to the United Kingdom, the comte de Flahaut, explained that London would have accepted mediation a few months before when the Federals were in trouble but that opinions had changed after Antietam.[71] Flahaut justified the British reserve by the Palmerston government's fear of irritating the North. Furthermore, the British cabinet considered that when coupled with the opening of the Southern ports, the truce lost all semblance of impartiality.[72] On November 13, Drouyn de Lhuys informed his agent in Washington that the French proposal had not won "immediate assent" from the two powers France had approached.[73] The proposal's rejection by London and St. Petersburg was officially announced on November 16.[74] Drouyn de Lhuys hastened to abandon the project.[75]

Almost immediately after the first attempt at mediation failed, a second was initiated. The Democrats' upsurge in the fall 1862 congressional elections reactivated French hopes for mediation. Both the French minister in Washington and the French consul in New York interpreted the election results as a clear demonstration of opposition to all-out war and suggested reviving the diplomatic option.[76] They cannot be accused of bias for this reading of the election's significance; the impression in the North was that the elections were a "near disaster" for the Republicans.[77] Although the Democrats made significant political gains in the House of Representatives, however, they did not win a majority, and they lost seats in the Senate.[78]

To revive the idea of mediation, two other elements needed to be taken into account, the first of which was Lee's victory at Fredericksburg on December 13, 1862. This "Antietam in reverse" clearly raised the prospect of the war's continuation. Was preserving the Union worth all this bloodshed? Public opinion in the North was much shaken by the carnage. Consul Paul in Richmond believed that the time for peace talks had finally come.[79] Moreover, in France, after the setback in November, Napoléon III had not given up on a diplomatic success. He also needed to show the French legislature that his government took seriously the difficulties caused by the disruption of trade with America.

On January 9, 1863, Drouyn de Lhuys sent a dispatch to Mercier containing the new mediation proposal. He was very cautious, abandoning the idea of a truce and instead suggesting that talks be conducted while the war continued. The foreign minister recalled the example of the American Revolution, when negotiations that began before the end of the conflict led to the provisional treaty of November 30, 1782, which contained the clauses of the Treaty of Paris.[80] The North could take the first steps toward discussions to be held under the supervision of France and England. Drouyn de Lhuys accepted that the Lincoln administration could decline the offer and restated that there was no consideration of forcing the hand of the Union, whose sacrifices, he recognized, had exhausted neither its resources nor its perseverance.[81] Regarding the content of the talks, Drouyn de Lhuys envisaged the North and the South seeking to establish whether their interests were definitively irreconcilable and whether separation could no longer be avoided.[82] On January 12, 1863, in his New Year's address to the two houses of Parliament, the emperor did not mention the mediation proposals.[83] The new offer of mediation was made public at the end of January 1863.[84]

The press reaction to the new mediation proposal was unanimously positive. Newspapers stressed the advantage for the opponents in conducting negotiations even as the war continued.[85] Those more reserved toward the imperial government considered these new overtures more acceptable and less adverse to the North than the first. Drouyn de Lhuys's letter was considered very reasonable; it did not pretend to wish more fervently for a peace that would lead to definitive separation than for a reconciliation that would give the North the political advantage.[86] The more conservative papers wagered that there would be a greater chance of success if France acted alone.[87] The tone was more pessimistic in the opposite camp, which speculated that the North would refuse to negotiate with an authority it took to be agents of rebellion.[88]

The Lincoln administration was also receptive to the terms used by Drouyn de Lhuys, who spoke of the warm feelings the Federal government had shown toward the French cabinet.[89] The French representative in Washington did not conceal his hope of seeing the offer accepted.[90] Yet this enthusiasm was soon quashed. In rejecting the French proposals, Seward argued that his government could not have its hands tied when it was poised to win. He did not see on what basis negotiations could take place given that the South did not wish to return to the Union. In his view, the only place for discussions was Congress, which the Southern states had left by seceding. Accepting France's suggestion would therefore amount to disregard for the Constitution, since it would mean negotiating with men who had violated it.[91]

Given these circumstances, as Drouyn de Lhuys deplored, all hope of reconciling the positions of North and South was abandoned.[92] France made no more offers of this nature. The Quai d'Orsay gave up initiatives that were not only vain but also were seen as failures of French diplomacy. Moreover — in proof that the intercession of the European powers was unnecessary — on February 3, 1865, at the Hampton Roads Conference, North and South established direct contact to discuss terms of a possible agreement to end the war.

Let us consider these two offers of mediation. Mercier advocated that France's good offices be proposed immediately after a Confederate success.[93] This was indeed the case for the mediation proposal in January 1863, which came after Lee's victory in Fredericksburg, but the French initiative the previous October followed the North's qualified victory at Antietam. It therefore cannot be said that France based its proposals on the victory of one side or the other. Yet in view of the outcome of these battles, the offers of mediation were less than equitable. The first undoubtedly favored the South because it proposed a six-month truce that would allow the Confederates some respite after the bloody battle at Antietam. Furthermore, opening the Southern ports would allow not only the transport of cotton to France but also the smuggling in of weapons and ammunition. Conversely, the offer of January 1863, which came after a Confederate victory, did not propose a truce. But perhaps we need not focus too closely on these military circumstances given that in both cases, the battles were part of a counteroffensive rather than an offensive. As such, the French overtures did not support a drive toward victory but rather the checking of an advance.

Without looking for overly complex explanations and covert schemes, it is important to stress just how worried diplomats and consuls were about the continuation of this seemingly endless war, so costly to Europe. As several historians have pointed out, the offers of mediation occurred at the height of the cotton crisis (see chapter 8). Their chief aim was thus less humanitarian than economic. In the mediation proposal of October 1862, the Quai d'Orsay referred to the economic interdependence that was causing a crisis as one of the principal reasons French wealth was drying up.[94] The French government needed to protect its nationals who were suffering the consequences of the crisis. Several times Thouvenel mentioned the public's growing concern about the conflict, which had prompted elected representatives to call for mediation.[95] It would appear therefore that the French intervention was first and foremost aimed at reassuring domestic opinion. The imperial government wanted to convince the working classes and the financial community that it was making every effort to ease their hardships. If the term were not anachronistic, we might say that the mediation announcements had to do as much with "communications" as humanitarian concern. Indeed, once the cotton crisis was over, the offers of peace talks disappeared.

Finally, we must not forget the personal aspect of the initiative. At a time when France was floundering alone in Mexico, the emperor, driven as always by the idea of fulfilling a destiny, was looking for a diplomatic success in America. Yet he had competition on the conciliation front. In September 1862, as the conflict deepened, the British government considered proposing mediation, while in late November Pope Pius IX offered his good offices to the representative of the Federal government.[96] If mediation were accepted, Napoléon III would enter history as the ruler who ended the American Civil War.[97] He well remembered the example of his uncle, who, through the 1803 Act of Mediation, managed to arbitrate between the irreconcilable positions of the Unitary and Federalist Swiss. And almost a century before, the fate of the future United States had been placed in France's hands. Why not again?

Yet one may wonder at the inconsequence of this highly unrealistic proposal. How could a margin for discussion be thought to exist when the North wanted to hear nothing of negotiations with its opponent? How was it conceivable that the North might accept for the South to take advantage of a truce and the opening of its ports to rebuild its forces? How could both belligerents be receptive to such an overture at the same time, when the fighting alternated between Northern and Southern victories? The initiative also lacked a forceful advocate. Thouvenel did not share the emperor's views. His preference was closer to a mission of conciliation or good offices, where the role of the third party would be limited to offering the means to arrive at a solution. He did not support the type of intervention in which a solution to the underlying issues would be proposed.[98] Note that Napoléon III waited for Thouvenel to be replaced before embarking on that path. As for Thouvenel's successor, he reluctantly defended a proposal that he would be careful to avoid repeating in the same terms two months later. Finally and most important, did it not seem a little late for mediation when the hostilities had been under way for a year and a half? Was it not when the secession began that it could have been justified, as the Southern states gradually abandoned the Union? There had been an opportunity, but it was not taken because the French government never imagined that the two sides would go to war.

But despite the failures, what counts is the impression these plans gave Richmond and Washington. For the former, they gave rise to the belief that Napoléon III was an ally of the Confederacy. In January 1863, Montholon, the general consul in New York, repeated to Drouyn de Lhuys the words of Jefferson Davis, thanking Napoléon for "the sympathy he has shown for the Confederate cause through his attempt at mediation."[99] The apparent good feeling toward the Confederates caused them to misjudge what should be read into the mediation. They were convinced that the proposal concealed a desire to recognize their government.[100] This was not a figment of their imagination. As we will see, the emperor was a strong supporter of diplomatic recognition.

NAPOLÉON III AND RECOGNITION OF
THE CONFEDERACY — JULY 1862

In the spring of 1862 Napoléon III began to talk to those favorable to the South about recognizing the Confederate government.[101] Benjamin Disraeli, the leader of Britain's Conservative party, told William Shaw Lindsay, a ship owner and member of Parliament, that such a diplomatic initiative from Napoléon would drive British public opinion to follow him and the Palmerston government to come around to this position.[102] This objective accounted in part for Lindsay crossing the Channel to see the emperor. On April 11, 1862, Lindsay, stressing the futility of the conflict for the warring parties and the unnecessary suffering it inflicted on both continents, suggested to Napoléon that France and Britain both recognize the Confederates. Lindsay thought that this action would end the war. According to Lord Cowley, the British ambassador to France and constant interlocutor of the imperial government since the beginning of the empire, the emperor adhered to this view.[103]

One month later, on May 14, Slidell thought he perceived a change in Thouvenel's stance, as he implied that France might take action if the South were to win a few decisive victories.[104] However, in a letter to his minister in Washington the next day, the foreign minister still refused to depart from his policy of strict neutrality.[105] This letter shows some double-dealing on his part. He used different language with his interlocutors depending on how close they were to the emperor. It is also proof that by spring 1862, the Tuileries Palace and the Quai d'Orsay were clearly opposed on the issue of Confederate recognition.

The emperor's choice was indisputably confirmed in July 1862 as a result of the reversal of the military situation in the Confederates' favor. Aside from the military context, the political situation seemed likely to bring France and England to take a diplomatic initiative in favor of the South. The two Confederate envoys, Slidell and Mason, wanted to make the most of the British Parliament's voting on Lindsay's motion for recognition of the Confederacy. On Wednesday, July 16, two days before the motion was tabled in the House of Commons, Slidell obtained an appointment with the emperor, who, as we have seen, was taking his cure in Vichy. During this interview the emperor blew hot and cold. On the one hand, he considered restoration of the Union impossible. He showed himself in favor of recognizing the Confederacy but said he could not act without England's cooperation. He said he had repeatedly expressed his wish for action in favor of the South but had never received a positive response from Britain. Napóleon III asked Slidell whether things might now be otherwise; Slidell, evoking the optimism of his colleague in Britain, earnestly assured the emperor of a change in the British position. He believed that the vast majority of the House of Commons was inclined to favor the South. On the other hand, Napóleon was less than encouraging because he judged that while simple recognition would have little benefit for France, it would result in a conflict with the North. Nonetheless, Slidell said he had prepared a request for official recognition of the South and that he would present it to Thouvenel. The emperor did not object.[106]

Since July 9, 1862, Thouvenel had been in London to attend an awards function and represent his government at the closing ceremony of an exhibition, a factor which was to prove important.[107] He did not return to France until July 16, the day of Slidell's meeting with Napóleon III. His absence raised all kinds of speculation because some assumed, without noting that he had left France before the interview, that the goal of his trip was to arrange a diplomatic action by Paris and London.[108] However, a certain episode proves the contrary. Immediately after his meeting with Slidell, Napóleon addressed a dispatch to his minister in London, but Thouvenel was already on his way back and did not receive it. It was Flahaut, the French ambassador to the United Kingdom, who did, but as the text was encrypted he could not read it and had to send it back.[109] We can therefore say with certainty that Thouvenel was not under instruction from Napóleon to discuss an action with the British on American affairs. If he had been, he would have stayed in London to await the outcome of the emperor's meeting with Slidell. This ineffectual dispatch proves that the emperor's decision to contact Thouvenel was made suddenly and without consultation. Moreover, on July 21, Thouvenel seemed almost relieved not to have received the dispatch in time and confided to Flahaut that he had invoked British neutrality to convince Napoléon not to break with French neutrality.[110] Flahaut replied that had he been able to decipher the contents of the emperor's dispatch, it would "have inspired absolutely the same feeling" in him.[111]

Slidell met with Thouvenel on July 25, while the day before, Slidell's colleague James Murray Mason had submitted his arguments for recognition to Palmerston, having done the same in a letter to the foreign minister.[112] Here the minister played a double game. Although he already knew the substance of the discussion between the emperor and Slidell, he questioned the latter on the result of the audience. Feigning ignorance, he let Slidell speak to find out just how far the emperor had gone. The envoy from Richmond said he counted on submitting an official request for recognition. The minister did not dissuade him but cautiously asked if, until then, he had kept the request secret. He argued for more time to take stock of the military situation but hinted to Slidell that in the event of an indisputable victory for the South, London might well cooperate with Paris. Slidell confirmed to Thouvenel that Mason, the Southern envoy to Britain, was submitting a concomitant request for recognition to the British government. Thouvenel approved this joint action and, when asked by Slidell, admitted that French public opinion did not believe that the Union would be restored. The Confederate envoy handed him the note on recognition, and the foreign minister said he would pass it on to the emperor. However, Thouvenel warned that Slidell should not expect a reply before August 12 or 15 because he had to accompany his wife to Germany.

Slidell was more optimistic than ever.[113] However, if Thouvenel endorsed the joint and simultaneous request for recognition that Slidell intended to present to his colleague Mason, it was because he anticipated its failure. The news from across the Channel emphasized the vigor with which Palmerston was fighting the Lindsay motion.[114] Furthermore, as would later become apparent, the foreign minister was careful to avoid holding talks with his British counterparts on the possibility of joint recognition of the Confederacy.[115]

On August 2, Russell sent Mason a note in which he refused to take sides on the issue of secession and stressed that the fluctuating events of the war made it impossible to secure recognition at that time.[116] On August 20, Pierre Cintrat, Slidell's informer within the Quai d'Orsay, told him in confidence that Thouvenel would not answer his request for recognition.[117] That same day, the minister expressed his satisfaction to Flahaut that his "policy of waiting and forbearance" was finally seen as "the only one possible." He hoped that once he was informed of it, this rebuff would discourage Slidell.[118] Nevertheless, he had to fight hard to have the other cabinet members see reason.[119] On September 11, 1862, he wrote to his agent in Washington of his delight that the "wise man's reserve" continued to prevail.[120] Not for long.

NAPOLÉON III AND RECOGNITION OF THE CONFEDERACY — JUNE 1863

Nine months later, Napoléon III again took the initiative. Moreover, with the Roebuck affair in June 1863, the controversy reached a climax.[121] Southern sympathizers in Britain wanted to take advantage of Lee's resounding success at Chancellorsville.[122] William S. Lindsay, the shipbuilder, was again behind the initiative. In late May 1863, he invited Mason, the Confederate agent in the United Kingdom, and British MP John A. Roebuck to his country house, Shepperton Manor. There, the three men decided to submit a motion for recognition of the Confederacy to the House of Commons on June 30. The schemers counted on Napoléon's support to win over the majority. However, a rumor circulated by a member of Parliament suggested that the French emperor had convinced himself it would be imprudent to recognize the South at that time.[123] Palmerston was to refer to this change in his speech on June 30. Hence arose Roebuck's idea of meeting Napoléon — of whom, he confessed, he was not a great admirer — to find out for himself if the emperor had changed his position or if this official denial was a trap set by London.[124]

To obtain this meeting for Roebuck, Slidell sought a new interview with Napoléon III. On Thursday, June 18, 1863, the latter received Slidell at the Tuileries Palace for half an hour. On this occasion, the emperor contradicted the rumor and said he was convinced "more than ever" of the soundness of Confederate recognition by the European powers. He agreed to receive Roebuck and Lindsay and even went further: he was willing to propose to England that both governments recognize the Confederacy.[125] Slidell was very optimistic. He believed that Palmerston would not dare take responsibility for the continuation of the war by rejecting Napoléon's offer.[126] The imperial cabinet meeting took place on the very evening of this meeting, but again the ministers were strongly divided.[127]

The lack of unanimity did not discourage the emperor, who believed, like Slidell, that a majority of Commons was in favor of British intervention in the conflict, and that Her Majesty's government would be obliged to follow this vote.[128] He therefore intended to force Russell's and Palmerston's hand the moment he believed the time had finally come for joint action. He clung stubbornly to this plan, and on June 20, 1863, he received Lindsay and Roebuck at Fontainebleau. Roebuck was not unknown to the imperial government, for a few years earlier he had defended with much fanfare another motion for a commission of inquiry into the interminable siege of Sevastopol.[129] The publicity that Roebuck was likely to make in defending his motion was of use to the emperor, as it offered him a platform in the British Parliament. It would allow him to confirm openly what certain rumors had contradicted in May: he remained a steadfast defender of the rights of the South. He asserted he was anxious to see the war end and wanted to act in concert with England. However, he refused to send a formal request to the British government; he was still smarting from London's rejection of his first mediation proposal. He said he had instructed the baron Jean-Baptiste Louis Gros, Flahaut's successor at the French embassy in London, to gauge British intentions on the subject of recognition and to suggest any mode of proceeding to achieve this. He authorized the two men to declare in Parliament that he wished to recognize the Confederate states if he could do so with England's cooperation.[130]

The version of this interview given by Lord Cowley, the British ambassador to France, which was based on the account by Drouyn de Lhuys, who had replaced Thouvenel at the Ministry of Foreign Affairs, differs significantly from the one above. It presents the emperor as much more passive, maintaining only that if England were to make him a proposal for recognition, he would probably not object to it. He wished for Gros to be so instructed.[131]

On June 21, Napoléon III's secretary, Jean-François Mocquard, informed Slidell that Drouyn de Lhuys had written to Gros, his ambassador to Britain, to sound out the head of the Foreign Office, Lord Russell, on the question of recognition of the South.[132] However, on the same day in an interview with Slidell, Drouyn de Lhuys expressed reservations. The minister did not hide his fears that London would hasten to communicate any diplomatic proposal that Paris might make to the Lincoln cabinet in order to embarrass France.[133] Although sources claimed otherwise,[134] Russell reiterated when challenged by several MPs that the baron Gros had not passed on any message to him.[135]

On June 30, 1863, the day the motion was debated, Roebuck tried to put Russell in an awkward position. He repeated before the parliamentarians the substance of the emperor's remarks and his willingness to recognize the South if Britain should do so. Roebuck stated that Napoléon III had asked his ambassador to inform the British cabinet as much. Furthermore, he informed the House that the emperor had authorized him to make these statements in his name. He wondered how it was possible for the queen's government to say it had received no communication of this nature. His allegations that it was concealing the truth triggered an uproar.[136] Indeed if, as it claimed, the British government was not aware of this communication, Napoléon's initiative looks like an attempt to circumvent its misgivings by using the parliamentarians to put pressure on the cabinet. That would in effect make a foreign country's parliament into his own platform. Meanwhile, William Dayton, the U.S. representative, met Drouyn de Lhuys, who assured him that "no official communication of any kind had recently passed on this subject between France and England."[137]

So who was telling the truth? Doubts were raised about the British ministers' statements but, curiously, the French diplomats were spared. Yet one might just as easily ask if it was Russell and Palmerston who were lying or whether Gros, the French ambassador to the United Kingdom, really had been instructed to approach the British cabinet. Those who reported on the emperor's interview with Lindsay and Roebuck are unanimous. Napoléon III did indeed speak of instructions sent to the diplomat. Even the press reported this, right up until Le Moniteur of July 5, which confirmed it.

To find an answer we must look to the ambassador in London. What did Gros say? Gros regretted that his approach to the British foreign minister had been misinterpreted. When asked by Drouyn de Lhuys, Gros told him that he had gone to the Foreign Office to discuss another topic, the Polish question. He took the opportunity in passing to communicate to Russell that the emperor was disposed to recognize the South.[138] So without formal instruction, Gros confirmed to Drouyn de Lhuys having visited Russell and mentioning, incidentally, recognition of the Confederacy. The fact that the meeting was unofficial led the British government to ignore the message. What is striking is that Gros spoke on his own behalf, not on behalf of his government. Was this attitude not due to the absence of instructions from Drouyn de Lhuys?

This certainly seems to be the case. Although the archives of the French Ministry of Foreign Affairs only contain a single dispatch from the foreign minister to his agent, dated July 1, 1863, U.S. historians who have studied the affair are confident that between June 22 and 26, Drouyn de Lhuys did send a telegram to instruct Gros.[139] According to them, the content of the dispatch can be inferred from the British ambassador's correspondence to his government. Indeed, Lord Cowley wrote that on June 23 Drouyn de Lhuys instructed Gros to meet Prime Minister Palmerston to correct the rumor that France had changed its position regarding recognition of the Confederacy. On this occasion, Drouyn de Lhuys is thought to have deliberately altered the emperor's

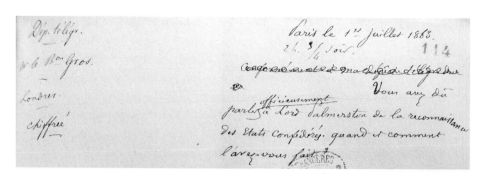

Telegraphic dispatch from Minister Drouyn de Lhuys.
Courtesy of the Ministère des Affaires Etrangères.

instructions. Instead of telling Gros to state unofficially that the ruler had resolved to recognize the Confederacy, he instructed him to tell Palmerston that
the emperor had no objection to recognizing the South.[140]

The problem is that this telegram cannot be found, and for good reason:
the minister never sent instructions. The hypothesis that a cable was sent in
June to Gros comes from a mistranslation of Drouyn de Lhuys's telegram. In
this message sent on July 1, 1863, the minister asked his ambassador, "Vous
avez dû parler officieusement à Lord Palmerston de la reconnaissance des
Etats confédérés. Quand et comment l'avez-vous fait?" ("You must have spoken unofficially to Lord Palmerston of the recognition of the Confederate
States. When and how did you do so?")[141]

This dispatch reveals the minister's ignorance as to the content of a meeting that he suspected to have taken place between Gros and Palmerston, but
of which he knew neither the date nor the proceedings. He mentioned Palmerston's name, not that of Russell, which shows he had nothing to do with the
meeting between Gros and Russell. If there had been instructions, Drouyn de
Lhuys would have named the right person; instead he spoke of Palmerston
because this is whom the emperor, in his note of June 22, recommended that
the French ambassador approach. It is possible that Drouyn de Lhuys, as a result of the persistent rumors and articles in the London press — sent to him by
Gros — concluded that an approach had been made without his knowledge.[142]

Drouyn de Lhuys's hostility to the idea of approaching the British government on joint diplomatic recognition of the Confederacy supports this
hypothesis. On June 18, having judged such an initiative inopportune, he expressed his disapproval by siding with the other cabinet members and carefully avoided sending a cable to his ambassador. On June 21, Napoléon III's
private secretary assured Slidell that Drouyn de Lhuys's telegram had indeed

The French Position

been sent off, yet on June 22 the question of its dispatch remained. To cover his back, he probably told Cowley that he had instructed Gros. Employing his predecessor's methods, he claimed to have contacted the British authorities though he had done nothing of the sort. Drouyn de Lhuys hoped that European events would distract the emperor from his designs. He was aware that for London and Paris alike, recognizing the Richmond government would be pointless, as such a move would not put an end to hostilities.[143] The affair would never have left the ministry archives if Roebuck had not been so lacking in discretion as to train a spotlight on the meeting between Gros and Russell. The Southerners, however, were not fooled. On July 6, 1863, Slidell wrote to Benjamin that he suspected Drouyn de Lhuys of not having carried out the wishes of his emperor.[144] Mason too entertained this hypothesis.[145]

The fact remains that Gros was indeed invited to meet with Russell. It may be assumed that the emperor, still smarting from Thouvenel's passivity the previous year, chose this time to bypass the reservations of Drouyn de Lhuys by contacting his ambassador directly to have him see Russell. This unofficial diplomacy put Gros in the very awkward position of acting without being able to refer the matter to his minister. Forced to acknowledge the facts when queried by Drouyn de Lhuys on July 1, Gros did all he could not to appear to be informing on the emperor. He claimed to have acted "incidentally," slipping Napoléon III's views into conversation almost by accident. His words betray the embarrassing situation in which he found himself, caught between the emperor's desire to have his position made known in London and Drouyn de Lhuys's evident reluctance. It was not the first time that Napoléon made direct contact with the ambassador to the United Kingdom without informing his foreign minister.[146]

The press got hold of the affair. The emperor's interview with Roebuck and Lindsay was revealed by the *Times* and taken up by *Le Journal des Débats*.[147] The conservative newspapers made little of the affair. *Le Constitutionnel* did not deny the emperor's overtures but emphasized their altruism; France was seeking a solution for humanity and the rest of the world.[148] The "opposition" press was divided. *Le Journal des Débats* believed the rumors of recognition were baseless and stressed the North's wrath at such an announcement.[149] Conversely, *Le Temps* was convinced that the baron Gros had submitted to Lord Russell on June 27 a formal proposal on France's behalf to recognize the South.[150] It treacherously published Roebuck's speech in the House of Commons.[151] It can be inferred that the newspaper wanted to highlight the "unofficial" diplomacy, which there was no longer any attempt to disguise, a form of diplomacy in which the emperor preferred to speak through dubious middlemen instead of an experienced diplomatic staff. However, overall, the press gave the incident little coverage, preoccupied as it was with the Polish question, over which England and France were opposed.

The imperial government decided to respond by publishing a paragraph in the unofficial part of Le Moniteur of July 5. Going back over the "incident that occurred in the House of Commons," it said that the emperor had not mandated Roebuck and Lindsay to speak before Parliament. No formal request for recognition had been made by Paris, which looked to London to introduce such a diplomatic initiative. The article therefore concluded that the emperor had not, as claimed by a certain element of the press, sought to influence the British Parliament through two of its members.[152] This was a clever statement because it turned the tables on Britain, passing London off as the decision maker. Napoléon III was not the one giving the starting signal, England was. The article in Le Moniteur had a mollifying effect. Both the press and diplomatic circles were satisfied.[153] However, the emperor's position, though already well known to diplomats and rumored among the public, had now been fully disclosed. Gros noted that presently "it is known, with no room for doubt, that the emperor is willing to recognize the independence of the Confederate States if England wants to act in concert with him."[154]

A telegram from the ambassador on July 14, 1863, informed Drouyn de Lhuys that Roebuck had withdrawn his motion.[155] On July 16, Gros wrote that the Roebuck affair could be considered closed.[156] According to Paul, the consul in Richmond, the Davis government seemed somewhat baffled by the French position.[157] For its part, Washington considered that France had crossed a line. Secretary of State Seward contacted Dayton, his agent in Paris, to have him express Seward's disapproval to Drouyn de Lhuys. In a thinly veiled threat, he wrote of the "serious complications" to which this policy could give rise.[158]

From the consuls' perspective, it was less Gettysburg than Vicksburg that sounded the death knell for Confederate hopes of triumph on the military front. While Consul Paul in Richmond felt it was still possible that General Lee would make another attempt to cross the Potomac despite his weakened forces, he thought Gen. Ulysses S. Grant had struck the Confederates a decisive blow in seizing their stronghold on the Mississippi River. Combined with the capitulation of Port Hudson, Paul predicted that the Confederacy would now be cut in two. He wrote that it was "sinking under the weight of this reverse." Only outside intervention could save it now.[159] As such, Vicksburg also sounded the death knell for Confederate hopes of triumph on the diplomatic front. Rumors concerning France's recognition of the Confederacy still circulated in September 1863, but no one seemed to pay them any more attention.[160]

Note that in both 1862 and 1863, Napoléon III chose a moment when the South was on a winning streak to break with neutrality. He anticipated victory for the Confederates and wanted to support them with a diplomatic decision. However, given the military context in Mexico, Napoléon was doubtless acting on a different strategy in 1862 compared to 1863. When he met with Lindsay on April 11, 1862, he had just learned of the conclusion of the Convention of La Soledad, signed with Benito Juárez on February 10 by delegations from the three European nations.[161] Juárez, supported by the United States, was de facto recognized as the legal president, which upset the emperor's plans for an empire in Mexico. For him, this convention presaged the coming defection of England and Spain, for he knew they were hostile to any intervention with a purpose other than to uphold their claims. France, if it wanted to see its political plan through, was therefore likely to find itself alone in Mexico. It was precisely at this point that he began to show the sympathy he felt for the South's fight in front of his guests and allowed the idea to spread that he might recognize its government.

At the interview he granted Slidell in July 1862, the emperor was worried not only by France's isolation but also by the difficulties the French advance was encountering in Mexico. On April 27, 1862, soon after France's allies had reembarked, Gen. Charles de Lorencez began his march on Mexico City. However, a few days later, on May 5, he clashed unsuccessfully with the first Mexican defenses on the outskirts of Puebla.[162] In Paris this failure came as a surprise. The Mexican campaign was seen by many, the emperor included, as a walkover, on a par with the Pastry War of 1838 that had lasted less than a year.[163] Napoléon III and Slidell met on July 16, thirteen days after the emperor had sent his instructions to Gen. Elie Forey, the newly appointed commander of the expedition. Faced with these unexpected obstacles, Napoléon desperately needed the South to remain passive. The Southerners had understood the emperor's concern about the situation in Mexico perfectly and intended to exploit it. At this very first meeting, Slidell mentioned the possibility of an agreement between the Confederacy and France on this matter. Moreover, a quid pro quo was established; the Confederates had their weapons transported through Mexico to bypass the blockade and Napoléon hoped for the

Confederacy's support in his Mexican plan. He overestimated their capabilities, so impressed was he by General Lee's victories that had managed to stop the invasion of Federal troops; he began to believe that Washington would agree to the independence of the states in rebellion.

In 1863, during the Roebuck affair, it was still the Mexican problem that motivated Napoléon III. This time, in light of events, the emperor was convinced that a grand alliance between Mexico and the Confederacy would materialize. The situation was very favorable. First, the emperor overestimated Roebuck's influence in Parliament. He thought that Commons would pass the Roebuck motion and force the Palmerston government to recognize the South. Second, the news from Mexico was finally satisfactory. On June 10, after a year of fighting, Napoléon had just learned that the French army had finally seized Puebla, a victory that presaged the taking of Mexico City.[164] Correspondingly, the Confederates' fortunes had been ascending since the winter of 1862, and in June 1863 confidential information obtained by the consuls indicated that Lee would lead a new offensive for what promised to be a decisive campaign.[165]

Only nothing went as expected. The Roebuck motion ended in failure and the Confederates suffered two successive defeats. News of Gettysburg reached Paris on July 17, 1863, followed four days later by that of the taking of Vicksburg. Moreover, this second battle, more than the first, alerted the imperial government to the fact that the war had reached a turning point. The Federals' control of the Mississippi River split the Confederacy. Though the noose was tightening on the South, the emperor did not yet despair of seeing the proponents of secession triumph. In 1864, he believed that there was still one last chance of success for the Southerners. Success, however, no longer would come on the battlefield but through the ballot box. He vainly counted on Lincoln's defeat in the presidential elections in November.

NAPOLÉON III AND THE CONSTRUCTION
OF CONFEDERATE WARSHIPS

Napoléon III did not simply want to recognize the South's independence. In defiance of the declaration of neutrality, he wanted to help the Confederates build a navy. In October 1862 Napoléon suggested to Confederate commissioner John Slidell that his compatriots use French shipyards to build a fleet, as they were doing in British ports. According to the emperor "a few ships would inflict fatal injuries on Federal trade." As a precaution, Napoléon envisaged such an order being placed on behalf of the Italian government and promised to consult his navy minister.[166] A few weeks later, as everything seemed to be stalled, Slidell approached the emperor's private secretary, Jean-François Mocquard, and reminded him of the emperor's suggestion. Mocquard confided to Slidell that after consulting his ministers, Napoléon had come up against great difficulties on this issue and could not for the moment give him any encouragement. However, on January 7, 1863, Slidell received a visit from Lucien Arman, owner of the biggest shipyard in Bordeaux, who offered to build battleships for his camp. Slidell was convinced that Arman had come at the emperor's request. He offered payment in cotton.[167] On February 23, things took a more concrete turn. Eugène Rouher, the minister of commerce, assured the envoy from Richmond that Confederate warships would indeed be built in French ports.[168] Given that in 1863 the British government banned the construction and equipment of ships for the Southerners in its territory, France was their only hope.[169]

On April 15, 1863, Arman and Southern envoy James D. Bulloch signed a contract for the clandestine construction of four armed cruisers in Nantes and Bordeaux, to be delivered within ten months. To finance construction, the Confederacy secured a loan from the Erlanger bank. As French law required ministerial authorization to install cannons onboard a merchant ship, Arman wrote to Minister of the Navy Prosper de Chasseloup-Laubat that these vessels were being built for a foreign ship owner who destined them for the service in the China seas and the Pacific; a ploy that violated French neutrality and was implemented with the concomitant consent of the commerce minister. On June 6, 1863, Chasseloup-Laubat gave his go-ahead to arm the ships.[170] On June 18, during his meeting with Napoléon III, Slidell thanked the emperor for sanctioning the contracts; the emperor reiterated his wish that their destination be concealed.[171] A month later a new agreement was concluded between Bulloch and Arman for the delivery of two ironclads. This time Arman believed there was no need to request approval from the Ministry of the Navy.[172]

When work on the four corvettes — the *Yeddo* and *Osaca* in Bordeaux, the *San Francisco* and *Shanghai* in Nantes — was well advanced, and the two battleships, the *Sphinx* and *Cheops*, were nearing completion, their construction in French ports was denounced to the U.S. legation, which obtained the documents to prove it.[173] A few days later, in mid-September 1863, U.S. minister to France William Dayton hurried to notify Drouyn de Lhuys. The flabbergasted foreign minister asked for a copy of the documents attesting to the imposture. On September 22, 1863, having examined the documents, he expressed his regret at not having been notified of Arman's requests. He hastened to inform his colleague at the Navy Ministry.[174] In his reply, Chasseloup-Laubat claimed to have granted his permission because Arman had told him that the ships being built in his shipyards were destined for a trade service between China, Japan, and San Francisco and had assured him that their armament was intended for defense against pirates.[175] However, knowing that Napoléon III was involved in the affair, he give no order to stop it.

Drouyn de Lhuys was nevertheless determined to prevent the vessels from being equipped with cannons, especially as the Americans had just sent a protest to the French government's agent in Washington.[176] The foreign minister considered it impossible not to satisfy the Federal authorities. In October, he informed the Lincoln administration that he had officially notified Lucien Arman and Jean-Simon Voruz of the withdrawal of authorization to arm the ships under construction.[177] At the same time he assured Dayton that the ships would not be able to sail without his permission.[178] However, when he sent a confidential dispatch to the finance minister, Achille Fould, calling on him to suspend authorization for the vessels to leave port, Fould replied that it was only possible to prohibit munitions from leaving. Ships were not concerned.[179] Things were further complicated when Slidell tried to have Napoléon III reverse the decision.[180] However, Drouyn de Lhuys maintained his objections.[181] As the builders refused to lose this deal without ensuring the ships that had been ordered could be sold, the foreign minister ordered Arman to sell them only to neutrals.[182]

Fearing a new maneuver by Napoléon III, early in the following year the U.S. diplomats attempted to alert opinion by making the chicanery public. The incriminating documents were handed over to *L'Opinion Nationale*, a newspaper that gave voice to defenders of the Northern cause. The article was published on April 30, 1864, with the title "The Southern Privateers." The paper received a warning from Interior Minister Paul Boudet, but it achieved its goal;[183] Rouher, the minister of commerce, solemnly assured Dayton that the ships would never be sold to the Southerners. For his part, Chasseloup-Laubat ordered that no ship of Arman's be allowed to sail without the authorization of the foreign minister.[184] In May 1864, Napoléon ordered Arman to sell the ships.[185] One of the ironclads, the *Cheops*, was sold to Prussia and the other, the *Sphinx*, to Denmark (the two countries were at war). Denmark also acquired two of the armed ships, the *Osaca* and *Yeddo*; the other two, the *San Francisco* and *Shanghai*, were sold to Peru.[186]

What can we learn from the "Arman ships affair"? As with the question of Confederate recognition, the emperor's attitude must be dissociated from that of his ministers, even if Napoléon III's position varied according to the diplomatic context. It does seem that in the fall of 1862, as he was on the verge of offering his mediation in the Civil War, the emperor appeared to have no qualms about diverging from the declaration of neutrality. For Napoléon, however, the building of the ships was subject to absolute secrecy; thus the leaks informing the Union representative irrevocably condemned Arman's ships to be sold to neutrals. If things dragged on, this was not to win time but simply because the emperor did not want to prejudice the owners of the Bordeaux and Nantes shipyards before they could see their orders honored. He was more concerned about the loss of a buyer for the shipbuilders than about breaking his word.

The Quai d'Orsay was completely ignorant of the plan and discovered it at about the same time as the Union representatives. From that moment, the determination and constant efforts of the foreign minister to enforce neutrality were decisive. He brought the case to his colleagues' attention and strove to overcome their reticence or hostility. He marginalized the emperor by assuring the minister of the Lincoln government that the ships would not be sold, even disarmed, to the South. His interests were served by the article Dayton had published in the *L'Opinion Nationale*, which, in calling the public and especially the legislature to witness the affair, helped accelerate the sale of the ships to neutrals. The resolve and obstinacy of the head of French diplomacy were what ultimately led the imperial government to change its view.[187]

This about-face was a severe disappointment for the Southerners, who saw it as "the violation of a commitment made in mutual trust."[188] In a final development, when in early 1865 the battleship *Stonewall*, formerly the *Sphinx*, was having damage repaired in Spain after a storm, it was curiously immobilized by the authorities.[189] Drouyn de Lhuys is believed to have convinced Mercier, the former agent in Washington who was by that time ambassador to Madrid, to put pressure on the Spanish government not to let the battleship leave. As Minister Plenipotentiary John Bigelow later acknowledged, had Arman's ships been seaworthy a year earlier (as the contracts originally foresaw), the course of the war might well have been affected.[190]

THE *RAPPAHANNOCK* AFFAIR

In the summer of 1863, France was confronted for the first time with the arrival of Southern ships in its ports. On August 23, 1863, the CSS *Florida* anchored at Brest to repair its machinery and caulk its holds.[191] The rules governing belligerent vessels' use of French ports were strict. The *Florida* was entitled to the full use of port facilities (and therefore could also buy coal, which was not treated as contraband of war), but its armament could not be increased, nor could Frenchmen be enlisted to supplement its crew. The latter condition was the most damaging because the *Florida* had suffered a mass exodus of its crew members. The ship failed to make up its original numbers and gathered just enough men to sail. To return to sea it had to evade detection by the USS *Kearsarge*, which was cruising continuously off the coast of Brittany.[192] Taking advantage of a moment of inattention from the *Kearsarge*, the *Florida* departed Brest on February 9, 1864.[193]

Other Confederate ships copied the *Florida*. In October 1863, the CSS *Georgia* anchored in Cherbourg, also for repairs. However, due to its miserable performance, the ship's captain wanted to get rid of it. The *Georgia*'s armament was in perfect condition, however, and was to be recovered. The CSS *Rappahannock*, which had left England to avoid being confiscated and fled to Calais, was finally chosen for this mission.[194] The transfer was to be made off the French coast. The arrival of the *Rappahannock* was immediately reported to the U.S. legation by its spies. As with London, which under pressure from the Federal government had closed its ports to Confederate ships, Dayton called for the minister of the navy to have the ship moved off. Chasseloup-Laubat replied that there was no reason to prevent the *Rappahannock* from staying in Calais. It was not contravening neutrality.[195] The foreign minister did not share Chasseloup-Laubat's opinion and sided with Dayton. On February 4, 1864, the *Rappahannock*'s commander was served with the order to leave the port of Calais, failing which the ship would be immobilized until the end of the war in America.[196]

However, once Drouyn de Lhuys understood that the *Rappahannock* was supposed to recover the *Georgia*'s armament off the French coast, he changed his mind. He called at that point for the ship to be immobilized.[197] Chasseloup-Laubat conformed to the opinion of Drouyn de Lhuys and ordered that the vessel not be allowed to leave, arguing that the *Rappahannock* had increased its crew by hiring British sailors and Confederate officers.[198] On February 17, he informed Drouyn de Lhuys of his decision, which met with the foreign minister's approval.[199] Faced with these changes of opinion, on February 26, 1864, the Confederates tried unsuccessfully to appeal to the foreign minister. John Slidell wrote to Drouyn de Lhuys challenging the number of enlisted sailors given (without denying the surreptitious increase that this proved).[200] He recalled that the *Rappahannock* had not violated neutrality because it was not armed. Without giving a substantive response, Drouyn de Lhuys replied that the arrangements were consistent with France's neutrality since the ships received "a welcome similar in every respect to that which was reserved for Federal ships."[201]

From that point on, things degenerated into an improbable diplomatic mess. To get around Drouyn de Lhuys's objections, the Richmond government's envoy mobilized all the supporters he had in the imperial cabinet. On March 14, 1864, Slidell returned to the attack, asking the minister of foreign affairs to authorize the *Rappahannock* to leave Calais.[202] He must not have expected much from this renewed request as the next day he alerted the emperor with a note to his private secretary, Jean-François Mocquard, demonstrating in several points that detaining the ship was a breach of neutrality.[203] Conscious that the wind was changing, the foreign minister resorted to tricks to delay the ship's departure. He entrusted the *Rappahannock* file to a committee of experts to determine whether the increase of the crew was a violation of neutrality, which at the same time made his lack of solid arguments obvious. To guarantee the committee's decision, Napoléon III chose a friend and member of the Privy Council, the lawyer, Senate president, and notorious pro-Confederate Théodore Troplong, to lead the debate.[204] When the committee authorized the *Rappahannock* to sail, Drouyn de Lhuys complied with this verdict and, on June 21, finally issued a favorable opinion.

This approval was only for show, however, for by late June nothing had yet happened. Slidell turned again to his contacts close to Napoléon III. On July 1 he met with Victor de Persigny, one of the emperor's most faithful servants, then Charles de Morny, the emperor's half-brother, to ask them to intervene. Slidell openly criticized Drouyn de Lhuys and both men promised to inform Napoléon. Finally, Slidell got what he was after; in a note written by Napoléon on July 7, just before the emperor left for Vichy to take his fourth cure, Persigny was told that instructions had been given to release the *Rappahannock*.

By July 9, no order had been passed on. Drouyn de Lhuys was deliberately ignoring the emperor's signal for the ship to be released. He preferred to remind him of his responsibilities. On July 10, 1864, he sent the emperor a report that restated his entire case.[205] Slidell then turned to Chasseloup-Laubat, the minister of the navy, who pledged his support and expressed surprise that there could be a difference of opinion between the emperor and the foreign minister. On July 11, the Confederate envoy again appealed to Drouyn de Lhuys, reminding him of the position he had held three weeks earlier.[206] Having received no response, on July 15 he wrote a note summarizing his fruitless efforts to Mocquard, who had accompanied the emperor to Vichy. In his reply of July 19, the emperor's private secretary indicated that the instruction had been given to let the ship leave. Nevertheless, this discounted the determination of the foreign minister, who decided to go to Vichy to convince Napoléon III not to give in to Southern entreaties. He devised a false pretext to prevent the *Rappahannock* from setting out to sea: if the ship's crew were limited to thirty-five men it would be impossible to maneuver, especially if it had to confront the *Kearsarge* that was lying in wait for the *Rappahannock*'s release off the French coast.[207]

Chasseloup-Laubat informed Slidell of this decision by reading him the letter that Drouyn de Lhuys had sent from the spa town. The minister of the navy indicated to Slidell that he did not approve the clause and deplored such harsh requirements. As soon as Drouyn de Lhuys returned, Chasseloup-Laubat promised to discuss the matter with him to have these draconian provisions softened.[208] Nevertheless, once back in Paris, the foreign minister, bolstered by his success in persuading Napoléon III, undertook to convince the other members of the cabinet. He eventually won over the empress to his views, and it was she who chaired the cabinet meeting. On July 28, 1864, Chasseloup-Laubat informed Slidell that the decision had been made to stick to the instructions given in February.[209] The case had been heard. The *Rappahannock* would remain in port until the end of the war.

In Slidell's opinion, Drouyn de Lhuys had bowed to pressure from the representative of the Lincoln administration. This is highly likely. The minister indeed feared that Washington would hold France responsible for any damages that the *Rappahannock* might inflict upon Union vessels.[210] Drouyn de Lhuys kept the U.S. authorities regularly informed of his actions, whether he was giving the order to release the ship or to immobilize it, insisting that his remarks be reported to Seward.[211] It was the Mexican situation that urged him to caution. He was considering the risks of serious friction with the North at a particularly sensitive time, as a new power was being established in Mexico City under French auspices. The threat was clear: as long as France remained neutral, the North would refrain from intervening against French interests in Mexico.[212] Paris was worried about the harm the Federals could cause by cutting the supply lines of the French expeditionary forces.

Looking at the facts, France had nothing to fear. If armaments were delivered to the *Rappahannock* out at sea by the *Georgia*, France's responsibility would not be incurred. It could even be said that the foreign minister went beyond the law and favored the North by delaying the *Rappahannock*'s departure. Confederate secretary of state Benjamin's anger was understandable; he fulminated, arguing that France had shown partiality and was respecting a tacit understanding between Paris and Washington.[213]

———

While at the start of the conflict, the Southerners thought that Spain, which had not abolished slavery, was the country most likely to form an alliance with them, they found in Napoléon III a champion to defend their cause in Europe.[214] However, the emperor had to reckon with the resolute opposition of Thouvenel and Drouyn de Lhuys, who regularly thwarted his plans. The *Rappahannock* affair was perhaps the acme of these convoluted negotiations. The Confederate envoys understood that at the highest echelons of state there was no consensus on the position to adopt toward the South. As they attentively followed the exercise of French diplomacy, they saw that it was possible to draw the actors into opposition, to hamper the foreign minister's efforts by encouraging his colleagues to contradict him, or even to appeal to the emperor and his entourage to achieve their ends.

» 3 «

THE ENTENTE CORDIALE
AND AMERICAN POLICY

Most U.S. historians consider that between 1861 and 1865, France could not have intervened alone in American affairs. The French government set too much store by the United Kingdom's foreign policy to act at variance with the British position. If France relinquished its aim of recognizing the government in Richmond, they maintain, this was due to Britain's refusal to depart from neutrality.[1] However, there are several major objections to this argument. First, the emperor's plan to return France to its former standing made any subordinate relationship unthinkable. The policy of grandeur was incompatible with such dependence, if not trusteeship. Second, far from complying with the British position, French foreign policy regularly broke with it. Third, despite efforts to coordinate the two countries' foreign policies, the Civil War did not erase past disagreements. Old quarrels regularly resurfaced to disrupt a climate that London and Paris would have preferred more cordial. The Anglo-French relationship was a checkered one. That being the case, what part did the entente with England play in the formulation of French policy toward America after 1860?

A CHECKERED RELATIONSHIP

With the accession of King Louis-Philippe in 1830, a rapprochement was initiated between France and Britain, known as the first "entente cordiale." How-

The Reception of Queen Victoria by Napoléon III at St. Cloud, 18 August 1855. Charles-Louis Müller, 1856. Courtesy of the Royal Collection Trust, Buckingham Palace, London, UK.

ever, this entente fluctuated greatly over time, and much depended on the men in power. In 1834, ties already began to slacken. Those in charge of foreign policy on either side of the Channel made no secret of their mutual dislike. Foreign Affairs Minister (and future president) Adolphe Thiers was not fond of England, while Minister of Foreign Affairs (and prime minister) Lord Palmerston remained very distrustful of France, which he still suspected of dreaming of conquest. To make matters worse, in 1840 diplomatic relations suffered from the Oriental Crisis.[2] Relations warmed significantly with the appointment as foreign minister of François Guizot, who found himself opposite the conciliatory Count of Aberdeen. In 1843 and 1845 Queen Victoria was hosted by Louis-Philippe, and he visited the queen in 1844. However, the affair of the Spanish marriages in 1846 disrupted this harmony and saw Palmerston return to the Foreign Office.[3]

The arrival of Louis-Napoléon Bonaparte to the French presidency seemed auspicious. He enjoyed England and made no fewer than five trips there under the July Monarchy. The country inspired him. He considered the English political system effective, was impressed by Britain's industrial development, which he aspired to replicate in France, and welcomed the free trade policy that was boosting commerce. Unlike his uncle, the prince-president and future emperor intended to make the English alliance a pillar of his foreign policy. He made considerable efforts and sought, without jeopardizing national interests, to keep the British happy. As a result, Napoléon III was often forced to make concessions to render his policy more acceptable to the English.[4] For instance, he gradually distanced himself from the cabinet in St. Petersburg, with which he had previously been on excellent terms.[5]

On June 2, 1853, the Entente Cordiale was reactivated, greatly facilitated by Aberdeen's return to office, this time as prime minister. The Crimean War marked the peak of the Entente. Prince Albert met Napoléon III in November 1854 in Boulogne, and in April 1855 the imperial couple was invited to London. In August the emperor returned the courtesy to Victoria, and during her visit to Paris, where she attended the World Exhibition, she paid tribute to the tomb of Napoléon I — a highly symbolic gesture.[6] In August 1857 Napoléon III, accompanied by Eugénie, was received at Osborne on the Isle of Wight. The queen returned to France at Cherbourg in August 1858.[7]

At the end of the 1850s, the relationship soured. London did not appreciate the emperor's adventurism in matters of foreign policy or his desire to permanently rescind the Vienna treaties.[8] Conversely, he felt a little too constrained by British inaction, not to say conservatism. The parting of policies is difficult to date, but it seems that Felice Orsini's attempted assassination of the emperor in 1858 had a real impact on Napoléon III's state of mind.[9] It was in England that the plotter had prepared his attack and obtained the bombs. Napoléon took advantage of this to demand that measures be taken against Republican refugees residing in Britain, which pleased no one.[10] Symbolic of this evolution was the course followed by Alexandre Walewski. As French ambassador in London, he had helped bring the two nations closer together, but once head of diplomacy he was less determined to keep up his efforts.[11] This was the result of having reassessed which partnership would be the most useful for France; he leaned more toward Austria.[12] It was also because the relationship suffered from Palmerston's return as prime minister, as his "brutal diplomatic behavior" during the Oriental Crisis was still fresh in Walewski's mind.

The Cobden-Chevalier Treaty on trade was little more than window dressing, for at the same time, with the launch of France's most powerful warship, the *Gloire*, England worried that the revival of the French fleet would challenge its maritime hegemony.[13] The countries engaged in an arms race, and in diplomatic matters the two powers did not always act in concert. Policy toward the United States was affected. As the minister of France in Washington, the comte de Sartiges, deplored, it seemed that from that moment on France could no longer rely on the British government to oppose U.S. plans, particularly in Central America or Cuba.[14] England's concerns turned to Asia, where it sought to consolidate its influence.[15] This new British strategy would not stop joint actions being considered, as in China. However, these were more a response to the need for mutual military support in distant expeditions than they were a translation of political objectives previously defined by the two cabinets.

COORDINATION EFFORTS

Nonetheless, in late 1860, faced with the unprecedented events that were rocking the United States, France and Britain sought to coordinate their policies on the American question. This was a common-sense measure, for each was aware that the conflict could seriously affect relations between the two continents. Thouvenel was able to rely on the experience of his ambassador to the United Kingdom, the comte de Flahaut, aged seventy-five. The two men shared a mutual respect. Flahaut admired Thouvenel's qualities and, in return, the minister did not hesitate to confide in a man over thirty years his senior.

In February 1861, Flahaut informed Thouvenel of his meeting with Lord Russell, the British secretary of state for foreign affairs. With regard to secession, Russell wanted the agents of both powers in the United States, Mercier for France and Lyons for the United Kingdom, to act in concert.[16] Thouvenel approved this approach.[17] The message was passed on clearly across the Atlantic.[18] Faced with the defection of several states, Thouvenel probed the British government to find out what position it intended to take.[19] At that time London had not decided anything. Flahaut highlighted Russell's indecision, which came from the latter's hostility toward the tariff policy applied by the North, on the one hand, and his disgust for the slavery practiced in the South, on the other.[20] However, once it became clear that secession had led to an armed conflict and England produced its declaration of neutrality, Paris announced it would do the same.[21] To decide on the protocol to follow in receiving the Southern envoys, Thouvenel asked Flahaut whether Russell had taken any special precautions in accepting to meet them.[22] Flahaut replied that the foreign secretary had received them unofficially.[23] Thouvenel followed suit when he granted Rost an interview in late June.

The foreign ministers on both sides of the Channel welcomed this convergence. In July 1861, in an official note to his agent in the United States, Russell reaffirmed his wish to make known that on the American question, the two governments would act together.[24] For his part, Thouvenel wrote in August to Flahaut that he "continued to walk in step with Lord Russell in American affairs."[25] In the first months of 1862, the intention to collaborate showed no signs of faltering. Without England's help, Napoléon III renounced the idea of breaking the blockade established by the North.[26] Thouvenel repeated to Flahaut that the emperor intended to do nothing about the United States without the full agreement of London.[27] Nor did he intend to do anything about recognition of the Confederacy. In June 1862, Adolphe Billault, the government's rapporteur before Chambers, reiterated to Slidell that to initiate such a step, British cooperation was essential.[28]

Can it be concluded that, with regard to American events, France's fate was tied to that of England? Napoléon III said so to Slidell on many occasions, and his actions did nothing to belie his words. However, it must be noted that he took this position with a military operation in mind, a solution first envisaged for breaking the blockade (see chapter 8). A diplomatic gesture in favor of the South also raised the strong possibility of military action to counter the reprisals that the Federal government would certainly unleash in return. In June 1863, Napoléon told Slidell that he did not want to act in discord with London because of the assistance that England could provide to protect the Mexican expedition, which the Federals would not fail to attack if France gave the South what it wanted.[29] It was, therefore, less the diplomatic question that depended on the British than the possible repercussions of this decision for France. In other words, if the emperor hesitated to recognize the South, it was not because the United Kingdom was unwilling but because without British support he would be left alone to face Washington. Napoléon's decision was not "blind conformity" but realism. What is more, invoking the necessary agreement of London was an ideal excuse to shirk all responsibility and leave the British government entirely accountable for the failure of Slidell's efforts.

For the Quai d'Orsay, the collaboration enabled it to compare views and agree on a diplomatic stance, then to best coordinate the action of the agents so a common front could be drawn. Thouvenel well understood that in relations with the two belligerents, France could only be strengthened by a joint position. It was not, however, a question of modeling the Quai d'Orsay's policy on that of the Foreign Office. British neutrality did not convince France but rather backed up its desire to refuse to recognize Confederate independence. Why would France, which had no major interests to defend in North America, get more involved than its neighbor? The British reserve therefore altered nothing in Thouvenel's thinking since he was convinced early on of the futility of such an act. However, he did make use of it to counter Napoléon. Without letting the opinion of the English authorities count unduly in determining its choices, the Quai played on the British position to avoid being dragged into a reckless venture.

DIVERGENT DIPLOMATIC CHOICES

It was not unknown for London to come round to the French position, especially as French foreign minister Thouvenel carried weight with his diplomatic counterparts. Early in the war, his insight helped him sniff out the trap set by the North when it proposed to adopt all the articles of the Declaration of Paris. It was he who warned the British of the dangers of a full ratification, which could advantage one of the belligerents in defiance of neutrality.[30] There were also times when the Foreign Office sought the support of Paris. During the *Trent* incident, England immediately adopted an unequivocal position and took the risk of causing a break in diplomatic relations. For its part, France played for time and preferred to work through the crisis diplomatically.[31]

Furthermore, Paris did not follow London blindly. The French declaration of neutrality was not directly modeled on the British one but drew on the findings of a committee of experts, which the French government had mandated to examine the situation created by secession. This in part explains why the text was published after the British government's proclamation. In the matter of a diplomatic intervention in favor of the Davis cabinet, some historians admit that following the Confederates' second victory at Bull Run on August 29 and 30, 1862, the British government was quite close to succumbing to the siren call of the Confederates.[32] The Union defeats cumulated with domestic problems caused by the lack of cotton.[33] In September, in a letter to his foreign secretary, Prime Minister Palmerston wondered whether mediation might be advisable. Working on the hypothesis that in the wake of Lee's offensive in Maryland, Washington and Baltimore would fall into Southern hands, he asked himself if it would not then be time for England and France to advise the warring parties to accept separation. If the North refused to negotiate, should the two powers not recognize the independence of the South as a fait accompli? Nonetheless, Palmerston wanted to await the outcome of Lee's invasion.[34]

Russell, for his part, considered offering mediation, followed, in the event of the Lincoln cabinet's refusal, by recognition of its opponent.[35] The foreign secretary planned a cabinet meeting for either September 23 or 30 to discuss mediation and asked his ambassador in Paris to bring up the possibility of the emperor's cooperation with the French foreign minister.[36]

Between September 30 and October 2, news of the mixed result for the Union at Antietam reached Europe. The reverberations of the bloody clash were not simply military. On October 2, upon hearing that the commander of the Army of Northern Virginia had retreated, Palmerston decided to give himself more time.[37] He did not abandon the idea of mediation, but, unlike his foreign secretary, on whom Antietam seemed to have had no effect, he wanted to wait for the situation to be clarified by more decisive events.[38] The Battle of Antietam was thus a turning point less in the diplomatic history of the war than in the British government's outlook.[39]

Was the imperial government tempted impulsively to imitate its counterpart across the Channel at the announcement of the Second Battle of Bull Run? Quite the opposite. France was not ready to cross the Rubicon. Thouvenel adopted a more cautious position than his British counterpart. On September 13, 1862, Russell instructed his ambassador in Paris to sound out the foreign minister on the possibility of a joint proposal for an armistice, followed, should the North reject it, by the threat of recognition of the South. The head of the Quai d'Orsay, guided by a report from Mercier, his minister in Washington, was not inclined in this direction. He recommended waiting for the midterm elections to be held a few weeks later in the Union states. He thought the North's disappointments might lead it to compromise. In choosing a diplomatic course, the French government focused less on the result of battles than on that of the popular vote.[40] Therefore, while the emperor's first mediation proposal was indeed an idea borrowed from the British government, but decided without consulting London, the next one was a purely French initiative.

Drouyn de Lhuys, Thouvenel's successor, also avoided following the British. On the question of building Confederate ships, he was particularly scrupulous in seeking to respect neutrality. Even if it meant going against Napoléon III, he did everything to ensure the warships were not delivered to the North's enemies (see chapter 2). Unlike the United Kingdom, at the end of the war France could congratulate itself for not having yielded to the South.[41] A few years later, before the arbitral tribunal in Geneva, the United

States would highlight the contrast between the two countries to prove that a different attitude had been possible.[42] Moreover, the Geneva tribunal ordered Great Britain to pay the United States reparations for the damage caused by the *Shenandoah* and *Alabama*.[43]

The gap between the two countries' American policies is understandable, as France did not have the same view of the United States as its neighbor across the Channel. British worries centered on increasing U.S. power, the threat it posed to Canada, and U.S. competition in the North American market. The two economies' growing interdependence may explain why, after 1815, they never let their squabbles fester to the point of war.[44] However, while France also feared the dynamism of the young country, which could focus its energies on expanding into Mexico, the French did not lose sight of the British hegemony that was built on France's own decline. Some contemporaries — starting with the emperor, who was no stranger to contradiction — noted that the United Kingdom had more to gain from the division of the Union than France. Napoléon III, though favorable to the independence of the Confederate states, was forced to admit to Slidell that the United States should be united to counterbalance England.[45] French recognition of the Confederacy would, therefore, be doubly counterproductive because in addition to focusing the North's wrath on France, which had nothing to gain from the Union's disappearance, it would also strengthen Britain's position in the world.

Thouvenel raised this inconsistency after the emperor authorized Slidell to submit a request for recognition of the Confederacy. On July 21, 1862, Thouvenel wrote to his ambassador in London, "I cannot conceive, in short, that we could be in a greater hurry than England, nor that we would risk taking sole responsibility for a task from which she would draw the profit and, in doing so, turn against ourselves the feelings it excites among Americans."[46] The liberal press was also quick to put forward this argument. The Civil War was a boon to England, which sought to weaken a rising power.[47] It recalled that Louis XVI had helped the colonist insurgents create a nation to compete with England on the shores of the Atlantic. By accepting the division of the Union, France would restore England in the land from which French ancestors had driven the English out.[48] After two wars against the United States, one lost and the other a draw, the Civil War would herald British revenge.[49]

A NOT-SO-CORDIAL ENTENTE

The character of relations between France and the United Kingdom fluctuated greatly over time. They could be warm or far from cordial. Inclement periods resulted primarily from changes in diplomatic leadership and the relationships between the men. The choice of Flahaut to replace Persigny at the head of the French embassy in London boded well since, like Walewski before him, he was a strong supporter of the entente with England.[50] However, the ambassadors of the imperial government in the United Kingdom suffered from having Lord Russell as their interlocutor.[51] Henri de La Tour d'Auvergne, appointed to this position in place of the baron Gros, encountered great difficulties with the British foreign secretary, whom he considered harsh and fickle.[52] In Washington, discord set in between Henri Mercier and Richard Lyons, the agents of France and the United Kingdom. According to Mercier, things began to sour in September 1861 because the British agent failed to consult with him, particularly on the issue of the blockade, with regard to which the two men were expected to work together.[53] This perhaps explains why, independently of his colleague, Mercier decided to go to Richmond, where he hoped to win a diplomatic success by opening discussions between the two parties. Lyons was surprised not to have been informed, and that it was not he but the minister of Russia whom the head of the French legation had asked to accompany him. Lyons inferred from this a change in his colleague's attitude.[54]

The difficulties also came from the top. Prime Minister Palmerston distrusted France, which he still saw through the lens of the Napoleonic epic. He was wary of the imperialist appetites of French leaders and suspected them of constantly seeking glory through domination or interference. This was already the case in the time of Louis-Philippe, after the serious friction that resulted from the Oriental Crisis and the affair of the Spanish marriages; it was even more obvious with the policy of grandeur the emperor intended to pursue. The French ambassador wrote that Palmerston had never concealed his lack of sympathy for the imperial government.[55] He despised Napoléon III, whom he called "the crafty spider of the Tuileries."[56] In a dispatch sent in April 1860 to Lord Cowley, his ambassador in Paris, Palmerston quipped that "the emperor's mind seems as full of schemes as a warren is full of rabbits."[57] This animosity may have been caused by the two occasions on which he was a collateral victim of tragic events in France. In 1851 Palmerston approved the Bonaparte coup while the British ambassador to France, Lord Normanby, condemned it. Subsequent to this diplomatic bungling, he had to submit his resignation to the queen. In 1858, following the Orsini bombing, Palmerston tried to pass a bill considered a threat to liberties but was defeated by Commons.[58]

Conversely, Thouvenel was well aware of Palmerston's resentment of him. He spoke of the latter's "false impressions" about him. Palmerston had not forgotten that in 1850, when Thouvenel was minister plenipotentiary in

Athens, he had protested against the presence of the British navy in the port of Piraeus. A little later, as ambassador to Constantinople, Thouvenel had led a latent battle against the British representative, which had led to the recall of the latter in 1858.[59] At the beginning of the American Civil War, Napoléon's foreign minister regularly complained to Flahaut about this climate of mistrust.[60] He wondered what benefit London could derive from such suspicion.[61] The poisonous atmosphere weighed on Thouvenel's mind, and he was not very enthusiastic about maintaining an entente cordiale.[62]

From mid-1862, Thouvenel's usually measured words betrayed a certain annoyance when he spoke of his relations with Lord Russell. He was irritated at Russell's self-important manner toward him. He wrote to the French chargé d'affaires in London, "Lord John Russell has lately formed a habit which I do not like: that of giving me reprimands and diplomatic lessons." He expressed his displeasure to Cowley, the British ambassador.[63] As for Thouvenel's successor, preservation of the entente with London was simply not a priority because he was above all a supporter of the Austrian alliance.[64] Meanwhile, across the Channel, from 1864 onward the British cabinet turned its attention back to internal affairs. During this period, nothing existed like the bond forged between Guizot and Aberdeen to coordinate their countries' foreign policy.

France's disappointment also stemmed from the fact that its intervention in the *Trent* affair had yielded no returns.[65] On November 8, 1861, the British paddle steamer RMS *Trent*, carrying Mason and Slidell, the Confederacy's new envoys to Europe, was boarded in the Bahamas by Commander Charles Wilkes of the USS *San Jacinto*. The *Trent* was allowed to continue on its way, but Mason and Slidell were taken prisoner and brought to the United States. In Europe the arrests aboard a neutral ship caused a considerable stir, as much in diplomatic circles as in the press.[66] The dispute took an alarming turn. On November 30, 1861, Palmerston and Russell prepared a threatening ultimatum.[67]

Thouvenel was aware of the consequences such a crisis might provoke. While he gave his support to the British government, he decided concomitantly to write a note to the Federal government to elicit its disapproval of the men's capture. The note was very well argued and clearly detailed why this incident was a breach of the rights of neutrals. Cleverly, he cast the Lincoln government as the victim of Captain Wilkes's impulsiveness.[68] With rather telling suspicion, the British were wary of Thouvenel's initiative to begin with and thought it possible that the imperial government was looking to stir up tension so a war would break out between the North and England.[69] Yet, in the end, the note was well received by the British diplomats and press.[70] Across the Atlantic, Seward suggested to Mercier that the emperor's attitude gave him hope for a possible compromise.[71]

Thouvenel's note arrived in extremis in Washington on December 25 and was immediately delivered to Lincoln's cabinet meeting.[72] The note helped the Federal government find a way out. Seward made use of it in his reply to the British. In his dispatch he recognized that international law had been violated and that, to respect its principles, the United States had decided to let Mason and Slidell go.[73] News of the Confederate envoys' liberation reached Paris on January 10, 1862. The British government and public opinion commended France's efforts.[74] The French agents were a little quick to credit the French intervention alone for the U.S. retreat.[75] This was highly presumptuous. While the Federal government initially adopted a bellicose posture, rising tensions soon forced it to weigh the risks of a conflict with Britain and reconsider Seward's hardline strategy. This led it to tame the anger aroused by the British note, which greatly facilitated Thouvenel's task.[76]

Thouvenel's assistance was not disinterested; he offered it to strengthen the entente with London. On December 26, 1861, he told his ambassador in London that he hoped France's conciliatory attitude would inspire "some remorse in Lord Palmerston and Lord Russell," and that he would not see a return to such mistrust in a hurry.[77] But the French government was sorely disappointed. In April 1862 the emperor was flush with resentment at the British refusal to break the North's blockade militarily (see chapter 8). He regretted that despite Thouvenel's dispatch concerning the *Trent*, which had resolved the crisis the previous December, Russell did not wish to cooperate with him. In July, Slidell reported that Napoléon III accused England of not having expressed sufficient gratitude for his intervention in its dispute with the United States.[78] He considered that his government had, in fact, allowed England to avoid a war. After the criticism, mistrust set in. Three months later, Napoléon III thought he perceived a certain Machiavellianism in British policy, suggesting to Slidell that he suspected London of attempting to poison relations between Paris and Washington.[79]

An incident that was revealed a year later, in July 1863, relating to the French mediation heightened the tensions.[80] The previous October, Napoléon III had taken up the idea Russell's suggestion of a month earlier to submit the North-South dispute to arbitration (see chapter 2). The British were irritated by the circumstances under which France communicated the mediation proposal. Drouyn de Lhuys sent a dispatch to London containing the conciliatory text on October 30, while Lord Russell was on leave. By the time Russell returned and was able to read it, the proposal had been made public. Drouyn de Lhuys denied having wanted to catch the British cabinet off guard. He explained that the French government had hastened to make the statement public simply to defuse the rumors of Confederate recognition circulating in the press. In addition, the Washington newspaper *Le Courrier des Etats-Unis* was to be shipped on November 13 with the mediation proposal included in its columns.[81]

On the French side, the resentment was due, first, to the Palmerston government's withholding of the text. It turned out that it had not seen fit to share the French mediation request with Parliament, and thus the text had remained in boxes at the Foreign Office. Second, the Tuileries cabinet was irritated by the circumstances under which the French offer of mediation was submitted to the Lincoln administration. It appeared that Richard Lyons, the British representative in Washington, had gotten hold of the proposal to submit himself to Secretary of State Seward. Given that the emperor was at the origin of this overture, the French believed they were entitled to be the first to advise the Federal cabinet via their minister in Washington.[82] Lyons's audacity was a breach of the laws of diplomacy.

—————

We must put these events in their proper context; the Civil War was not a priority of the diplomatic relations between London and Paris. The foreign ministries had more pressing concerns in the European theater.[83] A study of the agents' correspondence leaves no doubt as to the serious deterioration of the diplomatic climate between the two nations.

First there were the tensions in Syria. The imperial government was greatly disturbed by the murder of Christians with the Ottoman authorities' connivance. In the convention of September 5, 1860, it was decided that France would send an expeditionary force to the Middle East, but England, still touchy about Oriental affairs, set the condition that the force remain no more than six months. Yet in March 1861 the French were still present and Thouvenel had had enough of the British insistence that the troops leave the country.[84] But to calm London's growing irritation, born of concern that the expedition could lead to an extension of French influence in the Mediterranean just as construction of the Suez Canal was about to begin, the emperor repatriated his troops.

Second, London was worried about the French intervention in Italy. On the eve of Victor Emmanuel's appointment as the head of a kingdom that included northern and central Italy, Russell made it known that he disapproved of the imperial plan.[85] He continued to protest regularly against the occupation of Rome by French troops,[86] remarks that Thouvenel said made his government uncomfortable.[87] France's annexation of Savoy and the county of Nice aroused strong emotions in England.[88] London dreaded a new French expansion and feared France might set its sights on territory beyond the Rhine.[89] On several occasions, such as in April 1863, the British cabinet recalled that the Vienna agreements, which had sanctioned Napoléon I's defeat in 1815, were inviolable.[90] No alliance with France would lead England to abandon this system and risk making France a potential rival. In a speech a month later, Napoléon III responded to this warning by declaring that he "hated" the Vienna treaties and alluding to his plans to redraw the map of Europe.[91]

Other events the same year accentuated the gap between the two policies. The Polish uprising against the Russians divided the French and English.[92] Britain refused to join France in holding a conference, an idea that Queen Victoria described as "impertinence."[93] Poland was abandoned to its fate. This affair was followed in late 1863 by the question of the duchies of Schleswig and Holstein, which risked leading to a war between Denmark, Prussia, and Austria.[94] This time it was England that sought France's help, but the emperor would give no assistance.[95] Denmark lost its two duchies and two-fifths of its territory.

But it was the Mexican campaign that dealt the real blow to relations between London and Paris. In July 1861, following President Benito Juárez's decision to suspend payment of Mexico's foreign debt, including to the European powers, Madrid, London, and Paris resolved to use force against Mexico. The Spanish, British, and French governments sent troops that reached Vera Cruz in December 1861 and January 1862. But London and Madrid's sole aim in sending an expeditionary force was to uphold their financial claims. Paris felt the British were backtracking. Indeed, the British foreign secretary had initially favored the establishment of a stable government in Mexico but had changed his mind and now opposed an expedition that aimed to intervene in the country's internal affairs.[96]

The convention of La Soledad concluded on February 19, 1862, threw a little more oil on the fire. Signed by the Mexican government's envoy and representatives of the three Allied powers, it postponed the thorny problem of debt payments. Although the leader of the French expedition, Rear Admiral Edmond Jurien de La Gravière, had initialed the text, when the French government learned of the convention it expressed its disapproval.[97] The agreement presaged the withdrawal of the Spanish and British forces, a departure seen by the French as a sort of betrayal.[98] The emperor took it as a "capitulation."[99] The convention of Orizaba, signed on April 9, 1862, gave the signal for disengagement. Mexico agreed to repay its creditors. This promise allowed

Britain to follow the Spaniards' lead and reembark its men. When news of this repatriation was brought to his attention in June, Napoléon III made his bitterness known. The foreign minister, for his part, regretted that the two powers had been unable to present a united front in Mexico.[100] The situation became even more strained when it appeared that the British were sending arms to Juárez. The French ambassador to the United Kingdom protested but the English hid behind laws that prohibited their government from restricting trade with belligerent parties.[101] To top it all, Palmerston laid down draconian conditions for recognizing the government of Maximilian of Habsburg, the candidate chosen by France to sit on the Mexican throne. French diplomats wondered if this was not an excuse to sidestep the question.[102]

With so many disagreements, seeking unanimity on U.S. affairs was wishful thinking. In Washington, the cracks in the entente between the two countries did not go unnoticed. Seward, the head of Federal diplomacy, intuited very early on that the rivalry between France and England would render them incapable of collaborating.[103] He wondered how two countries with such different interests could appear willing to follow the same course.[104] In June 1861, in a dispatch to Thouvenel, Mercier wrote that he suspected Seward of wanting to drive a wedge into relations between the two countries. He noted that Seward refused to receive the two ministers plenipotentiary together and reserved his harshest words of resentment for England.[105] This difference in treatment was also highlighted by the French consul in Boston.[106] The following summer, Flahaut, the French ambassador to the United Kingdom, also shared his views on the subject with Thouvenel.[107] Flahaut said he was striving to impress upon the English government the need to quash any illusions the North might entertain of exploiting tensions between the two governments.[108]

Such illusions were shared by the Confederacy. Reminding Napoléon III of Richmond government's offer to supply cotton in exchange for war goods, John Slidell was quick to point out that such a proposal had not been made to Britain.[109] He even speculated that Le Havre could supplant Liverpool.[110] The two belligerents had understood that the united front put forward by France and England could easily be disrupted.

This less than cordial atmosphere perhaps explains the passivity of the Tuileries cabinet during the *La Blanche* affair. The ship had previously sailed under Confederate colors as the *General Rusk*, but it was sold on July 31, 1862, to a British subject who rechristened it. On October 4, 1862, *La Blanche* was taken for a blockade runner and inspected by a Federal ship in Cuban waters. A fire broke out onboard and the crew had to abandon ship. London reacted strongly, but the U.S. government considered that no one need be compensated for the fire because it was accidental. In the fall of 1863, the British government called for the French to act as intermediary in the crisis and to communicate with the Spanish government because the incident had occurred in its territorial waters. The British wanted France and Spain to join them in co-signing a declaration to be transmitted to the U.S. government, indicating that the neutral powers would deny it belligerent rights if it ignored the international obligations corresponding to those rights.[111]

The imperial government deliberately ignored Russell's dispatch. No instruction was given to the French ambassador in Madrid. The British were much displeased. Slidell surmised that this explained Queen Victoria's refusal to receive La Tour d'Auvergne, France's new ambassador to the United Kingdom.[112] Eventually, London's request was rejected and Drouyn de Lhuys announced that he refused to be associated with an approach he considered dangerous.[113] Unlike for the *Trent*, France would not intercede. It was to King Leopold that the British turned. The divorce was complete.

With regard to the unprecedented conflict in the United States, the attention devoted by the Tuileries cabinet to the position of its British counterpart nourished rather than governed its thinking. If France cooperated with London, it was to give more weight to French claims. France's demands that the rules of international law be respected were all the more compelling when associated with those of the leading world power. The entente was a means to protect the rights of neutrals, which both powers feared would be trampled by the warring parties given that the United States had not originally subscribed to the Declaration of Paris.

If we consider the state of mind of the protagonists, the emperor's position must again be distinguished from that of his foreign ministers. Napoléon III's desire to legitimize French action in favor of the South encouraged him to be attentive to the British position. He did not "follow" England strictly speaking, but he was dependent on its decision because he feared that a solitary initiative would isolate him diplomatically and, above all, militarily. However, after London's rejection of his first mediation proposal, with mistrust added to resentment, Napoléon resolved not to count on Russell and Palmerston to gain recognition of the Confederacy. He then placed his bets on the House of Commons to incline the British government to act in favor of the South. Getting the government to give in to parliamentary action — this position showed some nerve for an autocrat. It was a risky maneuver, for it could be seen as intolerable interference from the highest level. It could only further exacerbate the discord between the two countries.

For the two successive foreign ministers, the refusal to recognize the Confederacy was inspired not by England's position but by an objective evaluation of the benefit that France might draw from secession. Thouvenel and Drouyn de Lhuys both understood that the United Kingdom could profit a great deal from the American crisis. Defending the unity of the United States was a means to counterbalance the supremacy of British maritime trade and, indeed, British political hegemony. True, there was a fear of U.S. expansion, but British power remained a primary concern not least due to the preeminence of European interests. When he received Slidell in July 1862, the emperor himself admitted that the division of the Union could also bring disadvantages for France. He let slip the confidence that for French interests, the warring states should be reunited to counterbalance England.[114] These words show that the emperor was divided between his American ambitions and European realities. A contrary position would have put him at odds with the policy of his uncle, who had sold Louisiana to the United States in the hope that the country would eventually become a power to rival England.

Part Two

FRANCE'S VIEW OF THE SOUTH

» 4 «

MYTH AND REALITY

Southern propagandists hoped to rally the cream of French society to their cause. To do so, they sought to turn several factors to account. They stirred up the memory of French Louisiana, highlighted the North's stubborn refusal to let its rival leave the federation, recalled the South's adherence to free trade, seized upon the principle of national self-determination to present the South's struggle as that of an emerging nation that the North was attempting to suppress, and painted a picture of an aristocratic Dixie of European culture and customs. Yet these campaigners had to reckon with resolute opponents and the facts on the ground. The torments of the French nationals experiencing the war firsthand in the insurgent states gave the lie to the claims of the secessionist advocates. To what extent, then, was the French government influenced by a plea that had more to do with myth than fact?

A PRO-SOUTHERN ELITE

Napoléon III's aversion to the Northern states—the result of his unpalatable stay there in the late 1830s—was equaled by his partiality toward their opponents. Over and above his grand design, which he thought would be aided by the division of the Union, he expressed to John Slidell his sympathy for the Confederate States' struggle for independence.[1] The emperor's constant and emphatic support was no secret, and his pro-Southern leanings were common

Oak Manor Plantation, Alabama. Alex Bush, 1935. Historic American Buildings Survey. Courtesy of the Library of Congress, Prints and Photographs Division.

knowledge across the Atlantic from very early on.[2] Alfred Paul, the consul at Richmond, noted that this preference garnered Napoléon III the unequivocal goodwill of the government, the press, and the people of the South.[3] In January 1863, Jefferson Davis paid tribute to the "enlightened ruler of the French nation," to whom he felt indebted for the first official demonstration of sympathy for the suffering of his people.[4] The empress, who entered the political game in 1859 with the Italian affair, also revealed her propensity for the cause that Slidell so actively defended. Moreover, Slidell was surprised to find Eugénie so conversant in American affairs.[5]

Few members of the emperor's entourage expressed an opinion contrary to his. Thomas Evans, Napoléon's dentist, stressed in his memoirs that "the emperor was constantly surrounded by sympathizers of the South."[6] According to Adolphe Billault, one of three ministers without a portfolio, there was a significant contingent within the cabinet in favor of the states in rebellion.[7] Morny, the emperor's half-brother, professed to be won over to the Southern cause, as did the Interior Minister Victor de Persigny (a friend of Slidell's); Justice Minister Jules Baroche; Finance Minister Achille Fould; Navy Minister Prosper de Chasseloup-Laubat; Agriculture, Commerce, and Public

France's View of the South

Works Minister Eugène Rouher; as well as the former foreign minister, Alexandre Walewski.[8] Charles James Faulkner, U.S. envoy extraordinary and minister plenipotentiary to France until May 1861, noted that at the court balls, only friends of the South were present.[9] Elihu Washburne, later an ephemeral secretary of state under President Ulysses S. Grant before representing the United States in France from 1869 to 1877, reported that the Confederates were very popular in the capital as well as at the Tuileries Palace. A Confederate Woman's Aid Society organized by Southern women collected medical supplies and clothing in Paris for the Confederate army and staged fundraising concerts and bazaars.[10] In early 1862, the newly arrived Confederate emissary John Slidell is said to have received a standing ovation at the Bouffes-Parisiens Theater, while his Federal counterpart was booed.[11] Henry Hotze, the Southern propagandist in Britain, judged three-quarters of Parisian newspapers and a similar proportion in the provinces to be favorable to his government.[12] This picture drove the comte de Montalambert, one of the leading liberal figures, a legislator, and the editor of *Le Correspondant*, to despair. To Lucien-Anatole Prévost-Paradol, another brilliant opponent of the authoritarian empire, he wrote, "You would not believe how unpopular the North's cause is not only in the religious or fanatical world, but also in the political world—in our world."[13]

As for the diplomatic corps, the French minister to the United States, Henri Mercier, was presented by Slidell as very well disposed to his cause.[14] Mercier had many friends who were favorable to the South.[15] Despite his duty to show reserve, his partiality was nonetheless reflected in his account of events and descriptions of those involved. When writing his dispatches, the emperor's first agent had difficulty hiding the satisfaction he felt at the birth of a new republic in North America. He painted a very flattering portrait of Jefferson Davis, whom he considered "a true statesman" and contrasted in a caricatured manner to an inadequate and inexperienced Lincoln.[16] Mercier's bias was no secret because at the start of the war, one of his correspondents expressed to him a fear that the minister "had perhaps shown feelings overly favorable to the South." The writer thought this preference might weaken his influence with the Federal government.[17] By early 1862, Mercier could no longer ignore the accusations of partiality and had to defend himself. He rather inelegantly blamed his dubious assessments on the quality of the information provided to him by the consuls.[18] Thouvenel was forced to give Mercier a dressing down.[19] He admonished the agent to retain at least a semblance of objectivity in relating events and to resist being swayed by "the influence of articles in *Le Constitutionnel*."

Most French consuls likewise showed a preference for the Confederates.[20] The interim chargé d'affaires of the Charleston consulate identified himself on occasion with this camp.[21] In New Orleans, the comte Méjan's pro-Southern sympathies were common knowledge and were mentioned in the contemporary press.[22] Méjan estimated that secession could offer commercial opportunities in Europe by upsetting the hierarchy of the harbors of the United States. In this scenario New Orleans could replace New York for importing French goods to go around the tariff of the North. Convinced of this view, Méjan breached neutrality several times. For instance, he allowed French inhabitants to gather into militias and parade through the streets in a show of commitment to the Confederacy, which earned him Thouvenel's wrath. Thouvenel reminded Méjan that French residents had to abstain from "any interference whatsoever in the country's affairs."[23] The warning seems to have had little impact. During the fall of New Orleans, Méjan hid $405,000 in Confederate money in his consulate.[24]

WHY CHOOSE THE SOUTH?

In 1861 Henry Hotze convinced Judah P. Benjamin, then secretary of war of the Confederate States, to send him to Europe to create a propaganda network through which to popularize the Confederate struggle.[25] As they developed strategies to rally the political world and public opinion to their cause, these propagandists helped forge myths.[26] The most active propagandist in France was Edwin de Leon, who had letters published in the press and wrote articles for the newspaper La Patrie.[27] Alongside de Leon were natives of Louisiana, such as the Creole Paul Pequet du Bellet, whose first series of articles was published in February 1861 in Le Pays.[28] Slidell, the Confederate emissary to France, supported this approach. He well understood that wars are also won in the minds of the people.[29] The other camp was not to be outdone. Henry Shelton Sanford paid 500 francs per month to a certain Malespine, the Paris correspondent of Indépendance Belge, to defend the North in the columns of L'Opinion Nationale.[30]

Since many French people found the reasons for the Civil War obscure, the pro-South diplomats used a familiar point of reference: Louisiana. France had sold Louisiana to the United States in 1803, and this continued to form part of the collective memory under the empire. Mercier considered not only the French nationals living in that state (5 percent of the population) but all the residents of Louisiana to be French "in manners, language, and feelings."[31] Napoléon III spoke fondly to Slidell of these descendants of French settlers who still retained the old ways and language.[32] The conservative press also appealed to emotions, playing the card of the lost province. It portrayed Louisiana as a region of French culture and customs.[33]

The goal of these newspapers was to demonstrate an "affinity of races" and "original traditions" between France and Louisiana. The newspapers also evoked a need to defend these last vestiges of the Latin world and the Catholic Church from the threat of the Anglo-Saxon, Protestant Northern states.[34] This Pan-Latinist struggle was essential. The defense of the Latin world responded to a search for origins after the devastating Revolution, which had sought to make a clean break with the past. Many felt that the source of the French nation lay in Roman civilization, itself shaped by Greek and Christian contributions. Upon this foundation, a narrative could be constructed with which the French identified. During the Second Empire, a rediscovery of the Middle Ages helped forge a national history and give the Latin world a more identity-based meaning. But the Pan-Latinist agenda was more ambitious. Indissociable from the civilizational angle, it pursued political and economic goals on a European or global scale. In wanting to unite all the members of the great "Latin family," Pan-Latinism sought to recover a hegemonic position and thwart the growing power of the Germanic and Slavic peoples.

The idea of ethnic competition between Anglo-Saxons and Latins was reinforced in 1862, first by the French intervention in Mexico, and second by the occupation of New Orleans by Union general Benjamin Butler. Many saw the latter event as evidence of the North's desire to eradicate anything that might recall the French and Latin past. The Confederates appeared as the last barrier that could block the destructive advance of the Yankees toward Mexico. An alliance between France and the Confederacy was therefore essential for the defense of Pan-Latinism.[35]

The idea of an aggressive North became a leitmotif of diplomatic propaganda. The consuls believed that the Federal government's determination to favor the military option could only throw fuel on the fire. The consul in New Orleans predicted that Lincoln's decision to reinforce Fort Sumter would radicalize the separatists.[36] From this perspective, the bombing of the Federal position by the rebels was an act of self-defense.[37] From there it was a small step to rewriting history and saying that the North had declared war on the South. The French agents did not hesitate to follow Southern propagandists in describing the Union's fight against its rival as a "war of extermination."[38] The conduct of some Federal officers, such as General Butler's systematic bleeding of New Orleans, did half their work for them.[39] In this battle that pitted David against Goliath, some took pleasure in backing the underdog, especially if they thought the giant was hiding its true intentions. In Mercier's view, the blockade had only one goal: to protect the commercial interests of New York.[40] He believed the strategy betrayed the North's true motivation for war, namely, the fear of losing "a kind of colony." If the Federals reacted so forcefully it was because they were well aware that for them, the consequences of separation would be harmful, if not disastrous.[41]

Incongruous as it may seem, the South was also presented as the defender of freedom, given its conception of economic exchange. In February 1861 when the Confederacy was formed, the consul in New Orleans stressed the words of the new president, Jefferson Davis, in his opening address, when he asserted that the policy of the new republic should be based on the freedom of commercial transactions.[42] Unlike its opponent, the South did not propose a protectionist policy. This position struck a chord with the emperor, who was a supporter of free trade. Indeed, his idea of progress began with the abolition of customs borders to stimulate trade and bring peoples closer together, which should lead to the end of war. The reports submitted to the Quai d'Orsay suggested that the North's development owed nothing to its ability to innovate and everything to its prohibitive tariffs. The Southerners were gravely affected by the soaring customs duties that crippled consumers with a tax collected by the enemy.[43] With tariffs of 50 percent on wines, 40 percent on silks, and 25 percent on spirits, France also suffered greatly from the protectionism penalizing its exports.[44]

The South's destiny therefore seemed full of promise, for its independence meant a potential increase in trade. Mercier envisaged this prospect even before South Carolina seceded, as much in terms of finding a new market for French exports as of procuring cotton.[45] He saw the secessionist states' free trade policy as a golden opportunity for France to sell its products, which would not be subjected to tariffs at the new country's borders.[46] Alfred Paul, the consul in Richmond, reported the Southern authorities' claims that the nation that first recognized the new state would receive preferential treatment in commercial matters.[47] The boon for the business community was also described by Slidell in his letter to Thouvenel in July 1862.[48] Since the South did not have a merchant navy, its cotton could be transported under a European flag. The consul in New Orleans advised the French government to take advantage of the new state's emergence as a means to compete with England. Slidell wanted to give to the steamship line being planned between Le Havre and New York another, more profitable destination.[49] In the South everything remained to be built. As a liberated state, its potential was alluring. Mercier sent a book of statistics from the Federal capital showing that this region could benefit from French investment and expertise. The Southern states had everything to gain from secession.[50] Their valuable resources were just waiting to be exploited.[51]

To justify its fight, the South invoked the right of states to secede. Why would the American Union, formed by a federation of states, not let some of them leave if they so wished? The French representative in Washington, commenting on South Carolina's departure from the Union, said that neither the executive nor Congress could oppose the decision of a sovereign state.[52] The consul in New Orleans reached the same conclusion and considered Lincoln's policy illegal.[53] André Ernest Olivier Sain de Boislecomte, former French minister to the United States, also strongly questioned the legitimacy of action against the South. He believed that in writing "We the People of the United States" in the constitution, the Union had agreed to limit the federal tie by giving local representatives the greater power.[54]

The newspapers that supported the imperial government expanded upon these arguments. They vilified the military option preferred by the North and cast it as responsible for the war.[55] The Southerners' situation was likened to that of the Poles, both victims of a power that denied dissent.[56] The press hostile to Lincoln supported the rights of states, which it considered to have been flouted, and sided with the secessionists.[57] Even in the unreservedly pro-Union camp, it still seemed difficult to approve the North's inflexible refusal to let the states in rebellion go.[58] These newspapers did not dispute their right to leave the federation.[59] They believed that the North should think carefully before embarking on an enterprise whose human and material costs could be very high.[60] The conservatives expressed suspicion over the North's real intentions. For them, the tariff issue was the sole cause of a war encouraged by speculators and material ambitions.[61] Given that God had been banished from the business world in the United States, the Federals' resolve should come as no surprise.[62]

The friends of the South likened its fight to coming to the aid of oppressed nations. The idea took root all the more easily since secession occurred just as the Italians, with France's support, achieved their partial unification.[63] In July 1862, in the dispatch he sent to Thouvenel, Slidell expressed his view that it was time that France and England recognized his government because the Confederacy formed "an organized and independent people."[64] The nation allegedly differed from that of the North by virtue of its identity: an aristocracy of cultured, refined landowners steeped in tradition who were endeavoring — so the image went — to preserve a way of life and customs that came directly from Europe.[65] A North seen as impudent, uncultured, and greedy was contrasted with the pleasant manners, good education, and disinterest in material things of the Southern gentlemen. De Tocqueville had noted the same contrast in his day, when he opposed the Southern states with "the tastes, prejudices, weaknesses and grandeur of all aristocracies" to the Northern ones with the qualities and defects characteristic of "the middle class."[66]

The argument of the birth of a nation—which was to be taken up in October 1862 by the British chancellor of the exchequer, William Gladstone, in a famous speech—carried weight with the emperor.[67] A few months earlier, he had told Slidell that his sympathies had always been with the South because the people were fighting for the principle of self-government of which he was a "firm and constant advocate."[68] This was also the message that the Richmond government was pushing to French diplomats. In April 1862, during Mercier's visit to the Confederate capital, Confederate secretary of state Benjamin told him that the North and South now formed two distinct peoples.[69] The idea that a new nation was emerging in the South of the former United States, which the North was trying to crush, became the hobbyhorse of the pro-Southern press.[70] What earned the Confederacy all the more esteem was its unexpected strength, its Homeric tenacity, and the romanticism of despair. How could one not look kindly on a people struggling with such fierce will for their survival? Napoléon III saluted their courage.[71]

THE SOUTH'S CRITICS

Prévost-Paradol noted that part of the French public had been deceived by the South's propaganda. Never in France's history, he wrote, had there been a comparable blindness.[72] Yet because of the gaps in our knowledge of the subject, such a predilection remains difficult to establish. A study of French public opinion about the Civil War among the various social strata has yet to be conducted.[73] Moreover, the same social class can express opposite opinions depending on which of its interests are involved. The business community was just as concerned with preserving a good relationship with the North and its buyers of French products, despite the exorbitant tariffs applied, as it was worried by the lack of cotton. For many, the origins of the discord were difficult to grasp. It would seem that the average French person showed little interest in the Civil War.[74]

The South had to reckon with resolute and powerful opponents. The influence of men at court should not be overestimated. The progression of the authoritarian empire, to which they were attached, toward a liberal empire, is a reminder of this. It is clear that the Quai d'Orsay showed none of the enthusiasm of the emperor and some of his advisers toward the Confederates.[75] For

Thouvenel, the Southerners' practice of slavery made it impossible to embrace their cause. He was therefore naturally favorable to the North, but this did not prevent him from disapproving the forceful methods employed by the Lincoln administration to bring its opponents back into the Union fold.[76]

In October 1862, when Drouyn de Lhuys was appointed, Slidell wrote to Benjamin that the new French foreign minister had always been considered well-disposed toward their government.[77] Thouvenel, for his part, was worried about his successor's ignorance of American affairs and feared he would make hasty judgments influenced by the emperor.[78] Indeed, one of the new minister's first acts was to follow the emperor in proposing a mediation that advantaged the Confederates. Yet Drouyn de Lhuys was a conservative. He rejected all revolutionary movements. In this case, the principle that guided him was stability, and he was therefore instinctively opposed to the South's rebellion; all the more so if the rebellion was likened to the nationalist revolts that were sweeping across Europe, with which he felt no affinity.[79] He gradually distanced himself from the supporters of the Southern cause. In the spring of 1863 he informed Slidell that it was no longer appropriate for them to meet at the Quai d'Orsay.[80] By choice and by realism, those who formulated and implemented France's foreign policy were clearly hostile to the South. The South had not rallied the right players to its cause.

In addition, the Senate and the legislature were in favor of protectionism and did not share the criticisms of those who attacked the North's tariffs. Neither should we underestimate the role of certain figures, such as the emperor's cousin Prince Napoléon, who effectively counteracted the influence of Southern sympathizers on the emperor. Yet if Prince Napoléon's hatred of slavery put him on the Union's side, this did not make him an unconditional supporter. He criticized the North's individualism and love of money.[81] Nonetheless, he advocated its cause in his newspaper, L'Opinion Nationale.

There was also a section of the press favorable to the Lincoln government, and it attracted a fair audience. The majority of "liberal" and "Republican" newspapers were on the North's side, the most talented advocate of its cause unquestionably being Prévost-Paradol, who wrote for Le Journal des Débats. It was the same in Protestant circles. Although the control imposed by the regime prevented them from presenting their views without reserve, these newspapers nevertheless had an influence: Le Phare de la Loire mentioned L'Opinion Nationale, Le Siècle, La Revue des Deux Mondes, Le Journal des Débats, Le Temps, Le Nord, La Gironde, Le Journal du Havre, Le Progrès de Lyon, Le Mémorial des Deux-Sèvres, L'Union de l'Ouest, and L'Indépendance Belge as papers favorable to the North.[82] Le Courrier du Dimanche and Le Courrier de La

Rochelle can be added to these. Furthermore, the "semiofficial" papers far from exceeded the other organs in terms of circulation. *La Patrie* had a print run of 22,904 copies; *Le Constitutionnel*, 19,448; and *Le Pays*, 7,000;[83] while *Le Siècle* sold 52,300 copies — a little less than the other three put together[84] — *Le Temps*, 3,000; *L'Opinion Nationale*, 10,000;[85] *Le Journal des Débats*, 12,842 (almost as many as *Le Monde*, 13,982); and *La Revue des Deux Mondes*, 13,400.[86]

The objection could be made that a newspaper's influence depends on more than its circulation. But in fact, here again, the newspapers that criticized the Confederacy most strongly found a wider readership because their articles were often written by editors or journalists recognized for both their knowledge and their high-minded views. Judah Benjamin, the Confederate secretary of state, felt obliged to admit as much about *La Revue des Deux Mondes*.[87] Like Edouard Laboulaye, one of its greatest writers, the press at odds with Napoléon III's government believed that the outcome of the U.S. conflict was critical for Europeans. It considered the survival of the great republic essential, for it perceived this republic as a counterpoint to despotism and a unique political experiment.[88]

DIFFICULTIES FOR THE FRENCH
IN THE CONFEDERATE STATES

Among consular staff, support for the Confederacy was far from uniform or unqualified. The consuls denounced the Southerners for taking liberties with international conventions. For example, to be accepted as consul in Charleston, Durant Saint André was forced to disregard diplomatic practice: In order to avoid complications with the Confederate government, he did not go through Washington to receive his exequatur. In the spring of 1862, the consuls reported that Benjamin, the newly appointed head of Confederate diplomacy, was ordering them to request an exequatur from his government to be able to practice.[89] He received the support of the Confederate House of Representatives.[90] The consuls refused on the grounds that this procedure could only be demanded by a recognized government, which the Confederacy was not. Consequently, the Davis cabinet envisaged sending the consuls of France and England their passports. In the end this plan was abandoned, but the blunder left its mark.

The consuls were also provoked by the position of the Davis government toward French nationals living in the slave states. First, their business activities were targeted. In September 1861, article 2 of the instructions sent by the attorney general to his correspondents stipulated that nationals of neutral countries who traded with the states at war with the Confederacy would be considered "enemy aliens."[91] It therefore became impossible for the French people settled in the Southern states, who once traded with the North, to continue their profitable commerce. This discrimination was firmly condemned by the minister in Washington, who complained of it to Thouvenel.[92] The other cause of annoyance concerned the property of French nationals resident in the seceded states. While the Southerners were burning cotton, they also set fire to tobacco destined for export to Europe and owned by the Régie française des tabacs, the French national tobacco company.[93] From Boston to New Orleans, consuls and consulate secretaries denounced this gratuitous act for which, unlike for cotton, there was no justification.[94] Alfred Paul, the consul in Richmond, requested an interview with Secretary of State Benjamin to urge him to spare the French Virginia tobacco. Benjamin dismissed this request and promised that the imperial government would later be reimbursed for the losses it had incurred.[95]

The final cause for exasperation came as the Confederacy, foreseeing a shortage of manpower, decided to enlist French nationals into its armies. This was obviously contrary to the laws of war because foreign nationals had to be considered neutral. The consul in Boston observed that in none of the states loyal to the Union had any foreigner been obliged to do military service. Meanwhile, Thomas Moore, the governor of Louisiana, proposed on the basis of an old state law to incorporate all white men between the ages of eighteen and forty-five into the militia.[96] Consul Méjan objected.[97] Foreign Minister Thouvenel reacted vigorously, judging that it would be "monstrous" for the French to be exposed to abuse or ruin if they refused the draft.[98] Finally, in the autumn of 1861, Méjan got the state authorities to agree that the French of New Orleans—who numbered about 2,500—would be enlisted only to guard the city and maintain law and order.[99] However, when the city risked falling into the enemy's hands, those same authorities went back on their commitment. Méjan complained to his government.[100] In Richmond, Consul Paul equated this conscription to blackmail, since he believed it would be exercised as long as the new Confederacy was not recognized. He went further, accusing the police of the rebel states, who followed the orders of the governor of Virginia, of hunting Frenchmen down to force them to take up arms. Any who refused were sent to camps or prison. The consulate was besieged with French people who had not yet been affected by these measures. Paul agreed with his English colleague on a common approach toward the Confederate leaders. The Frenchmen were eventually released, but this belated leniency did not eliminate Paul's concerns.[101]

French nationals living in the Northern states who worried about being forcibly pressed into military service were soon reassured: the Federal government ruled out the enlistment of foreigners in the Union army from the outset. This was not the case in the South, where a law passed on April 16, 1862, provided for the conscription of foreigners. Although Jefferson Davis agreed to exempt them in November, abuses continued to be legion. Alerted by acts of violence taking place in Texas, at the beginning of the year Paul solicited the help of the secretary of state. Benjamin decided to intervene, but attempts to force the French to fight did not let up.[102] On the contrary, given the increasingly significant losses recorded by the South, the need for men was making itself even more keenly felt. After the summer of 1863, South Carolina reopened this explosive issue; in response the acting chargé d'affaires of the Charleston consulate proposed to offer the French the means to leave the Confederacy to avoid being subjected to this measure.[103] He sought the intervention of Gen. P. G. T. Beauregard, who eventually agreed to not take Frenchmen into his army, apart from volunteers, and to exempt them from military service.[104] The following year, after the act of February 17, 1864, extended military service to all men aged seventeen to fifty, the same consul was upset by the decree issued by the governor of Georgia under which all foreigners residing in that state who refused to mobilize for its defense would be forced to leave it within ten days.[105] The agent reported that Florida had taken a similar decision at the same time, but without allowing foreign nationals the choice to leave. Alabama followed suit.[106] It reached the point where the consuls' time was almost entirely taken up ensuring the protection of French nationals. The foreign ministers were prepared to assist them by sending Imperial Navy ships.[107]

THE BURDEN OF CONFEDERATE DIPLOMACY

The French government's view of the Confederacy was severely undermined by the personality of the heads of Confederate foreign policy and the agents they sent to Europe to represent them. There was no experienced figure who could forge close ties with the imperial government and boost the image of Confederacy. In the field of diplomacy, the ability to cultivate personal relationships is far from incidental.

Seen from Paris, the Confederate government left much to be desired. The naming of its president especially was greeted with caution. Jefferson Davis's time as secretary of war under the Pierce administration had aroused suspicion.[108] At the time, French agents had accused Davis of having accepted the position with a view to annexing Cuba or certain Mexican territories. The imperial government also found suspect his request that an American observation mission be sent during the Crimean War. For the then foreign minister—Drouyn de Lhuys—this smacked of espionage on behalf of Russia.[109] With the coming of the Civil War, some French consuls delighted in pointing out the shortcomings of the former senator from Mississippi. Alfred Paul, the consul in Richmond, made it his specialty. He regularly attributed to Davis all responsibility for the Confederacy's defeats. Already after Bull Run, he accused Davis of failing to take advantage of the confusion in the Northern camp to let General Beauregard score a decisive point on the battlefield.[110] Paul also criticized Davis's incomprehensible support of certain generals, such as Braxton Bragg.[111] The longer the conflict wore on, the more Davis's authoritarianism was disparaged.[112]

Until February 1862, at a time when the South needed continuity more than anything to deal effectively with the European powers, it was instability that prevailed. Three secretaries of state succeeded one another in one year. Unlike Lincoln's eternal secretary of state, William Seward, a former governor of New York who had acquired diplomatic experience on the Senate Committee for Foreign Affairs, who knew France and its government, and whose intelligence was noted (though his appearance criticized) by Prince Napoléon, Robert Toombs and Robert Hunter were poor choices, due more to their lack of motivation than to lack of skill.[113] The former would have been much better as secretary of the treasury, while Hunter reluctantly accepted a position that he had declined eight years earlier.[114] The third, Benjamin, seemed a much better choice; he combined intellectual agility and command of several languages with cosmopolitan savvy.[115] However, his support for cotton diplomacy (see chapter 8) and the Confederacy's actions against French consuls and nationals earned him the brunt of anger in Paris.[116] The longer the war continued and the less likely French recognition grew, the tenser the contacts between these agents and Benjamin became. Drouyn de Lhuys regretted that Consul Paul in Richmond had never seen Benjamin favorably disposed toward the French government.[117]

In early 1861, before Charles James Faulkner, who had been appointed by Secretary of State Lewis Cass to represent the United States in France the previous year, was recalled, Thouvenel discussed American events with him. Faulkner's convictions may well have offended Thouvenel—the American was a staunch defender of slavery. Yet it was mainly his indiscretions that irritated the French minister.[118] Thouvenel did not appreciate the fact that Faulkner leaked what was said between them.[119]

With regard to the various agents of the Confederacy in Europe, it must be said that the emissaries sent to France and England at the start of the war were unfamiliar with the diplomatic environment. True, Rost was of French extraction, but this former Louisiana judge and slave owner[120] was too direct, which embarrassed the Southern expatriates.[121] His attempt to appear nouveau riche and speak the native language offended the French court.[122] One might have thought that with John Slidell, who was well versed in French culture and fluent in the language of Molière, the South had finally found a representative of quality. This was all the more important given that, due to the difficulties encountered by the Confederate secretary of state in getting instructions to his agents (even going through Nassau, the blockade runners took several weeks to reach their destination),[123] Slidell often acted on his own initiative. But in fact it was not such a happy choice. First, because he was not very enthusiastic about going to France. He initially declined the proposal.[124] Next, Slidell did not have the makings of a good diplomat. Thouvenel, just as he had with Slidell's colleague Mason, emphasized Slidell's lack of expertise and remarked that his efforts in favor of Confederate recognition could not succeed.[125] Slidell's weaknesses were numerous. He was quick to get carried away and made mistakes. For example, he failed to perceive Napoléon's changeability and thought his intentions were definitive. Yet the emperor's desires and his acts were not the same thing. Even when what he said seemed sincere and he proposed to take initiatives, his decision was liable to change if someone countered it with a strong argument.

Slidell also lacked subtlety and took a long time to understand that the cabinet was not a monolith. His main defect was viewing diplomacy too much through the lens of personal relations and thereby neglecting the interests of nations. Above all, as de Leon recognized, his reputation was disastrous; he was known as a schemer.[126] When Slidell was first named to the post, Sartiges, former minister of France to the United States, offered to enlighten Thouvenel on his personality. We can suppose that the foreign minister lent a very attentive ear to Sartiges's consistently wise opinion. The latter warned Thouvenel that Slidell was a dangerous, violent, and "immoderately cunning" man who did not hesitate to use the most extreme means to achieve his ends and who inspired in Sartiges "distrust and even revulsion."[127] For once, Henri Mercier, the French representative in Washington, had to cast aside his Southern sympathies when he described Slidell, calling him "a clever man, very energetic but unscrupulous and of rather unsavory character."[128] Unsurprisingly, Slidell and Thouvenel did not get along.[129] It was the same for Thouvenel's successor, Drouyn de Lhuys, who did not appreciate Slidell's leaks to the press.[130]

All in all, the Confederate government did not give itself the means to win the diplomatic recognition it so ardently coveted. In terms of diplomatic effectiveness, the U.S. diplomats outperformed their Confederate counterparts.[131] To earn a place among the nations, the Confederacy counted much more on military success or the power of cotton, which it presumed to be absolute.[132] It deluded itself into thinking that Europe needed the South more than the South needed Europe. The Confederates were ignorant of the European and Mexican geopolitical affairs that modulated the diplomatic situation. They did not realize that events were following their course in parallel and that any credit they might hold could change according to circumstances.

A DESPOTIC SOUTH

The image that the propagandists tried to convey to European public opinion was too far removed from reality, too artificial a representation not to be laid open to doubt. The South as a defender of freedom? While certain historians might entertain this possibility,[133] the main witness of events in Richmond, the consul Alfred Paul, proffered quite the opposite opinion. Even before the outbreak of war, he was struck by the climate surrounding the execution of abolitionist John Brown. In his view, slavery revealed the true face of the South. Paul was outraged by the arbitrary actions taken against the few citizens of Virginia who showed support for Brown. According to Paul, this position was considered a crime. The consul reported that in response to the turmoil caused by the Brown case, abolitionist literature was prohibited there.[134] If any proof were needed beyond blacks being deprived of freedom, this decision demonstrated the incompatibility between democracy and slave republic.

As hostilities intensified, Paul saw authoritarianism as the hallmark of the Richmond government. We can, on this occasion, compare his singularly unbalanced judgment with regard to the suspension of habeas corpus by the Lincoln and Davis governments. It was Lincoln who took this step first in certain parts of Maryland on April 27, 1861, but Paul reserved his criticism for the Confederate government.[135] The consul in Richmond perceived a gradual shift toward the abuse of political power. It is true that rather than strengthening minority rights, the Confederate constitution tended to give the national government greater leverage.[136] Paul likened the regime to a "dictatorship" led with an "iron fist" by Jefferson Davis. In the consul's view, despotism was made all the easier to establish by the fact that the opposition was voiceless; Paul saw the Confederate Congress as little more than a rubber-stamp body.[137] In his opinion, Lincoln's reelection in November 1864 increased tensions and further strengthened the pressure on public opinion in the South. He worried over reports that the president of the Confederacy wanted to enlist newspaper editors and journalists to write his propaganda.[138]

The French press, as indulgent as it could be of the empire, nonetheless accused the South of antidemocratic practices. It observed that by not recognizing a legally elected president, the Southerners had failed to respect the Constitution.[139] Lincoln's reelection in 1864 was held up as an example by the most liberal newspapers. There was greatness in polling a people in the midst of war.[140] The stakes of the struggle therefore went further than a battle between two factions split over the issue of slavery, because it was clearly a question of preserving the oldest and most successful democratic model.[141] The French press also condemned the South's abuses of individual liberties. *Le Journal des Débats* and *Le Temps* were a little quick to write that despite Lincoln's suspension of habeas corpus, there had been no infringement of liberties. They noted that, unlike its enemy, the Federal government had not taken advantage of the war to employ harsh or arbitrary measures.[142] It goes without saying that the 13,535 citizens incarcerated in the North were unlikely to have shared this view.[143]

Despite their varying degrees of sympathy for the Confederates, the consuls agreed on the rebels' instinctive aggressiveness. The desire to do battle was thus another argument for the war against the South. When the first group of states seceded, the consul in New Orleans, though very favorable toward them, noted that he had heard nothing from Jefferson Davis to suggest any desire for reconciliation.[144] Paul, in Richmond, contrasted Davis's declaration with Lincoln's conciliatory exhortation in early March. He judged the president to be motivated by "good intentions" and was revolted that his statements had aroused indignation in Virginia.[145] It was therefore no surprise to him that the Southerners initiated the war by bombarding Fort Sumter. In doing so, they put their opponent in a position of self-defense.[146] Over the months, Paul warned his government against the deviousness of the South. At the time of the *Trent* affair, he found the absence of discretion about the two Southern envoys' departure suspect. He concluded that the Confederates had hoped the ship would be inspected so as to create the conditions for a break between London and Washington. Paul suggested that in its martial resolve, the South sought to drag France and England into the conflict.[147]

The liberal press tried to present the South as inherently aggressive. Because of its practice of slavery, which made brutality a habitual part of social relations, its use of violence was deep-rooted and impossible to suppress.[148] Moreover, the Confederates had demonstrated their refusal of all compromise when they disavowed the result of the November vote and attacked Fort

Sumter.[149] There was no coming to terms with them. Worse still, they might well disregard the laws of war. Newspapers condemned Jefferson Davis's threat to treat Northern soldiers as enemies of humanity.[150]

In contrast with the slow birth of the Union, the Confederate states organized themselves in three months. To the consuls, this haste appeared intended to present the new Lincoln administration with a fait accompli and, at the same time, to force the hand of Southerners less convinced by secession. At different moments during the crisis, French diplomats and consuls on the ground testified to the existence of unionist feeling in the Southern states. On the eve of the presidential election of November 1860, Mercier, referring to the threats of secession, had no doubt that in the South "the vast majority" wanted to maintain the Union.[151] A few days before the start of the war, Méjan, in New Orleans, wondered if a determined minority, in cahoots with the "cotton lobby," were in the process of deciding for a majority.[152] In November 1861, Consul Paul in Richmond reported a persistent attachment to the former Union among the Confederate population.[153] The following year, his colleague in Boston spoke of a fringe unfavorable to secession that had been silenced by hotheaded ringleaders but that was just waiting for a signal to be reawakened and renew ties with the North.[154] A few weeks before Lincoln's reelection, the dispatch from the New York Consulate repeated the analysis of a Frenchman that compared the process used at the conventions to the 1848 revolution which, he said, "was brought about by the clamor of a party that would not have counted 5,000 loyal voters."[155]

Even without reading the reflections of his agents, the minister of foreign affairs could draw on a number of results that revealed a continuing attachment to the Union in the South. The returns from Lincoln's first election, sent by Mercier, clearly indicated that the boundary between slave states and free states was not to be confused with loyalty or hostility to the Union. In Mercier's opinion, following the vote in November 1860 a majority of Americans were still in favor of the Union.[156] The example of the border states also fed doubts about the unanimity of which the Confederate leaders claimed to be custodians.

While the newspapers favorable to the imperial government were careful not to share this analysis, other organs denounced a theft of the vote.[157] This was no surprise for Le Journal des Débats. Moreover, the paper attributed the South's warmongering precisely to its being less imbued with democratic principles than its enemy.[158] This section of the press believed there was a particular resistance to secession in the states or state districts that had few slaves.[159] It argued that this explained the discord that was breaking out openly in certain states, especially when the threat of Federal troops became obvious.[160] The Unionist feeling called into question the legitimacy of rebellion. The liberal press regretted that the Union had suffered the onslaught of "fanatics."[161]

AN OBVIOUS MYTH

It soon became clear to the French that this was indeed a civil war. Although the antagonists in the American drama did not hesitate to use ethnic invective to discredit the enemy,[162] for the agents, the fact remained that those fighting each other were Americans, and their common origins could not be erased so easily. Confederate nationalism seemed to be a pure invention of the propagandists. The diplomats discerned no "ethnic" specificity in the South but rather observed what united the Americans: their language, traditions, memories, and a common project of Western expansion. When commenting on the South's fight, the consuls never used the argument of an emerging Southern nation; proof that they realized the concept was completely unsuited to the situation. Sain de Boislecomte, the former minister to Washington, analyzed the crisis as the separation of a part of the people from the rest of the nation.[163] The consul in Boston wondered how one could recognize the existence of two nationalities deriving from a single people.[164]

The press most distant from the imperial authorities also dismissed as inappropriate comparison of the South's situation to that of the Italians or Poles. On the contrary, the Southerners were incapable of breaking free from a shared past. Their flag was inspired by the star-spangled banner; they copied their laws from those of the Union, whose history they took for their own. These French papers recalled that the rebels had for years been content with the constitution. In 1861 they were largely inspired by the constitution of 1787, which they only amended in its language relating to slavery.[165]

Never did the French consuls paint a picture of an aristocratic South as the paragon of a refinement and distinction inherited from the Old World, as a land of balls and spinning crinolines to rival the imperial court. This stereotype bore no resemblance whatsoever to the social reality they observed. The consuls' dispatches instead depicted a very negative image of the Southern elite. A few days before the execution of John Brown in late 1859, the consul in Richmond described these patricians as follows: "They talk of the Virginians' chivalry! Oh! Let a man who was raised and had lived in the midst of a civilized society come and spend a week in this country and he would go away disgusted, sickened at such a sight!"[166] His colleague in New Orleans presented them as a band of schemers playing with secession so as to exclude North-

France's View of the South

ern capitalists from business and increase their fortunes.[167] His counterpart in Boston reduced them to an oligarchy of slave owners who worked for its own exclusive benefit. Starting with the first military setbacks in spring 1862, he enclosed with his dispatch the testimony of certain Confederate prisoners who regretted having fought for the cause of the rich.[168]

The liberal press was not fooled by the pro-Southern mystification and condemned admiration for those it saw as vulgar agitators.[169] For many of the writers in these newspapers, the origins of the war were to be found in the refusal of the Southern oligarchy to give up its political influence. They wrote that taking advantage of the cowardice of the North, which had yielded for too long to the blackmail of secession, the oligarchy had achieved dominance through iniquitous electoral privileges.[170] The rebellion was nothing but a power grab by slave owners determined to leave the republic rather than lose the leadership of it.[171]

———

News of Lincoln's death on Saturday, April 15, 1865, and, concomitantly, of the assassination attempt on Secretary of State Seward, arrived in France twelve days later. The reactions of astonishment, dismay, and indignation that this event solicited prove, if proof were needed, that the vision of a pro-Southern France should be qualified. It could always be argued that these demonstrations of warmth came once the conflict was over. But the emotion was deep and undeniably sincere. The assassination brought this comment from Drouyn de Lhuys: "History will not hesitate to rank him among the citizens who most honored their country."[172] Bigelow, who was in Brest when he learned the news, admitted he had not imagined the extent to which Lincoln's death would be felt in France.[173] On April 28, 1865, hundreds of students in Paris defied police to show their sadness. A public appeal resulted in a large number of pledges to fund a medal to be given to Lincoln's widow.[174] From this gold medal would arise the desire to offer a present to America, laying the groundwork for the gift of the Statue of Liberty.[175] On May 2, 1865, Eugène Rouher, the state minister responsible for the empire's policy of prestige, paid tribute to Lincoln. The president was also acclaimed by the members of parliament.[176] The emotion persisted for several weeks, all over France and among all social classes.[177]

For once, the press reaction was unanimous. From the most conservative to the most liberal, French papers praised Lincoln for his integrity, honesty, and sense of duty.[178] They paid tribute to a "good man, a great citizen who had faith in his mission," an "eternally illustrious man whom a heinous crime has stolen from the great American republic."[179] From then on, he was the first in the pantheon of American presidents. Although American democracy could withstand the blow, Lincoln's successor would struggle to fill the political vacuum.[180] These reactions suggest that we should not focus too much on the support that the Confederates were able to find within the imperial government. It is also important to keep in mind that sympathy rarely inspires foreign policy. The Southern lobby was mistaken to think that a certain elite's predilection for its cause would automatically lead to recognition of the Confederacy. In this regard, as Poland can testify, the defense of national interests always triumphs over feelings. Friendship creates a climate, not a policy.

» 5 «

THE WEIGHT OF THE
"PECULIAR INSTITUTION"
IN DIPLOMATIC RELATIONS

In France, slavery had been definitively abolished on April 27, 1848, with the issue of a decree by the provisional government of the Second Republic. Under the impetus of Victor Schoelcher, undersecretary of state for the navy and colonies, 248,500 slaves were suddenly freed. Consequently, it was difficult for observers at the time to imagine that in the United States, just a few miles from the French sugar islands, a practice could live on which they found hard to reconcile with the Americans' self-proclaimed democratic values. To the informed public, the slave system in the American South appeared both an anachronistic relic and an absurdity because it limited the region's economic potential. It is tempting to think that the French revulsion to slavery would make them incapable of recognizing a government that clung to it so fiercely. But given French confusion over the exact part slavery played in triggering the war, the difficulty many anticipated with sudden mass abolition, and its relatively low position on the scale of French concerns, "the peculiar institution" did little to penalize the rebel states. Perceptions of it as a morally disgraceful practice notwithstanding, the question is whether and to what extent slavery tarnished the South's image and obstructed recognition of its government.

Proclamation of the Abolition of Slavery in the French Colonies, 27 April 1848. François-Auguste Biard, 1849. Courtesy of the Château de Versailles, www.assemblee-nationale.fr.

SLAVERY WEAKENS THE SOUTH

In the years before the Civil War, two events occurred in less than a decade that shook up public opinion. The first was the resounding impact of *Uncle Tom's Cabin* in France.[1] Novelist George Sand wrote, "The book is in every hand, in every newspaper. There will be, there are editions in every format."[2] The liberal press duly noted the shock caused by reading of Tom's torments. French journalists considered the novel to have dealt a more severe blow to the cause of slavery than all the abolitionists' speeches put together.[3] They stressed the work's popularity in Europe.[4]

The other event that received major coverage was the struggle led by John Brown. A petition supported by Victor Hugo calling for leniency toward the Harpers Ferry assailant was widely publicized. From his island retreat, where he was ignorant of Brown's fate, Hugo wrote on the day of Brown's execution that, "viewed in a political light, the murder of Brown would be an irreparable fault. It would penetrate the Union with a gaping fissure which would lead in the end to its entire disruption. . . . For—yes, let America know it, and ponder on it well—there is something more terrible than Cain slaying Abel: It is Washington slaying Spartacus!"[5] The press that was at odds with the imperial regime took Brown's execution as a starting point to comment on slavery, drawing arguments from books on the "institution," or refuting the contentions of those who defended a form of ownership that could not be accepted without repudiating law, justice, and human dignity.[6] With the war and the question of Confederate recognition, the "opposition" press urged France not to cooperate with a republic that maintained such an "anachronistic practice."[7]

France's View of the South

The shame of it would be too high a price to pay to safeguard commercial interests.[8]

At the Quai d'Orsay, the positions of the two foreign ministers were unambiguous. On April 25, 1861, Thouvenel wrote to Henry Shelton Sanford, the U.S. minister to Belgium, of the incompatibility between the principle on which the Confederacy was based and the civilized world.[9] Just after assuming office, Drouyn de Lhuys reminded Dayton that he was no friend of slavery either.[10] Similarly, Alfred Paul, the consul in Richmond, wrote with the supporters of slavery in mind that "one must come to the south of the United States to witness such a deplorable blindness and hear, from gentlemen for example, that slavery is a divine, precious and sacred institution; that the countries that have them are privileged countries; that slavery must be defended and preserved now and always, that slaves are happy beings, that they know it and that they are ready to take up arms to remain slaves. This calumny, which affects a deprived and terribly unhappy population, whatever people may say of them, is blasphemy."[11] The conclusion drawn by the consul in New Orleans was that slavery could only alienate Europe from the South.[12]

This bad image aside, slavery weakened the South in many ways. Observers pointed out first of all that natural reproduction alone would be insufficient to renew the slave population. The Southern states, therefore, hoped to obtain a relaxation of the rules on slave trading, which the United States had outlawed.[13] Although before becoming emperor, Napoléon III had defended a slave trade that was organized and out in the open as preferable to smuggling, the Tuileries cabinet had since become as unfailingly vigilant as its British counterpart.[14] It unequivocally rejected the resumption of this trade and continued to give the issue a central place in discussions with London.[15]

Next, echoing Hinton Helper's arguments in *The Impending Crisis of the South*, the diplomats' reports stressed that the use of slave labor was an obstacle to the development of the Southern economy.[16] They considered it an unreliable mode of production, as it was based on a workforce that might defect with the war—a particularly worrying prospect when the economy depended so heavily on it.[17] It was also unproductive capital. Buying a slave was expensive with hardly any return on investment.[18] Slavery diverted money that would be better used for the states' development. Moreover, whereas in the North free labor encouraged men to be enterprising and increase their wealth, the South's refusal to question the system reinforced economic inertia.[19] The liberal press shared this view and believed that the profitability of free labor meant servitude was doomed.[20]

A final sign of weakness was that slavery reduced the South's military potential. First, it posed a threat to social stability. All throughout the war, the consuls feared a slave revolt—a fifth column that would be roused against the Confederacy at the most critical moment.[21] In October 1862, to win London and St. Petersburg over to his mediation attempt, Napoléon III raised the risk of a slave war as an argument to end the fighting as soon as possible; it was a fear he had already expressed to Slidell three months earlier.[22] Second, it was impossible for the Confederacy to enlist slaves; it therefore had to rely only on some 5 million whites for its defense. When, in the final months of 1864, the Confederate government envisaged offering black men their freedom to take up arms for the South, Consul Alfred Paul interpreted this as a blatant admission that the military situation was hopeless.[23]

THE CIVIL WAR, A WAR AGAINST SLAVERY?

Long before secession, the diplomats were aware that slavery was a bone of contention that could lead the Northern and Southern states to the brink of disaster. However, the possibility of a split was first seriously contemplated in the 1850s. For instance, after the laborious adoption of the Kansas-Nebraska agreement, Sartiges, who had headed the French legation since 1852, clearly raised the risk of separation.[24] By the end of the decade, skepticism had given way to certitude. In late 1859, the poisonous atmosphere surrounding the execution of John Brown convinced Sartiges's temporary replacement that South Carolina intended to unite all the slave states into a separate confederacy.[25] In reading these dispatches, the Quai d'Orsay was understandably tempted to see slavery as the key to understanding the conflict between the two sections of the Union. The ministry was all the more convinced when, in November 1860, the election of a new president known for his antislavery position added fuel to the fire.

Thus, when the crisis broke out, the consuls felt obliged to warn their government against misunderstanding its origins through a simplistic reading.[26] They pointed out that although Lincoln and the Republican Party defended the federal right to ban slavery in the territories and were opposed to new slave territories, Lincoln did not want to abolish slavery where it existed already because he was unwilling to interfere with the laws of states. The real grounds for the conflict was, therefore, slavery's expansion.[27] Indeed, in the end, Lincoln's position disconcerted the French agents as it blurred the image of a quarrel over the refusal or approval of slavery. They underscored the hypocrisy of the North, which denied the South's right to continue a practice that it was paradoxically prepared to tolerate in the border states to save the Union.[28]

The attitude of the French press also evolved. Initially, journalists expressed certainty that the issue of slavery was the primary cause of the war, since secession had been triggered by the election of an antislavery politician.[29] However, writers and editors gradually realized that this president had not been elected to pursue an abolitionist policy. The most conservative newspapers took malicious pleasure in pointing out that he called for the prohibition of slavery in the territories while toning down his demands for the states where it already existed.[30] Their liberal rivals were forced to concur; the Republicans did not denounce slavery so much as its extension.[31] However, these opposition newspapers managed to turn the difficulty on its head. In their eyes, it proved that the North was not acting as an aggressor, since it was not seeking to abolish the mainstay of the Southern labor system.[32] On the contrary, it had been willing to take conciliatory measures "to extremes" to keep the South in the Union.[33] This was a clever interpretation of events. By demonstrating that the revolt was unfounded, French liberals and Republicans depicted the Southerners as impetuous agitators who seized the most fallacious pretexts to leave the Union.

ABOLITION, A FRIGHTENING PROSPECT

The fierce battle at Antietam, which the Federal government considered a victory, offered Lincoln an opportunity to issue his preliminary Emancipation Proclamation five days later. French agents in America greeted the decree unenthusiastically, to say the least. Mercier saw it as directed at France and Britain, in case the latest military events had tempted them to recognize the South.[34] The vice-consul in St. Louis dismissed it as a belated act that aimed chiefly to weaken the enemy rather than help the slaves.[35] The consul in New York thought the gesture complicated the situation, as it was likely to spur the rebels to further resistance.[36]

Unsurprisingly, the Emancipation Proclamation of September 22, 1862, divided the conservative and liberal press. Conservative newspapers warned their readers not to be misled; it was not an abolitionist proclamation, first, because the border states were not affected, and, second, because it was a safe bet that if the rebel states put down their arms they would be allowed to keep their slaves.[37] The conservative French press argued that the easiest path to abolition was the independence of the South.[38] The anti-imperial press, in contrast, considered that Lincoln's proclamation was a step in the right direction, although some writers were dissatisfied and called it a half-measure.[39] However, as a whole, they maintained that Lincoln's statement marked a turning point in the war, whose outcome now was irrevocably linked to the fate of slavery.[40] Through his words, which would go down in history, Lincoln had taken his place in the pantheon of great men.[41] The Federal government was the stronger for it.[42]

How did the imperial government view abolition in general? In 1861, the difficulties that had arisen with the application of the Schoelcher decree thirteen years earlier remained a vivid memory. First, in 1848, the principle that France defended — setting foot in the country or its colonies automatically entailed emancipation — had proven problematic in the case of fugitive slaves who arrived on the French Caribbean islands.[43] Second, French slave owners in the U.S. South were required to manumit their slaves within three years or lose their French nationality. This time frame seemed too short. Certain members of Louis-Napoléon Bonaparte's government soon set to relaxing the decree. The act of February 11, 1851, lengthened the time limit for freeing slaves from three to ten years, while the following year the foreign minister — then Drouyn de Lhuys — wondered if it would be possible to add new amendments to the provisions of April 27, 1848.[44] This view was shared by the minister of the navy and colonies, who judged the provisions too stringent.[45] France had barely abolished slavery before Bonaparte's government began considering exemptions. Those in power were more concerned with the problems caused by abolition than with the progress of mankind.

French diplomats and consuls were also quick to point out the risks posed by abolition. As appalling as it was, slavery was nonetheless considered essential to the plantation economy. They felt that blacks alone, because of their origins, could cope with the sweltering heat of the plantations.[46] The agents also were uncertain what might replace slavery. Following Lincoln's election, the consul in New Orleans predicted that abolition would bring the death of the South, as it would kill Southern agriculture and therefore trade.[47] The argument that many agents found most compelling was that, in practice, the sudden emancipation of millions of human beings would be difficult to manage. Mercier argued that it was not enough to give blacks their freedom; serious thought had to be given to what would replace their bondage.[48] It is true that compared with late-1840s France, the issue of abolition in the slave states was of a different magnitude. Freeing almost 4 million slaves concentrated in one part of the country, and who constituted the majority of the population in states such as Mississippi and South Carolina, was a different matter than emancipating a few hundred thousand people scattered across islands from the Caribbean to the Indian Ocean.[49]

These statistics made the diplomats question the appropriateness of freeing the entire slave population en masse. For another much-feared consequence of abolition was the revenge that former slaves might take upon their liberation. In September 1861, Mercier, the French government's representative in the United States, wrote in his diary that by suddenly bringing about emancipation, the war would only lead to chaos.[50] He reiterated this view in early 1862, again warning against a hasty decision that "could only lead to terrible disorder, ruin, and massacres."[51] In America, fear of abolition was widespread because many dreaded it would trigger a slave uprising. It is no exaggeration to speak of a "Toussaint Louverture" syndrome, after the leader of the revolt that led to the emancipation of Haitian slaves in the late eighteenth century, though this was a dubious parallel because Toussaint's revolt preceded the first abolition by three years and not the reverse.[52] Nonetheless, the emancipation of slaves was identified with a climate of violence. Few doubted that as soon as the slaves were freed, they would turn on their former masters, if need be to take their place. The contradiction in such arguments is worth highlighting in passing: if the slaves were treated as well as some claimed, why, once freed, would they punish those who had enslaved them?

For this reason, the abolitionists were seen as sorcerer's apprentices. The diplomats and consuls did not recognize them as having moral sensibilities equal to most white Americans. They were perceived as dangerous men, not only because their ideas were a threat to the generally accepted social order but also because the goals of these "extremists" jeopardized the existence of a Union built through a succession of subtle compromises. In 1860, the consul in New Orleans feared they would again draw attention to themselves during that November's presidential election.[53] Mercier attacked the "little abolitionist church that is as fanatic as its congregation is outnumbered."[54] He went as far as to describe the abolitionists as "Northern separatists."[55]

Under the empire, the natural concord between French liberals and U.S. antislavery militants was viewed with suspicion. The abolitionist cause was accused of serving the designs of "perfidious Albion." Mercier spoke disdainfully of "England's usual maxims" and the "abolitionist concerns and scruples of Lord John Russell."[56] Being receptive to abolitionist arguments meant exposing oneself to accusations of collusion with the liberals and the British, that is, with the opponents of the regime within and beyond France's borders.

While all the articles on the subject condemned slavery, the French press as a whole was far from abolitionist. The conservative newspapers stressed that to deprive slave owners of a commodity they had legally acquired was an infringement of property rights.[57] Even liberal organs attacked the abolitionists for inflaming Southern opinion or for "fighting slavery in accordance with ab-

stract principles" rather than "pity for the oppressed race."[58] They wrote of
the difficulties that abolition would cause for the economy of not only the
slave states but also France. They warned against being influenced by purely
humanitarian considerations that ignored commercial realities, particularly
the issue of cotton. The possibility of blanket emancipation was therefore limited, they argued, by economic imperatives, as the South simply could not do
without these cheap workers who were the best adapted to the sultry climate
of Dixie.[59] Nor could the world risk a widespread uprising of blacks having re-
gained their freedom.[60]

It is important to note, however, that after the publication of *Uncle Tom's
Cabin* very few observers risked defending the "peculiar institution" or dis-
counting blacks' suffering. From the mid-1850s onward, most believed that the
freedom of the slaves was a goal toward which humanity should aim; what they
did not agree with were the terms proposed by the abolitionists. Immediate,
mass abolition was seen as problematic because many thought it would create
a sudden imbalance for Europe as well as the United States. The freed blacks
might choose to leave the plantations on which they had been kept by force,
causing a cotton shortage. Or they might demand to be paid, causing the price
of imported commodities to soar. Observers preferred progressive abolition,
or in the words of Napoléon III, "gradual apprenticeship,"[61] enabling slaves to
become accustomed to freedom little by little.

Following the Thirteenth Amendment passed by Congress on December 6, 1865, slavery was definitively abolished in the United States. While the
French foreign minister welcomed a measure "so consistent with the general
progress of humanity,"[62] the same cannot be said of his agents. For them, the
amendment was a source of concern, reflecting their deeply rooted prejudice
that blacks did not know what to do with freedom. According to Montholon,
who had just been appointed head of the French legation in place of Mercier,
the danger lay in the political rights that the newly freed slaves might obtain,
which could give them decisive power in states where they were numerically
dominant.[63] The minister plenipotentiary believed there could be no society
where whites and blacks lived on an equal footing.[64] He already foretold the
segregation that would follow. The consul in Charleston regretted the end of
slavery, saying that men of color now lacked occupation.[65] All abolition had
done, he maintained, was to encourage idleness.[66] One might think that as
time passed and the war was left behind, the diplomats would show more insight. Montholon's successor, Jules Berthémy, overcome by his aversion to the
idea of new freemen, feared that a "race war" would bring a "black oligarchy"
to power.[67] Such fear probably explains why the establishment of Black Codes

in some states was not greeted by the slightest whisper of protest from foreign diplomats.

A MARGINAL SUBJECT

What is looked upon today as the South's monstrousness was in fact hardly ever mentioned in the reports by French diplomats and consuls. Curiously enough, it takes much sifting through the dispatches to find a few brief allusions to the condition of slaves and their masters. Slavery was often only brought up to explain, and fairly schematically at that, the widening gap between the two sides of the Union. The consuls typically avoided airing their qualms in their correspondence with the ministry. They preferred to save that for private letters, as did the British consul in Charleston.[68] However, it is clear that in urban centers, where consuls rubbed shoulders with slaves, the trials of white Southerners carried far more weight than the South's special system of production. In the competition for compassion, the deprivation of citizens, the hardships of refugees, and the flood of wounded soldiers largely overshadowed the condition of slaves. In addition, French abolitionism mainly drew on Republican or liberal circles and did not enjoy the widespread support it had in England. The abolitionist struggle took place before the Second Republic, and the Schoelcher decree seemed to have extinguished any passions that the subject could arouse.

At the very start of the war, Mercier summed up the diplomats' position quite nicely by ranking slavery in a secondary position on the scale of concerns.[69] He wrote to Thouvenel on March 29, 1861, that "from the perspective of propriety, the monarchical governments of Europe are not linked to the United States by any principles of solidarity that might influence their behavior. I know that the North relies much on liberal governments' being loath to recognize a new state in which slavery would, in a way, be the fundamental institution. But however great their reluctance may be, as ultimately it cannot be the determining cause of the course to follow, it could not prevent any act commanded by higher interests."[70] As Slidell had perceived upon his arrival in France, the subject left many members of the imperial government indifferent.[71] Although Thouvenel and Drouyn de Lhuys were both hostile to slavery, this aversion counted little in their opposition to recognizing the Confederate government.

The emperor, for his part, showed himself to be more tolerant of the "peculiar institution." It is true that his uncle, of whom he liked to think he was the political heir, had restored slavery.[72] Napoléon III expressed the racist prejudices of his time, which precluded any conception of an egalitarian society. At the mercy of their masters, blacks' status was consistent with the inferiority that European societies commonly ascribed to them. In 1837, off the coast of Brazil, the future emperor observed slaves from afar. He delivered a judgment that fairly accurately reflects his contemporaries' instinctive revulsion for men of color: "Our pride would be hurt to see men who look like monkeys enjoying all our privileges."[73] He believed, like many observers, that black people were better adapted to the climatic conditions for picking cotton than whites. He also feared that freeing the slaves would result in an uprising in which the masters would be the first victims, and he attacked the philanthropists who criticized slavery in America without concerning themselves with the miseries of the people in France.[74] The question of slavery therefore never influenced his decisions concerning the Confederacy.

This was again confirmed in the last months of the war. In February 1865, the Davis government sent Duncan Kenner to Paris and London in a last-ditch attempt to obtain recognition of the Richmond government in exchange for abolition.[75] In accepting the end of slavery, the South was admitting its original error and questioning the very principle of its struggle. Unsurprisingly, the request was seen as an admission of powerlessness and was doomed to failure from the beginning. Slidell asked to meet with Napoléon III. The latter again assured him of his sympathies for the South but refused to take the initiative. Slidell asked whether the abolition of slavery would have any influence on him. The emperor admitted that Britain might be more affected by that decision than he would.[76]

We can therefore safely say that for French leaders — unlike their British counterparts — slavery was a secondary consideration. The French government treated slavery as a marginal issue that could on no account steer or determine its diplomatic policy. It would be anachronistic to examine France's diplomatic stance through the lens of human rights. While, as Lincoln foresaw, Great Britain was apt to be influenced by the Emancipation Proclamation, in France the diplomatic choice was unfettered by moral considerations. Besides, history showed that the practice of slavery was not incompatible with diplomatic recognition. Had the United States, like Brazil and Mexico, not been welcomed into the family of nations in its time without abandoning slavery?[77] Just as this practice did not penalize the South, it is equally safe to say that the fact the North had not made the war a crusade against slavery from the outset was not counted against it. Although the diplomats and consuls were indeed taken aback by Lincoln's attitude, the Republican president proving in their view a greater defender of the Union than of abolition, they were convinced that slavery was not one of the war's fundamental issues. A diplomatic position on it thus was not required to decide whether to recognize the Confederacy.

This does not mean, however, that slavery was completely absent from the French diplomatic position. At a time when Napoléon III had made his first liberal concessions by giving more power to the legislature, it was difficult for him to envisage a rapprochement with the slave states.[78] The emperor, who was judged on his ability to bring about changes in the imperial institutions, could not ignore the opposition's criticism of the South. The credibility of his venture was at stake. Also, the liberal opposition tried to draw a parallel between the violation of slaves' rights and the repression of freedom in France.[79] Under cover of their condemnation of the slave states, an opportunity emerged for the opponents of the empire to settle their scores with Bonaparte's despotic regime without being censored. By refraining from satisfying the Confederates' requests, Napoléon III deprived his opponents of a key argument. Thus, from the perspective of his American policy, at a moment when the emperor wanted gradually to let go of his discretionary powers, the credibility of his increased openness toward the opposition was at stake. His restraint in the American Civil War gained him allies at home.

» 6 «

NAPOLÉON III'S "GRAND DESIGN" AND THE CONFEDERACY

In 1862, Napoléon III sent an expeditionary force to occupy Mexico with the aim of establishing a Latin and Catholic empire in the region. Two years later Eugène Rouher — a significant figure of the Second Empire referred to by some as vice-emperor — described the speech before the legislature as the *grande pensée du règne* (the grand thought of the reign, commonly translated in English as the Grand Design).[1] This formulation makes clear how central this large-scale geostrategic plan was to the Second Empire's foreign policy.

The American Civil War, which ran parallel to this episode, served Napoléon III's purposes in many ways. First, the division of the Union neutralized the United States by rendering it unable to enforce the Monroe Doctrine. Second, the very favorable location of the new Confederacy, interposed between the states loyal to the Lincoln government and the Rio Grande, would protect Mexican interests. Third, faced with this interference in Mexican affairs, the insurgents showed their support for Napoléon's enterprise. In such a favorable context, it is fair to wonder at France's inaction. If the breakup of the United States was such a precious opportunity, why did Paris not seek to encourage this division?

The emperor, dismayed at the losses of Mexican territory in 1848, wanted to give Mexico the means to resist the potential advances of the United States. Mexico, he believed, must serve to contain U.S. expansion, much as the Crimea helped curb Russia's territorial ambitions.[2] Moreover, just as he had challenged Russian Orthodoxy, so Napoléon III wanted to make himself the protector of Catholics by forming a Latin bloc that would counter Anglo-Saxon Protestantism. For the emperor, the republican model symbolized both U.S. supremacy and the weakening of Mexico, and he saw a return to imperial rule as the only way to "regenerate" the country. The possibility of establishing a European prince on the Mexican throne had already been on the agenda under the July Monarchy. Napoléon III resumed the idea. His imagination was fired by the prospect of this grand design for Mexico, which the empress was the first to support.[3] From the summer of 1861, the candidate favored by the imperial couple was Maximilian of Habsburg, brother of the Austrian emperor Franz Josef.[4] The choice of this pretender to the Mexican throne served Napoleonic diplomacy more than the aspirations of the Mexicans themselves, even the most conservative.[5]

Napoléon III's plan, as he wrote to Gen. Elie Forey, commander in chief of the expeditionary force to Mexico, was designed above all to counteract U.S. dominance. In strengthening Mexico, France would secure its dominion over this part of the continent.[6] Napoléon III's ambition was apparently to remodel the American continent by establishing, in place of the United States, an entity comparable to the German Confederation that would divide the territory between the Union, the Confederacy, and Mexico, with the latter a bastion of French influence.[7] All this is difficult to verify, however, not least because the emperor's statements must be taken with a grain of salt. They were often fed to his interlocutors as a test without any in-depth study of the question. It, therefore, seems unwise to set too much store on the utopian designs he delighted in conjuring.

Napoléon III's Mexican policy did hold the key to his policy toward the South. Based on the brochure *La France, le Mexique et les Etats confédérés*, written by the economist Michel Chevalier but inspired by the emperor, it is possible to identify the three arguments that tempted him to recognize the Confederacy.[8] First, he thought the split of the United States into two hostile republics would guarantee the integrity of its neighbor. Second, Napoléon believed the Confederacy would form a barrier to prevent the United States from

Maximilian I of Mexico, 1864. Courtesy of the Library of
Congress, Prints and Photographs Division.

crossing the Rio Grande. Third, he surmised that the new Mexican government would need support to consolidate its power. Once the French troops had departed, the Confederacy's help would be useful in ensuring the survival of the new regime. The Confederacy would, therefore, play a dual role as a buffer state, usefully interposed between Washington and Mexico, and as a valuable ally to protect Maximilian's throne.

THE SOUTH'S CHARM OFFENSIVE

From the very start of the war, the Confederates and their sympathizers tried to cast themselves out as the natural allies of the new Mexican regime. They sought to demonstrate that the Southern Confederacy and a Mexico "regenerated" by France must come together to stand up to Yankee hostility.[9] The *Index*, a Confederate propaganda newspaper, defended Napoléon's policy on several occasions.[10]

In Slidell's view, this was the key to tipping the balance in favor of his camp. In July 1862 he explained to the emperor that the Confederacy could join forces with him against Benito Juárez and his party, which had the support of the Federal administration. He mentioned the Corwin Treaty that was soon to be considered by the Senate. Slidell cleverly portrayed this $11 million loan, which Washington presented as a means of stabilizing Mexican power and establishing peace, as disguised aid from Washington to Juárez.[11] A few days later, in his letter to Thouvenel requesting recognition of the Confederacy, Slidell again dwelled on how well disposed Richmond was to the imperial plans.[12] That same summer, in a confidential note to his government, he advocated an "offensive and defensive alliance between France and the Confederate States on Mexican affairs."[13] Such an alliance was of course highly unrealistic. How could the South possibly fight on two fronts? However, the difficulties facing the French expeditionary force at Puebla made the imperial government receptive to such offers.

On October 22, 1862, during his interview with Napoléon III in Saint-Cloud, Slidell proposed this rapprochement between the Confederacy and the new Mexican regime and raised the possibility of a pact. He mentioned the purportedly widespread idea that France was pursuing a much larger agenda than just Mexico, including, for example, occupying Haiti. He said that this prospect would probably displease Washington but not Richmond.[14] It is true that throughout the Civil War, there were rumors of French plans to resurrect an independent Texas or annex territory north of Mexico. Drouyn de Lhuys mentioned them only to brush them aside.[15] Added to these speculations were those concerning the transfer of territory from Mexico to France as compensation for its role in forming a new government.[16]

In June 1863, Napoléon III told Slidell how delighted he was to learn that the Confederate capital had reacted enthusiastically upon hearing of the capture of Puebla by French troops, unlike the North, which had shown some disappointment. The Southern envoy thought such a demonstration unlikely but did not contradict the emperor. Slidell reiterated the South's sympathy for the French venture and prophesied that the Confederacy would soon become the continent's great power. The alliance between his government and Mexico would then become essential.[17]

The Confederates' favorable view of the imperial scheme was confirmed by the consuls, beginning with Alfred Paul in Richmond. He reported that the successes of the French army in Mexico were well received not only in Richmond but throughout the South.[18] Arthur Lanen, the acting chargé d'affaires of the Charleston consulate, joined to his dispatch an issue of the *Atlanta Confederacy*, which he felt summed up the opinions of the Confederate press and population on the establishment of an empire in Mexico: "The Mexican question is, I think, the only one on which there is currently a consensus in the Southern States."[19] Many diplomats and consuls let themselves be seduced by the South's charm offensive.

In fact, Richmond's indulgence was purely tactical. To have any hope of European backing in their quest for independence, Confederate leaders recognized the need to forswear their intentions of southward expansion. Once embroiled in the war, they shrewdly suppressed any imperialist rhetoric or ventures rather than project an aggressive image that would be counterproductive.[20] The Confederacy could hardly alienate the French to its south while waging war against the Federals to its north, so it needed Mexico to remain neutral. After the loss of New Orleans, the Mexican port of Matamoros became the main conduit for cotton exports and imports of vital supplies for the Confederacy.[21] Confederates established regular trade between Europe and Matamoros, which the French closely observed.[22] Napoléon III's troops seized the port on September 26, 1864, just as the South's fight was nearing its end. The transport of arms then depended on French goodwill and the new occupants did everything they could to step up cross-border trading.[23]

This apparent benevolence can be ascribed to France's desire to prolong the conflict. Maximilian had just taken up his duties. It would be preferable for the war, which divided and weakened the United States, to continue a little longer in order for him to consolidate his power. As soon as it was over, Napoléon III's Mexican puppet would have to deal with pressure from Washington. He had to strengthen his regime before the North got its victory. This meant keeping the Confederacy going a few months more, and for that Matamoros had to be kept open to Confederate forces. So this was not, strictly speaking, an act of munificence toward the Confederates, who by 1864 had little to offer Napoléon III that might assist him in his Mexican venture.

THE SOUTH'S SINCERITY IN QUESTION

Despite Slidell's reassurances, the French also had their doubts about the sincerity of the South's support for their Mexican venture. In 1861, Robert Toombs, the Confederate secretary of state, instructed his agent in Mexico, former freebooter John T. Pickett, to assure President Benito Juárez of his government's friendship. Toombs explained that Juárez could always count on the goodwill of the Confederate States to maintain the principles of constitutional liberty that Mexico had successfully asserted.[24] Once the grand Napoleonic design began to take shape, it was with the French that the Confederates discussed the Mexican question. They stressed the need for popular support for the new government, but this was clearly the weak point of the imperial plan. In July 1862, in his request for recognition, Slidell wrote to Thouvenel that he was confident Napoléon III did not intend to impose in Mexico "a government that does not conform to the wishes of her inhabitants."[25] This recommendation was also expressed in late 1863 by the Confederate president in a speech to his Congress.[26] The diplomats were aware that in combining acceptance of Maximilian's empire and respect for popular sovereignty, the South was conditioning its support on a wish that was impossible to fulfill.[27]

Above all, the Confederates seemed just as attached to the Monroe Doctrine as the citizens of the free states, but both sides had to put the doctrine on the back burner. Despite the rhetoric, the Southerners struggled to hide their annoyance at the idea that a European power would set up a government in its pay on the Confederate border. In 1864, Charles Prosper Fauconnet, the chancellor of the French consulate in New Orleans, alerted Drouyn de Lhuys to the intentions of the Defenders of the Monroe Doctrine, a local group that appeared to be preparing an armed expedition from the city to come to the aid of Juárez's men.[28] A few weeks before the end of the war, the consul in New York, in turn, warned his government of the Southerners' duplicity. He said that the Monroe Doctrine was most strongly supported in the slave states because it had been from there that most expeditions of the freebooters who had threatened Cuba and Central America in the 1850s had departed. It was worth noting, he suggested, that it was in Virginia newspapers that the conquests in Mexico raised the most concern.[29]

Because the Lincoln administration and Congress were openly hostile to French intervention — in 1863 the Senate passed a resolution condemning the French intervention, and the following year Congress reaffirmed the legitimacy of Juárez — the imperial cabinet feared that peace between the warring sections would lead to a joint action against the French scheme. This concern was justified by Francis Blair's mission in 1864 and the Hampton Roads Conference on February 3, 1865. On each occasion, the reconciliation envisaged by the Southerners included a proposed anti-French initiative. Hearing leaks of these plans for reunification, through armed invasion of Mexico, the French diplomats were disturbed. In Washington, Mexico City, New York, and London, they all suspected the Monroe Doctrine of serving to unite Northerners and Southerners by waging an external war.[30]

In Paris, the Foreign Ministry wavered between concern over a possible coalition between the former enemies, for which France would pay the price, and the assurances offered by the Federal government's agents. Federal officials sought to mollify the French authorities by saying that it would be impossible to keep hundreds of thousands of men ready for action once hostilities had ended.[31] Drouyn de Lhuys hoped that the North would take into account France's efforts to respect neutrality and stay out of the Civil War.[32] On the Mexican question, then, Paris ended up perceiving the South as the more hotheaded of the two belligerents. The Confederacy also appeared to be playing a malicious double game. While the Hampton Roads Conference was under way, the Confederate government sent Duncan Kenner to Europe in an eleventh-hour attempt to secure recognition. But at the conference, the Southerners proposed to drive the French from Mexico in exchange for an armistice; their intentions were leaked and preceded Kenner.[33] His mission confirmed to the ministry, and perhaps even finally convinced the emperor, that the South could not be considered a serious partner in France's plans for Mexico.

A PREJUDICIAL EXPANSIONIST PAST

If the French diplomats questioned the Confederates' sincerity when the latter claimed to be sympathetic to the imperial design, this was also because the South's past did not speak in its favor. Until the eve of secession, Southern nationalism was reflected by an unremitting desire for conquest in the Caribbean, Mexico, or Central America.[34] Indeed, few diplomats doubted that the Southerners' temperament and interests were geared toward a vigorous defense of territorial expansion. In the preceding decade it had been the slave states that had most actively supported attempts to land in Cuba (ambitions against which France and Britain had taken a clear position). The French agents had, on many occasions, described Federal administrations being torn between pressure from Southerners to annex the island they considered an appendage of Florida and pressure from the North to restrain the expansion of the slave states.[35]

With regard to Central America, the comte Eugène de Sartiges, former French minister to the United States, noted not long before the war that in both the House of Representatives and the Senate, the Southern states considered the Central American territories "a natural annex of the Union."[36] They fervently defended the invasions of William Walker, the freebooter who dreamed of building another slave empire in Central America. For the diplomats, the connection between Walker's ambitions and the Southerners' plans was clear.[37] Sartiges stressed the extent of support for Walker in those states, particularly in Louisiana where his trial was taking place and where he was sure to be acquitted.[38] This danger was echoed and denounced by the French liberal press, which deemed the practice of slavery likely to extend the frontiers of the United States as far as the Isthmus of Panama.[39]

The consuls pointed out that during President Franklin Pierce's term, Walker's forays into Mexico had earned him much popular support in the Southern states.[40] As noted by the acting head of French legation in Washington, throughout the 1850s the Southern states hoped to take advantage of the political instability in Mexico to snatch new territories from their southern neighbor and thereby restore the sectional balance of power in the United States.[41] When James Buchanan was elected president in November 1856, the French agents feared that the slaveholders' plans for the conquest of Mexico would move forward. Although the new president was a native of Pennsylvania, Sartiges underscored his deference "to the Southern party," since he could not count on the North to support his plans for expansion.[42] Buchanan's declarations firmly substantiated the idea that the United States would annex Mexico's northern territories at the first opportunity, despite Mexico's abolition of slavery there.[43]

The French agents also pointed to the issue of the Isthmus of Tehuantepec, which the Southern states still aimed to control. They saw this as a venture financed and run by men of the South and which, by bringing the ports of California and New Orleans closer together, could give the latter city hope of becoming the main warehouse for U.S. trade.[44]

The McLane-Ocampo Treaty, signed in 1859, appeared to be the culmination of this annexationist policy. The Senate rejected the treaty in a vote that reflected the divide between the North and South. In early 1860 the acting head of the French legation in the United States, considering the increasingly likely assumption that the South would separate from the North, warned his government that this would change the global balance of power.[45] Henri Mercier, his successor as head of the legation, had to admit that the Southern states' economic and political necessities compelled them, more than the Northern states, to expand. He explained that far from being satisfied with their borders, they were spurred on by the search for new business opportunities and the desire to bolster their position on slavery by expanding its domain in places where it had been abolished.[46]

Given how attached France was to the territorial integrity of the former Spanish colonies, it is understandable that the Confederate officials made the Quai d'Orsay uneasy. When Jefferson Davis accepted the office of secretary of war under the Pierce administration, Sartiges did not hide his fears. Following the Gadsden Purchase, Davis had deplored the fact that the Union did not get more Mexican territory south of the Gila River.[47] In a dispatch to Drouyn de Lhuys, the minister to Washington said that Davis still had his sights set on adjusting the border with Mexico, which he had contested since the Treaty of Guadalupe Hidalgo.[48] In 1859 the calls to seize Cuba, taken up by men like Alexander Stephens, were another cause of concern to the French minister plenipotentiary.[49] Four years before the outbreak of war, the name Judah Benjamin was associated with a policy of aggression toward the Southern neighbor. *Le Moniteur* had reported his plan to build a railroad across the Isthmus of Tehuantepec.[50] On that occasion, Sartiges had revealed to the foreign minister the true purpose of Benjamin's trip. The latter, moreover, had made no secret of it as he had spoken to the French minister plenipotentiary of the independence of Mexico's northern states and their union with the Anglo-American federation.[51] Echoing Sartiges, the French representative to Mexico, Dubois de Saligny, also criticized Benjamin's maneuvers and reported them to Thouvenel.[52]

To complete this collection of pen portraits, the future Confederate envoy to France John Slidell had, in the 1850s, been regularly presented by Sartiges as a standard-bearer of the "extreme annexationist party" that defended the freebooters in their attempts to seize Mexican or Central American territories.[53]

AN INDELIBLE SUSPICION OF IMPERIALISM

Was there any reason to expect that an independent Confederacy would not pursue expansion? In principle, secession was likely to revive ideas of annexation. Slave owners thought that the establishment of an empire committed to slavery would be inevitable once their territory was separated from the North.[54] In a speech in Atlanta on February 21, 1861, did Jefferson Davis not envisage the Confederacy enlarged by portions of northern Mexico? Did article 4, section 3, of the Constitution of the Confederate States not authorize the acquisition of new territories and the institution of slavery within them?[55]

However, French consuls and diplomats, Mercier in Washington especially, were convinced that the splitting of the Union had wrecked the Southern states' territorial plans. The agents simply substantiated the ideas voiced by supporters of the Southern cause, who claimed that an immediate stop had been put to the expansionist policy.[56] Slidell reported this change when he wrote to Thouvenel in July 1862. France, which was so concerned about the expansion of the Union, he asserted, should rejoice in the new situation that served its policy toward the United States. The French government should consider the birth of the Confederacy a guarantee of the political balance in North America.[57]

The French liberal press did not share the diplomatic agents' optimism in the slightest. According to these newspapers, secession had not satisfied the insurgent states' appetites. The theme of proslavery expansionism became one of their leitmotifs.[58] It was impossible to peruse one of these newspapers or journals without seeing references to the threat the slave states posed to the territory south of the Rio Grande. In *Le Journal des Débats*, F. Camus was already outlining the expectations of these imperialist Southerners in January 1860: "Once [Southerners were] masters of Mexico, Central America, and Cuba, that is to say, an area five or six times the size of France and located in highly fertile regions, slavery would be proclaimed as the cornerstone of society and, populated quickly and cheaply, the slave trade would openly be restored there."[59] A year later, Camus believed that Lincoln's election, far from curbing Southerner's will to expand, would encourage them to forge ahead.[60] In early 1861, *La Revue des Deux Mondes* explained the South's visceral reaction as expressing slave owners' vital need to expand their empire by annexing Mexico and Central America.[61] Cotton production, which impoverished the soil, justified expansionism by always requiring new land. To geographically restrict cotton farming was therefore to deal it a fatal blow, since it could only survive by continually expanding into new virgin soil.[62]

Once war was declared, the advocates of the Federal administration placed the Confederates' expansionist plans at the heart of their case.[63] In his memorandum to the emperor, Gen. James Watson Webb asserted that the secessionists meant for nothing less than Mexico's total disappearance and replacement with the new slave Confederacy.[64] Federal supporters were not the only ones who felt that the South would not be content to develop its "peculiar institution" and assuage its hunger for land north of the Rio Grande. A few diplomats, all living outside the United States, took up the argument. In July 1861 Dubois de Saligny, the French minister to Mexico, reported that governors of the country's northern provinces had offered to attach their territory to the new Confederacy.[65] In late 1861, Sartiges, now ambassador in The Hague, told Thouvenel that Southern nationalism was still motivated by a need for new land. When associated with cotton production, slavery was therefore an engine of expansion. As long as it survived, Sartiges maintained, the slave economy would justify the policy of conquest.[66] He was anxious to warn Thouvenel about Slidell. Sartiges had not revised his judgment of the Confederate envoy, whom he saw even before the Civil War as the herald of expansionism. He reminded Thouvenel that three years earlier Slidell had emphatically expressed his desire to see the United States take over Cuba.[67] Slidell, in his letter to Thouvenel in July 1862, inadvertently substantiated the idea that an increase in territory for the slave states was essential as a counterweight to the power of the Northern states.[68] As such, Slidell's suggestion the following year that the Confederacy adhere to the tripartite treaty guaranteeing Spain's possession of Cuba could only be received with skepticism.[69]

In 1862, André Sain de Boislecomte, another former minister plenipotentiary in Washington during the Second Republic, also considered that secession opened opportunities for the slave states, which, after annexing Mexico, might continue toward the equator. In this case, the "European expedition to Mexico may well disturb their prosperous schemes."[70] The foreign minister was, therefore, aware that territorial expansion was a project that unified the South. He realized that its temporary suspension was due to the Civil War, which had conveniently brought a halt to the annexationist designs that had seemed so resolute before the outbreak of hostilities.

Northerners understood how much they could benefit from propaganda focused on this topic. In December 1861, Secretary of State Seward made public a telegram he had sent a few months earlier to Thomas Corwin, his representative in Mexico. It described the dangers awaiting that country now that the rebel and border states had broken away from the Union:

> The [Mexican] President could not fail to see that Mexico, instead of being benefited by the prostration or obstruction of Federal authority in this country, would be exposed by it to new and fearful dangers.
> ... A continuation of anarchy in Mexico must necessarily operate

France's View of the South

as a seduction to those who are conspiring against the integrity of the Union to seek strength and aggrandizement for themselves by conquests in Mexico and other parts of Spanish America. . . . The President can scarcely believe that the disaffected citizens of our own country, who are now attempting a dismemberment of the American Union, will hope to induce Mexico to aid them by recognizing the assumed independence which they have proclaimed, because it seems manifest to him that such an organization of a distinct Government, once that part of the present Union which adjoins Mexico, would, if possible, be fraught with evils to that country, more intolerable than any which the success of those desperate measures could inflict, even upon the United States. At the same time it is manifest that the existing political organization in this country affords the surest guarantee Mexico can have that her integrity, union and independence will be respected by the people of the American Union.[71]

Seward also made it clear that his government had no desire to take control of any part of Mexico.[72] After Thouvenel read it, this correspondence was carefully filed in the archives of the Ministry of Foreign Affairs.

Under these circumstances, separation would be anything but a guarantee against expansion. Indeed, it would create an imbalance by allowing the newly independent South to spread unhindered, provoking a situation more dangerous for the entire continent than the American Union. It would have been surprising had Southern expansionists not contemplated enlarging their territory and labor system into Latin America after their new nation was established.[73] Once again, it was Sartiges who gave Thouvenel an idea of these alarming prospects when he maintained that recognition of the Richmond government would not be enough to resolve "the question of limits." He stressed that if the Union were divided, the policy of the new Northern confederation would be to prevent the expansion of the South toward countries where slavery existed, had existed, or might come to exist.[74]

Thouvenel's remarks to Flahaut, his ambassador in London, show that, unlike his agents in the United States, he had not been taken in by the Southerners' reassurances that expansion was no longer on the agenda. The foreign minister was well aware of the danger that separation would entail. In the fall of 1861, with a possible breakup of the Union looming, he stressed the extent to which Mexico, so weakened politically, would afford "territorial compensation" to its neighbor. To prevent this from happening, he recommended that a "restorative government strong enough to stop internal dissolution" be formed in Mexico.[75] In February 1862, Thouvenel wrote in another letter to Flahaut that, should the slave states' departure from the Union be definitive, "the biggest challenge will be that of limits."[76] In July, the minister questioned Slidell on the issue of the Confederacy's borders. Thouvenel had probably already raised this point with Napoléon III because, in his meeting with Slidell a week earlier, the emperor had also mentioned the foreseeable difficulty of establishing the slave republic's borders.[77] This did not seem to disturb Napoléon to the extent it did his foreign minister, for the emperor continued to advocate for Southern independence. Like many diplomats, the emperor had been intoxicated by Southern propaganda. He believed the secessionists' guarantees that an independent Confederacy would renounce territorial conquest.

The heads of French diplomacy had identified the threat, and so too had the liberal press. Although a few journalists tried to undermine the North by holding it responsible for orchestrating expansion, all in all, such indictments were exceptional, the stance of its opponent over the previous decade having done much to put the North in the clear.[78] The French press, generally favorable to the government in Washington, went back over the history of Southern aggression. It dated the awareness of the Southern expansionist danger back to the presidential candidacy of Republican John Fremont in 1856. That was when the North began to oppose the incessant usurpations. It could not look with equanimity on its peace with other nations being endangered by the ambitions of an "aristocracy of slave owners," who talked of annexing Cuba, the Caribbean, Mexico, and all of Central America.[79] The same newspapers pointed out that the North was not fighting to found an empire; it was fighting for principles.[80] Even more than the citizens of the North, it was the Republicans, because they were abolitionists, who were stopping Southern encroachments.[81] Through their efforts, the press maintained, they were preventing the formation of a vast slave empire that would give the Southerners the key to the continent and the supremacy of the two seas.[82] The liberal newspapers were grateful to the North for protecting European interests by endeavoring to maintain an overall balance.[83]

MAXIMILIAN KEEPS HIS DISTANCE

In the summer of 1863, with the entry of French troops into Mexico City, *Le Journal des Débats* wrote a little hastily that in neither New York nor Paris was there any doubt that as soon as the new Mexican government was formed, it would hasten to recognize the Confederacy, provided it was recognized in turn.[84] On January 7, 1864, Confederate secretary of state Judah Benjamin

France's View of the South

sent credentials to Gen. William Preston to represent him before Maximilian. Benjamin issued Preston with authorization to recognize Maximilian's government. The members of the Lincoln cabinet were gravely concerned by Preston's mission.[85] It would seem they were mistaken, for Maximilian's stance toward the Confederates was unambiguous, and during his visit to Paris he refused to meet with Slidell. En route to Mexico, Preston stayed in Cuba, where he learned that Maximilian preferred to remain neutral. Preston decided to abandon his mission in Mexico and embark for Europe.[86]

Slidell was convinced that Maximilian had been pressured by Napoléon III not to grant Preston an interview. He explained this rejection by the French government's hope to obtain support for the new Mexican regime from the Federal government. The latter had supposedly hinted at this support to Mercier, provided that France not enter negotiations with the Confederacy.[87] Is this possible? In light of previous statements and the constant aversion shown by the Federal government toward the Napoleonic design, this idea seems highly improbable. Moreover, in March 1864 at a reception given by Napoléon III at the Tuileries in honor of Maximilian and Charlotte, the U.S. representative, William Dayton, was conspicuous in his absence.[88]

Another question arises: Had the French government maneuvered to prevent Maximilian from being tempted to recognize the Confederacy? Ambrose Dudley Mann, the Confederate emissary to Belgium, had allegedly discovered proof that Napoléon III had ordered Maximilian not to establish relations with the Confederate government in France or Mexico.[89] However, both the foreign minister and the emperor assured Dayton that the archduke had never talked of recognizing the South.[90] Such a conviction would, therefore, have made any pressure unnecessary. The first hypothesis nonetheless seems more likely because Maximilian had no strong views and it was Napoléon III who outlined the course he should follow.[91] At the same time, *Le Courrier des Etats-Unis*, on the strength of leaked information, held that the French government did not think it appropriate for the new Mexican empire to recognize the South. This can be explained by the timing. When Maximilian finally took office in the summer of 1864, the outcome of the Civil War was becoming inevitable on the military front and the South's support was no longer of any use.

Once he was crowned emperor, Maximilian feared any attempts to dismember Mexico. His concern was justified a year later when, at the end of the war, idle former Confederates looked to settle in northern Mexico, some of them with colonization in mind.[92] The new Mexican authorities perceived this immigration as a threat, to say the least. A report from the minister of war recommended either preventing expatriation from taking place or setting draconian rules, for example by obliging all new arrivals to lay down their arms before crossing the border.[93] In June 1865 at a meeting with Maximilian, the comte Dano, French minister in Mexico City, noted that the emperor was very concerned about the former Confederates' entreaties to settle in the country. He wanted to allow them nothing but the region in central Mexico and justified this by their tendency to break free of the central government to then detach themselves from the country. "What would happen after a few years when a dense population, entirely Anglo-Saxon in language and origin, had become firmly established in my border departments? . . . The plan for a Republic of Sierra Madre, so often brandished, could then be achieved despite all our efforts on a much larger scale, taking from us all our Northern departments from Tamaulipas to the Sea of Cortés and Baja California."[94] Maximilian added that the destruction of the Confederacy could have very positive consequences for the future of Mexico and was pleased he had remained neutral.[95]

———

Napoléon III may have thought that a divided and distracted United States promised to protect the establishment of Maximilian's power and ensure the success of his Grand Design. In fact such a result was dependent on the simultaneous success of the French expedition and the Confederate rebellion. This synchronism was an impossible goal because the advancement of the imperial project was inversely proportional to the Confederacy's successes. In 1863, when the war turned in favor of the North, the French succeeded in seizing Mexico City. The limitations of this policy became apparent quickly enough to informed observers but not to the emperor himself, who insatiably constructed grandiose and romantic plans without objective examination.

French diplomats and consuls in the United States may have been convinced that the Civil War had quashed the Southern states' desires for new territory, but the Quai d'Orsay did not share this position. The Foreign Ministry continued to see the new republic as inherently expansionist. Secession itself was an indirect expression of expansionist tendencies, as it marked a refusal to remain confined within existing territorial boundaries. The founding of the Confederacy was an act of geopolitical ambition.[96] It was therefore felt to be a threat to the Mexican design. The foreign ministers had observed that Southerners were careful not to define the limits of the Confederacy and that the spirit of this new republic remained driven by an imperialist dynamic, which its supporters, despite their overtures, never managed to erase. The Quai d'Orsay saw the men the South had chosen to lead its destiny and its diplomacy as staunch expansionists. They embodied everything that France had been trying to fight for over twenty years. The Confederates lacked discernment—to put it mildly—in failing to perceive that they could not have made worse choices in the leaders and representatives they sent to France. That is why the outcome of the war was so important for the Quai d'Orsay; a Confederate victory would signal the resumption of Southern conquests to fuel a slave empire. The incompatibility between an independent slave republic alongside the new Mexican empire was a key argument to use against the emperor, who found the reconstitution of a French empire in the heart of the Americas very tempting.

While the conquest of new lands was a unifying project for the South, the North, opposed to the expansion of slavery, seemed more respectful of borders. In retrospect, the vision French diplomatic leaders developed was binary and oversimplified. They envisioned a peaceful North as guarantor of Mexico's borders and a South prepared to use any pretext to cross them.[97] They did not understand that Northerners also harbored expansionist aims. From this perspective, it was essential that the Union born of the War of Independence survive because it provided a solid framework to counter the intense expansionist desires of the slave states' citizens.[98] France had to keep the Federals happy. The North did not have a pressing need to acquire new territory in Mexico; it had the West.

Part Three

THE FUTURE LIES IN UNION

» 7 «

THE FUTURE OF THE
DISUNITED STATES

As tensions in the United States came to a head in the winter of 1860–61 with the secession of several states, observers showed little surprise. Since the Nullification Crisis — South Carolina's initial attempt to use secession for blackmail — and the events of the 1850s that had widened the gap between the two sections of the Union, they had been expecting a break in the federal ties. This scenario had been envisaged so often by fire-eaters from the slave states that the republic seemed fated to split. French agents had long been alerting their government to the risk of separation, becoming more insistent whenever the issue of slavery flared up with particular vehemence. Charles Sain de Boislecomte, the former French minister to Washington, believed, for instance, that "everything tended toward this event [separation] and that its raison d'être lay in the public organization, the laws, and the morals of the nation."[1] While they were taken aback by the rush to extremes when Lincoln was elected, they were in no way surprised to see a group of states gradually seceding from the Union to form a separate entity. From that point, the imperial government had two main concerns: determining whether the Union was, in fact, a dead letter, while at the same time contemplating a future with two republics instead of one.

U.S. Capitol in March 1861. Courtesy of the Library of
Congress, Prints and Photographs Division.

A DIFFICULT DEATH CERTIFICATE TO ISSUE

In October 1860, a few days before Lincoln's election, Mercier, the French
minister in Washington, warned Thouvenel that the vote could lead the slave
states to "give in to the advice of despair." However, he also thought it possible
that the aggressive talk could be put down to electioneering.[2] After November 6, however, the excitement aroused in the South by the election of the
former lawyer from Illinois left Mercier in no doubt as to the seriousness of the
situation.[3] He told Thouvenel that nine out of ten congressmen had expressed
the conviction that the Union would not survive the crisis.[4] The consuls were
just as pessimistic. Alfred Paul in Richmond also mentioned the possibility of
a split as a result of this vote.[5]

The Future Lies in Union

The French press was not surprised either at the unrest that swept briskly through the South. Four years previously, it had already had a chance to gauge the consequences to which the election of an antislavery figure like Fremont might lead. Unlike the diplomats, the press did not agree on the ramifications of Lincoln's election, news of which reached Paris on November 24, 1860. Most organs believed that pro-Union feeling would be stronger than the separatist tendencies of Southern extremists. The scenario of a split had been written about so many times as to make it seem unlikely. Interests were too mixed on both sides and the South would likely obtain great advantages in exchange for remaining in the Union.[6] Few newspapers anticipated the fatal repercussions of the Republican victory.[7]

Once secession began, the process seemed unstoppable to many French observers. On December 20, 1860, South Carolina's withdrawal from the Union only reinforced Mercier's conviction that "the American Union was in its death throes." He thought it likely that the new president would be forced to ratify the split at his inauguration.[8] Those Mercier questioned in Washington were of the same opinion.[9] At the sight of the secession process under way, the consuls became more alarmed and expected many other states to defect. Consul Paul in Richmond noted that even in Virginia, where the population was usually of calmer spirit than in other Southern states, "there is no longer any talk of Union or of compromise or of any attempt to keep the federation intact."[10] The consul in New Orleans was of a similar view; the political transition would be fatal to the Union.[11] In February, the failure of the conference convened under the auspices of former president John Tyler in a final effort to avoid war only heightened the defeatist sentiment.[12] After the birth of the Confederacy, Mercier recommended that the European powers settle their future interests based on the assumption the South would achieve separation.[13] Paul in Richmond deemed it futile for the North to go against the South's choice; it had to let the secessionist states leave the Union.[14] These remarks confirm the French diplomats' belief that with secession, the expansion plans of the slave states had been definitively buried.

When news arrived of the first act of secession, the press reviewed its judgment of the consequences of the November vote. The scale of the crisis could no longer be ignored. Lincoln's election appeared to be only the first act in a terrible tragedy driven by the two sections' refusal to remain united. The breakup of the Union was regrettably probable.[15] While the press was unanimous in recognizing the seriousness of the crisis, however, newspapers were divided over its origins. Those most hostile to the imperial regime saw the events of 1861 as a settling of scores from previous years. They thought the premises of the war could even be traced back to the formation of the United States, even if, through the actions of the Southerners, the gap between the two sections of the Union had gradually widened.[16] For the more conservative press, opposed to a republic in principle, it was less the North/South divide that was at fault than the nature of the regime.[17] Apart from these conservative organs, which welcomed the American troubles, prior to May 1861 newspapers from all sides deplored what they saw as the tragedy of secession and recalled France's pride in having contributed to the Union's formation.[18]

At the Quai d'Orsay, Foreign Minister Thouvenel was worried by the results of the presidential election and the announced defections that followed South Carolina's.[19] In the first months of the conflict, he repeatedly expressed his hope that the work of the founding fathers would remain intact. He wrote to Mercier, "Our feelings are all in favor of the Union. I would consider this dissolution a great catastrophe, a blow to freedom and progress."[20] He did not hide this preference from Confederate envoys.[21] Far from remaining indifferent to separation, Thouvenel hoped he could help avert it.[22]

As we have seen (in chapter 2), the emperor was publicly cautious. In front of Faulkner, the U.S. representative whom he knew to be pro-South, he explicitly showed himself loyal to the old order.[23] He even said he was prepared to offer his services to help resolve the emerging conflict.[24]

After the summer of 1861 in Washington, Mercier no longer doubted the demise of the Union, but the Quai d'Orsay did not heed his opinion and maintained its position of neutrality.[25] Thouvenel solemnly reiterated to the agents from Washington his desire to see the Union remain the framework of the American federation. This determination gave Seward cause to salute the good intentions of France and its foreign minister.[26] In February 1862, Thouvenel spoke in a similar vein to the new Confederate envoy, John Slidell.[27] So much so that in March, Slidell believed that Napoléon III hoped for a reconciliation.[28]

The series of Northern victories in the first half of 1862 suggested that if the parties failed to come to an agreement, defeat would compel the South to submit to force. In March 1862, the consul in Boston reported numerous accounts of people convinced that "the war would be over in three months," while Paul in Richmond maintained that the powder and gun supplies the South had just received would not reverse the outcome.[29] In April, for the first time, he mentioned the threat weighing on the Confederate capital, while in May his colleague in Boston promised that the end was at hand.[30] In the same month, Mercier confirmed this feeling when he wrote, "I think we have finally come to the decisive moment of the crisis. Before long the Federals will be in Richmond, there is no longer the shadow of a doubt."[31] In early June, he barely mentioned the Confederate victory in the Shenandoah Valley, focusing instead on the advance of McClellan's troops, who were camped on the outskirts of Richmond preparing to deliver the decisive blow.[32] Meanwhile, Seward provided his minister in Paris, William Dayton, with a complete picture of the military situation so he could "demonstrate to Mr. Thouvenel that it entitled the friendly nations to regard the failure of the uprising as a certainty."[33] In late June 1862, the minister of foreign affairs, relying largely on the reports of his consuls and his minister in Washington, had no doubt as to the outcome of the war.

A clear change occurred after Lee's Seven Days' campaign. Paris was expecting word of the taking of Richmond, but the news that reached France was of the assailants' retreat. Mercier now doubted that the North could soon achieve military successes of any importance.[34] The content of the consuls' dispatches, except for those of Paul in Richmond, was suddenly reversed. In July, the agent in New York described a situation full of uncertainty for the North, as much in financial as military and political terms.[35] In August, he judged that the situation could turn in favor of the rebels.[36] The Confederate representatives' arguments about the death of the Union now received close attention. Napoléon III combined these statements with his own thoughts on the benefits to be gained for Mexico from this unprecedented situation. In their meeting in July 1862, he told Slidell that he considered the restoration of the Union impossible and that final separation was just a matter of time.[37] Thouvenel, for his part, even if he admitted the North's unexpected failure to make the South yield and the Confederates' unwavering refusal to give in, took a more nuanced approach. Remembering "events which, at a solemn moment in the history of the United States, closely tied that country to France," Thouvenel continued to deplore the blow to the American Republic.[38] Though he increasingly believed that it would be impossible to restore the Union, he only meant in its previous form. He was inclined to favor a relationship between the North and the South established on a new basis.[39]

In the fall of 1861, the press hostile to the imperial regime joined Le Constitutionnel and its ilk in writing that the Union was irreversibly divided. The First Battle of Bull Run sent shockwaves through the opposition press because the South had shown it was capable of holding out against its opponent. These newspapers did not see any interest in prolonging the fight. Because the South no longer wanted to be united to the North, it was useless to try and compel it, through the strength of arms, to return to the Union.[40] However, while the press as a whole agreed that the diagnosis was terminal, views unsurprisingly diverged on how France should react to the disappearance of the Union. The newspapers close to the government wanted to take advantage of the Union's wounds to recognize the South, while their rivals were of the opinion that this decision was the Federal government's alone to make, either voluntarily or by the force of military events.[41]

Given the uncertainty surrounding the outcome of the recent fighting and the fate of the war as a whole, the Quai d'Orsay was loath to acknowledge the Union's demise. Between the summer of 1862 and the summer of 1863, the Foreign Ministry found it difficult to get a firm idea of the military situation, which went through several phases without one belligerent or the other taking a clear advantage. After Antietam, Mercier wrote to Thouvenel that the war seemed "about to reach its climax, only then to rush off in one direction or another."[42] The consuls admitted their bewilderment at the North's inability to subdue its opponent and were equally puzzled at the South's inability to make its enemy give up.[43] There was no way to predict definitively how particular battles would impact the outcome of the war. While the French agents believed the Union to be in its death throes, the challenge for them was to determine the time of death. The American republic was perhaps finished, but the Confederates had not forced the Federals to abandon the struggle. In these circumstances, the diplomats preferred to wait and see, as recognition of the South depended on the disappearance of the Union, itself conditional on the North giving up its pursuit of a seemingly endless war.

Given this situation, should the French government anticipate events and decide on diplomatic action in favor of the South? After Lee's victorious campaign in the early summer of 1862, that is just what the Confederate agents tried to bring about. John Slidell wrote to Thouvenel that the course of events justified the hope and expectation that his government would be recognized by France.[44] As the war dragged on without definitive result, Mercier recommended diplomatic recognition if only as a reward for the Confederates' stubbornness in their struggle for independence. Mercier felt that since the South had proven it could hold out against the North, its tenacity should be enough to tip the balance.[45] However, Thouvenel was not of a mind to jump the gun. In the very first hours of the conflict, he determined a course of action from which he would not waiver. He wrote to Mercier that France would not take the political risk of anticipating the developments of the war. He would finalize his position once separation had become "irrevocable."[46] When Thouvenel first received Slidell on February 7, 1862, he expressed himself in the same terms.[47] In May, he reaffirmed to his ambassador to the United Kingdom that

The Future Lies in Union

no decision would be made as long as "uncertainty weighed on the final con-sequences of the conflict."[48]

For Thouvenel and his successor Drouyn de Lhuys, it was the demo-cratic process more than a Southern military feat that could decide the fate of the Union, and Thouvenel awaited the outcome of the midterm elections in November 1862 to adopt a definitive position.[49] Whereas for the British, a decisive military event could have led the government to propose an arrange-ment on the basis of separation, the French were counting more heavily on the pressure of public opinion to achieve this result.[50] In any case, Napoléon III's foreign ministers may have considered the Union moribund but felt it was not up to France to issue the death certificate so long as the North was not itself resigned to separation.

WHAT FUTURE FOR A DIVIDED UNION?

Did a divided Union have a future? In July 1862, in the dispatch he sent to Thouvenel, Slidell judged that the Confederacy offered "sufficient elements of order and stability" to give it the right to take its place among the family of nations.[51] However, this view was by no means shared by all observers. In 1861, following his travels in the Northern states, Prince Napoléon wondered what would become of the country if the Union were to split.[52] The consuls also seriously doubted the potential of a divided Union. The consul in New York summed up in one stroke what many diplomats did not dare say out loud: "In my opinion, the Southern Confederacy is not viable."[53] The agent best placed to confirm or refute this judgment was Alfred Paul, the consul in Richmond, who agreed with his colleague in New York. Paul was one of the first consuls to give his opinion on the process initiated on December 20, 1861, and was very critical from the start. South Carolina's secession appeared to him a foolish decision.[54] He reproached the other Southern states for their passivity when they failed to disavow the insurrection.[55] Paul sensed early on that breaking away from the federal framework was an act of madness that could only end in a fiasco. Stressing the South's past lack of unity and its highly diverse com-ponents, he painted a pessimistic picture of the new entity. If by chance the slave republic did manage to establish itself outside the federal framework, its future, he felt sure, would be bleak. The Confederacy would find itself having to deal with an inherent conflict between the principle of the states' rights and the increased centralization of its Federal government. There would also be conflicting interests between the agricultural states of the Deep South and the border states which were inclined toward becoming free-labor manufacturing.[56]

Many French observers saw the link that joined the states to the central government as the Confederacy's primary structural weaknesses.[57] The French could not fully understand the autonomy given to the states within a federal framework. Since its revolution, France followed a Jacobinist tradition that invested strong centralized power in Paris. From the capital, the emperor decided the future of France. It was, therefore, difficult for French observers to sympathize with the South's provincial rebellion. Paul highlighted the Confederate government's difficulties in countering the "thoughtless desires and embarrassing pretensions of States or categories of States." He was referring to the use of local militias, which the state governors alone could decide to employ. In his opinion, they were an obstacle to the conscription decreed by the government in Richmond. He observed, moreover, that the link between the states in rebellion was tenuous. Paul wondered whether, apart from slavery, there was a common denominator between those whose homes bordered the free states and those living near the Gulf of Mexico.[58] He noted that specific characteristics outweighed the general interest. The rebel states protected their own interests above all, and this self-involvement was not without consequence for the Confederacy's survival. Would it suffer from the rights it granted to states? Would the Confederacy fall victim to the principle upon which it had been founded?

Another weakness identified by the diplomats lay in the future coexistence of a slave republic and a free republic. Sain de Boislecomte, the former minister to Washington, was emphatic on this point: if the South triumphed, it would do nothing to change the difficulties of the political situation. Indeed, a permanent state of tension would take hold between the federation established in the north and the one in the south.[59] The quarrels that punctuated the 1850s, particularly over the issue of fugitive slaves, showed that there could be no appeasement as long as men were deprived of their liberty on one part of American territory.

The arguments of the liberal press stemmed from one main observation: since secession had taken place outside the rule of law, the government it led to had no legal basis. Some newspapers considered that a federation could not be dissolved without the consent of the authority that coordinated and centralized its policies. President Lincoln was only doing his duty in defending the Union since he had taken an oath to uphold the U.S. Constitution.[60] Furthermore, accepting the principle of secession would lead to the Union's breakup into multiple sovereignties. It would introduce a principle of anarchy that would endanger the order and security of states.[61] Finally, the superiority of individual states was a myth because none could claim the attributes of sovereignty regarding monetary, foreign, or defense policy. There was only one sovereignty, and it was invested entirely in the president, the Supreme Court, and Congress. Southerners forgot that while the states (as colonies) had existed before the Union, they had changed their relationship to the Federal government when the people ratified the Constitution. Besides, this chronological priority was only true for the thirteen original states; twenty more had been added from federal territory.[62]

Next, the press hostile to Napoléon III deemed the formation of a new entity from the eleven rebel states fanciful. The Confederacy, these writers claimed, would not survive.[63] Several articles discussed the South's dependence on Northern banks. Separated from the North, it would never be able to finance its investments.[64] Once again, the argument underscored the overall weakness of the Confederacy due to the Confederate government's weak authority over the states. The authors took pleasure in pointing out that the slave states had taken up arms on the strength of their sovereignty but, in a historical irony, these states' rights now turned against the Davis government.[65] The liberal newspapers also expected the future of two republics in North America to be ridden with conflict. The confrontation would come from the Confederate states' need to extend slavery to territories still spared the practice, from a commercial rivalry over how to share the Mississippi River, and from the economic, demographic, and material imbalance that would continue to grow between the two sections.[66] As such, the success of the Southern rebellion would bring a perpetual struggle between the Union and the Confederacy.

THE UNION MUST BE REBUILT

Given these circumstances, the preservation of a federation was deemed preferable. Napoléon III may have dreamed of a confederacy of North American States in four equal parts; yet this was a plan to which Thouvenel and his successor had never subscribed.[67] Besides believing that an independent Southern republic was both unrealistic and a threat to Mexico, one of the reasons for Thouvenel's and Drouyn de Lhuys's hostility to the Confederacy was the desire to maintain an international balance.

It is therefore understandable that French diplomats, trying to imagine what might replace the defunct Union, had never seriously envisaged two strictly separate entities. Instead, they had always wanted to maintain some kind of framework linking the two republics. Henri Mercier was the first to suggest a customs union, that is two self-governing nations with a common economic market but separate administrations.[68] A few months later he returned to this idea, wondering if France might not accept the political independence of several states, but again conditioning its acceptance on a customs union.[69] The ministry's departments worked on this idea and drafted a project they submitted to Thouvenel on July 4, 1862. It was a plan for the delimitation between North and South that, in the event of a separation, would follow the division already established by slavery. A full account of military successes would go into the reconfiguration of the separate nations. Missouri, Kentucky, Tennessee, and part of Virginia would return to the North; eleven states would remain in an independent South. The two separate countries would still operate as one economic unit, according to this scheme, with a single border for customs and a uniform tariff. Each of the republics would bear a proportionate share of the debt of the former United States.[70]

Thouvenel read the plan a month and a half later. He decided to make alterations to it in case France was asked to mediate a peace. Far from endorsing separation, Thouvenel wished to reconstruct the Union on a new basis. He deliberately used the oxymoron "two federated confederacies." In his mind, the two republics would benefit from the same diplomatic representation and a unified customs framework, and at the political level a chamber representing both sides would settle disputes.[71] On September 12, 1862, Thouvenel met with Dayton, the U.S. representative to France. Referring to what was still only a framework, he took his idea of strengthening the union of the two states even further and proposed that they be united for defense in addition to foreign relations.[72] He was inspired by the United Principalities of Moldavia and Wallachia, which had merged to form Romania. They had adopted common legislative institutions and had each elected the same leader.[73]

For Drouyn de Lhuys, the splitting of the Union was no more a matter of course than it had been for his predecessor. In the mediation proposal he drafted in January 1863, he appealed to the North and South to consider whether the memories of a common existence, the links of all kinds that had made them a single state and brought this state to "a high degree of prosperity," were not more powerful than the causes that had led them to take up arms against each other.[74] Reframing his offer in a historical perspective, he recalled all that the United States had gained by federating. In *Le Constitutionnel* of January 20, 1863, an article written by Paulin Limayrac but published at the request of the foreign minister, expressed the hope of seeing the restoration of "the great American confederation in its entirety."[75] Thouvenel and Drouyn de Lhuys believed that the struggle of the states in rebellion went against the

The Future Lies in Union

march of history. They could not resign themselves to the disappearance of the Union.

———

Accepting the end of the Union required the French to determine the moment of its demise and contemplating what should replace the former United States. There was uncertainty on both points: uncertainty about the definitive disappearance of the Union, which was impossible to officially endorse as long as the North remained determined to put down the South's rebellion; and doubt about the sustainability of the Confederacy, which had not demonstrated its ability to survive the Civil War. In March 1862, the consul in Boston summed up in a few words what quickly became clear to the ministry: the restoration of the Union was "the only [outcome] possible, the only one desirable, for Americans and for the foreign powers."[76]

Of course, in the summer of 1862, faced with the Southerners' unexpected resistance and the Union's failure to make them yield, the Quai d'Orsay did briefly envisage the breakup of the United States. This was a matter of resignation, not choice. Paradoxically, it was just as the Union appeared most vulnerable to defeat that its existence was seen as essential to a peaceful future for the continent. A peaceful United States was far more reassuring than two rival republics in perpetual conflict. The disturbing prospect of continued conflict explains why the scheme for what Thouvenel called "two federated confederations"—a plan that could be submitted to both parties in the event of mediation—proposed no more than a reorganization of the federal framework. This reconstruction, which made something new with the old, was ultimately reassuring and shows just how inconceivable it was for the ministry that the South would not maintain strong ties with the North. For both Thouvenel and Drouyn de Lhuys, the future of the United States lay in a new union, not a division between two republics. What kind of union could this be? The question troubled the Americans themselves.[77] Lincoln had an answer. In publishing his Emancipation Proclamation in September 1862, he proved that he, too, aspired not to restore the antebellum federation but to give rise to another, as the accomplishment of a second American Revolution. The winds of change, fanned by Lincoln, and the distinct lack of prospects for a slave republic demonstrated that the idea of an independent South was illusory.

THE SOUTH, A TRADE PARTNER?

A major source of wealth for the United States, North American cotton was also crucial for Europe, representing over 80 percent of its total cotton purchases in 1860.[1] The old continent had neglected to diversify its suppliers to meet the demands of its growing textile industry, to the extent that the South had become its almost only supplier. France had the second-largest cotton industry in Europe, though well behind Britain, and was more dependent than Britain for its imports on the South's "white gold."

Cotton dependency gave the slave-owning elites leverage. In 1855, the title of a book by journalist David Christy gave rise to the expression "King Cotton," a slogan taken up a few years later by South Carolina senator James H. Hammond.[2] He believed that cotton gave the South considerable power, as without this essential raw material for their textile industry, France and England would see their economies collapse. Once hostilities began, the Confederates hoped to inspire a diplomatic choice in their favor through economic pressure. France and Britain felt the effects of the "cotton famine." The Tuileries cabinet tried to determine the origin of the shortage while assessing the real impact of the crisis on the workforce. However, it did not lose sight of trade in wheat and other products with the states loyal to the Federal government. This concern for trade with the North explains why France, like the United Kingdom, confounded Southern expectations by not recognizing the Confederacy or otherwise intervening in the conflict.

Colonel Ellet's Ram Fleet on the Mississippi, 1862. Line engraving
after a sketch by Alexander Simplot, published in *Harper's Weekly*,
1862. Courtesy of the U.S. Naval Historical Center.

THE COTTON FAMINE

The French cotton industry, which employed 379,000 workers,[3] was concentrated in three regions: Normandy, Alsace, and the Nord. Of the total volume of cotton, 90 percent was imported from the southern United States and almost all of it — 95.5 percent — landed in Le Havre.[4] In 1861 cotton represented the largest item of import expenditure (11 percent of purchases).[5] Yet French imports were modest compared with England's, absorbing only 10 percent of the South's cotton production. At the start of the war, the foreign minister estimated France's annual cotton requirements at about 400,000 bales, nearly six times less than Britain (2.5 million bales).[6]

The decrease in cotton supplies began to make itself felt in France in late 1861. With scarcity came a gradual inflation in price. In November, Rouher, the commerce minister, noted that the progressive rise in cotton prices had amounted to an increase in excess of 40 percent over a few months.[7] Looking beyond the numbers, people started to suffer. From the fall of 1861, the reports of the *procureurs généraux* (district attorneys) and their deputies began to get the attention of the imperial government. In Normandy, they mentioned a decrease in working hours or wages.[8] The deputy *procureur* of Colmar, in Alsace, made the same observation.[9] Rouher's pessimism for the coming months was not misplaced, since the worst was still to come.[10] The economic situation deteriorated throughout 1862. By then, where working hours were not reduced, employers were laying workers off. In Alsace, the reports noted "significant worker layoffs," while in the Nord and the Aisne the situation seemed equally alarming.[11] Many mills stopped running, and in Roubaix only a quarter of workers were on the job.[12] In Rouen, the capital of Normandy, 55 percent of cotton workers were unemployed.[13] At the end of 1862, only 271,570 bales had been imported; total cotton purchases had halved.[14] The first months of 1863 seemed to promise no respite. Whereas under normal circumstances North American cotton fetched around 4 francs per kilogram, in early 1863 prices reached 6.74 francs per kilogram. The deputy *procureur* of Caen welcomed efforts by public charities to alleviate the increasing poverty.[15]

The French government received appeals from all sides to help the victims of the "cotton famine." Employers' federations and chambers of commerce were concerned about the effects of the American Civil War on French trade and petitioned their government for cotton imports to be resumed.[16] The fate of the working class was of major concern to the emperor (he was the author of *L'extinction du paupérisme*), and he did not remain indifferent.[17] At a cabinet meeting in October 1861, he expressed his dismay at the country's economic and financial situation.[18] The foreign minister, for his part, wrote to his minister in Washington that "our industry is suffering horribly and, for many reasons, the malaise of our working classes does not leave us as cold as our neighbors."[19] The imperial government's consideration of social suffering was also motivated by its need to limit discontent and ward off potential popular uprisings.

This fear of social unrest explains why Napoléon III and his ministers made every effort to alleviate the workers' hardship. The government took measures to relieve distress at both the departmental and national levels. On January 25, 1863, the commerce minister presented a bill to the legislature for an appropriation of 5 million francs for cotton workers. In May 1863 an additional 1.2 million francs were granted.[20] While the press hostile to the empire nonetheless welcomed this state assistance, it denounced the paucity of private donations and the selfishness of the wealthy in the face of such poverty.[21] The liberal press made comparisons with the philanthropic behavior of the British and hoped that a fraternity of classes would grow out of the crisis to foster national unity.[22] Starting in February 1863, collections for charity were finally undertaken throughout France.[23]

WAS THE BLOCKADE TO BLAME?

Before a solution to the "cotton famine" could be found, the causes had to be determined. In September 1861, Thouvenel naturally blamed the North's blockade of Southern ports.[24] What France could do about the blockade was not so clear. Henri Mercier advocated a Franco-British initiative to persuade the Lincoln administration to relax the blockade and let some cotton through.[25] In Paris, the Quai d'Orsay was in favor of making a direct request to Seward to permit foreign provisions of the much-needed cotton. It felt that Washington had everything to gain from doing so, as the moral effect would be in its favor.[26] The minister kept business circles informed of his requests.[27] On several occasions, Thouvenel told William Dayton, the Union's minister plenipotentiary in Paris, of the "troubles" and "suffering" of the French population and called for the blockade to be eased.[28] Although Dayton assured him that his government was giving the French request serious consideration — the North made it known that it was doing its utmost to procure cotton for neutrals and that it planned to seize a Southern port — no progress was forthcoming.[29] On the contrary, the Northerners decided to use blockships — the Stone Fleet — to block access to the ports. In January 1862, in a letter to his ambassador in London, Thouvenel still believed that the Mississippi cotton harvests might reach Matamoros, but by April he had given up hope.[30]

The diplomatic initiatives toward Washington having failed, France considered military action against the blockade. Montholon, the consul in New York, drafted a report reviewing the best means to break the blockade. He wrote that "combined squadrons would easily disperse the Federal forces that have closed the southern ports of the United States."[31] Despite rumors of a Franco-British intervention to break the blockade in February 1862, it was two months before the two countries took the next important step.[32] On April 11, British member of Parliament William Shaw Lindsay, one of the leading shipbuilders in England and very favorable to the South, met with Napoléon III. The latter said that Thouvenel had twice proposed to Lord Cowley, the British ambassador, that he suggest joint action against the blockade to his government but that London had not responded to the proposal. Still, the emperor had not given up the military option and indicated that if Britain were to join him, he was prepared to break the blockade with a sizable fleet up to the mouth of the Mississippi River.[33] It is likely that Napoléon wished to take advantage of the Mexican campaign to take action against the blockade, which he blamed for ruining the French economy and impoverishing workers. Since January 7, 1862, British, French, and Spanish ships had been anchored in the harbor of Vera Cruz.[34] It would be easy for London and Paris to use some of them to disperse the Union vessels that were preventing access to the port of New Orleans. However, Napoléon wanted Lindsay to act as intermediary because he considered that "the ground was not well enough prepared for his government to send proposals to the queen's ministers."[35]

Lindsay went to see Cowley and returned on April 13 to report to the emperor on their interview. The British ambassador, he said, had dismissed the idea of such an intervention. Napoléon III advised him to return to England and talk directly with Russell, the foreign minister, and Palmerston, the prime minister. He recommended that Lindsay also meet with two members of the opposition, Lord Derby and Benjamin Disraeli. When Lindsay arrived in England, Disraeli welcomed Napoléon's proposal and suggested that much of Parliament would support it and could force the government to accept it, but Russell turned down the request point blank. Russell reminded Lindsay that all communication between France and England must go through diplomatic channels, and he refused to negotiate outside of them. Back in Paris, Lindsay met the emperor for the third time on April 18, 1862, and informed him of this rebuff. The ship owner hoped that Napoléon would pursue his objectives independently of England, but the emperor suggested that France and England send a friendly request to the U.S. government asking that the ports be reopened. Napoléon realized that the Union seizure of New Orleans could make this measure unnecessary.[36]

By May 13, 1862, the emperor seemed to have definitively abandoned the plan; he told Cowley nothing was to be done for the moment "apart from observing events."[37] Slidell raised the possibility of armed intervention against the blockade at his first meeting with Napoléon III in July 1862. Napoléon III rejected the idea, arguing that opening the Southern ports by force would constitute an act of war.[38] At their second meeting in October 1862, Slidell, highlighting the weakness of the Federal defenses, repeated his request, but the emperor did not respond.[39] In his speech of January 12, 1863, at the opening of the legislative session, Napoléon III simply linked the textile industry's woes to the American war and asked that the legislature relieve workers' adversity with an exceptional appropriation.[40]

Why was the armed intervention abandoned? The first reason was Napoléon's reluctance to act without England. Although far more concerned by the lack of cotton than France, London was checked by Seward's firm, even aggressive stance.[41] England categorically refused to risk a conflict with the United States by breaking the blockade. What is more, the British government suspected that the blockade had little to do with the disruption of supplies.[42] Napoléon III understood that he only had his own forces to rely on to open the Southern ports. All the more so for the fact that, as the Convention of Soledad had given reason to expect, the British and Spanish ships had just cast off from Vera Cruz.[43]

Second, while some businessmen called for aggressive action against the blockade, just as many argued for nonintervention and neutrality. Manufacturers in the Haut-Rhin, for example, were benefiting from high-priced cotton and the last thing they wanted was an intervention that would cause prices to plummet.[44]

Finally, Thouvenel must be given credit for having changed the emperor's mind. In addition to the risk of a very dangerous conflict with the United States, Thouvenel stressed that the connection between the decline in cotton shipments to Europe and Lincoln's closure of the Confederate coast was unfounded. The consuls' reports on the successes of the blockade runners were piled high on his desk. They had convinced Thouvenel that the blockade established along the Southern coast was in fact extremely porous.[45] Based on these facts, the foreign minister managed to persuade the emperor that any action against the blockade would be not only dangerous but also useless.

However, Napoléon III's bellicose inclinations were such that Thouvenel had been forced to counter the emperor's plans. First, by failing to transmit to Cowley the emperor's offer to propose a joint intervention to his government. Cowley categorically denied to Lindsay that France had ever suggested to Britain that together they put an end to the blockade. For his part, Thouvenel told Cowley on April 14 that he had not written a note to that effect but had, on the contrary, tried to show the emperor and Rouher that interference would inevitably lead to a clash.[46] Slidell had confirmation of this a few weeks later, when Charles Wood, a member of the British government, denied that Paris had ever made overtures to London to end the blockade.[47] Thouvenel then endeavored to tone down the emperor's words to Lindsay for the British government, as he wanted the French position of nonintervention to be unambiguous.[48] Finally, he persuaded Napoléon III to amend his stance. It is likely that Thouvenel only became aware of it in conferring with Cowley after the interview with Lindsay. He subsequently tried to dissuade the emperor from going too far, which explains the more moderate position the ruler adopted during his last meeting with Lindsay.

THE SOUTH'S RESPONSIBILITY UNCOVERED

The French foreign minister was already aware of the porosity of the blockade (see chapter 1) during his first meeting with Slidell on February 7, 1862. He asked the envoy why, if so many vessels managed to get through, so little cotton was reaching neutral ports. Slidell emphasized the small tonnage of the vessels that slipped through the cracks and many sailors' fear of being captured, but these arguments were unconvincing.[49] When on May 1, 1862, the

Northerners seized the main port for U.S. cotton exports, the hopes of the diplomats and consuls soared.[50] The Federal government quickly indicated that it would lift the blockade on New Orleans and start shipping cotton.[51] Yet the French agents were soon disillusioned. It became obvious that the conquest of this port would change nothing; in fact, the cotton crisis only got worse. On June 5, 1862, Thouvenel confessed his disappointment.[52]

Why did nothing change? According to Paul in Richmond, the lack of a Southern commercial fleet might mean there were no ships to transport the cotton.[53] Paul, like his counterpart in New Orleans, also blamed the drop in supplies on the disruption of trade due to the blockade. The consuls asserted that the European vessels that usually transported cotton preferred to turn away rather than be subject to the controls of the Northern fleet, echoing the claims of the Confederate secretary of state.[54] Apparently the argument hit home, because in April 1863, in a letter to the minister of the navy, this was the interpretation given by the new foreign minister, Edouard Drouyn de Lhuys.[55]

However, another reason was put forward to explain the decline in imports. The diplomats and consuls wondered whether cotton producers were not surreptitiously withholding their crop. They also wanted to ascertain whether the Davis cabinet approved such a move. Paul's suspicions were raised in the fall of 1861. He was surprised to see that the Confederate government, though keen to prove that the blockade was a sieve, was not promoting the sale of cotton.[56] His counterpart in New York accused the Southern leaders of closing their eyes to those hindering cotton exports.[57] While in Richmond in April 1862, Mercier, who had until then been hesitant to implicate the Confederate leaders, received direct confirmation from the Confederate secretary of state that his government endorsed the embargo.[58] In July 1862, Slidell himself provided proof that the cotton supply was being limited with the Southern leaders' assent. In his declarations to Napoléon III and the French foreign minister, he conditioned the South's cotton exports to France on an acknowledgment of his government.[59] Slidell inadvertently let it be understood that, in accordance with state governors and planters, the embargo had not only been approved but decided and organized by the Davis cabinet. As such, Napoléon III was persuaded that the Confederate leaders wanted to use cotton as a bargaining chip to obtain a diplomatic decision in their favor. Without beating around the bush, he told Slidell, "If you do not give it to us, we will not be able to find it anywhere."[60] The British government was also convinced of the Confederate leadership's involvement in the embargo.[61]

The other explanation for the drying up of cotton deliveries was the planters. The diplomats and consuls protested that planters often preferred to destroy their cotton rather than see it fall into the hands of Northerners and be sold to the European powers; an extreme measure that Seward reported to the imperial authorities.[62] The agents were outraged by the destruction of such a valuable resource and wrote countless dispatches to that effect. The consul in New Orleans first mentioned this deliberate policy in late 1861 and noted that it had the firm support of the Confederate population.[63] The following year, the capture of the city only confirmed what he had foreseen. Before cotton could leave the port, the Southerners took care to burn both the stocks in the warehouses and the cargo on the ships. The consul called it a "sad spectacle" of "very doubtful" utility to the Southern cause.[64] For the consul stationed in New York, this willful destruction proved that lifting the blockade would have no effect on the dearth of cotton shipments to Europe.[65] In Washington, Mercier provided Thouvenel with news of the fires and made no attempt to temper his gloom.[66] In June 1862, the diplomat indicated Seward's willingness to take action in order to get cotton through to Europe. But Mercier doubted the initiative would be successful because of the Southern planters' resolve.[67] Five months later, the plenipotentiary hinted at his defeatism to Thouvenel's replacement. He confirmed to Drouyn de Lhuys that whatever interventions the Northerners undertook to seize the cotton and have it transported to the major markets in the North, the cotton would be burned.[68]

Although, by the summer of 1863, Union forces controlled the Mississippi River, the chancellor of the New Orleans consulate considered it unlikely that France would see any cotton arrive, as the burning of white gold showed no sign of slowing down. He too described at length to his minister the devastation caused by the rebels.[69] The Southerners' retreat was accompanied by desperate acts. In the areas reclaimed and rehabilitated by the Federals, the consul accused the Southern guerrillas of causing damage to prevent cotton from growing.[70] When the raids did not manage to reach the plantations, they preyed on ships descending the Mississippi and its tributaries.[71]

In Paris, this fierce resistance was of utmost concern to the government. On March 25, 1862, the emperor invited Dayton, the Union representative, to meet him to discuss his worries about the determined action of the cotton growers. Henry Shelton Sanford, the U.S. minister in Brussels, did not conceal from Thouvenel his government's powerlessness to stop the collapse in exports of a product that the Europeans so badly needed.[72] The foreign minister put these depredations down to a desire for revenge. In his view, the Confederates were expressing their resentment of France, perhaps due to its inaction in the face of a blockade they considered illegal.[73] He spoke to his consul in Richmond of the disastrous effects "the use of these desperate measures" entailed.[74] Whatever the Northerners' willingness to supply Europe, his successor, Drouyn de Lhuys, was under no delusions and believed France must give up on Southern cotton.[75]

Did the Confederate authorities endorse the destruction of these 2.5 million bales?[76] In March 1862, the consul in Charleston sent the Quai d'Orsay an indignant dispatch containing information obtained by his British colleague. It pointed to the Confederate secretary of state, Judah P. Benjamin, referred to as "the party leader willing to risk everything."[77] Two months later, the consul in Boston backed up these accusations with a letter from Benjamin in which he appeared explicitly complicit in these "barbaric practices used as a system of defense."[78] In Richmond, Paul stressed the popularity of the conflagrations—encouraged, moreover, by the Confederate Senate, which passed a law to make them mandatory. He wrote that they were coordinated by public safety committees, backed up by local committees, to check that the cotton was not secretly sold to blockade runners.[79] In the summer of 1863, the chancellor of the New Orleans consulate informed his government that new orders had been given by the Davis administration to burn all the cotton stored in Southern warehouses.[80] The consul in Charleston saw this as utter stupidity because the Confederacy was depriving itself of the only resource with which it could earn foreign currency.[81]

In the last months of 1861, the liberal French press also denounced the embargo imposed by Southern authorities.[82] It considered that there was collusion between the Confederate government and the state governors, in Louisiana for instance, to confine cotton to the plantations.[83] These revelations were by no means trivial. They sought to emphasize the Machiavellianism and selfishness of the Southerners, who were using cotton for economic blackmail without concern for the embargo's consequences for European countries. However, from the spring of 1862, the talk was less of the withholding of cotton than of its destruction. Newspapers were scandalized by the "incendiary frenzy," especially after the capture of New Orleans, where several thousand bales went up in smoke.[84] There was no longer any question of blaming the lack of cotton on the North and its blockade.[85]

The diplomats and consuls had trouble understanding the Confederate strategy. Indeed, by 1863, conscious that the embargo had failed to trigger the expected diplomatic decision, the rebels seemed to want to make concessions to meet their financial needs. In January 1863 the consul in New York noted that the South registered a debt of nearly $1 million, with not a cent in its coffers.[86] It took out a loan to be repaid in cotton. The loan was granted by the Franco-German banker Emile Erlanger.[87] Far as it was from the big financial institutions such as Rothschilds, Barings, and Hottinguers, the choice of Erlanger's bank was likely due to his personal connection to Slidell.[88] The loan was for a total of 75 million francs, divided into bonds, repayable over twenty years at 7 percent interest.[89] On March 19, 1863, the first bonds were put on the market in London, Liverpool, Amsterdam, Paris, and Frankfurt. The issue was a success. However, together with the setbacks suffered by the rebels in mid-1863, the strengthening of the blockade, the reluctance of British capitalists to buy the bonds of slave states, and the speculative nature of the transaction caused the bonds to drop in the fall to less than 40 percent of their nominal value.[90]

In September 1863, Benjamin proposed to Slidell to sell cotton directly to the French for $8 million or $10 million.[91] Yet at the same time, the Confederate government maintained its embargo. On February 15, 1864, the consul in Richmond learned that the Confederate Congress had passed two bills, signed by Jefferson Davis, prohibiting the export of cotton and tobacco under penalty of forfeiting all means of transporting these goods.[92] In October of that year, Fauconnet, the chancellor of the French consulate in New Orleans, notified his government that the Southern administration had softened its position but had to reckon with the guerrillas who bypassed the Northerners' outposts to destroy cotton, which continued to be set ablaze before Maj. Gen. William Tecumseh Sherman's advance in Georgia.[93] The diplomats and consuls wondered whether Davis and his government were still in control of the situation and concluded that only the North's successes would enable the large-scale return of white gold to Europe.[94]

A COTTON CRISIS?

Accounts coincide to date the end of the French cotton crisis in the late winter of 1862–63. If we look at the press, some organs saw the situation improving in the first months of 1863, and even earlier in Britain.[95] The same is true for the *procureurs*. Their reports show a gradual recovery in manufacturing, which was faster in some regions than others (in Mulhouse an improvement was observed in January 1863; in Rouen, Nancy, and Colmar the upturn was confirmed in October, while in Caen and Belfort the crisis came to an end in early 1864).[96] So how is it that France overcame the difficulties caused by cotton diplomacy?

One oft-cited explanation is the existence of a cotton surplus in France and England right before the Civil War. The South could not have chosen a worse moment to secede. While the Confederates were gradually establishing their embargo in 1861, France and Britain suffered relatively little from the cotton crisis. Bumper crops before the war had saturated the markets, and both countries had taken advantage of the drop in cotton prices to build up their stocks.[97] By September and October 1861, petitions from the textile industry were urging Thouvenel to prepare for a shortage of cotton for the French textile industry.[98] However, while the foreign minister had been worried in September, in late October he reviewed his position and judged that the cotton stocks were not exhausted; on December 1, 1861, France still had 143,345 bales, which is probably an underestimate.[99] Indeed, while the French requirements were slightly higher than 400,000 bales, in 1860, 594,000 bales of cotton were imported to Le Havre and, despite a collapse from the summer of 1861, 516,000 bales still reached the Norman port in the first year of the Civil War.[100] So France could easily draw on its stocks to offset the cotton shortage. The imperial government nonetheless became alarmed, which was proof of its difficulty establishing an accurate estimate of remaining cotton stocks. In November 1861, Rouher, the minister of agriculture and commerce, assessed them at six months' worth, in January 1862, the wife of Justice Minister Jules Baroche heard it said that France had no more than six weeks' worth, and in April 1862 Thouvenel evaluated them at two months' worth.[101]

Another way out of the crisis was to turn to suppliers outside Dixie, which allowed an increase in cotton imports in 1863 and the following years. From the 271,570 bales imported into France in 1862, the figure slowly rose to 381,539 in 1863 — almost as many as the already high 1860 level (400,000 bales) — and 460,880 in 1864.[102] Looking at the trade tables, we can confirm this by expenditure. In the second half of 1862, France purchased 26,296,380 francs worth of cotton, and 58,206,056 francs worth in the first half of 1863. On a full-year basis this gives 126,158,877 francs in 1862, 177,170,622 francs in 1863, and 315,606,000 francs in 1864.[103] In other words, France bought three times more cotton between July 1 and December 31, 1863, than between January 1 and June 30, 1863.

From where did salvation come? Some newspapers recommended making Algeria a land of cotton, but this alternative did not fulfill its promise. In 1861 and 1862 fewer seedlings were planted there than in 1854.[104] If the crisis were to continue, Mexico could be a solution. Without writing it explicitly, the emperor, in his letter of July 1862 to General Forey, commander of the expeditionary force in Mexico, made the connection between the Mexican plan and the search for new agricultural areas: "We are seeing today, through sad experience, how precarious is the fate of an industry that is reduced to seeking its raw material on a single market, of which it suffers all the vicissitudes."[105] The two successive foreign ministers looked into this possibility.[106] However, the complications related to developing land and, above all, pacifying the territory, forced them to put this idea on the backburner.

So there would be no French cotton. France had to rely on the British cotton from India that arrived in Le Havre after being delivered to Liverpool. While in 1860 only 30,000 bales were imported from England, the following year this figure quadrupled.[107] By 1863 Anglo-Indian cotton was replacing that of the Southern states and supplying the European markets.[108] The Confederate envoys, forgetting that the South had used and abused the cotton threat, attempted to arouse indignation among the French at the blow to their national honor of becoming so dependent on England's goodwill. In July 1862, in the request for diplomatic recognition he presented to Thouvenel, Slidell hinted that Britain had every interest in letting the war continue to gain a monopoly of this essential material with its Indian production.[109] France, by looking to Britain for its supplies, at least partially escaped its dependence on American cotton.[110] But the introduction of cotton from India had its drawbacks, as the fabrics made from this material were too light and difficult to print on. Looms had to be modified, and French manufacturers had to import English looms.[111]

The effects of the cotton crisis on workers were also less dramatic than first expected. In the 1860s there were 4,384,000 industrial workers in France.[112] Despite the considerable size of the construction industry, textiles remained by far the largest industrial sector in France. One third of workers, or 1.5 million people, were indirectly dependent on cotton, with those directly dependent on it numbering fewer than 400,000 (1 percent of the French population), that is, only a quarter of textile workers and less than 10 percent of the entire working population.[113] So the number of workers harmed by the suspension of cotton imports was in fact relatively low, and not all of these workers lost their jobs. On April 15, 1863, the total number of unemployed in France, all sectors included, was around 223,336; in February 1864, it was 174,052.[114] The total number of unemployed workers in the cotton industry therefore never exceeded 55 percent of its workforce. Finally, the situation in France, with its 5 million looms, was in no way comparable to that of Great Britain (31 million looms) and the 16 percent of Britons who depended on the cotton trade.[115] The French textile industry in general, and the cotton industry in particular, was still in its infancy.

Also, the difficulties encountered varied widely. The crisis affected certain sectors more than others: weaving more than spinning and hand loom weaving more than mechanical weaving. The trouble experienced by workers also varied from region to region. Normandy was more adversely affected by the crisis than Alsace.[116] Adjusted working arrangements helped to relieve the suffering. Reductions in working hours and in already miserable wages nonetheless allowed people to keep their jobs. Unemployment, when it did occur, was often partial. Moreover, urban textile manufacturers still relied on the performance of many tasks at home, most often in rural areas.[117] This meant many workers could supplement their income with agricultural work.[118] Indeed, the working class was not at all concentrated and the craft sector accounted for 70 percent of production.[119] Finally, there was the possibility for workers to be hired in the booming wool or linen industries.[120] The launch of public works projects was also a timely substitute for the lack of jobs and played a welfare role. For instance, major projects were launched in Alsace (such as the construction of the railway line from Belfort to Guebwiller and the canal from Colmar to Neuf Brisach) and in Normandy (the line from Caen to Flers). On May 25, 1863, a journalist from *L'économiste français* wrote that "public works have become the principal and true resource for cotton workers."[121]

All this explains why the gloomy forecasts made by the imperial government in the winter of 1861–62 were not borne out. It is likely that, fearing the reaction of the working class, French authorities overestimated the impact of the crisis. Their apprehension caused them to act quickly, and this diligence in providing assistance to those most exposed to the cotton shortage helped defuse potential conflicts.

We should also note that not all those who made a living from the cotton industry thought the origins of the crisis were quite so clear-cut, and France's American policy benefited from this lack of clarity. Many workers believed that there was not necessarily a lack of cotton but rather that the industrialists, considering the poor sales due to rising prices, reduced the quantities of cotton they were buying. This interpretation was taken up by the press, which further implied that a shortage might have been organized to encourage speculation; unscrupulous financiers were allegedly behind the disruption of supply.[122] Some workers also mistakenly blamed the reduction in sales of cotton textiles to competition from the British fabrics that flooded into the market as a result of the Cobden-Chevalier Treaty, a free trade agreement between France and England signed in 1860. The *procureurs'* reports emphasized the confusion in the minds of some workers, particularly in Rouen, "the citadel of protectionism," which had strongly opposed the treaty.[123] Thus, for the working classes, the cotton crisis may have appeared to have little connection with the fratricidal conflict in the New World; a war whose circumstances were, for many, so difficult to grasp that their attempts at analysis left room for the unfounded interpretations. This misunderstanding was of use to the imperial government, which was spared from having to conduct a more active American policy.

On the eve of the Civil War nearly 12 percent of U.S. exports went to France (compared to 45 percent to the United Kingdom and 6 percent to Germany).[124] The South may have sold France the cotton it needed, but this must not overshadow all that trade with the Union represented. France was just as dependent on its exports to America as on its imports of white gold (and tobacco) — an argument readily taken up by members of the Lincoln administration. With regard to economic interests, they contended, France and England had everything to gain from the Union's remaining intact.[125] In 1861, therefore, the American Civil War seemed to be a double scourge for Europe: it could not only dry up the sources of production but also close off an important market. In May 1861, Thouvenel wrote that the emperor anticipated with grave concern the "extreme disruption" that a conflict between the two parts of the Union would cause in trade relations.[126]

In 1859, with regard to maritime trade, Le Moniteur ranked the United States second, just after England.[127] At the beginning of the Civil War, French exports to the United States totaled 221 million francs worth of goods, while imports amounted to 241 million francs.[128] However, following the conflict and the reduction of cotton shipments, the trade balance was reestablished. French exports to the United States were mostly luxury items that can be classified into three categories. First, textiles: silks (especially from Lyon), for which, in 1861, the United States was France's top buyer for soft furnishings, as well as patterned fabrics (in 1862) and wool yarn (which accounted for one-third of exports). Second, wines and spirits: in 1861, the United States was the leading destination for French exports of table wines and vintages, as well as wines from the Mediterranean territories under French control. The United States was the second-leading buyer of French pure alcohol, as they were for spirits from 1862 onward. The third category was industrial products, such as watches and clocks from Montbéliard, as well as leather, carpets, gloves, and shoes from Rouen, and knives, pottery, and porcelain from Limoges. For these goods, the United States accounted for a quarter of all French exports. For dyes, the United States bought a third of French exports.[129]

For the United States, France contributed 40 percent of total silk imports, 66 percent of wine imports, and 55 percent of watch imports.[130] Without a doubt, silk fabrics were of fundamental importance. Silk was to France what cotton was to America; it was by far the leading French export, with sales totaling 332,891,322 francs in 1862 (ahead of wine, 195,922,795 francs; and woolen fabrics, 187,999,169 francs). And this value kept increasing. At the start of the war, silk fabrics represented nearly 20 percent of all French sales abroad, with the United States buying a quarter of the total.[131]

The North accounted for the lion's share of all this commercial activity. As evidenced early in the war in a report commissioned from Montholon, the consul in New York, its population was larger and richer than the South's. The Northerners were the ones buying luxury items. "The markets of the slave states obviously cannot offer our products sufficient outlets," Montholon wrote. "Unlike in the North, in the South people hardly consume our products at all."[132] We must not be fooled by the image of the great Southern plantations and their wealthy owners, attracted by the luxury and refinement of old Europe. This was a small minority. The South was so short of cash that it concentrated its purchases on war supplies. On February 15, 1864, Alfred Paul, the consul in Richmond, reported that the Confederate Congress had passed a resolution in a secret session prohibiting the importation of luxury items starting that March 1.[133] There was no doubt that, as the agents implied, the future lay in the North. Even Virginia, the state of the first presidents, no longer stood out for its "profound decadence."[134] Moreover, in the United States, the vast majority of French nationals resided in the free states.

It is not hard to understand why Napoléon III also worried about the consequences of a French diplomatic action in favor of the South. His concern about the North's reaction was apparent, if inexplicit, in the interviews he granted to the Confederate envoy. In October 1862, he told Slidell that if France acted alone its trade would be destroyed. On June 18, 1863, although the emperor claimed to be increasingly convinced of the soundness of recognizing the Confederacy, he put forward the same argument: a break with the United States would have grave consequences for French trade.[135] But while Napoléon came to this conclusion after a year and a half of war, his foreign minister had been much quicker to understand the relative weight of the North and South. In April 1861 Thouvenel said to Faulkner, the U.S. representative who was about to leave Paris, "I believe that maintaining the Federal Union in its integrity is to be desired for the benefit of the people North and South, as well as for the interest of France." Shortly after this, Sanford, the U.S. minister in Belgium who was overseeing the U.S. legation in Paris pending Dayton's arrival, pointed out to Thouvenel that France sold more to the North than the South, and the latter agreed.[136] No doubt Thouvenel had listened to the argument repeated several times by the U.S. secretary of state that the sacrifice of cotton was considerably less serious for Europe than would be the absence of trade with the North.

In Paris, there were fears that French decisions would provoke retaliation by the North. It was still possible for the current Federal government to increase the tariff established by the previous administration. On July 23, 1862, the day Slidell came to submit a proposal for recognition of the Confederacy to Thouvenel, the foreign minister wrote to his agent in Washington that he feared a toughening of the tariff by the North that would lead "almost to the closure of the U.S. market."[137] What is more, as noted in Montholon's report, France depended on the North to ship its products. Its merchant marine was modest; the tonnage of French steamers represented only one-tenth that of U.S. steamers in 1857, and its trade movements remained geographically concentrated in Europe.[138] Given that the North's merchant fleet was many times larger than its opponent's, Sartiges, the former French minister to the United States, exaggerated little when he remarked, as Montholon had, that trade with Europe was entirely in the hands of the Union merchant marine.[139]

Besides, goods arrived almost exclusively in the North. Appropriate infrastructure and the construction of railways had led to an increasing concentration of trade in the ports of the Northeast. New York benefited most of all, as the city carved out a predominant role in the trade flows between Europe and the United States. New York was the leading port for U.S. foreign trade, with 83 percent of imports; the main gateway for wine and alcohol (60 percent), woolen goods (90 percent), and silks (93 percent).[140] In his report, Montholon considered that Franco-American trade was conducted "almost entirely through the North's ports, particularly New York, which centralizes more than half of the trade flows of the entire Union with foreign countries," a fact with which Sartiges concurred.[141] Consul Paul noted from Richmond that New York received "four fifths and a half" of all luxury goods and spoke of New York as "America's Paris."[142] The consul in New York was very impressed by the profits of its trade and banks, and described a city that had "never displayed more wealth and activity," with railways "crammed with freight," wharves "laden with goods," and "unaccustomed luxury on show everywhere." As far as he could tell, the most expensive items found buyers most easily.[143] Such unrivaled prosperity backed up the conclusions drawn by Paul, who, already before the war, had contested the profitability of a planned transatlantic steamship line linking Saint-Nazaire to Norfolk.[144] He preferred to see the Le Havre–New York link consolidated.

Finally, in the other direction, the North's shipments to France were far from insignificant. While the role that cotton played was obviously unique, the South's once essential share of trade with France fell sharply in the decade just before the war. Until 1850, Southern products accounted for 80 to 90 percent of French purchases from the United States, but by around 1860 the future Confederate States only provided 60 percent of exports to France.[145] Among the products from the North, potash and food were the leading exports. The United States was the second-largest supplier of wheat and flour to France and the first for fats (lard). The Montholon report recalled that American grain shipments were crucial for France because they "help to mitigate, to a very large extent, the deficit of the last harvest." The consul in New York wrote in his preamble that if the South achieved its goal, "factories might have cotton cheaper than before, but their workers and the whole French population would certainly pay much more for their bread."[146] This was particularly true given that France's 1861 wheat crop was the worst of the decade, while exceptional weather conditions brought the United States a record harvest in 1860. The grain crisis also affected the United Kingdom, which came to need the North's wheat more than the South's cotton.[147] The agents came to the conclusion that France was more in need of bread and of a market for its products than of cotton imports.[148] It was therefore in French interests to keep the Union intact.[149]

What possible advantage could there be, then, in weakening a rapidly developing country with such a promising future? Why would the empire, which was constantly seeking new economic opportunities, risk undermining this up-and-coming market? Napoléon III, for all his Southern sympathies, was perfectly aware of this. In May 1861, Thouvenel, reporting the emperor's remarks on the American crisis, wrote to Mercier that, "His Majesty desires that the United States lose nothing, through a political subdivision, of the character of a great power, and abdicate nothing, to the detriment of the general interests of civilization and humanity, of the role already assigned to them by their fast and outstanding development."[150] The emperor took up this argument again a year later in his letter of July 3, 1862, to General Forey: "In the current state of the world's civilization, America's prosperity is not immaterial for Europe because it feeds our industry and sustains our trade. We have an interest in the Republic of the United States being powerful and prosperous."[151] "Powerful and prosperous"—if this was what America must be, division was doomed, since both the power and the prosperity came from the union of the states.

The roles the North and South played in the French economy were made evident in newspapers across the political spectrum. Their writers were aware that French commercial interests swung between the South, which provided France with cotton, and the North, which consumed French manufactured goods and wines and supplied France with wheat.[152] In-depth investigations conducted by "liberal" journalists showed that for the French Empire, the importance of imports from the South must be analyzed comparatively. Certain

The Future Lies in Union

facts could not be denied; Northern ports were indeed the hub of transatlantic trade.[153]

———

In retrospect, the South's intransigent King Cotton diplomacy appears absurd. Southerners, forgetting that just before the war France and England had built up their stocks, deluded themselves about the impact that a sharp decrease in cotton shipments would have on European economies. The two nations only really felt the effects of the decline in cotton exports starting in 1862, so an immediate "cotton famine" was impossible. The Confederates also underestimated the Europeans' ability to get cotton from elsewhere. Moreover, one may well wonder whether the South was not more severely penalized by the financial impact of the embargo than were the two powers.[154] This blunder was stressed by the consul in Richmond, who could not understand how a people at war could willingly go without such income.[155] Also, France felt the impact of the crisis less acutely than its neighbor across the Channel. The as-yet protoindustrial French economy afforded some protection. Through agriculture and large public works projects, French workers found extra income to cover the drop in their wages.

Not least, the Southerners committed a serious error in making the supply of cotton to France and England contingent on diplomatic recognition. King Cotton was not enough to force France to recognize the Richmond government. To start with, if, as the ministry thought early in the war, the collapse in imports of white gold was a result of the blockade, cotton could not circulate in any event. In this case, a military operation would have been more effective than diplomatic intervention, but the martial option was unthinkable given the British reservations and the Mexican expedition. Later, looking at the statistics of the blockade runners so generously provided by the Davis administration, the Quai d'Orsay understood that the blockade could not alone be blamed for the shortage of cotton. The Southerners' strategy, which sought to bring the powers to challenge a blockade deemed ineffective under maritime rules, was ill-conceived. By stressing the permeability of the Union's blockade, the Confederates were committing a serious error, making it apparent that their goal was to drag European nations into their war against the United States. This hardline policy, with cotton bales ablaze in the background, did much to undermine their image, for they were willing to risk provoking an economic crisis in Europe to achieve their own ends. As such, the Confederates accompanied their request for recognition with an insulting attempt at blackmail. To give in to pressure from the South was diplomatically and morally unacceptable.[156] It was an alternative to which the imperial government, for reasons of prestige but also of realism, could never agree. Indeed, the French government did not forget the other side of the commercial equation: trade with the United States, in which the North held a prominent place. Satisfying the Confederates would expose France unnecessarily to a protectionist counterattack by the Federal government, which would dry up a key market for French exports. By focusing as much on the possibility of declining exports as on the shortage of cotton imports, the French government put the South's threat into perspective and acknowledged the North's true place in the economy. From that point on, the only possible way to procure cotton was not to recognize the government of the rebel states but to stop the war. That would be the task of mediation.[157]

» 9 «

THE IMBALANCE OF POWER

From the very start of the war, the French agents in the United States compared the two enemies. Their efforts clearly demonstrated the North's demographic, economic, financial, and technological superiority. However, faced with the staunch determination of the enemy troops, the Union's military superiority remained to be demonstrated. The question for the South, then, was whether a warlike predisposition and unshakeable resolve would be enough. From the beginning, Consul Alfred Paul in Richmond replied in the negative. His analysis—which today would be judged far too deterministic—gradually shaped the view of the Tuileries cabinet on the overall military situation. The French government understood that prolonged hostilities would seriously jeopardize the rebellion's chances. The observation missions delegated by the French Ministry of War testified to its surprise but also to the new standing it granted to the Union armies. Under these circumstances, the imperial government considered that the South's chances of winning its independence depended on the Federal government's either backing out in the face of the rebels' prodigious effort or being rejected through the ballot box. Was the Lincoln administration willing to make enormous sacrifices? Would Northern public opinion tolerate heavy losses? Paris realized the extent of the North's potential when Lincoln's persistence in the war was rewarded with electoral triumph, strengthening his administration. This powerful position meant entering into conflict with the Federals would be folly.

The first factor in the French assessment of the American war was the disparity between the populations of the twenty-three states loyal to the Union and the eleven that had left it.[1] The 1860 census summaries left the diplomats no doubt that the demographic imbalance weighed markedly in favor of the North. Thouvenel judged the gap at 5 to 6 million whites in the rebel states compared to 20 million in the Union. He was not far off the mark.[2] And as the consul in New York pointed out, the demographic gap was only getting bigger. In his report titled "Note for the Minister on the Possible Consequences of a French Intervention in the Anglo-American Conflict," he established that European emigration almost exclusively benefited the North.[3] As well as being larger, he noted that the North's population was more urban, wealthy, and industrial than the still-rural South.[4]

The diplomats also noted the gulf between the two economies. The figures reported to the ministry showed that the North was home to all the major industrial centers and accounted for 70 percent of the value of U.S. manufactured goods, while the South produced only 16 percent. Observers were unanimous in describing the Southern economy as traditional, based entirely on the monoculture of export crops.[5] The agents pointed out that the South's relationship to the North was one of subordination. According to their information, the North sold the South $150 million worth of manufactured goods and manufactured and exported the yarn from the cotton harvested in the South.[6] The statistics available to the Quai d'Orsay showed the same subordination on the financial front. The North held the most significant financial resources, and it was in Northern banks that the slave states' money was invested.[7] The Federals therefore could dry up credit to Dixie, which, according to the consul in Richmond, was precisely what they did in the first days of the conflict.[8] And besides, as observers noted, the Federals had access to an additional resource: they could rely on the gold from California to settle their purchases in Europe and quadruple their defense spending.[9] Although cotton meant the relationship was more balanced when it came to trade, Montholon, the consul in New York, pointed out that this was relative, because the South depended on the North to ship it.[10] The Northern economy was also well served by its ports and highly developed rail network.[11] While the scale of the French rail network (16,465 km in 1870) was comparable to that of the rebel states, Montholon assessed the Northern states' network at more than twice the size of their opponent's over an area half as large, with tracks of far better quality.[12] In addition to this advantage, Sartiges, the former minister to Washington, noted that the

North had a comprehensive system of inland navigation free of any military pressures, which was not the case on the Mississippi River.[13]

Yet the South was not without assets. Napoléon III was impressed by the superiority of the officers who came from its strong military tradition and by the deep conviction of the states in rebellion that they were fighting for their existence.[14] The diplomats compared the Northerners' lack of enthusiasm for the fight to the combative fervor that roused the white Southern masses.[15] In their view, this deep faith in the legitimacy of their struggle could make up for the disparity between the two camps.[16]

THE VISIONARY VIEWPOINT OF CONSUL ALFRED PAUL

It would be apt at this point to acknowledge a truly great diplomat, Alfred Paul. During the Civil War, the content of the dispatches written by the consul in Richmond found an unexpected echo among the leaders of French diplomacy.[17] The foreign ministers came to rely on his first-class accounts, which were especially valuable in that Paul described the facts with objectivity, accuracy, and foresight. His talents combined perceptive analysis and sound judgment. At age thirty-four he was sent by the Second Republic to Philadelphia, then to Richmond in 1852, where he was to work half of his career as second- and later first-class consul (from August 27, 1857).[18] Even as he fulfilled his standard duties, which were heavy enough in themselves and mainly concerned the collection of economic data and the delivery of French tobacco for the Régie française des tabacs, Paul carefully observed the rising tensions within the Union. He then witnessed their development into fratricidal conflict. At the outbreak of hostilities, he was advantaged by his location. By choosing to set up their government in Richmond, the Southerners gave de facto primacy to a post with only consular status. Paul found himself in a privileged position to witness the Confederacy's four-year struggle.[19] As the foremost observer and interpreter of the conflict, he became an essential intermediary between his government and that of Richmond.

From the outset of tensions, Paul demonstrated a rare ability to take the true measure of events. He never doubted that disunion would lead to civil war. In December 1859 during John Brown's trial, he was already envisioning this possibility, and on November 6, 1860, he did not hesitate to predict the partition of the Union as a result of Lincoln's election. He did not underestimate the determination of the Southern population, who saw this electoral success as a provocation.[20] While secession was still in its infancy—on January 9 only Mississippi had joined South Carolina—he foresaw no outcome of the crisis other than the dissolution of the federal pact.[21] Faced with the pending collapse of the Union, the question was what the new administration's position would be when it took office in March. Paul's view conflicted with that of his colleagues. He thought no reconciliation was possible. He did not believe that, as in the past, the divorce between the two sections would be postponed by a providential compromise; he sensed instead that the federation was about to lance the boil that had been undermining its foundations for decades. He recognized the resolve of the new Federal administration and told his government that, this time, the North would not back down.

As early as December 22, 1860, Paul warned Thouvenel that secession could not take effect without a civil war, which would be "more horrific here" than anywhere in the world.[22] After the fall of Fort Sumter, the news that Washington was mobilizing significant forces to crush the rebellion confirmed his views. Not without a certain vanity, Paul congratulated himself on the accuracy of his predictions.[23] Yet he did not approve of the use of force against the unruly states.[24] In this, he shared the view of certain liberal French thinkers. He believed it was better to let the rebels leave the Union in order for them to realize the thoughtlessness of their political project.

Paul did not underestimate the difficulty of the struggle; he was well aware that the South was fighting for its existence. He recognized that there was a fundamental psychological element playing in the Southerners' favor: the North was invading their land and they were determined to defend it to the bitter end. A few days after the attack on Fort Sumter in April, he predicted that no Northern intervention could be accomplished without the loss of many men, for the South would defend its ground valiantly and energetically.[25] This war, he said, would take on "proportions never before seen in history" because "the South [would] resist any coercion until the last breath of the last man."[26] He foresaw a bitter conflict in which the North would only manage to "subjugate" the South after a war that would be "long, fierce, and ruinous for the whole country."[27] In the summer of 1861 he already understood what many would realize two years later: the North would have to throw all its strength into the battle to subdue its enemy, who would fight every inch of the way to repel what it saw as an invader. Union forces would face a tenacious opponent in an extensive, hostile territory.

At the same time, Paul made it clear very early on that in his view, no matter how hard the war might prove for the North, it could not be defeated; the rebellion of the insurgent states was doomed to failure. As he saw it, if no European power came to the South's aid, it would be forced to give in. His dispatches provided a long list of Confederate weaknesses. From the start, the rebels' inferiority seemed to him so "obvious, blatant, and undeniable" before a "force which is set to become colossal" that the fate of arms was sealed.[28] This view was based solely on his assessment of the balance of military, demographic, economic, financial, and material power, all of which favored the North. He was already applying this reasoning in 1861 when the number of combatants on each side was still quite balanced. In fact, this inequality would only have an influence once the North and South had settled into a long war. By focusing solely on the gap between the two sections, Paul was anticipating the strategy of attrition, which was not applied systematically until the North finally began to deploy overwhelming resources in 1863. This deterministic vision neglects the psychological aspects and contingencies of war, the outcome of which can never be determined in advance. Unexpected reversals occur, and did in this conflict on several occasions when the Confederates were able to take the fight north of the Potomac. They managed to delay the final outcome for four years, which was no mean feat.

Paul acknowledged the valor of the "Gray Coats," starting with their leader, Gen. Robert E. Lee, whom he considered "the most eminent man to head the Confederate army."[29] However, this narrow focus on certain figures, and the belief that through their ability alone they could foil the Northern forces' plans, made the demise of the best Confederate men seem all the more tragic for the South. The news of Lee's victory at Chancellorsville was immediately marred by the death of Gen. T. J. "Stonewall" Jackson. Paul saw this "irreplaceable loss" as a disaster for the Confederates.[30] A few months later, he attributed the defeat at Gettysburg in part to the absence of Jackson, whom Lee sorely missed.[31]

Furthermore, Paul reliably attributed the military setbacks of the Confederate armies to Jefferson Davis. He made a specialty of denouncing the tactical errors and lack of overall strategy of a president who changed his secretary of war six times while Lincoln kept the same one throughout the conflict. Already after Bull Run, he blamed Davis for failing to take advantage of the confusion in the Northern camp to let General Beauregard advance toward the North. Paul sent to Thouvenel the general's report saying that his momentum was checked by order of the president.[32] He also criticized Davis's incomprehensible support for certain generals. In December 1863, Paul found it irresponsible to maintain Gen. Braxton Bragg in his position when the general had suffered a serious defeat the previous month.[33] Paul also emphasized the many shortcomings of the rebel army.[34] In June 1862 he described the regiments stationed in the Southern capital in these terms: "an exhausted army, poorly fed, poorly clothed, burdened by want and disease, subjected to privations that exceed anything that human, physical, and moral strength can withstand." He compared the poor condition of Southern soldiers to the Union troops, who he thought must be the best fed in history.[35] According to the consul, even the most illustrious officers were no better off, Lee included.[36] Unlike many of his colleagues, who were intoxicated by the victories of the Army of Virginia, he never lost sight of the whole theater of operations. This broader view led him to qualify the supposed deficiency of the Union's military skill. Although he found them fainthearted, Paul conveyed a more tempered view of what many supposed was the "inferiority" of the Northern armies' officers.[37] Besides, because the North did not always have the best men, it learned to train and organize them with skill. Paul described its offensive strategy that brought superior forces and equipment together at a given point, relying on the railway to transport its troops quickly and en masse. He was also struck by the firepower deployed by the North, such as its use of river gunboats armed with thirteen guns.[38] The only failing he acknowledged was Lincoln's decision to blockade the Confederate coast. Given the extent of coastline, he believed that interdiction efforts could only be porous and futile.

Paul's fixed opinion on the war can also be explained by his unique vantage point in Richmond. Of all the French diplomats, he was the best placed to witness the hardships the South faced. He was able to compare this with Washington, which he visited during the war. He observed that a part of Richmond's population lived in abject poverty. Southern citizens bore the full brunt of inflation and could not get essential products. From the end of 1861, he began scrupulously reporting the complications that affected all areas of daily life. He noted that the South "wanted literally for everything." The price of staple goods soared by 200 percent.[39] He began 1862 by noting, "We have nothing left. We no longer even have the paper for treasury bills."[40] Famines were recurrent and riots broke out not only in Richmond but also in Petersburg and Raleigh.[41] In Paul's eyes, the difficulties faced by civilians betrayed the desperation of the Confederates' struggle. The French minister in Washington, Henri Mercier, admitted that it was only after going to Richmond in April 1862 that he became aware of these troubles, implicitly recognizing that from Washington he could not accurately diagnose the situation.[42] Since Paul accentuated the rebels' hardships, his perspective was sometimes distorted. Witnessing from the front row the successive sieges of Richmond—in his office he could hear the Federal guns pounding the city—he regularly predicted the fall of the capital and, in its wake, the Confederacy.[43] However, he underestimated the city's defenses, which were sufficiently robust to repel the Northerners' repeated assaults.

We can compare Paul's analysis in the first months of the war to that of Mercier, which pointed to the directly opposite conclusion. Mercier's sympathy for the Confederates often led him to make alarmist statements about the North's dire military situation. In October 1861, Mercier considered that the North could not long sustain "the extraordinary efforts it is making at the moment" and would have to hurry to get a result.[44] Downplaying the capture of New Orleans and forgetting that in the West, after victory at Shiloh, Tennessee, the Federals were laying siege to Corinth, Mississippi, he focused on General Jackson's offensive in the Shenandoah, which he rather hastily predicted would take him to the gates of the Federal capital.[45] Conversely, Paul described the fall of Port Hudson, Louisiana, as a "terrible and fatal blow to the Southern Confederacy."[46] When the Seven Days' Battles (June 26–July 1, 1862) helped loosen the Federals' stranglehold on Richmond, Paul was not swayed. He maintained that the gap between the two sides would ultimately decide the fate of arms. He wrote to Thouvenel, "We must not lose sight, Sir, of the fact that the North's resources for waging the war are huge and that those of the South are almost nil." He felt strongly that the Union would besiege the Southern capital again.[47] Even after Lee inflicted a heavy defeat on his enemy at Fredericksburg in December, Paul kept his eyes trained on the overall theater of operations and continued to write that without a cessation of hostilities or outside support, "the Northern armies will end up completely overrunning the Confederate States."[48]

In a dispatch dated January 1864, Paul took stock of his observations thus far and noted that his predictions had all proven accurate. Force was triumphing over bravery and heroism, a perhaps prosaic but largely predictable outcome. Now, more than ever, nothing could stop the Northern steamroller from crushing its enemy:

It [the North] knows it is the strongest. It has a larger army, a first-class navy, open ports, lots of money, vast amounts of credit, a submissive population accustomed to everything that has been undertaken over the last three years in transforming the country, facilities of all kinds which, the more they are used and abused, seem to spread the general welfare by increasing the resources of the Treasury. The spectacle is striking when one arrives in the South. All this is obvious, undeniable, palpable. The North has everything in hand while the South is beginning to have nothing, nothing, nothing but the desperate efforts in Richmond and, everywhere else, everything running out, a despondency justified by the simple and inexorable reason that human strength has physical and mental limits, and that after three years of continuous but powerless heroism for a cause that has not always had everyone's sympathy, a state of prostration fatal for that cause is bound to come.[49]

Grant's march on Richmond between May and July 1864 resulted in a series of setbacks for the Union commander, defeated by Lee in May (at Wilderness and Spotsylvania) and June (at Cold Harbor and Petersburg). Yet in Paul's view the Overland campaign, though costly, ended unquestionably in the Union's favor.[50] He recognized the effectiveness of Grant's strategy. While the Federal commander suffered more losses, he managed to bleed his opponent dry while "effortlessly" renewing his own numbers.[51] For the consul, the fall of Atlanta in September spelled the end of the Confederacy.[52] Given these circumstances, four months before Lee's surrender, Paul forecast the end of the conflict that had bathed America in blood for almost four years. He saw this outcome as confirmation of what he had prophesied since the beginning of the war: "I have consistently written in such a way as to suggest that the North would achieve its ends if no foreign intervention came to put an end to this war or tip the balance in favor of the Southern states."[53]

Paul's detailed and accurate reports regularly earned him the approbation of his minister. In late 1861, Thouvenel praised the accuracy of Paul's information, which he felt would be of great benefit to the ministry's services, and in early 1862 he thanked Paul for meticulously portraying the situation in the Southern states.[54] In 1863, it was Edouard Drouyn de Lhuys's turn to praise his agent's dispatch, having read with particular interest the comments on the warring parties' respective positions and the information provided on the battle of Chancellorsville and the military operations before Charleston.[55] The emperor himself, in his response to Slidell in October 1862, drew arguments from articles in a Richmond newspaper that had been sent by Paul through consular channels.[56] It eventually became common practice for the minister to send the dispatches from the consul in Richmond to his correspondents so that they could get a clear idea of the conditions of the war.[57] Paul's talents were hailed at the highest level. In 1863, the emperor rewarded him for his good work by raising him to the rank of officer of the Legion of Honor. But this credit had a downside. Early in 1864, when Paul wanted to return to France to his mother's bedside, the foreign minister denied him six months' leave, claiming his presence was essential to the proper functioning of the service.

Did the other French witnesses to the American drama share Paul's predictions? Prince Napoléon, the cousin of Napoléon III who visited the United

States in 1861, used the same arguments as Paul and predicted a Union victory.[58] Among the consuls, besides Jules Souchard in Boston, few were as categorical so early on. But Souchard's certainty of a Northern victory came as much from a personal wish (he was deeply hostile to the slave states) as from a rigorous examination of the warring forces' relative strength. It was only after the summer of 1863 that other consuls fell into step with Paul and Souchard. For example, in November 1863, after the North's setback at Chickamauga, Louis Borg from the New York consulate wrote that the Federal cause would owe its triumph as much to its fortune of arms and its countless resources as to its military advantages.[59]

In Paris, besides the consuls' reports, the Tuileries cabinet was subjected to active lobbying from Union supporters, who steadfastly insisted on their champion's invincibility. The first to take up this refrain was Gen. James Watson Webb, a friend of the emperor's. In his memorandum of the summer of 1861, he said that the South was sure to succumb for it did not have the North's means and could not hold out for long caught between the blockade and the western territories, where the Northerners would inevitably secure control of the Mississippi River. Watson mentioned Napoléon's knowledge of the situation; the emperor was perfectly informed on all these subjects.[60] Dayton, in his interviews with Thouvenel and later Drouyn de Lhuys, reiterated Seward's insistence on the indisputable superiority of the Northern forces and the predictable success of its armies, albeit at enormous cost.[61] He also repeated this to the emperor and empress when the occasion presented itself.[62]

THE NORTH'S MILITARY CAPACITY SEEN FROM FRANCE

Although Thouvenel did not foresee a Union victory as clearly as Paul did, some of his comments show that he was fully aware of the imbalance. In May 1862, when speaking to Dayton, he referred to the disparity between the forces to explain the Federal troops' string of successes. For the foreign minister, there was no doubt that the North had overwhelming military and material resources, as well as an access to credit that the Southern states could not dream of equaling. Judging simply by the efforts to which the North had so easily consented since the beginning of the war, he presumed that it was in a position to stretch itself even further.[63] After the summer of 1862, which saw balance restored to the military situation between the warring parties, the emperor was aware that, as hostilities continued, the South would come to lack troops; each of the Confederate dead eroded a little more its already weakened human resources. Napoléon III expressed this concern to Slidell, comparing these losses to those at the bloody battles of Solferino and Magenta, during his own 1859 Italian campaign.[64] Drouyn de Lhuys also mentioned "the disparity of numbers and financial means," counterbalanced by the vigor with which the South resisted and which gave the war its "indomitable fury."[65]

Gradually, the French authorities became aware that the Federals were waging an astonishingly modern war. Again, the consuls' reports had much to do with this realization. Paul's colleagues were as impressed as he was by the power of the North's artillery. The consul in New York remarked that the fortifications of the Confederate ports could not withstand enemy fire much longer.[66] In the summer of 1863, Consul Maurice Durant Saint-André in Charleston was staggered to witness the Northern troops' systematic bombardment of the city with projectiles containing flammable liquid. He was forced to take refuge aboard a ship anchored off South Carolina.[67]

Prince Napoléon, after his stay in the United States, had recommended that the emperor take a keen interest in the Northern armies.[68] This advice must have been heeded because the imperial government sent delegates to observe. Between November 1863 and March 1864, Capt. Charles Pigeard, a veteran of the Crimean War, stayed in the United States to gather information on the Federal navy.[69] In his report to the minister of the navy, Pigeard highlighted the power of the U.S. Navy, which he considered "far ahead of Europe" for local defense. The U.S. naval artillery appeared to him the only one to have proved its worth. It could overcome "all the battleships put into action in France and England thus far."[70] As the Second Empire was making a considerable effort to provide France with a navy, the Civil War confirmed to the French government the absolute necessity of constructing a fleet of battleships.[71]

After Pigeard's observation of the Federal navy, Lt. Col. Victor Felix Adolphe de Chanal, a graduate artilleryman of the Ecole Polytechnique who was married to an American, took over, this time to record his impressions of the Union army.[72] He sailed for the United States in March 1864 and returned eight months later. De Chanal was amazed by the North's capabilities, organization, and discipline and the modernity of the war it was fighting. The Union had revolutionized tactics hitherto employed in Europe. He emphasized the Union's enormous offensive capacity, the firepower of its artillery, its ability to organize a defense by building trenches or fortifications, the precision of its mapping based on rigorous topographic surveys, the speed of communications thanks to aerial signals and particularly the telegraph, the use of the railway to carry troops, and the efficiency of health and medical treatment services, and so on.[73]

Many French newspapers thought a Northern defeat was highly unlikely. At worst, with the heroism of the South's efforts compensating for its deficiencies in resources, some journalists wrote that the situation would end in a status quo. The conservative press barely concealed its satisfaction at the prospect of a fight with no winner or loser weakening the American Republic.[74] Other authors were forced to recognize that the Northern states had means incomparably superior to those of their enemy. Despite the South's exploits, if it received no reinforcements, these journalists predicted, it would succumb.[75] More generally, they denounced Lincoln's "war of extermination"—a rebuke that could be seen as an admission. In 1863 the situation of the Poles persecuted by their Russian neighbor offered a timely point of comparison.[76]

In 1862, after the first year of war, the French liberal press started to highlight the supremacy of the Northerners. Until the winter of 1861–62, to liberal journalists the conflict seemed more like "a war of skirmishes and partisans."[77] However, with the beginning of the spring offensive in 1862, it became clear to them that the mobilization of the North's resources would be decisive.[78] The South could not win on its own.[79] Following the reversal in the summer of 1862, while these observers were surprised by the Confederates' stamina, they recalled that the North had not yet put its entire arsenal into action (for instance, unlike the South, it had not yet instituted a draft).[80] As the war wore on, liberal journalists concluded that the North did not know how to exploit its undeniable supremacy, or was using it badly. They explained that if the Union armies failed to defeat their enemy it would be the fault of pusillanimous generals.[81] In the summer of 1863, after Lee's defeat at Gettysburg, they sensed that the South would have trouble leading a new offensive because it had no resources left to embark on another undertaking of similar ambition.[82] The capture of Richmond came as no surprise to them because "the North's resources were far greater and practically inexhaustible."[83]

THE SOUTH INCAPABLE OF WINNING ALONE

Thus, for many contemporaries, by vanquishing its enemy, the North was simply fulfilling its destiny. It was acting out a preordained history, which nothing could impede so long as the South received no external support. This view was shared by Consul Paul who, from the beginning, saw that the rebellious states were incapable of winning unaided; the outcome of the struggle depended on whether or not France or Britain became involved.[84] From 1863 onward, other colleagues joined him.[85] The rebels' hopes for military European involvement in the war were futile.[86] In fact, it seems clear that European action was never conceivable beyond a diplomatic level. France never considered an armed intervention in favor of the South. The only threat of military intervention, which Napoléon III supposedly insinuated, concerned not assistance to the Confederate forces but only sending French ships to break the blockade. Even then, as we have seen, this option was quickly set aside following pressure from the Quai d'Orsay. As Paul implied after the first French mediation proposal, some believed that a diplomatic action to interrupt the fighting could save the South.[87] By 1863, however, following the failure of the French initiative and the reversal of the war in the North's favor, Paul felt that the chances of such intervention by European powers were dwindling.[88]

French diplomats wondered whether the Richmond government, behind its requests for recognition, was not secretly banking on the likelihood that a diplomatic intervention would slide into a military one because it would be taken as a casus belli by the North. This disingenuous bid for reinforcements proved to the diplomats that the South conditioned its success on external help. As determined as the Confederacy was in its goals, it nonetheless betrayed its inferiority to the European powers because its own forces were not sufficient to resist the North's attacks. What is more, the South's compelling need for one of the two nations, or both together, to compromise themselves for its benefit suggested that, as it had demonstrated during the *Trent* affair, it would do anything to drag them into the war. Thus the Confederates sought doubly to take advantage of France and England by leading them to believe, first of all, that their war for independence had a chance of success and, second, that their request for recognition would not involve European military intervention. For this reason, the Quai d'Orsay firmly maintained its policy of neutrality.

THE NORTH'S DETERMINATION IN QUESTION

The end result of all these observations was to reinforce, on the military level, a conviction the Quai d'Orsay had already firmly established based on the demographic and economic data, namely, that it was physically impossible for the South to defeat the North. The Southerners' only hope was to prolong the war to the point that its cost to the North would become unbearable. As the diplomats had understood, barring a surprise, the key to the war was not to be found on the battlefield but in the North's resolve. The French government was sure of the South's determination to resist the North, but was the opposite true? In defense of principles, rather than interests, was the North prepared to see a ruinous war through to the bitter end?

The Future Lies in Union

When the crisis broke out, the agents wagered that the new occupant of the White House would remain passive. First, such an attitude seemed to many to be natural and inevitable. Did de Tocqueville not, in his day, use the example of Jackson—a man of sturdy character—to show that the federal government would invariably cede to the states' demands?[89] Second, Mercier felt that Lincoln inspired little respect and did not seem to be equal to the occasion.[90] Some observers, citing previous situations in which the fate of the Union had been in danger, still believed that the Union would sign a last-minute agreement giving satisfaction to the insurgents by guaranteeing the future of slavery. Méjan, the consul in New Orleans, defended this optimistic view in April 1861; he did not imagine that the fight could end otherwise than by an arrangement.[91] Others, referring to the defection of the seven original Confederate states, banked on the weakness of the new administration and Lincoln's submission before the fait accompli. Had his predecessor not pleaded in favor of maintaining the Union while refusing to take any coercive action against secession? Mercier believed, as Buchanan had, that Lincoln would accept the split rather than launch the ruinous war that would otherwise result.[92] The only dissenting voice was that of Alfred Paul, who envisaged a civil war as early as December 1860.

In Paris, Confederate sympathizers tried to persuade the foreign minister that Lincoln would not react. They based this belief on the president's inaugural address on March 4, when he reiterated his commitment to the Union and his refusal to abolish slavery in the Southern states, a position that perhaps augured a peaceful outcome to the crisis. The present dispute, like those that preceded it, could still end in an honorable compromise. Charles James Faulkner, the U.S. minister to Paris, implied the same thing in April before being recalled by his government for his Confederate leanings. He assured Thouvenel that coercion would not be used against the states in rebellion because the majority of Americans were in favor of respecting states' self-government and sovereignty. The American minister believed that constitutional changes would resolve the crisis and commit the separatist states to a peaceful return to the Union. Seward was obliged to contradict him.[93] At his meeting with Mercier of June 6, 1861, Seward confirmed his government's determination to crush the rebels and refused to consider the dissolution of the Union.[94]

Actions as well as words showed that the new administration would not simply watch the Union disappear. As news of the attack on Fort Sumter reached Paris, so too did word of Lincoln's decision to resist. The president's call for 75,000 militiamen and the decision to blockade the Southern coast confirmed to Paul what he had sensed from the beginning.[95] This was indeed the start of a civil war. "The illusions about Washington's alleged weakness are beginning to fall," he wrote.[96] For the imperial government, Bull Run marked a turning point. It was clear that Lincoln would not be a new Buchanan. Two days after his army's defeat, the president announced that further efforts must be made to render the blockade effective and reinforce the Union troops in Virginia to prepare an invasion. The memorandum by General Watson Webb called attention to this resolve. Webb wrote that Lincoln was prepared to use a million men if necessary.[97] The consul in New York also confirmed this renewed determination.[98]

After the winter, the Northern victories in the first half of 1862 and the march on Richmond revealed the Federal government's radical intentions. France's ambassador to London was dismayed at the Lincoln administration's uncompromising position.[99] The reversal of the summer of 1862 by no means sapped the morale of the Union's defenders, and that is perhaps what most impressed the diplomats. On the contrary, the North responded to each set of bad news with even stronger mobilization. Nothing seemed to shake the confidence behind its will to fight or its assurance of overcoming secession.[100] Thouvenel acknowledged that the tremendous energy the North was putting into the war "testified to the Federal government's steadfast confidence in the imminent return of fortunes."[101] In early 1863, Drouyn de Lhuys attributed the failure of his mediation proposal to the Federal government's tenacity.[102] The Union may have just suffered a major setback in Fredericksburg, but the war's continuation had not weakened the Union's confidence in the ultimate success of its efforts.[103]

Unlike the diplomats, the French press did not wait for the first battle to acknowledge the stubbornness of the new president and his cabinet. Far from seeing any indecision in Lincoln's inaugural speech, the conservative newspapers thought his words rang like a death knell. He would not recognize the fait accompli.[104] The liberal press also believed that war was likely.[105] Lincoln's proclamation calling out 75,000 men after the surrender of Fort Sumter only confirmed this belief.[106] However, while the liberal newspapers welcomed Lincoln's obstinacy, their conservative counterparts stressed the senselessness of wanting to bring "10 to 12 million individuals" back into the federation through armed action.[107]

COULD THE NORTH COUNT ON PUBLIC OPINION?

Did the Federal government have the support of the Northern public? The diplomats thought the South's only chance of winning independence was for the Lincoln cabinet to be repudiated by the electorate. In July 1862, extrapolating on the position of the Northern government, which would soon face the vote of its fellow citizens, Mercier wrote, "If the wind changed, it [the Federal government] would change with it, I do not doubt that for a moment."[108] A month before the congressional elections in November 1862, Dayton spoke to Thouvenel of the Northern people's support for their government, but the foreign minister expressed his doubts. Thouvenel felt the best way to settle the question was to evaluate this alleged support in light of the popular vote.[109]

Even if the midterm elections reflected a sharp upsurge for the Democrats, the Republicans retained the majority. Lincoln was spared having to deal with a hostile Congress and kept both hands on the controls; yet the results gave Paris the impression that war-weariness was setting in among Northerners. From that moment, the ministry was even more watchful for any sign of a reversal of opinion in the North. The new foreign minister, Drouyn de Lhuys, asked his consuls to keep him informed of any swings in public opinion in the states loyal to the Union.[110] Such a swing seemed to materialize in 1864. Alfred Paul reported a stirring of public dissent in the North following the series of Union defeats in the first half of the year. In early July, just after Lincoln was named Republican Party candidate at the Baltimore convention, Paul raised the possibility of a Democratic success in the upcoming congressional elections if the South managed to hold on until November.[111] After Confederate Gen. Jubal Early's raid in the Shenandoah Valley, Geofroy, the first secretary of the legation, was more confident than Paul that the death toll of recent months would benefit the peace Democrats.[112]

In France, the conservative press — focused as it was on the Northerners' setbacks — also doubted Lincoln's reelection, sensing he would fall victim to the peace party.[113] The opposition newspapers were more cautious, not stopping at the South's apparent triumphs but considering the theater of operations as a whole. They pointed out that despite the North's setbacks, Sherman's raid in Georgia and the taking of Atlanta in September had suddenly turned the tables in favor of the Lincoln cabinet. The Confederacy was on its last legs.[114]

Napoléon III took a keen interest in the race for the White House, which pitted Abraham Lincoln against his Democratic challenger, Maj. Gen. George McClellan, and the emperor openly favored the latter. According to a New York newspaper enclosed with a dispatch from Charles-Henri-Philippe Gauldrée-Boilleau, the French consul in New York, to Drouyn de Lhuys, the U.S. legation in Paris thought that if McClellan won, Napoléon would move to recognize the Confederacy.[115] In fact, it seems clear that the emperor, along

William Sherman and Staff. Photograph by Mathew Brady, between June 1, 1862, and 1865. Courtesy of the Library of Congress, Prints and Photographs Division.

with most observers, was mistaken. McClellan may have been the most power-ful symbol of opposition to Lincoln's policy of all-out war, but he was no less committed to the Union. In Paris, however, it was believed that his clemency left the door open for an arrangement to loosen the federal ties. From Rich-mond, Consul Paul cautioned those in France who saw McClellan as Lin-coln's strict opposite. He advised them not to mistake the intentions of the two parties competing in the presidential race. After the sacrifices of the war, unionism was common to most party platforms. The fall of Atlanta brought a Northern victory within reach, making it difficult to imagine a negotiation be-tween the Lincoln administration and the Confederacy. It did not take long for the Union's military feats to toughen the fainthearted and fortify Lincoln.[116] The electoral rout over McClellan closed the possibility of Northern defeat at the polls.

While the French government believed that a defeat for Lincoln might change something, the press was more doubtful. It was aware that on the heart of the issue—restoration of the Union—the contenders were of the same

The Future Lies in Union

mind. They only disagreed on how to achieve it, through force or negotiation, and on the question of emancipation.[117] Lincoln's reelection did not surprise observers, especially because, as the conservative newspapers underscored, Southern citizens were excluded from the vote.[118] What remained was how to interpret this victory. For the conservative organs, it meant all-out war and a shift from democracy to tyranny. Conversely, for the Republican and liberal press, the North emerged stronger from the poll.[119] This renewed mandate would allow it to finish the war, restore the Union, and eradicate slavery for good.[120]

Let us reconsider the position taken by Napoléon III. In late 1864, he had not abandoned his desire to intervene somehow in the American conflict. He did not envisage a restoration of the Union and, as with the first mediation proposal in 1862, he was counting on Democrats to rout Republicans at the ballot box. He believed that if the Federal government was deprived of political means, an overture toward the South was still possible. This time, he expressed these views in front of a Northern diplomat in the hope that they would be made public, an expectation that was inevitably fulfilled. By siding with McClellan, he meant for his preference to tip the balance in favor of the camp that seemed to him most willing to accept a negotiated peace between the warring parties and confirm the separation. Two lessons can be drawn from this final attempt by the emperor to enter the diplomatic game of the American Civil War. First, his belief that his voice would be not only heard but also listened to by Northern voters shows that he overestimated his influence across the Atlantic. Second, he underestimated the inroads made by the Federal troops: the front was closing in on the last Confederate strongholds, giving voters ample reason to back Lincoln. On these two points, it is no exaggeration to say that the emperor singularly lacked lucidity.

POSTWAR VICTORY FOR THE SOUTH

One argument put forward by Southern sympathizers was that the North's war on the South was pointless because whatever the result, reconstruction of the Union would be impossible. After the war, the North would have to maintain troops indefinitely in the eleven former secessionist states, which would not stop seeking to break free of the federal framework.[121] The consuls were of the same opinion. The postwar period would bring with it new tribulations for the North; another conflict would follow on from the Civil War because the secessionist states would never agree to reenter the Union. The dispatches contained numerous predictions of this grim future. Three days before the fall of Fort Sumter, the consul in New Orleans considered the scenario in which the Federal government decided to resist. He suggested that even if the South were put down, the split would still be definitive. It might not be so in fact, but it already was in spirit.[122] Ten months later, the consul in New York explained the war's futility using the same argument: any aspirations of bringing the rebel states back into the Union were illusory.[123] In 1864 the vice-consul in St. Louis noted how weak federal feeling was in his state even though Missouri had remained loyal to the Union.[124]

In 1862, ambassadors and ministers plenipotentiary in Europe likewise feared the repercussions of a Northern victory. The comte de Flahaut, French ambassador to the United Kingdom, wrote to Thouvenel that if the North won, it would be unable to maintain the Union except by force.[125] André Sain de Boislecomte, former minister to Washington, believed that the North's triumph could only be secured by the total "subalternization" of the South.[126] The same year, the current minister to Washington, Henri Mercier, described for Thouvenel some influential politicians who recognized that the North, after its victory, would be obliged to reincorporate the South by force or else accept the principle of separation.[127] All these comments convinced the foreign minister that the North, in wanting to obtain the adherence of all the states, would not be able to dominate its opponent without reinventing the Union. Perhaps he already had in mind his plan for "two federated confederations" when he told Mercier in May 1862 that "it is impossible, on the contrary, not to anticipate that the day when the war in the United States ends with the conquest of all the states who claimed to form a separate union, the regime that follows that conquest can no longer be the one that existed before the conflict, the one in which the rest of the Union has continued to live."[128]

The French press, also looking ahead to the future, became aware early on that the conflict had erected obstacles between the belligerents that would make it difficult to restore the antebellum republic. Despite its triumph, the Northern army would not find men of goodwill in the South to help with postwar reconciliation by forming a party that would support the reestablishment of Federal authority.[129] For the Lincoln administration, victory on the battlefield would therefore mark the beginning of interminable troubles.[130] How, after the war, could it make men from Georgia and Massachusetts serve in the same Congress? Some newspapers evoked the risk of despotism when imagining that the winners would seek to bring the rebel states back into line and prevent another secessionist crisis.[131] The likelihood of a "perpetual struggle" gave the more conservative papers grounds to argue, once again, for an honorable compromise on the basis of separation.[132]

Some observers felt that what could save the South was, paradoxically, a victory for the North, which as long as it failed to subjugate its enemy, as long as it put the principle of federalism first, would not realize that reconstructing the Union was impossible. Only after having crushed the opponent whose ambitions of independence it disputed would the North understand its blindness and discover that the split ran so deep that the war had ultimately been in vain. Time would prove the South right in seeking to form a separate confederacy, which would inevitably impose itself anyway. According to this line of thinking, it would be pointless to anticipate recognition of a Southern government because, sooner or later, the North would have to grant it.

FRENCH FEARS CONFLICT WITH THE NORTH

As we have seen, given the North's determination to crush the secession, France's recognition of the Confederate government would have consequences. The Lincoln administration, which hoped that diplomatic isolation would force the eleven rebellious states to see reason, would see the formalization of diplomatic relations with the Confederacy as encouraging the rebellion. French recognition of the South would inevitably lead to a break in relations between France and the defenders of the Union.

From the outset of the crisis, William Seward, the U.S. secretary of state, brandished the threat of an engagement against any European power that supported the secession. On July 4, 1861, he sent the fiercest warning yet to British leaders: if their government recognized the Confederacy he would "wrap the world in fire."[133] Considering the Unionist feeling that remained in the states in rebellion, he believed the Union could reunite around the defense of the nation.[134] Given the Southern states' stubborn commitment to forming an independent association, he had to give up on a unifying war but did not abandon the idea of dissuasive action toward the powers. He stated emphatically that his government, though in the midst of a civil war, would not hesitate if it also needed to wage an external conflict. He took pains to impress upon the European powers the risk and cost to them of such a cataclysm.[135] In the early summer of 1862, when the North had just suffered its first major setback and had to give up on capturing Richmond, Seward spoke in strong language to Dayton so that the latter would use similar terms with Thouvenel: "If intervention in any form shall come, it will find us in the right of the controversy and in the strong attitude of self-defense."[136]

Henri Mercier regularly warned his government of the Americans' touchiness and of Seward's antagonism. For example, he informed Thouvenel on

May 23, 1861, that the secretary of state would take a dim view of a French interference.[137] After the summer, rumors of French or English recognition of the Confederacy were spreading in Washington. Although Mercier was favorable to recognition in principle, he put his government on its guard and recommended handling the Federal authorities with care. "I have repeated to you several times," he wrote, "that with an eye to the future, we must avoid offending the North."[138] He said so again in the spring of 1862, when there was even less question of upsetting Washington since it seemed obvious that, in the coming weeks, the Northerners' momentum would bring them to Richmond: "Let us be careful not to quarrel with them; without forgetting the present, let us think of the future."[139] Six days later he added, "We must make friends of these people. . . . We do not know where their warlike humor might lead them."[140] The following year, Mercier again mentioned the threats by the Federal government, which had emerged stronger from the summer of 1863.[141]

Thouvenel noted Mercier's many warnings in his letters to Flahaut, his ambassador to the United Kingdom. The foreign minister also had no doubt that recognition of the South could lead to war with the North. He envisaged needing Flahaut's backup to help to prevent France and England from "risking war with the United States." He confided to Flahaut, "I may need your help to spare us a venture that would be more serious than the one in Mexico."[142] Thouvenel thought it useful to send Mercier's dispatch to Napoléon III, who agreed with him.

The danger of a war with the North was not only on the minds of the diplomats. French liberal newspapers repeatedly brought up the risks of recognizing the Confederacy. They advised France to "think twice" before committing such a severe breach of neutrality, which would be taken as a casus belli.[143] What would the losses and suffering of the cotton industry be next to the harm caused by an undertaking sure to be longer and more difficult than the Crimean expedition?[144] Les Débats remarked that there must be a reason why England, which hoped to see the United States dismembered, was nonetheless reluctant to go to war with it. These journalists believed the British were taking into account the distance to be traveled and remembering their past struggles.[145]

The fear of a duel with the North concerned not the present but the future, since for the moment the war hindered the Federals and deprived them of their best units. Although the French fleet was second only to the British, Paris was well aware that the United States was taking advantage of the Civil War to close the gap. In 1865, with 671 warships, of which 71 were ironclads, they had the largest navy in the world.[146]

The Future Lies in Union

In addition to the contest of military strength and a possible confrontation with the winner of the Civil War, Paris feared the distance to transport troops to the North American continent, the difficulty of surrounding one of the Federal ports, which the British had already experienced, and the cost.[147] The example of the two wars the British had fought against the Americans was not only dissuasive but instructive. The foreign ministers' opposition was based above all on the existing military situation. France was getting bogged down in Mexico. In the spring of 1862, Thouvenel wrote, "The affair has started badly but it is not possible to stop halfway."[148] The conflict appeared more obviously each day to be an expedition for which the difficulties and risks had been underestimated; a decision taken lightly and founded more on an adventurous vision than on a duly considered calculation.[149] Added to the Spanish and British defections were the unforeseen difficulties that hindered the progress of the French expeditionary force. In June 1862, the French press published the report of the troops' leader, Gen. Charles de Lorencez. He wrote of an arduous campaign and "complications"—a euphemism—before the city of Puebla.[150] News of that failure reached Paris on July 2, 1862.

If the emperor wanted to see his "grand design" realized, he had to refrain from provoking Washington, which was in a position to defeat the imperial initiative. If the Confederate government was legitimated by French recognition, the diplomats and consuls feared that, in retaliation, the Federals would first send ships to impede the transportation of troops to Mexico and, second, would support the Juarist cause against the new authority installed by France. The report presented by the consul general in New York at the beginning of the war and mentioned at the beginning of this chapter bears the evocative title "Note for the Minister on the Possible Consequences of a French Intervention in the Anglo-American Conflict." It highlighted the risk of seeing the Northern forces employing naval means against France.[151]

It was indeed this latter argument—the importance of not complicating the Mexican Expedition—that the Quai d'Orsay regularly used with Napoléon III. Hardly had the French expeditionary force landed at Vera Cruz than, in a letter to Flahaut, Thouvenel said he wanted to have examined whether the taking of Matamoros would lead to complications with Washington.[152] Six months later, when the regiments were stalled before Puebla, Thouvenel confided to Flahaut his fervent wish to keep Washington happy. "The more I consider the matter," he wrote, "the more I think of the financial and other difficulties of the Mexican expedition, the more I see our throwing ourselves into conflict with the United States as an inopportune and dangerous act."[153] Flahaut shared this position entirely, agreeing that France was sufficiently en-

tangled with its intervention in Mexico and hardly needed to make itself another enemy.[154]

Foreign Minister Drouyn de Lhuys was as cautious as his predecessor.
He had shown himself to be wary of costly conflicts in the past, during the
Crimean War, for instance.[155] In March 1853 he disapproved of sending part of
the French fleet, and he later sought to end hostilities in Crimea with a compromise peace agreement.[156] It seems that he did not consider the Mexican
expedition opportune.[157] After the taking of Puebla, he wanted to build on
this French success to negotiate with the legal government and get out of the
Mexican quagmire while France was still on top.[158] The emperor, who wanted
a change of regime, ignored his advice.

Drouyn de Lhuys was equally opposed to a military venture against the
North. Like Thouvenel, he refused to risk complications with the Federal government, fearing its capacity to jeopardize the troops engaged in Mexico. On
June 21, 1863, he told Slidell that he was worried Washington would encourage
the departure of a volunteer corps to Mexico, a move that would aggravate the
situation even further. He conjectured that faced with such an incursion, the
emperor would be forced to declare war on the North, to the great benefit of
England.[159] In a letter to the minister of the navy, Drouyn de Lhuys expressed
himself clearly about the stance to adopt toward Washington: "I do not need
to stress the political interest of the highest order there is for the Emperor's
government, in the present circumstances, not to overexcite this hostile tendency on the other side of the Atlantic. It could cause the most serious difficulties for us, which we must work to avoid as much as possible by giving the
Washington government no justified grievance, no plausible excuse for more
violent recriminations against our attitude and our alleged ulterior motives."[160]

To dissuade the emperor from his diplomatic plan in favor of the Confederate government, each foreign minister cleverly established a connection
between the American and Mexican policies. Apparently the message got
through. Napoléon III was finally convinced that the impact of a conflict with
the United States would be disastrous at a time when his troops were getting
hopelessly embroiled in Mexico. At his second meeting with Slidell on October 28, 1862, Napoléon stressed the risk of a clash with the United States.[161]
When he received Slidell once more on June 18, he again used this argument
against diplomatic action in favor of the South.[162]

In July 1863, with the military situation turning in favor of both the North,
after Gettysburg and Vicksburg, and the imperial army, after the capture of
Mexico City, the decision to maintain a position of mutual neutrality was
now thoroughly justified. It served the interests of both powers: of France

by paving the way without complications for its candidate in Mexico and of Washington by obtaining a definitive renunciation of any form of intervention in favor of the South. On November 9, 1863, Drouyn de Lhuys made it clear to Slidell that France would not risk a military engagement in Anglo-America and would maintain its neutrality.[163]

It is also important not to lose sight of the storms gathering in European skies and the difficulties in several parts of the continent that warranted the full attention of the imperial government. Shortly before leaving the Foreign Ministry in October 1862, in a final dispatch to his minister in Washington, Thouvenel again recommended that choices be made. France could not orchestrate everything at the same time. "Mexico, the American question and, on top of everything, the Rome business is really too much at once," he wrote.[164] A few days later, the emperor indicated to Slidell that he could not focus solely on the American dispute because he needed to concentrate on the situation in Europe, especially the events taking place in Italy and Greece.[165] The following year, the attention of Napoléon III was still primarily focused on Europe. In August 1863, Slidell regretted that the Polish question overshadowed all others; in November, he was disappointed because the emperor's speech to Parliament had focused only on European matters; in late December, he mentioned the risk of war in Europe that was monopolizing the emperor's attention.[166] It was undoubtedly the tireless work of the foreign ministers that brought Napoléon's focus back to European events, particularly the question of the duchies, the rising Austro-Prussian antagonism, and the negotiations concerning Italy.[167]

While tensions on the European continent occupied government officials' attention, Asia was not absent from their thoughts. In the 1850s and 1860s a decisive step was crossed in the Far East. Westerners broke Japan's isolation, forced China to open its market, and, in 1859, France began its conquest of the Indochinese peninsula. The situation of Japan that Mercier briefly mentioned early in the war compelled the Western powers to join forces.[168] In 1854, the Americans managed to conclude a treaty with the Tokugawa shogunate (the Treaty of Kanagawa signed by Cdre. Matthew C. Perry). Four years later, the agreement was supplemented with new clauses concerning a treaty of friendship and commerce. But with the decline of the shogunate, the imperial court increasingly relied on the antiforeign party.[169] On June 5, 1863, the emperor of Japan decided to expel Europeans and Americans, whose vessels were targeted between the islands of Honshu and Kyushu.[170] The situation required cooperation between all the powers; the English, French, Dutch, and American naval forces came together to retaliate. This collective action led to the Franco-American bombardment of Shimonoseki followed by the landing of troops to destroy the batteries at the entrance of the strait. The emperor of Japan was forced to defer his order of expulsion.[171] Napoléon III, in his speech of February 15, 1865, at the opening of the legislative session, welcomed this collaboration, stating that, "in Japan, our navy, united with those of England, Holland, and the United States, had given further proof of what it can and what it will do."[172] It was therefore impossible for France to antagonize this partner if it wished to develop its projects in the Far East. Besides, was it not better to remain on good terms with the United States at a moment when the Tuileries cabinet was concerned about the increasing Russian influence in China and Japan? On December 30, 1864, Drouyn de Lhuys sent a report providing an update on this question to La Tour d'Auvergne, his ambassador to the United Kingdom.[173]

———

It is undeniable that by engaging in Mexico, Napoléon III closed the door to recognition of the Confederate government. French policy toward the United States had thus become a contradiction: the Confederate rebellion had made the intervention in Mexico possible, but the success of that intervention required not recognizing or siding with the Confederacy for fear the United States would intervene. France could not add a dispute with the United States to its Mexican difficulties. It was less a fear of the North that precluded action in favor of the South than the detrimental conjunction of two engagements. As far as the Quai d'Orsay was concerned, war with the North was an event that had never been envisaged, regardless of the Mexican context. First, with or without Mexico, the military option was completely ruled out by the two successive foreign ministers as an unrealistic and foolish alternative. The virtue of the Mexican plan was to have come at the perfect time to provide the diplomats with an argument to which Napoléon III was particularly receptive, and which could be used to deter him from taking his initiatives too far. Second, it was from this perspective that the North's supremacy took on its full significance; the foreign ministers were convinced very early on that the Federal government could prevail and must therefore be handled carefully in preparation for the postwar period. France, in basing its policy on the prospect of success for the Washington government, had to consider the future of relations with the United States. It needed to strengthen its economic ties with this important partner and maintain good diplomatic relations in order to continue joint undertakings, such as in Asia, or simply to sustain Maximilian's regime, which Washington contested. At the start of the French expedition, Seward, drawing

The Future Lies in Union

on the Monroe Doctrine, highlighted U.S. objections to three features of the Napoleonic plan: (1) the imposition of a government by European powers, (2) the installation of a foreign sovereign in Mexico, and (3) the establishment of a monarchical form of government not properly chosen by the Mexican people.[174] Paris hoped its neutrality would be rewarded by a change in the Federal cabinet's position. It was deluding itself.

CONCLUSION

One might legitimately be surprised that the imperial government focused solely on French national interests in determining its policy on the American crisis. Nowadays, democratic nations cannot define their foreign policy without taking into account public opinion. No such obligation existed during the Second Empire, where the antidemocratic nature of the regime meant that decision-makers discussed external affairs in the closed sphere of the Quai d'Orsay or the Tuileries Palace. It was only toward the very end of his reign, on May 11, 1868, that Napoléon III granted newspapers greater latitude by doing away with prior authorizations and warnings. The same goes for the regime's definitive evolution toward parliamentarianism, which came after the *sénatus-consulte* of September 8, 1869. In any case, on the American question, the emperor took advantage of his subjects' ignorance about world events.[1] Contemporary accounts show that the French paid only marginal attention to the conflict, much less than the British, who were keenly interested in the outcome of the war.[2]

The government of Napoléon also showed little concern for the fate of its nationals living in the United States. Certainly, it proposed to protect those living in the states close to the Atlantic coast by sending warships. But it completely ignored the Frenchmen serving under the flag of either side, even though the declaration of neutrality prohibited the French from enlisting at the risk of losing their nationality. It is true that their numbers were negligible and their contribution insignificant. Unlike the 200,000 Germans and 150,000 Irish who fought, French participation remained very modest, at around 15,000 to 20,000 combatants (13 to 18 percent of the French living on American soil, mainly in the Northern states).[3] Camille de Polignac, who enlisted in the armies first of General Beauregard and then General Bragg, and the prince de Joinville and his two nephews, the comte de Paris and the duc de Chartres, who fought under General McClellan, failed to match the celebrated Revolutionary War exploits of the comte de Rochambeau and marquis de Lafayette.[4]

To determine its course of action during the American Civil War, the French Ministry of Foreign Affairs relied solely on its assessment of how France could best benefit from the situation created by the crisis, a judgment that it based on the dispatches of its diplomats and consuls. Well, no advantage could be gained from a division of the Union; no valid reason could prompt the French Foreign Ministry to side with the states in rebellion. If observers today are surprised that slavery did not count against the South as much as they might expect, this was because foreign policy, far from being a matter of feelings and morals, obeys interests above all. If anything penalized the South, it was its expansionist proselytizing. Despite the Confederate government's overtures, both French foreign ministers were aware that Napoléon III's Mexican plan came into competition with the Southerners' land-grabbing tendencies. The Quai d'Orsay did not cede to their entreaties. It always suspected the proponents of the peculiar institution of wanting to constitute a slave empire. From the start of the crisis, the reasons for their secession could be taken as an admission. The rebels refused to accept that slavery be confined to the states that practiced it and showed that they had not given up their expansionist aims. The diplomats and consuls also doubted the viability of the Confederacy, which would have trouble surviving outside the federal framework. The new republic's inability to control its maritime borders, hemmed in by the blockade, and its land borders, squeezed by the Federal forces, showed it was incapable of establishing its sovereignty. While the architects of France's foreign policy pleaded for the association of states to be established on a new basis, Lincoln's desire to reinvent the Union by ridding it of the burden of slavery was surely a move toward regeneration. When considering the commercial aspects, the Quai d'Orsay, though certainly sensitive to cotton dependency, could by no means overlook the market the North represented for French exports. Above all, the diplomatic staff found it hard to imagine that, unless the North gave up, it would fail one day to bring its opponent back into the Union.

Napoléon hoped for a victory for the secessionists, but his blindness was offset by the foresight of the French foreign ministers—backed up by the dispatches from Richmond—who understood that the South, like the thirteen colonies in times past, could not win alone. Napoléon III would not be another Louis XVI. The memory of that monarch's aid to the rebels of the New World was dissuasive, as the cost of the episode at the time was ruinous for both the treasury and for the regime. The American Revolutionary War finished off the Bourbon monarchy; the American Civil War would not seal the fate of the Second Empire. Finally and most important, the Quai d'Orsay was well aware that adding a dispute with the states loyal to the Union to the difficulties of the Mexican expedition would be an irreparable blunder. The North had the power to cause a great deal of trouble for the French forces. The Foreign Ministry's caution confirmed the effectiveness of Secretary of State Seward's dissuasive strategy.

The Union victory upset Napoléon's hopes. The emperor would have liked to weaken the United States by dividing the country, but the resurrected Union cemented the nation and forged its power. With Napoléon III, anti-Americanism became an integral principle of Bonapartism. Far from being extinguished by the fraternity of combat in two world wars, France's challenge to U.S. dominance was reinforced and asserted itself after Yalta, especially when General Charles de Gaulle returned to power in 1958. The great historian René Rémond was the first to highlight the lineage between the Bonapartist and Gaullist right wings. The founder of the Fifth Republic denouncing American hegemony recalled the views of Emperor Napoléon III a century before. Napoléon's fear of possible U.S. expansion to the Gulf of Mexico, expressed in his letter to General Forey, was echoed in de Gaulle's travels to Latin America and his desire to establish a privileged partnership with Mexico, and again by the Phnom Penh speech denouncing the U.S. intervention in Vietnam.[5]

Napoléon III had to revise his American policy under the influence of his foreign ministers, who made him realize that France would not benefit from the dismemberment of the United States. It took all their talents if not energies to get the emperor to hear reason. Despite many temptations, nonintervention prevailed. This policy reveals the powers of persuasion of Thouvenel and Drouyn de Lhuys. France's American policy not only provides valuable insight into how the imperial government worked, it also demonstrates that the ministers' influence often balanced and contradicted that of the emperor. Both men managed to steer Napoléon III in a prudent direction. They made him perceive the pointlessness, for French interests, of recognizing the Confederacy, and the danger there would be in creating tensions with the Northern government. They took advantage of his indecision, his weak character, and the kidney stones from which the emperor began to suffer in 1863 and that only increased in severity.[6] In his weakened state, Napoléon dithered. He would have liked to recognize the Confederacy but, convinced by his ministers' arguments, would not see this choice through if it meant being isolated on the international stage. In the end, he understood that he did not have the means to conduct his American policy.

Thouvenel and Drouyn de Lhuys did not merely contradict the emperor; they resisted his impulses by not complying with his instructions. France's American policy also raises questions about the real weight of Napoléon III's personal power because the emperor, though fully aware of the latitude that his ministers gave themselves, asked neither of them to hand in their portfolio. On the contrary, as the years passed, Napoléon grew more attached to his ministers and was increasingly reluctant to change them.[7] He preferred to bypass their reservations through unofficial intermediaries such as Lindsay, or establish direct contacts with the diplomats stationed abroad. These parallel negotiations contravened the normal functioning of diplomacy and greatly complicated the efforts of his ministers. Thouvenel bemoaned "a dual policy which is never explained."[8] He admitted his repugnance for the go-betweens chosen by the emperor, saying that they "spoil more affairs than they help with."[9]

The "emperor's secret," the parallel diplomacy he was introducing without sanction from his ministers of foreign affairs, was well known to those involved at the time, and the Southerners above all. When Mercier traveled to Richmond, the Confederates suspected the emperor of having instructed the agent directly without notifying Thouvenel.[10] The use of overlapping and conflicting channels made for disorganized diplomacy and blurred the message that France intended to deliver. This duality gave other governments the impression of a confused, ambiguous, and contradictory French policy. Between the emperor's rash plans and the more cautious approach favored by Thouvenel or Drouyn de Lhuys with regard to American events, foreign cabinets were unsure which policy prevailed. The imperial government's representative in London reported that in the House of Commons, members wondered if there were not two French embassies, one of which was accredited by the Foreign Office.[11] Even as the heads of the Quai d'Orsay resisted Napoléon's temptations, they constantly had to redefine diplomatic policy by denying the emperor's intentions. In this respect, the Second Empire's American policy during the Civil War was emblematic of the relationship between Napoléon III and those responsible for French diplomacy.

Although France did not wish to recognize the Southern states, the hostilities could only serve French interests. The war limited the actions of the Federal administration just as France was struggling to impose itself in Mexico.[12]

From 1864, the continuation of the fratricidal war left Maximilian's regime time to consolidate. The diplomats understood that although the Union was satisfied with the borders of Mexico, it conformed just as much to the Monroe Doctrine as its rival. The North was no more tolerant than the South of seeing a neighboring country reduced to a vassal state by a European power. They feared that once peace returned, the Federal government would seek to intervene actively in the Mexican question. It would not only be in a position to prevent supplies from reaching the expeditionary force in Mexico, it could also trigger hostilities to drive the French out of the country, carrying the eleven vanquished states along with it. After the split in the Union, such a conflict would indeed have the virtue of facilitating national reconciliation. The scenario was particularly worrying given that the new Mexican regime had no solid foundation whatsoever. That is why once Maximilian was established in Mexico, although the Civil War was in its last months, the advice from the French legation in Washington was to encourage the South to maintain its resolve and not to yield "on the question of absolute separation."[13] The diplomats were aware that prolonging the fighting between North and South would help consolidate Napoléon III's "grand design."

This desire to protect Maximilian also explains why France was slow to reconsider the right of belligerency granted to the Confederates. In late April 1865, as news of Lee's surrender arrived in Europe, the Federal government sent the maritime powers a formal demand that they finally rescind the Confederate States' right of belligerency.[14] The Quai d'Orsay refused to do so. It justified this by the sporadic fighting that still continued—a fallacious argument that displeased the U.S. representative.[15] In mid-May, given that the war had ended, a note to the minister recommended that the clause concerning belligerence be lifted.[16] However, the ministry did not follow this advice. This time, it referred to the British position that conditioned the withdrawal of belligerent rights on the withdrawal of the right of visit that the Federals applied to neutral ships.[17] Again, the rationale was questionable because the French commercial fleet was affected very little by the state of war in America. However, on May 30, 1865, the Foreign Office believed it was no longer possible to observe a state of war in America and informed its ambassador in Paris.[18] France waited until June 8 to adopt the same position.[19]

It took two months for France to withdraw belligerent status from the secessionists. One can surmise that this delay was due to the political situation in the United States, which had appeared uncertain to the imperial government since Lincoln's assassination and the failed attempt to assassinate Secretary of State Seward in April. The loss of these statesmen could result in a new team taking over the Union's foreign policy, which might prove less lenient toward the regime that France had established in Mexico. Until Drouyn de Lhuys was sure of the policy that Washington intended to adopt toward Maximilian's government, he did not want to give up his only bargaining chip. Once the minister received assurances that the United States would maintain a benevolent neutrality toward the new sovereign, he was quick to inform Mexico City.[20] From then on, there was no question of maintaining a diplomatic posture that the facts on the ground had long made obsolete.

Nevertheless, the end of the Civil War marked the entry of the Napoleonic plan into an uncertain phase. Weakened, without popular support, the Habsburg emperor could not envisage a future in Mexico without gaining Washington's support. But the Federal cabinet obstinately refused. As such, while the French had just finished conquering the territory, Lee's surrender at Appomattox brought them face to face with their inability to adapt the political situation to a military one. This conclusion convinced the French that they should withdraw from Mexico. So ironically, if, by tearing each other apart, the Americans gave the starting signal to land an expeditionary force in Vera Cruz, four years later they held in their hands the countdown to the French evacuation.

Acknowledgments

It is customary to express one's gratitude to those who have given their support during the ambitious undertaking of writing a book. However, in writing these lines, I am not merely respecting a well-established tradition through a sense of obligation. Rather, it is with sincere pleasure and some emotion that I address my thanks to those who helped me to prepare the English edition of this book.

I would first like to thank Anne Bryan Faircloth and Frederick Henri Albert Beaujeu-Dufour, who were willing to cover the costs of translation. By their generous act, they have offered a second lease of life to these works of diplomatic history originally published in French. I take this opportunity to acknowledge the conscientious work of this book's translator, Jessica Edwards, and to thank her for her diligent and fruitful collaboration.

I would also like to express my gratitude to Don Doyle, who contributed a great deal to getting this book under way. Without his constant encouragement and friendly support, I likely would not have embarked upon this venture. Together with the major contribution he has made to U.S. history, heightened by his comprehensive approach to events, it is to his great personal qualities that I would like to pay tribute here. His help has been precious. His involvement has been constant. He has been an invaluable support.

I am very appreciative of the confidence that Mark Simpson-Vos and UNC Press have shown me in publishing this book. Over the four years it has taken to finalize this project, they have been patient, understanding, and constantly available despite their workload.

I thank Howard Jones for his wise counsel and availability; Aaron Sheehan-Dean and David Wetzel for their enthusiasm and scrupulous reading of the manuscript; the late René Rémond, who suggested I work on France's foreign policy toward the United States after 1830; and André Encrevé, who supervised my doctoral dissertation. I thank Betje Klier for his valuable recommendations and help; Baron Gilbert Ameil, who proposed these books for the Prix Napoléon III; and Gerald Sim, author of an excellent study dealing with activities of the French consular staff and diplomatic agents, who regularly answered my questions. And, of course, I cannot forget to express my gratitude to the historian Serge Noirsain, the leading francophone specialist on the Civil War, who is always willing to assist researchers.

A book such as this one also owes much to library and archive staff. I would especially like to thank the staff of the archive department at the French Ministry of Foreign Affairs, who diligently answered my questions and more than fulfilled my expectations. I also greatly appreciated the attentiveness of the information department of the Library of Congress, whose services I regularly requested.

And, finally, I am grateful to Mylane, who shares my life and although far removed professionally from diplomatic history, nonetheless agreed to read the manuscript.

Chronology, 1848—1870

France	United States	Interactions between America, Europe, and Asia*
1848		
February 22–25. Revolution overthrows King Louis Philippe. Second Republic proclaimed.	*January 24.* Gold discovered in California.	*January 1.* The British seize Greytown (Nicaragua).
April 24. Election of the Constituent Assembly.	*November 7.* General Zachary Taylor (Whig) elected president.	*February 2.* Treaty of Guadalupe Hidalgo.
April 27. Abolition of slavery.		
June 22–26. Workers' uprising in Paris.		
November 4. National Assembly adopts constitution inspired by U.S. Constitution.		
December 10. Louis-Napoléon Bonaparte becomes first president of French Republic.		
1849		
May 13. Election of legislature. In following months, freedoms are restricted.	*January 19.* French socialist Etienne Cabet founds a community in Nauvoo inspired by his utopian novel.	*July.* Naval force dispatched to Smyrna.
July 4. French seize Rome, ending republic. They restore Pius IX.	*March 5.* Zachary Taylor inaugurated twelfth president of United States.	
July 10. Rio de la Plata Affair.		
August 12–September 5. French fail in attempt to capture Hawaii.		
October 12. British and French naval support given to Sublime Porte.		
1850		
May 31. Law restricting universal suffrage.	*January 29.* Henry Clay's Compromise.	
July 16. Law restricting freedom of the press.	*April 19.* Clayton-Bulwer Treaty.	

1851

July 18–19. Assembly refuses to revise constitution to allow president to run for second term.

December 2. Louis-Napoléon Bonaparte stages coup d'état.

December 20–21. Plebiscite approves Louis-Napoléon Bonaparte's coup.

July 9. Zachary Taylor dies. Vice President Millard Fillmore becomes thirteenth U.S. president.

September 18. Fugitive Slave Act.

September 17. First Treaty of Fort Laramie.

1852

January 21. Constitution approved by plebiscite.

February 29 and March 14. Legislative elections result in total victory for Louis-Napoléon Bonaparte.

November 21. Plebiscite approving reestablishment of Empire.

December 2. Louis-Napoléon Bonaparte takes name Napoléon III.

March 20. Publication of *Uncle Tom's Cabin*.

November 2. Franklin Pierce (Democrat) elected president.

September 17. Marines land at Buenos Aires.

1853

January 29. Napoléon III marries Eugénie de Montijo.

September 24. New Caledonia becomes a French colony.

March 4. Franklin Pierce inaugurated fourteenth president of United States.

March 11–13. U.S. intervention in Nicaragua.

July 8. Perry expedition to Japan.

March 11–13. U.S. intervention in Nicaragua.

April 20. Santa Anna resumes Mexican presidency for the last time.

October 15. William Walker's incursions into Baja California and Sonora.

France	United States	Interactions between America, Europe, and Asia*
1853 (continued)		
		November 3. Walker seizes La Paz and makes it capital of Republic of Baja California, which is then integrated into Republic of Sonora.
1854		
March 27. United Kingdom and France declare war on Russia. Crimean War.	*February 28.* Creation of Republican Party. *March 31.* Treaty of Kanagawa. *April 4 to June 17.* American and English ships land forces in Shanghai. *May 30.* Kansas-Nebraska Act. *June 5.* Canadian-American Reciprocity Treaty. *December 30.* Gadsden Purchase.	*February 13.* William Walker pushed back to Sonora. *July 13.* American bombing of Greytown. *October.* Walker tried and acquitted after eight minutes' deliberation. *October 9.* Ostend Manifesto.
1855		
April. Napoléon III visits London with his wife, Eugénie. *August.* Queen Victoria and her husband, Prince Albert, received in Paris.	*August 7.* Creation of Fourierist colony in Texas. *September 12–November 4.* U.S. naval force lands in Fiji Islands. *November 21.* Wakarusa War begins in Texas. *December 20.* Third Seminole War.	*August 9.* Santa Anna overthrown. Mexico inaugurates liberal reform. *October 13.* Walker takes Granada (Nicaragua). *November 25–29.* U.S. and European intervention in Uruguay.
1856		
March 16. Birth of the imperial prince. *March 30.* Treaty of Paris. End of the Crimean War.	*May 21.* Riots in Lawrence (Kansas). *May 22.* Caning of Charles Sumner. *May 24 to 25.* Pottawatomie massacre (Kansas). *June 2.* Battle of Black Jack (Kansas).	*April 15.* Marines land in Colombia (Panama). *May 20.* President Pierce recognizes Walker's provisional government.

April 16. International declaration prohibiting privateering.

August 25. State of war declared in Kansas.
August 30. Battle of Osawatomie (Kansas).
November 4. James Buchanan (Democrat) elected president.
November 16–24. Marines deployed in Canton.

July 12. Walker proclaims himself president of Nicaragua.

1857

June 21. Elections to legislature. Only five members of Republican opposition elected.
July 11. France puts end to Algerian resistance.
July 18. France begins occupation of Mali.

March 4. James Buchanan inaugurated fifteenth president of United States.
March 6. Supreme Court delivers Scott v. Sandford decision, taking a firm proslavery position.

February 12. Federal Constitution of United Mexican States ratified.
May 1. Walker surrenders to U.S. troops.

1858

January 14. Orsini's attempted assassination of Napoléon III.
May 22–August 19. Paris conference to establish United Principalities of Moldavia and Wallachia.
July 20–21. Plombières meeting.
November 17. France annexes Clipperton Atoll.

April 22. Demonstration in New York for "World Republic."
May 19. Marais des Cygnes massacre (Kansas).
August 16. Transatlantic telegraph cable works for only 20 days.
October 6–16. Marine expedition in Fiji Islands.

January 21. Benito Juárez becomes president of Mexico. Start of War of the Reform.
January 2–27. Two U.S. warships land in Uruguay.

1859

February 18. Beginning of French conquest of Cochinchina.
May 3. Beginning of Italian campaign. France fights against Austria alongside Piedmont.

July 31–August 2. Naval force lands in Shanghai to protect American interests.
August 27. Oil discovered in Titusville.
October 18. John Brown taken prisoner at Harpers Ferry.
December 2. Execution of John Brown.

November 28. Wyke-Cruz Treaty between Honduras and United Kingdom.
December 14. McLane-Ocampo Treaty.

France	United States	Interactions between America, Europe, and Asia*

1860

France	United States	Interactions between America, Europe, and Asia*
January 23. Free trade agreement with United Kingdom.	*May 16.* Abraham Lincoln named Republican Party candidate for president.	*September 12.* Walker executed by firing squad in Honduras.
March 24. Treaty of Turin giving Duchy of Savoy and County of Nice to France.	*June 1.* Census estimates population of United States at 31,443,321, including 3,953,761 slaves.	*September 27–October 8.* U.S. naval forces land in Colombia (Panama).
August 30. French expedition in Syria and Lebanon.	*June 18–28.* Democratic Party convention splits between two candidates, Stephen A. Douglas and John C. Breckinridge.	
October 6. Capture of Beijing by Anglo-French forces.	*November 6.* Lincoln elected.	
November 24. Napoléon III's first liberal reforms.	*December 20.* South Carolina secedes.	

1861

France	United States	Interactions between America, Europe, and Asia*
May 13. United Kingdom proclaims its neutrality in U.S. Civil War.	*January 9–February 1.* Secession of Mississippi, Florida, Alabama, Georgia, Louisiana, and Texas.	*January 1.* Benito Juárez enters Mexico City.
June 10. France proclaims neutrality in U.S. Civil War. Right of belligerency granted to South.	*February 4.* Formation of Confederate States of America.	*March 18.* Spain annexes Dominican Republic.
	February 9. Jefferson Davis becomes president of CSA.	*March.* Benito Juárez reelected president of Mexico.
	March 4. Abraham Lincoln inaugurated sixteenth president of United States.	*July 17.* Juárez suspends payments of foreign debt for two years.
	April 12. Battle of Fort Sumter. Start of Civil War.	*July 27.* France and Britain break off diplomatic relations with Mexico.
	April 15. Abraham Lincoln declares state of insurrection and raises 75,000 volunteers.	*October 31.* Convention of London. France, United Kingdom, and Spain decide on armed intervention in Mexico.
	April 17. Virginia secedes.	*December.* Spanish contingents land in Vera Cruz.
	April 19. Blockade of Southern ports decided.	

April 20. Robert E. Lee resigns from U.S. Army.
April 27. Abraham Lincoln suspends writ of habeas corpus.
April 29. Maryland decides to stay in Union.
May 6–20. Secession of Arkansas and North Carolina.
May 8. Richmond made capital of Confederate States.
May 20. Kentucky proclaims its neutrality.
June 8. Tennessee secedes.
June 19. West Virginia joins Union.
June 28. Foundation of Central Pacific.
July 21. First Battle of Bull Run ✕
August 10. Battle of Wilson's Creek ✕
November 1. George McClellan becomes commanding general of U.S. Army.
November 8. Inspection of the Trent.
December 27. Mason and Slidell released.

1862

July 16. First meeting between Napoléon and Slidell.
October 28. Second meeting between Napoléon and Slidell.
November 10. Napoléon unilaterally proposes six-month armistice between belligerents in U.S. Civil War.

February 6–16. Battles of Forts Henry and Donelson ☆
February 20–21. Battle of Valverde ✕
March 6–8. Battle of Pea Ridge ☆
March 8–9. Battle of Hampton Roads.
March 17. Start of Peninsula campaign.
March 23–June 9. Jackson's Shenandoah Valley campaign. ✕
April 6–7. Battle of Shiloh. ☆

January. British and French troops land in Vera Cruz.
February 19. Convention of la Soledad. United Kingdom and Spain reembark their troops in Mexico. France alone continues war under command of General de Lorencez.
April 28. Battle of Las Cumbres. Victorious French troops reach Puebla.

France	United States	Interactions between America, Europe, and Asia ✲
1862 (continued)		
	April 25–May 1. Capture of New Orleans. ☆	*May 5.* First Battle of Puebla. French defeated
	May 20. Homestead Act.	by Mexican general Ignacio Zaragoza.
	May 31–June 1. Battle of Seven Pines. ☆ ✗	*June 13–14.* French victory over Mexicans
	June 25–July 1. Seven Days' Battles. ✗	at Battle of Cerro del Borrego.
	July 13. First Battle of Murfreesboro. ✗	*July 3.* General Forey replaces General de
	July 15–16. Battle of Apache Pass.	Lorencez and assumes functions of French
	July 13. Henry Wager Halleck becomes	minister plenipotentiary in Mexico.
	commanding general of U.S. Army.	
	August 28–30. Second Battle of Bull Run. ✗	
	September 17. Battle of Antietam. ☆✗	
	September 22. Abraham Lincoln proclaims the	
	partial and conditional emancipation of slaves.	
	November 9. Ambrose Burnside becomes	
	commander of the Army of the Potomac.	
	December 13. Battle of Fredericksburg ✗	
	December 31–January 2, 1863. Second	
	Battle of Murfreesboro. ☆	
1863		
January 28. New proposal of French	*January 1.* Lincoln signs Emancipation	*March 16–May 17.* On their second
mediation to end U.S. Civil War.	Proclamation.	attempt, the French take Puebla.
April 13. Secret contract between Lucien	*January 26.* Joseph Hooker becomes	*April 30.* Battle of Camarón, Mexico, feat of
Arman and James Bulloch.	commander-in-chief of Army of the Potomac.	arms of the French Foreign Legion.
May 31. Legislative elections. 17	*February 3.* Battle of Dover. ☆	*June 7.* French troops enter Mexico City.
Republicans elected.		

June 18. Slidell meets with Napoléon for third time.
June 26–July 5. Roebuck affair.
July 17. New agreement between Arman and Bulloch.
November 27. CSS *Rappahannock* arrives in Calais.

February 25. Establishment of national banking system.
March 3. Enrollment Act passed in the North. ✗
April 27–May 6. Battle of Chancellorsville. ✗
May 13. "Stonewall" Jackson dies.
May 18. Siege of Vicksburg begins.
June 24–July 3. Battle of Hoover's Gap. ☆
June 28. George Meade becomes commander-in-chief of Army of the Potomac.
July 1–3. Battle of Gettysburg. ☆
July 4. Surrender of Vicksburg. ☆
July 3–16. New York City draft riots.
August 21. Lawrence massacre (Kansas).
September 7–9. Battle of Cumberland Gap. ☆
September 18–20. Battle of Chickamauga. ✗
November 7. End of Bristoe campaign. ☆
November 19. Gettysburg Address.
November 23–25. Battle of Chattanooga. ☆

July 10. "Assembly of Notables" meeting in Mexico City offers crown to Maximilian of Habsburg.
July 16. General Bazaine appointed commander-in-chief of expeditionary force in Mexico.
July 16. Battle of Shimonoseki Straits fought by USS *Wyoming* against Daimyo's fleet.
July 22. Juárez government decrees sale of public lands in Mexico.
August 16. Dominican Restoration War between nationalists and Spain.

1864

May. Napoléon orders Arman to sell ships being built for South to other buyers.
May 25. Right to strike instituted.
June 19. Confederate privateer CSS *Alabama* sunk outside Cherbourg by USS *Kearsarge*.
July 28. CSS *Rappahannock* unable to sail.
August. Emperor suffers attacks of colic and nephritic hemorrhages. Empress Eugénie's influence becomes preponderant.

February 20. Battle of Olustee. ✗
March 9. Ulysses S. Grant becomes commanding general of U.S. Army.
March 10–May 22. Red River campaign. ✗
May 5–6. Battle of the Wilderness. ✗☆
May 9–12. Battle of Spotsylvania. ✗☆
May 11. Battle of Yellow Tavern. ☆
May 23–26. Battle of North Anna. ✗☆
May 24–25. Battle of New Hope Church. ✗

April 10. Maximilian of Austria accepts imperial crown and signs Treaty of Miramar with Napoléon III.
April 14. Start of Spanish–South American War between Peru and Spain following Spain's conquest of Chincha Islands.
May 28. Archduke Maximilian lands in Vera Cruz, Mexico.

France	United States	Interactions between America, Europe, and Asia*
1864 (continued)	*May 24–June 4.* Battle of Dallas. ☆ *May 31–June 12.* Battle of Cold Harbor. ✗ *June 27.* Battle of Kennesaw Mountain. ✗ *June 9–March 25, 1865.* Siege of Petersburg. *June 11–12.* Battle of Trevilian Station. ✗ *July 11–12.* Battle of Fort Stevens. ☆ *July 20.* Battle of Peachtree Creek. ☆ *July 22.* Battle of Atlanta begins. *August 5.* Battle of Mobile Bay. ☆ *August 14–15.* Second Battle of Dalton. ☆ *August 17.* Battle of Gainesville. ✗ *August 31–September 1.* Battle of Jonesborough. ☆ *August 28–October 28.* Price's Missouri Raid. ☆ *September 2.* Atlanta falls to Union. *September 21–22.* Battle of Fisher's Hill. ☆ *October 19.* Battle of Cedar Creek. ☆ *November 8.* Lincoln reelected. *November 15–December 22.* Sherman's March to the Sea. ☆ *November 29.* Sand Creek massacre. *December 5–7.* Third Battle of Murfreesboro. ☆ *December 15–16.* Battle of Nashville. ☆ *December 23–January 15, 1865.* Fort Fisher Battles. ☆	*June 12, 1864.* Maximilian and Charlotte of Habsburg, emperor and empress of Mexico, arrive in Mexico City. *September 4–14.* Naval forces of United States, United Kingdom, France, and the Netherlands force Japan to allow the Straits of Shimonoseki to be used by foreign shipping in accordance with existing treaties.

1865

March 4. Final meeting between Napoléon and Slidell.

June 8. France withdraws Confederate right of belligerency.

January 31. Robert E. Lee becomes general-in-chief of Armies of the Confederate States.

February 3. Hampton Roads conference.

February 16–17. Burning of Columbia (South Carolina).

February 18. Union seizes Charleston.

March 2. Confederate defeat at the Battle of Waynesboro. ☆

March 4. Abraham Lincoln begins second term.

March 6. Battle of Natural Bridge. ✕

March 16–21. Carolinas campaign. ☆

March 25. Battle of Fort Stedman. ☆

March 31–April 9. Appomattox campaign. ☆

April 9. Robert E. Lee signs terms of surrender.

April 14. Lincoln assassinated.

May 10. Jefferson Davis arrested.

May 13. Battle of Palmito Ranch. ✕

June 23. Stand Watie surrenders.

November. Mississippi introduces first black code.

December 18. Thirteenth Amendment ratified.

December 24. Ku Klux Klan founded.

January 17–February 8. Mexico expedition. Siege of Oaxaca. Bazaine obtains surrender of Porfirio Díaz.

March 3. Spain renounces annexation of Dominican Republic.

March 9–10. U.S. forces sent to Panama to protect American residents.

April 11. In Mexico Belgian Legion defeated by Juarists at Battle of Tacámbaro.

July 16. The Belgian Legion takes revenge on the Juarists at the Battle of Loma.

November 6. Seward declares that Maximilian's government runs counter to U.S. interests.

1866

April 9. Congress passes Civil Rights Act.

June. Beginning of Sioux revolt.

July 24. Tennessee reintegrated into Union.

January 4. In Mexico, Bagdad falls into hands of Juarists with support of U.S. military.

France	United States	Interactions between America, Europe, and Asia*
1866 (continued)		
	July 27. Second transatlantic cable. *December 21.* Fetterman massacre.	*February 12.* Washington calls for withdrawal of French troops from Mexico. *April 5–6.* French government announces withdrawal in three stages of French troops from Mexico. *June 20–July 7.* In China U.S. expeditionary force counters attack on U.S. consulate at Newchwang. *July 27.* First transatlantic telegraph cable connects United States to Europe. *September 25.* Belgian Legion defeated by Juarists in Ixmiquilpan. *October 18.* Porfirio Díaz victorious against French and conservative Mexicans at Battle of La Carbonera.
1867		
November. French military expedition to Rome to protect Pope Pius IX.	*March 2.* Period of radical reconstruction begins. South divided into five Union occupation districts under Reconstruction Act.	*February 5.* French army evacuates Mexico City. *February 4–June 13.* In Japan, U.S. forces landed several times to protect American interests. *Marines intervene in Nicaragua.* *March 11.* Last French troops leave Mexico. *March 30.* United States purchases Alaska from Russia.

France signs friendship treaty with Madagascar.

1868

April 29. Treaty of Fort Laramie.
May 16. Impeachment of Andrew Johnson postponed.
June–July. Six former Confederate states reintegrated into Union.
July 9. Fourteenth Amendment ratified.
November 3. Ulysses S. Grant (Republican) elected president.
November 27. Battle of Washita River.

May 15. Capture of Querétaro. Maximilian taken prisoner.
June 13. Punitive expedition by United States to Formosa.
June 19. Maximilian and his remaining followers shot.
July 15. Juárez enters Mexico City.
August 28. United States seizes Midway Islands.

May 24. Election of legislative body. Opposition gains in strength. Napoléon intensifies liberal reforms.
November 17. Empress inaugurates Suez Canal, built by French.

1869

March 4. Ulysses Grant inaugurated eighteenth president of United States.
May 10. First transcontinental rail link.

February. In Uruguay U.S. forces protect foreign residents during rebellion.
April. U.S. forces protect passengers and goods in Colombia.

France	United States	Interactions between America, Europe, and Asia*
1870		
January 2. Republican Emile Ollivier called on to form a ministry.	*January–July.* Last four secessionist states reintegrated into Union.	
April 20. Establishment of bicameral parliamentary system.	*March 30.* Fifteenth Amendment ratified.	
May 8. Plebiscite massively approves new constitution.	*May 18.* Ku Klux Klan assassinates N.C. state senator John Stephens.	
July 19. France declares war on Prussia.	*June 1.* Census reports that United States has population of 38,555,983.	
September 2. Emperor taken prisoner, capitulates at Sedan.		
September 4. In Paris, emperor's dethronement announced and republic proclaimed. Government of National Defense continues war.		
September 18. Two Prussian armies begin siege of Paris.		
1871		
January 26. Armistice signed between France and Prussia.		
May 10. Treaty of Frankfurt ends war between the two countries. France loses Alsace and part of Lorraine.		

X = Confederate victory; ☆ = Union victory; ☆X = inconclusive battle

*For the chronology of U.S. interventions abroad, see Gerstein, *Securing America's Future*, 190–92.

Notes

ABBREVIATIONS

ADPEU Affaires Diverses et Politiques, Etats-Unis
CCC Correspondances Consulaires et Commerciales
CPA Correspondances Politiques, Angleterre
CPEU Correspondances Politiques, Etats-Unis
CPM Correspondances Politiques, Mexique
CPCEU Correspondances Politiques des Consuls, Etats-Unis
LJEU Livres Jaunes, Etats-Unis (1861–66)
LJM Livres Jaunes, Mexique (1862)
MDEU Mémoires et Documents, Etats-Unis
ORN *Official Records of the Union and Confederate Navies in the War of the Rebellion*, ser. 2, vol. 3, *Proclamations, Appointments, etc. of President Davis, State Department Correspondence with Diplomatic Agents, etc.* (Washington, D.C.: U.S. Government Printing Office, 1922).
PR Papiers d'Eugène Rouher
PS Papiers du Comte Eugène de Sartiges
PT Papiers d'Edouard Thouvenel
RDDM *La Revue des Deux Mondes*

1. Nagler, Doyle, and Gräser, *The Transnational Significance of the American Civil War*, 5.

2. Was Napoléon III in fact the nephew of Napoléon I? Recent DNA tests have revealed an absence of male kinship between the two emperors.

3. Seguin, *Louis Napoléon le Grand*, 431.

4. Besides French, Napoléon III was fluent in English, German, and Italian. Leduc, *Louis-Napoléon Bonaparte*, 110. His uncle did not speak English.

5. Sainlaude, "La politique étrangère de la France à l'égard des Etats-Unis," 247.

6. Renouvin, *Histoire des relations internationales*, 547.

7. Duroselle and Renouvin, *Introduction à l'histoire des relations internationales*, 308. Thouvenel neatly summarized his state of mind with this paradoxical assessment: "His resolution is very hesitant." Thouvenel, *Le secret de l'Empereur*, 2:379.

8. Hamon-Jugney and Oudin-Doglioni, *Le Quai d'Orsay*, 2–6.

9. Case, *Edouard Thouvenel*, 59.

10. Thouvenel's downfall came in mid-October 1862 after he implored Napoléon III to end the occupation of Rome. He died in 1866 on the eve of his probable return to the Quai d'Orsay. Bruley, "Thouvenel," in *Dictionnaire du Second Empire*, 1260.

11. Anceau, *L'Empire libéral*, 1:129.

12. D'Harcourt, *Les quatres ministères*, 4.

13. Drouyn de Lhuys dominated the imperial Foreign Ministry, which he headed for over six years (one-third of the Second Empire). His previous ministerial term had been dominated by France's engagement in the Crimean War. De Lhuys was made foreign minister again in 1862 but resigned in 1866, leaving the political scene definitively, over disagreements with Napoléon III about how to respond to the formation of the North German Confederation. He died in 1881. Choisel, "Drouyn de Lhuys," in *Dictionnaire du Second Empire*, 444–45. He was buried with his wife in a corner of the park of the Mettray penal colony (near Tours), now an institute for medical and vocational rehabilitation. Information provided by the author, who was present when the minister's grave was discovered.

14. Case, *Edouard Thouvenel*, 247. De Tocqueville spoke of Napoléon III's mind as "incoherent, confused, filled with great but ill-assorted thoughts." De Tocqueville, *Souvenirs*, 315.

15. Quoted in Price, *The French Second Empire*, 407.

16. The title of ambassador was reserved for first-class posts. Under the Second Empire, there were seven embassies and twenty-five legations. It was not until 1893 that the French mission in the United States became an embassy, reflecting the new U.S. role in the world.

17. In 1865 for instance, two young diplomats, Charles Baudin and the marquis de Châteaurenard, turned down this promotion, preferring to remain secretaries in Europe. Bruley, "Un spectacle des plus intéressants," 23.

18. The *exequatur* is a patent issued by the government of the host country. It recognizes a consular officer in his or her official capacity and confers upon the consul the right to exercise his or her functions in the country. The agent is thus bestowed with both a jurisdiction and an authority. Without the issuance of this patent, the consul cannot undertake any official act. Calvo, *Dictionnaire manuel de diplomatie*, 178–79. For more information on the activities of French consuls during the American Civil War, see Sim's "La présence diplomatique et consulaire française aux Etats-Unis," 157–87 and 476–508.

19. Thouvenel to Mercier, Paris, January 24, 1861, CPEU, 124:37; Thouvenel to de La Forest, Paris, May 16, 1861, CPCEU, 8:192. Edouard Henri Mercier de Lostende (1816–86) was born in Baltimore, where his father was consul for Louis XVIII. His diplomatic career reached a turning point after Bonaparte's coup. Before taking up his post in Washington in 1860, he headed the legations in Dresden, Athens (where he was in touch with Thouvenel, who headed the embassy of Constantinople), and Stockholm. His mission ended in late 1863, before the end of the Civil War. Papiers du Personnel, 1st ser., no. 2848; Carroll, *Henri Mercier and the American Civil War.*

20. As in August 1863, for example, when the French consular agent Nicholas Portz died at Mobile and the consul Maurice Durant Saint André hurriedly left his post in Charleston to take refuge aboard a French warship. On November 2, 1861, the consul at Richmond wrote that he had not been able to send his dispatches for three months. Paul to Thouvenel, Richmond, November 2, 1861, CPCEU, 9:259. Alfred Paul was born in Marseille in 1817. In 1852 he was assigned to the Richmond consulate, first as second-class consul, then as first-class consul. He was to spend half his career there. He was the only consul to serve during the entire Civil War. He was also the only diplomat to cross the front lines to deal with tobacco exports of the Régie française des tabacs. During secession and the Civil War, he proved himself to be a great diplomat (see chapter 9). He died in September 1868 of yellow fever in Havana, where he had just been posted as consul. For more details, see Sainlaude, "Alfred Paul: Un diplomate français dans la guerre de Sécession."

21. Sainlaude, "La politique étrangère de la France à l'égard des Etats-Unis d'Amérique."

CHAPTER 1

1. Thouvenel to Méjan, Paris, February 7, 1861, CCC New Orleans, 13:278. Comte Eugène Méjan (1814–74) was born in Milan. He headed the consulate in New Orleans from 1856 to 1862. He was well established in upper Louisiana society thanks to his wife, whom he married in New Orleans in 1860. He was recalled to France following the tensions with General Butler. He spent his later career in Havana, where he died of yellow fever (like his colleague Paul).

2. Thouvenel to Mercier, Paris, April 25, 1861, CPEU, 124:161–63.

3. Hahn, *A Nation without Borders,* 219.

4. Jenkins, *Britain,* 1:109. Adams, *Great Britain,* 1:94.

5. The clauses are discussed in the third part of this chapter. Stoeckl to Gorchakov, Washington, May 29 and June 10, 1861, in Case, *Edouard Thouvenel,* 351. Baron Edouard Stoeckl had been Russia's minister to Washington since 1854. Alexander Gorchakov was the Russian minister of foreign affairs. He was appointed in 1856 and remained in office for more than twenty-five years. The two men would negotiate the sale of Alaska to the United States in 1867.

6. Thouvenel used the French word *dissidences.*

7. U.S. Bureau of the Census, *Country of Birth of the Foreign-Born Population,* 3:695; Bodelle, *Petite(s) histoire(s) des Français d'Amérique,* 299.

8. Thouvenel to Mercier, Paris, May 11, 1861, LJEU, 1861, 93–94; CPEU, 124:194–206.

9. *Archives diplomatiques,* 1862, 1:271–72; Thouvenel to Mercier, Paris, June 10, 1861, LJEU, 1861, 97.

10. Lyons to Russell, Washington, June 14, 1861, in Case and Spencer, *The United States*

and France, 58. Lyons represented His Majesty's government in Washington. Russell was the British foreign minister.

11. Rousseau, *Droit international public*, 601.

12. McPherson, *La guerre de Sécession*, 421.

13. Drouyn de Lhuys to Bigelow, Paris, May 20, 1865, LJEU, 1866, 87–92.

14. Verhoeven, "La reconnaissance internationale," 105.

15. Thouvenel to Mercier, Paris, May 21, 1862, *Archives diplomatiques, 1863*, 1:275–77.

16. That is how it was interpreted by both the Northern and Southern authorities. Ferris, *Desperate Diplomacy*, 75; Spencer, "Recognition Question," 541–42.

17. Case and Spencer, *The United States and France*, 56–57; Drouyn de Lhuys to Barrot, Paris, November 10, 1863, ADPEU, 45:131v–32v.

18. Flahaut to Thouvenel, London, August 12, 1861, PT, 8:173. Charles de Flahaut de La Billarderie (1785–1870) was appointed French ambassador to the United Kingdom in 1860. This former general of the First Empire who participated in several prestigious battles (including Austerlitz, Iena, the Russian campaign, and Waterloo) was the natural son of Talleyrand, Napoléon I's brilliant foreign minister who had also represented France to the British government (1830–34). Flahaut's diplomatic career took off under the July Monarchy. He was also the lover of Hortense de Beauharnais, Napoléon III's mother, with whom he had a son, Charles de Morny, who was therefore the emperor's half-brother. Bernardy, *Flahaut*, 383.

19. Seward to Dayton, Washington, May 30, 1861, in Case and Spencer, *The United States and France*, 66–67; Ferris, *Desperate Diplomacy*, 45–46.

20. For example, Seward to Dayton, February 19, 1862, April 15, 1862, ADPEU, 30:172, 45:30–v.

21. Seward to Dayton, Washington, March 26, 1862, ADPEU, 30:137–38.

22. Mercier refers to the meeting in his dispatch to Thouvenel on March 31, 1862, *Archives diplomatiques, 1863*, 1:266–67.

23. Thouvenel to Mercier, Paris, May 21, 1862, *Archives diplomatiques, 1863*, 1:270–75.

24. Thouvenel to Mercier, Paris, July 4, 1861, CPEU, 124:368–69.

25. Thouvenel to Delangle, Paris, May 24, 1861, ADPEU, 33:10.

26. Russell to Lyons, London, July 1861, ADPEU, 44:8–11v.

27. Zorgbide, *La guerre civile*, 72.

28. Thouvenel to Flahaut, Paris, July 29, 1861, CPA, 720:127. Similarly, Great Britain recognized the belligerent status of Santo Domingo because of the Spanish blockade. La Tour d'Auvergne to Drouyn de Lhuys, London, December 19, 1864, CPA, 731:193v. La Tour d'Auvergne became French ambassador to London in 1863.

29. Drouyn de Lhuys to Bigelow, Paris, May 20, 1865, LJEU 1866, 87–92. Bigelow, consul general, was appointed U.S. minister to France in 1865. Bigelow rejected Drouyn de Lhuys's argument and pointed out that the Federal government had not declared war on the South. Bigelow to Drouyn de Lhuys, Paris, May 29, 1865, LJEU, 1866, 89.

30. Jules Grenier, in *Le Temps*, July 18, 1861. The pro-government mouthpieces were *Le Constitutionnel*, *La Patrie*, and *Le Pays*. The best-known liberal newspapers were *Le Journal des Débats* and *La Revue des Deux Mondes*. Bear in mind, however, that under the Empire the press was subject to tight control and regular censorship.

31. Jules Grenier, in *Le Temps*, July 18, 1861.

32. J. J. Weiss, in *Le Journal des Débats*, January 9, 1862.

33. *RDDM*, 1862 (1/2), 430.

34. For example, Gaillardet, in *La Presse*, June 20, 1861, in Blackburn, *French Newspaper Opinion*, 36.

35. Sanford's account explained that Faulkner remained in charge and blocked or delayed Sanford's negotiations with French officials.

36. Owsley, "Henry Shelton Sanford," 211–28.

37. Thouvenel to Seward, Paris, April 25, 1861, ADPEU, 30:24.

38. Bigelow, "John Bigelow and Napoleon III," 154–65.

39. Doyle, *The Cause of All Nations*, 297–98.

40. Priestley, "Mort insolite à Paris," 15.

41. Carroll, *Henri Mercier*, 5–6.

42. D'Hauterive, "Le prince Napoléon," 244.

43. Foreman, *A World on Fire*, 80, 187.

44. In 1867, Lyons was appointed British ambassador to France, which he would remain for nearly twenty years. In December 1863, Mercier was hastily recalled (the legation was still receiving invitations from the State Department addressed to him as he embarked for France). *Le Temps* wondered if this return should be interpreted as a repudiation. Edouard Hervé, in *Le Temps*, October 9, 1864. Daniel Carroll, who wrote his dissertation on the minister plenipotentiary, sees no particular significance in Mercier's departure for France. Carroll, *Henri Mercier*, 348, 354. In 1864, Mercier was given a substantial promotion to head the embassy in Madrid, which suggests that his recall was not in fact a sanction. The Republic relieved him of his duties six years later. Papiers du Personnel, 1st ser., no. 2848.

45. Dickey, *Our Man in Charleston*, 267.

46. Paul: 1st ser., no. 3192; Sainlaude, "Alfred Paul," 1:3–15.

47. This former lawyer was elected to the House of Representatives before being sent to Mexico in 1845 to negotiate an agreement between the two countries and obtain territorial concessions for the United States. The Mexican government's refusal caused the United States to declare war in 1846. Slidell was later elected and reelected as a Democratic senator from Louisiana until 1861. At the start of the Civil War, he was appointed to represent the Confederate government in France and was taken prisoner, with his colleague James M. Mason, during the Trent affair. He was released and made it to Paris in early 1862.

48. Slidell to Benjamin, Biarritz, September 22, 1863, *ORN*, 905–7.

49. Baillou, *Les affaires étrangères*, 1:587, 648, 707, 716, 721, 733. The Pickett papers contain several notes by Cintrat. See, for example, Slidell to Benjamin, Paris, May 3, 1863; and June 2, 1864, *ORN*, 756, 1139–41. Pierre Cintrat began his diplomatic career in 1814 at age twenty-one. In 1849, Drouyn de Lhuys appointed him director of the diplomatic archives department, which he ran for seventeen years. He therefore saw all the dispatches of the foreign ministers and their agents. He was highly regarded by his superiors. Officially, he was against the publication of any correspondence. He obviously had fewer scruples when it came to reporting their content to Slidell. Cintrat (Pierre): 1st ser., no. 961.

50. Slidell is buried in the cemetery at Villejuif, Benjamin in Père Lachaise in Paris.

51. Thouvenel to Mercier, Paris, April 25, 1861, CPEU, 124:161–63.

52. Mercier to Thouvenel, Washington, May 23, 1861, CPEU, 124:225–27, 229–30. Seward's threats were made public and published in *Le Moniteur* on June 16, 1861.

53. Thouvenel to Mercier, Paris, June 20, 1861, LJEU, 1861, 99.

54. Thouvenel to Mercier, Paris, April 29, 1861, CPEU, 124:16.

55. Mercier to Thouvenel, Washington, April 13, 1862, LJEU, 1862, 120; Thouvenel to Flahaut, Paris, May 1, 1862, CPA, 721:163. This episode is described in chapter 2.

56. Flahaut to Thouvenel, London, April 30, 1862, PT, 8:337. According to Lyons, Mercier asked Russia's minister to join him.

57. Thouvenel to Flahaut, Paris, May 1, 1862, CPA, 721:163.

58. Note by Villefort, Paris, March 31, 1863, ADPEU, 45:55–61. Villefort was the ministry's head of legation.

59. Declaration by Napoléon III, Paris, June 10, 1861, ADPEU, 43:141–44; Thouvenel to Flahaut, Paris, June 1, 1861, ADPEU, 43:122–24. Article 21 of the Napoleonic Code pronounced that those who took up service abroad without permission would lose their French nationality. Thouvenel to Delangle, Paris, May 24, 1861, ADPEU, 33:15.

60. In November 1861, Federals and Confederates clashed in the bay of Saint-Pierre in a battle between the steamers *Iroquois* and *Sumter*. Chasseloup-Laubat to Thouvenel, Paris, December 17, 1861, ADPEU, 46:27–42v. A year later, on November 22, 1862, a similar battle was fought in the bay of Fort-de-France between the South's *Alabama*, commanded by the former commander of the *Sumter*, and the frigate *San Jacinto*. Chasseloup-Laubat to Drouyn de Lhuys, Paris, December 22, 1862, ADPEU, 46:126–38.

61. Drouyn de Lhuys to Cowley, Paris, June 12, 1863, ADPEU, 45:82–v, and *Archives diplomatiques, 1864*, 2:430–32. Lord Cowley was appointed British ambassador to France in 1852. He would remain in the post for fifteen years.

62. Edouard Manet, *The Battle of the "Kearsarge" and the "Alabama"* (1864), Philadelphia Museum of Art. Noirsain, *La naissance du C.S.S. Alabama*, 48–56. The report on this episode can be found in the file ADPEU, 52, "L'*Alabama* à Cherbourg" (1864).

63. Mercier to Thouvenel, Washington, March 29, 1861, CPEU, 124:124.

64. Drouyn de Lhuys to Chasseloup-Laubat, Paris, December 5, 1864, ADPEU, 45:139v.

65. Thouvenel to Chasseloup-Laubat, Paris, Mai 30, 1861, ADPEU, 33:24v–25.

66. Paul to Drouyn de Lhuys, Richmond, January 15, 1863, CPCEU, 15:19–21; Montholon to Drouyn de Lhuys, New York, January 17, 1863, CPCEU, 13:25–v, and *Archives diplomatiques, 1863*, 1:398. Charles de Montholon-Sémonville was the second son of the famous general who, with his no-less famous wife, Albina, accompanied Napoléon I to St. Helena. Before being appointed to the consulate general of New York in 1853, he had already spent time in the United States as attaché at the legation in Washington and consul in Richmond. In 1863 he was sent to Mexico and two years later became France's minister plenipotentiary to the United States. Papiers du Personnel, 1st ser., no. 2980.

67. For example, Benjamin to Slidell, Paris, September 1863, ADPEU, 32:159v.

68. For example, Drouyn de Lhuys to La Tour d'Auvergne, Paris, December 5, 1864, ADPEU, 45:139v.

69. Thouvenel to Flahaut, Paris, May 11, 1861, ADPEU, 43:80–81.

70. Mercier to Thouvenel, Washington, April 26, 1861, CPEU, 124:164–75.

71. Thouvenel to Flahaut, Paris, May 13, 1861, CPA, 719:377–79.

72. Adams, *Great Britain*, 1:158–59. On this specific issue, Thouvenel was wrong to suggest a partial adoption. Indeed, as Villefort recalled two years later, it had been agreed at the signing of the Declaration of Paris that accession would be indivisible and that the powers that wished to accede must do so for all four principles, failing which their acceptance would be declared void. Note by Villefort, Paris, March 31, 1863, ADPEU, 45:

52v–54. That is why in 1856, since the United States expressed reservations over article 1, they were exempt from all of them.

73. Paul to Thouvenel, Richmond, September 5, 1861, CPCEU, 9:239–v.

74. Thouvenel to Dayton, Paris, September 9, 1861, ADPEU, 44:103–5.

75. Seward to Dayton, Washington, September 10, 1861, ADPEU, 44:126–28.

76. *Archives diplomatiques, 1861*, 2:365–66.

77. Case, *Edouard Thouvenel*, 356. At the time, James Watson Webb, a former soldier and journalist, was about to be appointed head of the U.S. legation in Brazil. He was pro-North. The emperor knew him from the time he had spent in the United States in 1837.

78. Adams, *Great Britain*, 1:247; Thouvenel to Mercier, Paris, August 19, 1861, CPEU, 125:23; Geofroy to Thouvenel, Washington, August 13, 1861, CPEU, 125:17. François Henri Louis de Geofroy was born in 1822. He had been first secretary of the legation since 1860. He briefly replaced Mercier, who took leave to visit Niagara Falls by invitation of Secretary of State William Seward. In May 1862, he left Washington for Athens but returned in late 1863 as first-class secretary. After the departure of the minister plenipotentiary, he handled routine business while waiting for Mercier's replacement to arrive in Washington. A few days before the outbreak of war between France and Prussia, he was appointed envoy extraordinary and minister plenipotentiary to China and then to Japan. In 1880, he became chairman of the French and American Claims Commission for Civil War Compensations. As the top post of the French legation to the United States continued to escape him and his mission weighed heavily on him, he asked for permission to retire in 1883. 1st ser., no. 1806.

79. According to Rouher, the minister of agriculture, trade, and public works, France had proposed to England twice without success that it take action against the blockade: the first time in the summer of 1861 and the second in the spring of 1862. In April 1862, Napoléon III seemed to confirm this. In both cases, the remarks were reported by Slidell. Slidell to Benjamin, Paris, April 14, 1862, *ORN*, 393–95. Thouvenel confirmed the statement. Thouvenel to Mercier, Paris, August 19, 1861, CPEU, 125:23.

80. In the first months of the Civil War, Europeans saw a sharp drop in cotton supplies from the South.

81. For example, Belligny to Thouvenel, Charleston, August 18, 1861, CPCEU, 8:260–61v. Pierre Joseph Belligny de Sainte-Croix (1810–77) was named consul in Charleston in 1856. In April 1861, he witnessed the bombardment of Fort Sumter. He got along well with his British colleague Consul Robert Bunch, with whom he sought to coordinate his actions. He was replaced the following year because he failed to give a detailed account of the crisis following South Carolina's secession. Papiers du Personnel, 1st ser., no. 3635; Berwanger, *The British Foreign Service*, 39; Geofroy to Thouvenel, Washington, September 6, 1861, CPEU, 125:64. See also the commander of the *Lavoisier* to the minister of the navy for the Gulf of Mexico. La Roncière to Chasseloup-Laubat, Paris, November 9, 1861, ADPEU, 46:8–17.

82. Paul to Thouvenel, Richmond, April 15, 1862, CPCEU, 12:53–v.

83. Geofroy to Thouvenel, Washington, September 6, 1861, CPEU, 125:64. Geofroy based his note on the report by Rear Admiral Reynaud.

84. Paul to Thouvenel, Richmond, September 6, 1861, CPCEU, 9:226v, 228–33v; Paul to Thouvenel, Richmond, November 2, 1861, CPCEU, 9:254v; Paul to Thouvenel, Richmond, November 8, 1861, CCC Richmond, 5:11–14, CPCEU, 9:263. It was Robert Hunter, the Confederate secretary of state (from July 1861 to February 1862), who gave these figures to Paul.

85. Belligny to Thouvenel, Charleston, January 16, 1862, CCC Charleston, 7:212.

86. Belligny to Thouvenel, Charleston, March 15, 1862, CCC Charleston, 7:232; Paul to Thouvenel, Richmond, April 15, 1862, CPCEU, 12:52–55.

87. Lanen to Drouyn de Lhuys, Charleston, May 29, 1864, CCC Charleston, 7:367. At the beginning of the war Louis Charles Arthur Lanen (1835–1908) served as assistant to the consul general of New York. Two years later the inexperienced diplomat headed the Charleston consulate after the flight of Durant Saint André. In addition to English he was fluent in Spanish, German, and Italian. Along with his colleague Geofroy, he represented France on the Franco-American Joint Commission for Civil War Compensations in 1880. Papiers du Personnel, 1st ser., no. 2405; Sim, *La présence diplomatique et consulaire française aux Etats-Unis*, 164.

88. Rost, the Southern envoy, gave the emperor's government the list of vessels that had run the blockade up until August 20, 1861. He spoke of 400 ships that had gotten through without difficulty. Rost to Thouvenel, 1861, ADPEU, 32:3–4. The following year John Slidell submitted a similar document to Thouvenel, *Mémorandum au sujet du blocus du littoral des Etats confédérés proclamé par le gouvernement des Etats-Unis respectueusement soumis à son excellence M. Thouvenel* (Paris, 1862), ADPEU, 32:85–88v. However, these figures may have been exaggerated.

89. Paul to Thouvenel, Richmond, January 22, 1862, CPCEU, 12:6–v; Slidell to Thouvenel, Paris, July 21, 1862, ADPEU, 32:57v–58. Slidell's memo, in Slidell to Benjamin, Paris, July 25, 1862, ORN, 481–87.

90. When on April 11, 1862, the emperor received Lindsay, a British ship owner, the sovereign admitted he would have long declared the blockade "ineffective" and, had he received the support of England, would have taken the necessary steps. Slidell's memo, in Slidell to Benjamin, Paris, April 14, 1862, ORN, 393–95. In July 1862, Slidell, the Confederate special commissioner to France, made another attempt. Napoléon III again regretted that France had respected the blockade, but he dismissed the idea of launching an operation to run it, as that would constitute an act of war. Slidell's memo, in Slidell to Benjamin, Paris, July 25, 1862, ORN, 481–87.

91. McPherson, *War on the Waters*, 49.

92. Russell to Slidell, London, February 10, 1863, ADPEU, 32:103. Dispatch given by Slidell to Drouyn de Lhuys. Russell to Lyons, London, February 15, 1863, ADPEU, 32:115.

93. Russell to Slidell, London, February 10, 1863, ADPEU, 32:103v.

94. Thouvenel to Flahaut, Paris, July 29, 1861, CPA, 720:126–28.

CHAPTER 2

1. Fenton, *Napoleon III*, 125–26.

2. Dansette, *Louis-Napoléon Bonaparte*, 131.

3. Milza, *Napoléon III*, 104–5.

4. Case, "La sécession aux Etats-Unis," 294.

5. Girard, *Napoléon III*, 40.

6. "choqué, froissé, vexé, mortifié, dépaysé, matérialisé, pétrifié, stalactisé, aurifié, argentifié, canalisé, vaporisé, et cela dix fois par jour." Dansette, *Louis-Napoléon Bonaparte*, 131.

7. In the political climate at the time, with Bonapartism regaining ground, Louis-Napoléon Bonaparte thought it possible to seize power. He hoped to rally the garrison

of Strasbourg and then march on Paris, but he failed to win the troops' support. The king, keen to avoid making him a martyr by imprisoning him, magnanimously heeded a suggestion by the conspirator's mother to send her offspring away from Europe. The nephew wanted to repeat his uncle's "Flight of the Eagle." In April 1814, after his defeat against a European coalition, Napoléon I was forced to abdicate and was exiled to the island of Elba. However, on March 1, 1815, he reclaimed power. "The Flight of the Eagle" is an expression that describes the journey he made from the Mediterranean coast to Paris on March 20, where he was triumphantly received.

8. Milza, *Napoléon III*, 103.

9. In March 1829 the new president of the United States, Andrew Jackson, believed it was time for France to pay compensation for the losses suffered by U.S. maritime trade during the Napoleonic Wars. By a treaty signed on July 4, 1831, the government of Louis-Philippe agreed to pay 25 million francs in six annual installments. The U.S. Senate quickly ratified the agreement, but the French Chamber of Deputies was slow to vote for it, which led the two countries to break off diplomatic relations in 1835. Only pressure from business circles anxious to preserve bilateral trade managed to prevent the animosity from escalating. Still, it took six years for the crisis to be resolved.

10. Girard, *Napoléon III*, 39. He would keep this letter in his wallet all his life. Hortense died on October 5, 1837.

11. Giraudeau, *Napoléon III intime*, 70.

12. Bruyère-Ostells, *Napoléon III et le Second Empire*, 55.

13. Fenton, *Napoleon III*, 126.

14. Dansette, *Louis-Napoléon Bonaparte*, 131. Letter to Queen Hortense of April 24, 1837. D'Hauterive, "Le prince Napoléon," 247.

15. Fenton, *Napoleon III*, 126. Letters from Napoléon III to Narcisse Veillard.

16. Binder, *James Buchanan*, 204. John Young Mason (1799–1859) is not to be confused with James Murray Mason (1798–1871). John Mason was best known for his role as secretary of state for the navy under Presidents John Tyler and James Polk. He represented the United States in France from 1853 until 1859, the year he died in Paris.

17. Tooley, *The Peace That Almost Was*, 223–42.

18. On May 11, Foreign Minister Edouard Thouvenel delivered the emperor's reaction, suggesting that a compromise be sought between the two camps. Thouvenel to Mercier, Paris, May 11, 1861, CPEU, 124:194; Thouvenel to Mercier, Paris, May 16, 1861, CPEU, 124:216–17, and *Archives diplomatiques, 1861*, 1:110; Dayton to Seward, Paris, May 23, 1861, *Archives diplomatiques, 1861*, 1:340.

19. Mercier to Thouvenel, May 28, 1861, ADPEU, 30:25.

20. Mercier to Belligny, Washington, June 5, 1861, CPEU, 124:390–v.

21. Mercier to Thouvenel, Washington, June 10, 1861, CPEU, 124:301; Thouvenel to Mercier, Paris, August 8, 1861, CPEU, 125:15–16v; Mercier to Thouvenel, Niagara, September 9, 1861, PT, 13:387–v. In November 1861 once again Mercier called for French intervention. Mercier to Thouvenel, Washington, November 7, 1861, CPEU, 125:186.

22. Flahaut to Thouvenel, London, September 22, 1861, PT, 8:183v–184.

23. *Le Temps*, January 28, 1862; *Le Journal des Débats*, January 28, 1862; *La politique impériale*, 358.

24. Billaut, one of the three ministers without portfolios, confirmed the emperor's reserve. L. Alloury, in *Le Journal des Débats*, June 15, 1862.

25. Sartiges to Thouvenel, The Hague, February 1, 1862, ADPEU, 30:102v–103. Comte

Eugène de Sartiges (1809–92) was probably the most skilled minister plenipotentiary sent by France to the United States between 1840 and 1870. He was appointed to head the Washington legation in 1851. Sartiges already had vast diplomatic experience and was a skilled negotiator. He was a keen observer of American affairs, which he grasped very clearly and judged with lucidity and prudence. His transatlantic mission was the longest of his career. During his time in the United States, he married an American woman from a prominent Boston family. He was not recalled until eight years later to head the legation in the Netherlands. To crown his career, in October 1863 he was appointed ambassador to the Holy See. He then became a senator in 1868. Papiers du Personnel, 1st ser., no. 3666.

26. Thouvenel to Flahaut, Paris, February 10, 1862, in Thouvenel, *Le secret de l'Empereur,* 2:236–37.

27. Thouvenel to Mercier, Paris, February 27, 1862, *Archives diplomatiques, 1863,* 1:263–65; Thouvenel to Mercier, Paris, March 6, 1862, LJEU, 1862, 116. These successes were the taking of Forts Henry and Donelson.

28. The *Times* (London) of February 17, 1862, denounced this interference. CPEU, 126:168.

29. Mercier to Thouvenel, Washington, April 13, 1862, LJEU, 1862, 121, and *Archives diplomatiques, 1863,* 1:269–71.

30. Mercier to Thouvenel, Washington, April 28, 1862, CPEU, 127. Benjamin's remarks are transcribed over about thirty pages in the form of a dialogue.

31. *RDDM,* 1862 (5/6), 496.

32. A. Hébrard, in *Le Temps,* April 29 and 30, 1862.

33. J. J. Weiss, in *Le Journal des Débats,* May 6, 1862.

34. A. Hébrard, in *Le Temps,* May 16, 1862; *RDDM,* 1862 (5/6), 496.

35. Slidell to Benjamin, Paris, May 15, 1862, ORN, 419–20.

36. Thouvenel to Flahaut, Paris, May 2, 1862, in Thouvenel, *Le secret de l'Empereur,* 2:299.

37. Thouvenel to Mercier, Paris, May 15, 1862, *Archives diplomatiques, 1863,* 1:273.

38. Paul to Thouvenel, Richmond, May 30, 1862, CPCEU, 12:93–94.

39. Thouvenel to Mercier, Paris, June 12, 1862, *Archives diplomatiques, 1863,* 1:278, and LJEU, 1862, 130. Thouvenel was unaware of the successes of "Stonewall" Jackson's troops in Shenandoah between May 23 and June 9. Mercier to Thouvenel, Washington, July 1, 1862, CPEU, 128:6, and *Archives diplomatiques, 1863,* 1:282–83.

40. Paulin Limayrac, in *Le Constitutionnel,* May 8 and 22, and June 8, 11, 12 and 20, 1862, in West, *Contemporary French Opinion,* 74–75, 81; *Le Pays,* June 10, 1862, in Blackburn, *French Newspaper Opinion,* 81.

41. L. Alloury, in *Le Journal des Débats,* June 9, 10, and 12, 1862.

42. A. Hébrard, in *Le Temps,* May 16, 1862; L. Alloury, in *Le Journal des Débats,* June 14 and 15, 1862.

43. A. Nefftzer, in *Le Temps,* June 15, 1862; L. Alloury, in *Le Journal des Débats,* June 16, 1862.

44. Delord, in *Le Siècle,* May 5, 1862, in West, *Contemporary French Opinion,* 74.

45. De Tocqueville wrote: "The words one addressed to him were like stones thrown down a well; their sound was heard, but one never knew what became of them." De Tocqueville, *Souvenirs,* 350.

46. Slidell's memo, in Slidell to Benjamin, Paris, July 25, 1862, ORN, 481–87.

47. Thouvenel to Flahaut, Paris, July 21, 1862, ADPEU, 30:215-v; Mercier to Thouvenel,

Washington, July 19, 1862, PT, 13:471v; Mercier to Thouvenel, New London, August 26, 1862, PT, 13:490v.

48. Graebner, "Northern Diplomacy and European Neutrality," 68.

49. Thouvenel to the chargé d'affaires at the French embassy in St. Petersburg, Paris, July 23, 1862, ADPEU, 30:216–17v. Mercier put forward the same idea in late July; it is possible that Thouvenel took it from him. Mercier to Thouvenel, New London, July 29, 1862, PT, 13:480.

50. Crook, *The North, the South*, 223.

51. Thouvenel to Mercier, Paris, September 11, 1862, in Thouvenel, *Le secret de l'Empereur*, 2:387–88.

52. Thouvenel to Mercier, Paris, September 18, 1862, CPEU, 128:93–95, *Archives diplomatiques, 1863*, 1:285.

53. Thouvenel to Flahaut, Paris, September 27, 1862, CPA, 722:115.

54. Paul to Thouvenel, Richmond, October 10, 1862, CPCEU, 12:129v–31.

55. Paul Becquet du Bellet, *Le Pays*, September 11 and 17, 1862, in Blackburn, *French Newspaper Opinion*, 95–96.

56. L. Alloury, in *Le Journal des Débats*, July 26, 1862; Clément Duvernois, in *Le Temps*, July 24, 1862.

57. Slidell's memo, in Slidell to Benjamin, Paris, October 28, 1862, *ORN*, 574–78.

58. Jones, *Blue and Gray Diplomacy*, 215–16.

59. Montholon to Thouvenel, New York, September 30, 1862, CPCEU, 10:202; De La Forest to Thouvenel, Philadelphia, September 12, 1862, CPCEU, 10:257v–58. During the 1850s Alphonse Lacathon de La Forest (1812–84) was consul in Boston. In 1869, he moved to New York, where he headed the French consulate. Papiers du Personnel, 1st ser., no. 2276.

60. Drouyn de Lhuys to Flahaut and Montebello, Paris, October 30, 1862, LJEU, 1862, 142–43, and *Archives diplomatiques, 1863*, 1:288–90, and CPA, 722:138–40v. See also the memo "Mediation in America," Paris, July 8, 1863, CPA, 725:153. This memorandum, written nine months later, went back over the whole affair. Drouyn de Lhuys to Mercier, Paris, October 30, 1862, CPEU, 128:148.

61. Drouyn de Lhuys to Flahaut, Paris, November 6, 1862, CPA, 722:137.

62. Drouyn de Lhuys to Mercier, Paris, November 13, 1862, *Archives diplomatiques, 1863*, 290–91, and LJEU, 1862, 145.

63. A. Grenier, in *Le Constitutionnel*, November 10, 1862, in West, *Contemporary French Opinion*, 87. For provincial papers, see Blackburn, *French Newspaper Opinion*, 39, 96.

64. A. Gaïffe, in *La Presse*, November 11, 1862, in West, *Contemporary French Opinion*, 88; J. J. Weiss, in *Le Journal des Débats*, November 11, 1862; A. Hébrard, in *Le Temps*, November 13 and 14, 1862; L. Legault, in *Le Temps*, November 15, 1862.

65. Prévost-Paradol, in *Le Journal des Débats*, November 23, 1862.

66. A. Gaïffe, in *La Presse*, November 8, 10, and 16, 1862, in Blackburn, *French Newspaper Opinion*, 100; Prévost-Paradol, in *Le Journal des Débats*, November 14, 1862.

67. Prévost-Paradol, in *Le Journal des Débats*, November 23, 1862.

68. A. Hébrard, in *Le Temps*, November 13, 1862.

69. Dayton to Drouyn de Lhuys, Paris, November 16, 1862, ADPEU, 30:225v–28; Drouyn de Lhuys to Mercier, Paris, November 27, 1862, *Archives diplomatiques, 1863*, 1:292.

70. Paul to Drouyn de Lhuys, Richmond, December 19, 1862, CPCEU, 12:136–40v.

71. Flahaut to Drouyn de Lhuys, London, November 11, 1862, CPA, 722:174–75v. The Emancipation Proclamation and public reaction against Gladstone's Newcastle speech also had an influence.

72. Flahaut to Drouyn de Lhuys, London, November 13,1862, CPA, 722:176v–77.

73. Drouyn de Lhuys to Mercier, Paris, November 13, 1862, 1863, 1:290–91.

74. *Le Moniteur*, November 10, 13, and 16, 1862.

75. Drouyn de Lhuys to Mercier, Paris, November 13 and 18, 1862, LJEU, 1862.

76. Mercier to Drouyn de Lhuys, Washington, November 10, 1862, LJEU, 1862, 148; CPEU, 128:151v–54v; Montholon to Drouyn de Lhuys, New York, January 4 and 13, 1863, CPCEU, 13:4–v, 10–12v, 23–v.

77. McPherson, *La guerre de Sécession*, 612.

78. Risley, *The Civil War*, 148.

79. Paul to Drouyn de Lhuys, Richmond, December 19, 1862, CPCEU, 12:136v–40; Paul to Drouyn de Lhuys, Richmond, January 4, 1863, CPCEU, 15:4v–6v.

80. Mention of the War of Independence was not particularly propitious, as in that conflict the rebels won against an incomparably stronger power.

81. Drouyn de Lhuys to Mercier, Paris, January 9, 1863, LJEU, 1863, 112–13.

82. Drouyn de Lhuys to Mercier, CPEU, 129:15.

83. *Discours prononcé Par S. M. l'Empereur à l'ouverture de la Session Législative.*

84. *Le Journal des Débats*, January 30, 1863.

85. Paulin Limayrac, in *Le Constitutionnel*, January 28, 1863, in West, *Contemporary French Opinion*, 96; J. J. Weiss, in *Le Journal des Débats*, January 29, 1863.

86. *Le Temps*, January 28, 1863; J. J. Weiss, in *Le Journal des Débats*, January 29, 1863.

87. Moreau, in *L'Union*, January 30, 1863, in Blackburn, *French Newspaper Opinion*, 103.

88. *Le Temps*, January 28, 1863; J. J. Weiss, in *Le Journal des Débats*, January 30, 1863.

89. Drouyn de Lhuys to Mercier, Paris, January 23, 1863, CPEU, 129:41.

90. Mercier to Drouyn de Lhuys, Washington, January 23, 1863, CPEU, 129:42.

91. Mercier to Drouyn de Lhuys, Washington, February 10, 1863, CPEU, 129:88–90; Mercier to Drouyn de Lhuys, Washington, March 1, 1863, CPEU, 129:116.

92. Drouyn de Lhuys to Mercier, Paris, February 26, 1863, LJEU, 1863, 114.

93. Mercier to Drouyn de Lhuys, Washington, November 18, 1862, CPEU, 128:182.

94. Drouyn de Lhuys to Flahaut and Montebello, Paris, October 30, 1862, CPA, 722: 135v–36. Montebello, or Auguste Louis Napoléon Lannes (1801–74), was the son of the first duc de Montebello, Jean Lannes, one of Napoléon I's brilliant officers who was mortally wounded at the Battle of Essling. Louis Napoléon Lannes was ambassador to Russia from 1858 to 1864. Papiers du Personnel, 1st ser. no. 2962.

95. Thouvenel to Mercier, Paris, June 12, 1862, *Archives diplomatiques, 1863*, 1:278; Thouvenel to Flahaut, Paris, July 21, 1862, ADPEU, 30:215. The elected members of the General Council of Haut-Rhin expressed the wish that the government take steps to help stop the war. Colmar, August 30, 1862, ADPEU, 30:222.

96. Alvarez, "The Papacy in the Diplomacy of the American Civil War," 227–48.

97. Girard, *Napoléon III*, 191.

98. Thus it is possible to accept good offices and reject mediation. De Martens, "Du rétablissement de la paix," 2:402; Guillaume-Hofnung, *La médiation*, 16.

99. Montholon to Drouyn de Lhuys, New York, January 17, 1863, CPCEU, 13:26.

100. Benjamin to Slidell, Richmond, December 11, 1862, ADPEU, 32:126–28.

101. With regard to this subject, Billaut implied to Slidell that recognition of his

government had been postponed as a result of Union forces taking New Orleans. Slidell to Benjamin, Paris, June 1, 1862, *ORN*, 428–29.

102. Mason to Benjamin, London, April 18, 1862, *ORN*, 397–99.

103. Cowley to Russell, Paris, April 13, 1862, in Adams, *Great Britain*, 1:289–92. Note that Slidell's memorandum recounting this interview does not mention these remarks. Slidell to Benjamin, Paris, April 14, 1862, *ORN*, 393–95.

104. Slidell to Benjamin, Paris, May 15, 1862, *ORN*, 419–20.

105. *Archives diplomatiques, 1863*, 1:273. See also Thouvenel to Mercier, Paris, May 15, 1862, CPEU, 127:151–52.

106. Slidell's memo, in Slidell to Benjamin, Paris, July 25, 1862, *ORN*, 481–87. Bigelow rightly notes that Napoléon III did not compromise himself or commit to anything. Bigelow, *France and the Confederate Navy*, 125.

107. Thouvenel was absent from July 9 to 16. Thouvenel to Gramont, Paris, July 8, 1862, and Thouvenel to his wife, London, July 10, 1862, in Thouvenel, *Le secret de l'Empereur*, 2:331–32, 333–34.

108. Thouvenel, *Le secret de l'Empereur*, 2:349. That is what David Paul Crook means when he asserts that the telegram Napoléon III sent Thouvenel would have changed history if it had arrived before Thouvenel left London. Crook, *Diplomacy*, 81.

109. Flahaut to Thouvenel, London, July 23, 1862, PT, 8:371v–72v.

110. Thouvenel to Flahaut, Paris, July 21, 1862, in Thouvenel, *Le secret de l'Empereur*, 2:338–40.

111. Flahaut to Thouvenel, London, July 23, 1862, PT, 8:371v–72v.

112. Mason to Russell, London, July 24, 1862, *ORN*, 500–501. James Murray Mason (1798–1871), former representative and senator from Virginia, was the Confederate envoy to the United Kingdom. During the Trent affair he was imprisoned by the Federal authorities for some time with his colleague Slidell. According to Slidell, the new military situation warranted a review of the opinion on the South's ability to prevail. Slidell to Thouvenel, Paris, July 21, 1862, ADPEU, 32:47v.

113. Slidell to Benjamin, Paris, July 25, 1862, *ORN*, 479–81.

114. There was no doubt that the motion would be rejected. Clement Duvernois, in *Le Temps* of July 19, 1862, expressed his doubts about the success of the Lindsay motion in Parliament.

115. Indeed, three months later, Slidell learned that Lord Cowley, the British ambassador to France, denied having ever been aware of emperor's views on the subject. Slidell to Benjamin, Paris, October 20, 1862, *ORN*, 560–61.

116. Slidell to Benjamin, London, August 2, 1862, *ORN*, 503–4.

117. Slidell to Benjamin, Paris, August 20, 1862, *ORN*, 518–20.

118. Thouvenel to Flahaut, Paris, August 20, 1862, in Thouvenel, *Le secret de l'Empereur*, 2:364.

119. Indiscretions revealed to the Southerners the considerable discord over recognition within the imperial cabinet. Slidell to Benjamin, Paris, August 12, 1862, *ORN*, 511–12.

120. Thouvenel to Mercier, Paris, September 11, 1862, in Thouvenel, *Le secret de l'Empereur*, 2:387–88.

121. For a detailed account, see Sainlaude, *Le gouvernement impérial*, 101–15.

122. Blackett, "African Americans," 76–77.

123. This was Seymour Vesey-Fitzgerald, a conservative friend of Mason's and MP for Horsham.

124. Roebuck to Lindsay, Paris, June 18, 1863, *ORN*, 814.

125. Slidell's memo, in Slidell to Benjamin, Paris, June 21, 1863, *ORN*, 812–14.

126. Slidell to Mason, Paris, June 29, 1863, in Sears, "A Confederate Diplomat," 272.

127. Persigny to Slidell, note of June 19, 1863, in Slidell to Benjamin, Paris, June 21, 1863, *ORN*, 811. The imperial cabinet met on Tuesdays and Thursdays. It was again Cintrat who gave Slidell this confidential information. Slidell to Benjamin, Paris, June 21, 1863, *ORN*, 810–11.

128. Slidell was not alone in thinking that Parliament would agree to recognition. Mason wrote that "at least four-fifths" of the members of the House of Commons were favorable toward the South. Mason to Benjamin, London, July 10, 1863, *ORN*, 837.

129. At the time, the French ambassador to London, Walewski, had informed his foreign minister — then Drouyn de Lhuys — of the actions of this character. Walewski to Drouyn de Lhuys, London, January 25, 1855, CPA, 699:121–22. The commission of inquiry indeed took place and Prime Minister Aberdeen had to resign.

130. Slidell to Benjamin, Paris, June 25, 1863, *ORN*, 820–21.

131. Cowley to Russell, Paris, July 2, 1863, in Case and Spencer, *The United States and France*, 413–15.

132. Note from Mocquard to Slidell, Fontainebleau, June 21, 1863, in Slidell to Benjamin, Paris, June 21, 1863, *ORN*, 812. On June 26, British ambassador to France, Lord Cowley, also informed Russell that Drouyn de Lhuys had instructed Gros. Cowley to Russell, Paris, June 26, 1863, in Case and Spencer, *The United States and France*, 417–18. Jean-François Mocquard knew the mother of the future emperor well. He became Bonaparte's confidant from the time of his election. Mocquard wrote Bonaparte's speeches and correspondence, prepared dossiers, and played a discrete part in covert schemes such as the coup. He remained Napoléon III's principal private secretary until his death in 1864.

133. Slidell to Benjamin, Paris, June 21, 1863, *ORN*, 811.

134. Cintrat confirmed to Slidell that Gros had been instructed to remind Palmerston of France's willingness to join Britain in recognizing the Confederates. Mason to Benjamin, London, July 2, 1863, *ORN*, 824–27. On June 29, 1863, Roebuck asked Gros if he had received such a dispatch. The ambassador remained vague and referred to an informal proposal. Mason to Benjamin, London, July 2, 1863, *ORN*, 824–27.

135. Hubbard, *The Burden*, 145.

136. Gros to Drouyn de Lhuys, London, July 1, 1863, CPA, 725:115v–17v.

137. Dayton to Seward, Paris, July 2, 1863, in Case and Spencer, *The United States and France*, 421.

138. Gros to Drouyn de Lhuys, London, July 1, 1863, CPA, 725:117v–18. Russia's harsh repression of the Polish insurrection beginning in January 1863 had been causing considerable concern among the public. Gros met Russell to discuss contingency measures to be taken should Russia not surrender to the friendly representations of France and England.

139. Owsley thought the telegram was probably sent to Gros on June 22, 1863. Spencer leaned more toward June 23, and in any case before June 26, when Cowley told Russell that Drouyn de Lhuys had instructed Gros. Owsley, *King Cotton Diplomacy*, 460–61; Case and Spencer, *The United States and France*, 417–18. Spencer qualified this judgment somewhat fifteen years later, when he wondered at Drouyn de Lhuys's passivity in sending this telegram. Spencer, "Recognition Question," 542.

140. Cowley to Russell, Paris, June 26 and July 7, 1863. "Cowley's Memorandum on

Correspondence Shown Him by Drouyn de Lhuys," dated July 14, 1863, enclosed with the dispatch from Cowley to Russell of the same day, in Case and Spencer, *The United States and France*, 417–18.

141. Drouyn de Lhuys to Gros (telegram), Paris, July 1, 1863, CPA, 725:114. Case mistranslated the start of the sentence as "You were to have spoken unofficially." Case and Spencer, *The United States and France*, 418. For his part, Owsley made a double mistake by writing, "You should have spoken officially." Owsley, *King Cotton Diplomacy*, 461. To cover himself, Drouyn de Lhuys went in for some trickery. He wrote at the top of his dispatch, "In accordance with my instructions of" but did not mention a date and took care to cross these words out, although they remain decipherable. Knowing that the text might be read, he showed in this manner that he had followed the emperor's instructions but deleted the phrase so that the telegraph operator would not transmit this false information and mislead his ambassador.

142. Gros to Drouyn de Lhuys, London, July 1, 1863, CPA, 725:115.

143. Drouyn de Lhuys to Mercier, Paris, July 8, 1863, CPEU, 130:147.

144. Slidell to Benjamin, Paris, July 6, 1863, *ORN*, 832–34.

145. Mason to Benjamin, London, July 10, 1863, *ORN*, 837–38.

146. In July 1860, for example, keeping Thouvenel in the dark, the emperor directly contacted Persigny, then posted in London, with a handwritten letter for the British government stating his sympathies for the Piedmont cause. Dethan, "La politique italienne d'Edouard Thouvenel," 269–73.

147. *Le Journal des Débats*, June 27, 1863. This article was based on the one in the *Times* (London).

148. E. Simon and H. Marie Martin, in *Le Constitutionnel*, July 2 and 3, 1863, in West, *Contemporary French Opinion*, 101–2.

149. L. Alloury and J. J. Weiss, in *Le Journal des Débats*, June 29, July 1 and 3, 1863.

150. L. Legault, in *Le Temps*, June 30, 1863. *Le Temps* was repeating the conclusions of *Le Mémorial Diplomatique* of June 29, 1863.

151. A. Nefftzer, in *Le Temps*, July 3 and 4, 1863.

152. *Le Moniteur*, July 5, 1863.

153. Gros to Drouyn de Lhuys, London, July 6, 1863, CPA, 725:135.

154. Gros to Drouyn de Lhuys, London, July 16, 1863, CPA, 725:183–84.

155. Gros to Drouyn de Lhuys, London, July 14, 1863, CPA, 725:178.

156. Gros to Drouyn de Lhuys, London, July 16, 1863, CPA, 725:183–84.

157. Paul to Drouyn de Lhuys, Richmond, August 24, 1863, CPCEU, 15:69v.

158. Seward to Dayton, Washington, July 8 and 10, 1863, in Van Deusen, *William Henry Seward*, 363–64; Seward to Dayton, Washington, July 29, 1863, ADPEU, 31:52.

159. Paul to Drouyn de Lhuys, Richmond, 1863, CPCEU, 15.

160. Drouyn de Lhuys to Mercier, Paris, September 13, 1863, LJEU, 1863, 123.

161. Dubois de Saligny to Thouvenel, Vera Cruz, February 16, 1862, CPM, 58:146. Dubois de Saligny was the French minister in Mexico.

162. Napoléon III was poorly informed. The emperor thought that Puebla was a small town of no importance, when in fact at that time it had 80,000 inhabitants, the population of a city like Lille at the start of the empire.

163. The "Pastry War" of 1838–39 was in fact in no way comparable to the 1862 action as it had no political objective and was limited to taking Vera Cruz. In the 1830s, French merchants living in Mexico, including a pastry chef named Remontel, whose shop in

Tacubaya was ruined, complained of looting and acts of violence. Having failed to obtain the slightest compensation, in 1838 Louis-Philippe's government sent a squadron to blockade the Mexican ports. The French troops landed at Vera Cruz. Mexico promised to pay the victims 600,000 pesos in damages, and the French forces withdrew the following year. However, this sum was never paid. The debt would serve, among other arguments, as justification for the French intervention in Mexico in 1861.

164. In a letter to General Forey, Napoléon III wrote from Fontainebleau on June 12, 1863, that news of the victory at Puebla had reached him "the day before yesterday," so June 10, 1863. Napoléon III to Forey, Fontainebleau, July 3, 1862, LJ-M, 1862, 191. Drouyn de Lhuys wrote to Dubois de Saligny on June 15, 1863: "Sir, by the time you receive this letter, our victorious armies will no doubt have entered Mexico City." CPM, 60:145.

165. Montholon to Drouyn de Lhuys, New York, June 16, 1863, CPCEU, 13:49v–50.

166. Slidell's memo, in Slidell to Benjamin, Paris, October 28, 1862, ORN, 574–78.

167. Slidell to Benjamin, Paris, January 11, 1863, ORN, 638–39.

168. Slidell to Benjamin, Paris, March 4, 1863, ORN, 705–7.

169. Noirsain, La flotte européenne, 51.

170. Spencer, The Confederate Navy, 148–49.

171. Slidell's memo, in Slidell to Benjamin, Paris, June 21, 1863, ORN, 810–14.

172. Noirsain, La flotte européenne, 158.

173. Clapp, Forgotten First Citizen, 232; Spencer, "Drouyn de Lhuys," 322–23.

174. Drouyn de Lhuys to Chasseloup-Laubat, Paris, September 25, 1863, PR, 8.

175. Chasseloup-Laubat to Drouyn de Lhuys, Paris, October 12, 1863, PR, 8.

176. Mercier to Drouyn de Lhuys, Washington, October 5, 1863, CPEU, 130:203–6v.

177. Drouyn de Lhuys to Mercier, Washington, October 20, 1863, CPEU, 130:217–18.

178. Drouyn de Lhuys to Dayton, Paris, October 22, 1863, PR, 8.

179. Drouyn de Lhuys to Fould, Paris, October 22, 1863, PR, 8; Fould to Drouyn de Lhuys, Paris, October 31, 1863, PR, 8.

180. Slidell to Benjamin, Paris, October 25, 1863, ORN, 937–39.

181. Drouyn de Lhuys to Mercier, Paris, November 9, 1863, CPEU, 130:223.

182. Spencer, "Drouyn de Lhuys," 328–30.

183. Noirsain, La flotte européenne, 160–61. Paul Boudet replaced Persigny in this office on March 23, 1863.

184. Spencer, "Drouyn de Lhuys," 334.

185. Spencer, The Confederate Navy, 172.

186. On the question of ships built in France and denounced by the United States as intended for sale to the Confederates, see file ADP, no. 53.

187. Drouyn de Lhuys's opposition is also the explanation James D. Bulloch gives for the failure. Bulloch, The Secret Service, 287–88.

188. Spencer, "Drouyn de Lhuys," 314–41, 330.

189. On the Sphinx, see file ADP, no. 54.

190. Bigelow, France and the Confederate Navy, 194.

191. On this question, see ADP, no. 49.

192. This was the same Kearsarge that would inflict heavy damage on the Alabama off the coast of Cherbourg in June 1864.

193. This led Paris to forbid belligerents from weighing anchor more than twice a month in the same port. Noirsain, La flotte européenne, 164–67.

194. On the Georgia and the Rappahannock, see ADP files, nos. 50 and 51; La Dépêche de

Washington, Direction Politique, no. 3, Washington, January 25, 1864, CPEU, 131:23; Merli, *Great Britain*, 131.

195. Note from Foreign Affairs to the Ministry of the Navy, Paris, December 19, 1863; PR, 8.

196. Drouyn de Lhuys to Dayton, Paris, February 4, 1864, PR, 8.

197. Drouyn de Lhuys to Chasseloup-Laubat, Paris, February 4, 1864, PR, 8.

198. Chasseloup-Laubat to Drouyn de Lhuys, Paris, February 5, 1864, PR, 8.

199. Chasseloup-Laubat to Drouyn de Lhuys, Paris, February 17, 1864, PR, 8; Drouyn de Lhuys to Chasseloup-Laubat, Paris, February 19, 1864, PR, 8.

200. Slidell to Drouyn de Lhuys, Paris, February 26, 1864, PR, 8. He spoke of forty men in all, including twenty-five stokers and mechanics. The remaining fifteen was the normal crew required to handle a steamer.

201. Drouyn de Lhuys to Treilhard, Paris, February 27, 1864, CPEU, 131:37. In 1857, Vicomte Jules Etienne Joseph Treilhard (1824–82) became the first secretary of the legation in Washington, where he remained for three years before getting married to the daughter of a New York businessman. In 1862, still secretary, he returned to Washington and remained in the position for more than a year before being replaced by Geofroy after Mercier's departure. In 1870, he represented France in the United States as plenipotentiary minister. Papiers du Personnel, 1st ser., no. 3972.

202. Slidell to Drouyn de Lhuys, Paris, March 14, 1864, PR, 8.

203. Slidell's memo to Mocquard, Paris, March 15, 1864, *ORN*, 1055–56.

204. Slidell to Benjamin, Paris, May 21, 1864, *ORN*, 1118–20.

205. Noirsain, *La flotte européenne*, 178.

206. Slidell to Benjamin, Paris, July 11, 1864, *ORN*, 1169–71.

207. Noirsain, *La flotte européenne*, 178.

208. Ibid.

209. Slidell to Benjamin, Paris, August 1, 1864, *ORN*, 1181–83.

210. Drouyn de Lhuys to Chasseloup-Laubat, Paris, February 4, 1864, PR, 8.

211. Drouyn de Lhuys to Dayton, Paris, February 4, 1864, PR, 8; Drouyn de Lhuys to Treilhard, Paris, February 27, 1864, CPEU, 131:37.

212. Treilhard to Drouyn de Lhuys, Washington, March 13, 1864, CPEU, 131:44.

213. Merli, *Great Britain*, 225–26.

214. Bowen, *Spain and the American Civil War*, 2.

CHAPTER 3

1. In 1970, Lynn Case and Warren Spencer judged that the main explanation for the South's disappointment lay in the alliance between France and Great Britain. Case and Spencer, *The United States and France*, 5, 335.

2. Muhammad Ali, the ruler of Egypt backed by France, sought to free himself of the authority of his suzerain, the Ottoman caliph. Great Britain feared that this emancipation would provoke a crisis within the Ottoman Empire. The London Convention of July 15, 1840, and an Anglo-Turkish military intervention constrained Muhammad Ali's ambitions. For a time, the Egyptian dispute led to speculation that war might erupt between London and Paris.

3. Droz, *Histoire diplomatique*, 320–40. France and England were divided over which husbands should be given to Queen Isabella II of Spain and her younger sister. In the end,

France won out. The queen married her cousin, and the infanta married Louis-Philippe's youngest son. The announcement of these marriages caused a crisis between Paris and London.

4. Smith, "Angleterre," 63.

5. Theis, "Entre besoin de repos et désir de gloire," 583.

6. Médard, "La visite d'Etat de Victoria en août 1855," 14.

7. D'Arjuzon, "Napoléon III et l'Angleterre," 408.

8. Soutou, "L'Europe de Napoléon III," 367–68.

9. Smith, "Angleterre," 64. On January 14, 1858, as the emperor was on his way to the opera on rue Le Peletier, the Italian patriot Felice Orsini and his accomplices threw three bombs at the imperial procession. The attack killed twelve people. The emperor and his wife were unharmed.

10. Brown, "Palmerston," 683.

11. Poirson, *Walewski*, 191–95.

12. Bernardy, *Walewski*, 181.

13. Tombs and Tombs, *La France et le Royaume-Uni*, 64.

14. Walewski to Sartiges, Paris, April 30, 1857, CPEU, 116:167.

15. Sartiges to Walewski, Washington, November 21, 1857, CPEU, 117:191v.

16. Flahaut to Thouvenel, London, February 5, 1861, PT, 8:152–v.

17. Thouvenel to Flahaut, Paris, July 6, 1861, CPA, 720:63.

18. Mercier to Thouvenel, Washington, April 15, 1861, CPEU, 124:157.

19. Thouvenel to Flahaut, Paris, April 17, 1861, CPA, 719:280.

20. Flahaut to Thouvenel, London, April 19, 1861, PT, 8:112–v, and CPA, 719:305–6.

21. Flahaut to Thouvenel, London, May 13, 1861, PT, 8:140; Thouvenel to Mercier, Paris, May 16, 1861, CPEU, 124:218.

22. Thouvenel to Flahaut, Paris, June 5, 1861, CPA, 720:7.

23. Flahaut to Thouvenel (telegram), London, June 5, 1861, CPA, 720:18.

24. Flahaut to Thouvenel (telegram), London, July 9, 1861, CPA, 720:79–v.

25. Thouvenel to Flahaut, Paris, August 19, 1861, in Thouvenel, *Le secret de l'Empereur*, 2:159–60.

26. Slidell's memo, in Slidell to Benjamin, Paris, April 14, 1862, *ORN*, 393–95.

27. Thouvenel to Flahaut, Paris, April 14, 1862, CPA, 721:132v–33; Thouvenel to Flahaut, Paris, May 2, 1862, in Thouvenel, *Le secret de l'Empereur*, 2:299.

28. Slidell to Benjamin, Paris, June 1, 1862, *ORN*, 428–29.

29. Slidell's memo, in Slidell to Benjamin, Paris, June 21, 1863, *ORN*, 812–14.

30. Thouvenel to Dayton, Paris, July 20, 1861, ADPEU, 44:26; Thouvenel to Flahaut, Paris, August 19, 1861, ADPEU, 44:59. Sainlaude, *Le gouvernement impérial*, 29–32.

31. Sainlaude, *Le gouvernement impérial*, 61–68.

32. Jones, *Blue and Gray Diplomacy*, 215–16.

33. Brauer, "British Mediation," 49.

34. Jenkins, *Britain*, 2:167.

35. Jones, *Union in Peril*, 163; Adams, *Great Britain*, 2:38.

36. Brauer, "British Mediation," 55; Foreman, *A World on Fire*, 291.

37. Jones, *Union in Peril*, 177. Adams, *Great Britain*, 2:43–45.

38. Brauer, "British Mediation," 58.

39. Crook, *The North, the South*, 224.

40. Thouvenel to Mercier, Paris, October 2, 1862, in Thouvenel, *Le secret de l'Empereur*, 2:414–16.

41. La Tour d'Auvergne to Drouyn de Lhuys, London, April 24, 1865, CPA, 732:239v; note for the minister, Paris, November 1866, ADPEU, 48:71–v.

42. Bulloch, *The Secret Service*, 286. On this issue, see also Celozzi Baldelli, "The Decisions of the Arbitration Commissions," 261–344. The arbitral tribunal met on March 8, 1872, and declared admissible U.S. claims against Britain for building Confederate ships in its shipyards that went on to cause heavy losses among the North's merchant ships.

43. Merli, *Great Britain*, 95.

44. Thistlethwaite, *The Anglo-American Connection*, 97.

45. Slidell's memo, in Slidell to Benjamin, Paris, July 25, 1862, *ORN*, 481–87. Seward also used this reasoning with Mercier: Mercier to Thouvenel, Washington, June 4, 1861, CPEU, 124:294.

46. Thouvenel to Flahaut, Paris, July 21, 1862, in Thouvenel, *Le secret de l'Empereur*, 2:339–40.

47. Prévost-Paradol, in *Le Journal des Débats*, December 7, 1861, and July 5, 1863.

48. *Le Journal des Débats*, August 27, 1862.

49. *RDDM*, 1862 (5/6), 497.

50. Bernardy, *Flahaut*, 333.

51. D'Arjuzon, "Napoléon III et l'Angleterre," 408.

52. Lesueur, *Le Prince de La Tour d'Auvergne*, 178.

53. Mercier to Thouvenel, Niagara, September 9, 1861, PT, 13:385v.

54. Flahaut to Thouvenel, London, April 30, 1862, PT, 8:337.

55. Gros to Drouyn de Lhuys, London, May 24, 1863, CPA, 724:213–v.

56. Jenkins, *Lord Lyons*, 165.

57. Ashley, *The Life and Correspondence of Henry John Temple*, 2:386.

58. Brown, "Palmerston," 683.

59. Thouvenel to Flahaut, Paris, April 23, 1861, in Thouvenel, *Le secret de l'Empereur*, 2:72.

60. Ibid., 2:71–72.

61. Thouvenel to Flahaut, Paris, August 19, 1861, in Thouvenel, *Le secret de l'Empereur*, 2:159–60.

62. De Viel Castel, *Memoires*, 874.

63. Thouvenel to Chateaurenard, Paris, August 26, 1862, in Thouvenel, *Le secret de l'Empereur*, 2:370.

64. Girard, *Napoléon III*, 251.

65. For a more comprehensive account, see Sainlaude, *Le gouvernement impérial*, 61–67.

66. Thouvenel to Mercier, Paris, December 3, 1861, CPEU, 125:241; A. Hébrard, in *Le Temps*, November 28 and 29 and December 1 and 4, 1861; L. Alloury and X. Raymond, in *Le Journal des Débats*, December 1, 3, and 27, 1861; *RDDM*, 1862 (1/2), 421–43; F. Gaillardet and Limayrac, in *Le Constitutionnel*, November 29 and 30 and December 2, 1861; Chantrel, in *Le Monde*, November 30, 1861; A. Esparbié, in *La Patrie*, December 1, 1861; A. Lomon, in *A. Esparbié. Le Pays*, December 6, 1861, in West, *Contemporary French Opinion*, 41–44; Gavronsky, *The French Liberal Opposition*, 101–15; Blackburn, *French Newspaper Opinion*, 46–47.

67. Ferris, *The Trent Affair*, 29; Jones, *Blue and Gray Diplomacy*, 102.

68. Thouvenel to Mercier, Paris, November 28, 1861, CPEU, 9:114; Thouvenel to Mercier, Paris, December 3, 1861, CPEU, 125:241–44v; LJEU, 1861, 99–102; Thouvenel, *Le secret de l'Empereur*, 2:197–200; Thouvenel to Flahaut, Paris, December 4, 1861, CPA, 720:362–v; Thouvenel to Montholon, Paris, December 5, 1861, CPCEU, 8:178v–79v.

69. Ferris, *The Trent Affair*, 80.

70. Flahaut to Thouvenel, London, December 6, 1861, CPA, 720:366–v.

71. Mercier to Thouvenel, Washington, December 23, 1861, CPEU, 125:309.

72. Case, "La France et l'affaire du Trent," 72–73.

73. Case and Spencer, *The United States and France*, 222.

74. Flahaut to Thouvenel, London, January 11, 1862, CPA, 721:6–9; Flahaut to Thouvenel, London, January 9, 1862, PT, 8:266–67v; Flahaut to Thouvenel, London, January 11, 1862, LJEU, 1861, 105, and PT, 8:269.

75. Mercier wrote, "We have singularly facilitated a retreat that had become necessary." Mercier to Thouvenel, Washington, December 29 and 30, 1861, PT, 13:419, 420v. See also Souchard to Thouvenel, Boston, January 2, 1862, CPCEU, 12:147–v. Jules Etienne Souchard (1818–84) was a first cousin of Rouher. A year after he married an American woman from Boston, in 1856, he was appointed consul there. Boston was his only diplomatic post, which he held until 1867. Ironically, he spoke very bad English. Then ailing, he requested and was granted sick leave. Since his poor health did not allow him to resume his consular duties, he retired in 1869 and received the cross of the Légion d'Honneur. Papiers du Personnel, 1st ser., no. 3793.

76. Sainlaude, *Le gouvernement impérial*, 66.

77. Thouvenel to Flahaut, Paris, December 26, 1861, in Thouvenel, *Le secret de l'Empereur*, 2:215–16.

78. Slidell's memo, in Slidell to Benjamin, Paris, July 25, 1862, *ORN*, 481–87.

79. Slidell's memo, in Slidell to Benjamin, Paris, October 28, 1862, *ORN*, 574–78.

80. Gros to Drouyn de Lhuys (telegram), London, July 3, 1863, CPA, 725:131.

81. Drouyn de Lhuys to Gros, Paris, July 6, 1863, CPA, 725:133–v; Drouyn de Lhuys to Gros, Paris, July 8, 1863, CPA, 725:144–48. See also *Le Temps*, July 2, 1863.

82. Gros to Drouyn de Lhuys, London, July 3, 1863, CPA, 725:131.

83. To take just one example, volume 720 of political correspondence with England, though it covers a key period of the Civil War as it includes relations from the spring to the end of 1861, begins with Italian affairs and the death of the sultan.

84. Thouvenel to Flahaut, Paris, February 21 and March 11, 1861, in Thouvenel, *Le secret de l'Empereur*, 1:441–42, 485.

85. Thouvenel to Persigny, Paris, March 1, 1860, CPA, 715:214.

86. Russell to Cowley, London, October 31, 1862, CPA, 722:147–v; Gros to Drouyn de Lhuys, London, May 24, 1863, CPA, 724:213v.

87. Thouvenel to Flahaut, Paris, February 21, 1861, May 27, 1862, in Thouvenel, *Le secret de l'Empereur*, 2:35–36, 306–7.

88. Russell to Cowley, London, February 1860, and Persigny to Thouvenel, London, February 3, 1860, CPA, 715:68, 117–19.

89. Eichhorn, "The Rhine River," 149.

90. For example, Gros to Drouyn de Lhuys, London, April 9, 1863, CPA, 724:27.

91. Chassaigne, *La Grande-Bretagne et le monde*, 33.

92. In January 1863 the Poles rose up in opposition to their conscription into the Russian army.

93. Smith, *Napoléon III*, 270.

94. Drouyn de Lhuys to Gros, Paris, April 11, 1863, CPA, 724:29.

95. Drouyn de Lhuys to Napoléon III, Paris, June 21, 1864, CPA, 730:176, coded; Theis, "Entre besoin de repos et désir de gloire," 604.

96. Cunningham, *Mexico*, 48; Flahaut to Thouvenel, London, September 29, 1861, PT, 8:180v.

97. Gouttman, *La guerre du Mexique*, 93–95.

98. Knight, "La pérfida Albión," 266.

99. Thouvenel to Flahaut, Paris, March 21, 1862, in Thouvenel, *Le secret de l'Empereur*, 2:259–60, 266.

100. Thouvenel to Flahaut, Paris, June 12, 1862, CPA, 721:246.

101. Gros to Drouyn de Lhuys, London, April 22, 1863, CPA, 724:72–76.

102. La Tour d'Auvergne to Drouyn de Lhuys, London, March 14, 1864, CPA, 728:351; La Tour d'Auvergne to Drouyn de Lhuys, London, August 8, 1864, CPA, 731:13v.

103. Ferris, *Desperate Diplomacy*, 22.

104. Thouvenel to Mercier, Paris, June 6, 1861, CPEU, 124:301.

105. Mercier to Thouvenel, Washington, June 18, 1861, CPEU, 124:339–44v.

106. Souchard to Thouvenel, Boston, June 29, 1861, CPCEU, 9:305v–6.

107. Flahaut to Thouvenel, London, July 9, 1861, CPA, 720:80.

108. Flahaut to Thouvenel, London, August 6, 1861, PT, 8:176.

109. Slidell's memo, in Slidell to Benjamin, Paris, July 25, 1862, ORN, 481–87.

110. Confidential note by Slidell, Paris, July–August 1862, ADPEU, 32:91.

111. Russell to Grey, London, October 10, 1863, ADPEU, 45:117.

112. Slidell to Benjamin, Paris, October 25, 1863, ORN, 937–39.

113. Drouyn de Lhuys to Barrot, Paris, November 10, 1863, ADPEU, 45:127–31.

114. Slidell's memo, in Slidell to Benjamin, Paris, July 25, 1862, ORN, 481–87.

CHAPTER 4

1. Slidell to Benjamin, Paris, June 1, 1862, ORN, 428–29.

2. Napoléon III made no secret of the affinity he felt toward Slidell. Slidell to Benjamin, Biarritz, September 22, 1863, ORN, 905–7; Niboyet to Thouvenel, New York, June 11, 1861, CPCEU, 8:31. Paulin Jean Alexandre Niboyet (1825–1906) was vice-consul. After retiring in 1880, he devoted himself to writing.

3. Paul to Drouyn de Lhuys, Richmond, December 19, 1862, CPCEU, 12:136–40v.

4. Paul to Drouyn de Lhuys, Richmond, January 15, 1863, CPCEU, 15:20, and *Archives diplomatiques, 1863*, 1:404.

5. Slidell to Benjamin, Biarritz, September 22, 1863, ORN, 905–7.

6. Evans, *Memoirs of Dr. Thomas W. Evans*, 118.

7. Slidell to Benjamin, Paris, June 1, 1862, ORN, 428–29.

8. Slidell to Benjamin, Paris, August 20, 1862, ORN, 518–20. Note concerning the interviews with Thouvenel, Persigny Baroche, and Fould in Slidell to Benjamin, Paris, February 11, 1862, ORN, 339–41; Slidell to Benjamin, Paris, July 11, 1864, ORN, 1169–70; Slidell to Benjamin, Paris, March 10, 1862, ORN, 356.

9. Willson, *America's Ambassadors to France*, 259. This is significant because participants had to get through a draconian selection process. Six hundred people were at each ball but 3,000 to 4,000 invitations were sent. Girard, *Napoléon III*, 203.

10. McCullough, *The Greater Journey*, 244.

11. Doyle, *The Cause of All Nations*, 200. This remains to be confirmed. Doyle expressed doubts over the truth of this anecdote recounted by Beckles Willson.

12. West, *Contemporary French Opinion*, 108.

13. Guiral, "Prévost-Paradol," 296–97. Charles Forbes, comte de Montalembert (1810–70), was a liberal Catholic. Until his last-minute conversion in 1870, Antoine Prévost-Paradol (1829–70) was one of the most brilliant liberal opponents of the empire. At the time of the Civil War, he was writing for *Le Journal des Débats*.

14. Slidell to Benjamin, Paris, January 25, 1864, *ORN*, 1011–12. Carroll was less affirmative. Carroll, *Henri Mercier*, 356–59.

15. Carroll, *Henri Mercier*, xv.

16. Mercier to Thouvenel, Washington, February 25, 1861, CPEU, 124:78; Mercier to Thouvenel, Washington, March 17, 1861, CPEU, 124:105. Note that even keen partisans of the North, such as Prince Napoléon, painted an unflattering portrait of Seward and Lincoln. The former seemed to Prince Napoléon like "a little old man with the air of a badly brought up schoolmaster, vain and smug, very messily attired"; the latter like "an expedient president, with the air of a bootmaker, poorly turned out, a man without elevation or much knowledge," "a sad specimen." "What a difference between this sad representative of the great republic and its first founders!" D'Hauterive, "Le prince Napoléon," 256–58. Prince Napoléon met them in July 1861.

17. Summary of a letter from a correspondent of Mercier's, Paris, May 28, 1861, ADPEU, 30:25v.

18. "I think, Sir, that you must be a little wary of my impulses." Mercier to Thouvenel, Washington, February 24, 1862, PT, 13:431–v.

19. Thouvenel to Mercier, Paris, July 24, 1862, in Thouvenel, *Le secret de l'Empereur*, 350.

20. Dunning, "The French Consuls in the Confederate States," 84.

21. Lanen to Drouyn de Lhuys, Charleston, December 25, 1863, CCC Charleston, 7:324v.

22. "A French Count," *New York Times*, December 16, 1862.

23. Thouvenel to Méjan, Paris, July 13 and 18, 1861, CPCEU, 9:81–82.

24. Parton, *General Butler in New Orleans*, 377–81.

25. Burnett, *Henry Hotze*, 16.

26. Cullop, *Confederate Propaganda in Europe*, 27–29.

27. De Leon, *Secret History*, xii–xvii.

28. Nacouzi, "Les créoles louisianais défendant la cause du Sud à Paris."

29. Slidell's memo, in Slidell to Benjamin, Paris, July 25, 1862, *ORN*, 481–87.

30. Balace, *La Belgique*, 1:200.

31. Mercier to Thouvenel, Washington, November 26, 1860, CPEU, 123:377.

32. Slidell's memo, in Slidell to Benjamin, Paris, July 25, 1862, *ORN*, 481–87.

33. Gaillardet, in *La Presse*, February 25, 1861, in Blackburn, *French Newspaper Opinion*, 32; Gaillardet, in *Le Constitutionnel*, November 12, 1861, in Gavronsky, *The French Liberal Opposition*, 78.

34. *Le Constitutionnel*, December 13, 1861. *La Patrie*, January 12, 1864, in Roger, *L'ennemi américain*, 127.

35. Mercier, *Du Panlatinisme*, 31.

36. Méjan to Thouvenel, New Orleans, April 11, 1861, CPCEU, 9:53.

37. Paul to Thouvenel, Richmond, October 10, 1862, CPCEU, 12:129v–31; Paul to

Drouyn de Lhuys, Richmond, January 4, 1863, CPCEU, 15:11. Note that Paul disapproved of the North's use of force to subdue its opponent but had no sympathy for the states in revolt.

38. Montholon to Thouvenel, New York, May 12, 1862, CPCEU, 10:75v; Du Bellet, *Lettre au corps législatif*, 4. Mercier, *Du Panlatinisme*, 11.

39. In 1862, Méjan came into conflict General Butler. Butler's abuses led to his recall, but the general complained of Méjan's conduct to his government. Seward threatened to revoke his exequatur. In January 1863, France's minister in Washington, Henri Mercier, negotiated Méjan's departure and granted him a leave of absence. Papiers du Personnel, 1st ser., no. 2830.

40. Mercier to Thouvenel, Washington, April 26, 1861, CPEU, 124:164–75.

41. Mercier to Thouvenel, Washington, May 12, 1861, CPEU, 124:210. Analysis of a book of statistics passed on by Mercier, 1861–62, ADPEU, 30:2–13.

42. Méjan to Thouvenel, New Orleans, February 20, 1861, CCC New Orleans, 13:286.

43. Analysis of a book of statistics passed on by Mercier, 1861–62, ADPEU, 30:2–13.

44. E. Bellot des Minières, "Lettres sur la question américaine," Paris, May 7, 1861, MDEU, 25:193v–94; Fohlen, "La guerre de Sécession," 259–70, 266.

45. Mercier to Thouvenel, Washington, November 26, 1860, CPEU, 123:377.

46. Méjan to Thouvenel, New Orleans, January 9, 1861, CCC New Orleans, 13:261–62v; Méjan to Thouvenel, New Orleans, February 12, 1861, CPCEU, 9:23v–24v. See also A. de Lauzières, in *Le Pays*, February 28, 1861, in West, *Contemporary French Opinion*, 33.

47. Paul to Thouvenel, Richmond, May 30, 1862, CPCEU, 12:97v–98.

48. Slidell to Thouvenel, Paris, July 21, 1862, ADPEU, 32:56.

49. Méjan to Thouvenel, New Orleans, January 9, 1861, CCC New Orleans, 13:261–62v.

50. Analysis of a book of statistics passed on by Mercier, 1861–62, ADPEU, 30:2–13.

51. Méjan to Thouvenel, New Orleans, January 12, 1861, CPCEU, 9:8.

52. Mercier to Thouvenel, Washington, December 31, 1860, CPEU, 123:414–16.

53. Méjan to Thouvenel, New Orleans, April 29, 1861, CPCEU, 9:64v.

54. Sain de Boislecomte, *De la crise américaine*, 15. André Ernest Olivier Sain de Boislecomte (1799–1882) came from a family of diplomats. In 1849, de Tocqueville, who was then minister of Foreign Affairs, appointed Sain de Boislecomte minister plenipotentiary in Washington to settle a dispute between France and the United States known as the "Poussin affair." He did not please. After Bonaparte's coup d'état, he remained loyal to the Republic, which ended his short-lived diplomatic career. However, he was a friend of Drouyn de Lhuys. He wrote his book about the Civil War in 1862. Papiers du Personnel, 1st ser., no. 3667.

55. Edouard Gaulhiac, in *Le Constitutionnel*, May 7 and 16, 1861; F. Gaillardet, in *Le Constitutionnel*, May 19, 1861, in West, *Contemporary French Opinion*, 28–29.

56. *La Patrie*, 1863. Delamarre, the newspaper's owner, claimed that Napoléon III had endorsed this article. See Roger, *L'ennemi américain*, 125.

57. Edouard Gaulhiac, in *Le Constitutionnel*, May 16, 1861, in West, *Contemporary French Opinion*, 29; Paul Becquet du Bellet, in *Le Pays*, September 11 and 17, 1862, in Blackburn, *French Newspaper Opinion*, 95–96.

58. Baudrillart, in *Le Journal des Débats*, June 3, 1861; Jules Grenier, in *Le Temps*, July 18, 1861.

59. Baudrillart, in *Le Journal des Débats*, June 3, 1861; F. Camus, in *Le Journal des Débats*, April 24, 1862.

60. F. Camus, in *Le Journal des Débats*, June 24, 1861.

61. Lomon, in *Le Pays*, August 27, 1862; Melvil, in *Le Pays*, January 9, 1863; Galland, in *La Patrie*, May 9, 1865, in Blackburn, *French Newspaper Opinion*, 63, 74, 112.

62. Coquille, in *Le Monde*, September 1, 1861, in Blackburn, *French Newspaper Opinion*, 36.

63. De Leon, *La vérité*, 5–6.

64. Slidell to Thouvenel, Paris, July 21, 1862, ADPEU, 32:47v.

65. Doyle, "Slavery or Independence," 110.

66. De Tocqueville, *De la démocratie en Amérique*, 1:495.

67. Grant, *The War for a Nation*, 115.

68. Slidell's memo, in Slidell to Benjamin, Paris, July 25, 1862, *ORN*, 481–87.

69. Mercier to Thouvenel, Washington, April 28, 1862, CPEU, 127:50–78.

70. Gaillardet, in *La Presse*, February 25, 1861, in Blackburn, *French Newspaper Opinion*, 32; Gaillardet, in *Le Constitutionnel*, November 19, 1861; Louis Bellet, in *La Patrie*, June 15, 1861, in West, *Contemporary French Opinion*, 29, 37–38.

71. Slidell's memo, in Slidell to Benjamin, Paris, June 21, 1863, *ORN*, 812–14.

72. Guiral, "Prévost-Paradol," 296–97.

73. The working class is thought to have sided with the South. Sancton, "The Myth of French Worker Support," 58–80. But ultimately, apart from workers in the textile and wine-growing industries, few felt the effects of the crisis.

74. Case and Spencer, *The United States and France*, 43.

75. See Sainlaude, *La France et la Confédération sudiste*, 79.

76. Thouvenel, *Le secret de l'Empereur*, 2:339.

77. Slidell to Benjamin, Paris, October 20, 1862, *ORN*, 560–61.

78. Thouvenel, *Le secret de l'Empereur*, 449.

79. Price, *The French Second Empire*, 408; Darimon, *L'opposition libérale sous l'Empire*, 281.

80. Slidell to Benjamin, Paris, March 4, 1863, *ORN*, 705–7.

81. D'Hauterive, "Le prince Napoléon," 243, 251.

82. E. Mangin, in *Le Phare de la Loire*, November 26, 1864, in West, *Contemporary French Opinion*, 109, 112.

83. Charle, *Le siècle de la presse*, 95.

84. Giving it the largest circulation in the Parisian press. Ibid., 96.

85. Joseph Sablé, "Centre d'études du 19e siècle français / Centre for 19th Century French Studies" (2001), http://sites.utoronto.ca/sable/.

86. Blackburn, *French Newspaper Opinion*, 9; Feyel, *La presse en France*, 118.

87. Benjamin to Hotze, Richmond, January 9, 1864, in West, *Contemporary French Opinion*, 109–10.

88. Doyle, *The Cause of All Nations*, 140.

89. Saint-André to Thouvenel, Charleston, March 23, 1862, CPCEU, 11:33. The baron Maurice Durant Saint André (1823–75) was the son of a former French consul of New York. In 1861 he was appointed consul in Charleston, where he replaced Belligny. It was to be his last post as a diplomat. In 1863 he left his post and returned to France without authorization from the ministry, claiming as the reason his concern for his family's safety. In fact, he chose to come back to France and gave up diplomacy to work in the finance administration department. Sim, *La présence diplomatique et consulaire française aux Etats-Unis*, 164.

90. Paul to Thouvenel, Richmond, April 3, 1862, CPCEU, 12:48v.

91. Paul to Thouvenel, Richmond, September 14, 1861, CPCEU, 9:243v–44.

92. Mercier to Thouvenel, New York, September 29, 1861, PT, 13:408–v.

93. We must not forget the role of tobacco in French imports. Until the Civil War, U.S. tobacco accounted for almost 75 percent of total consumption in France. Blumenthal, *A Reappraisal*, 104.

94. Souchard to Thouvenel, Boston, May 13, 1862, CPCEU, 12:189–v; Fauconnet to Drouyn de Lhuys, New Orleans, September 4, 1863, CPCEU, 14:268v–69. Charles Prosper Fauconnet (1818–89) was assigned to the United States for the first time in 1849 as chancellor of the Charleston consulate. He became chancellor of the New Orleans consulate in 1860. He assisted Méjan in softening relations with the authorities. He was appointed vice-consul in Galveston in 1866 and returned to New Orleans in 1868. He remained in the United States for more than twenty years. He did not obtain the rank of consul until 1877. Papiers du Personnel, 1st ser., no. 1566. Brasseaux, *Ruined by This Miserable War*, xi.

95. Paul to Thouvenel, Richmond, May 14, 1862, CPCEU, 12:78v–80.

96. Souchard to Thouvenel, Boston, June 29, 1861, CPCEU, 9:303–v.

97. Bodelle, *Petite(s) histoire(s) des Français d'Amérique*, 304.

98. Thouvenel to Niboyet, Paris, June 4, 1861, CPCEU, 8:38v–39v.

99. Noirsain, *La Nouvelle-Orléans française*, 90; Méjan to Thouvenel, New Orleans, October 4, 1861, CPCEU, 9:94v–95. When in April 1862, having heard of the Federals' arrival, rioters swept through New Orleans, looting, these militias were called in by the mayor and helped secure the city. Bodelle, *Petite(s) histoire(s) des Français d'Amérique*, 305.

100. Méjan to Mercier, New Orleans, February 24, 1862, CPC New Orleans, 11:196.

101. Paul to Thouvenel, Richmond, March 23, 1862, CPCEU, 12:25–27v.

102. Paul to Drouyn de Lhuys, Richmond, February 8, 1863, CPC Richmond, 15:28.

103. Lanen to Drouyn de Lhuys, Charleston, October 5, 1863, CPCEU, 14:79–80.

104. Lanen to Drouyn de Lhuys, Charleston, November 16, 1863, CPCEU, 14:103–5v.

105. Lanen to Drouyn de Lhuys, Charleston, August 9, 1864, CPCEU, 18:286–89v.

106. Lanen to Drouyn de Lhuys, Charleston, August 13, 1864, CPCEU, 18:291–92.

107. Thouvenel to Méjan, Paris, April 3, 1862, CPCEU, 11:216–17; Drouyn de Lhuys to Lanen, Paris, September 9, 1864, CPCEU, 18:308–v.

108. Sartiges to Drouyn de Lhuys, Washington, April 8, 1855, PS, 8.

109. Sartiges to Drouyn de Lhuys, Washington, April 8, 1855, PS, 8; Vaillant to Drouyn de Lhuys, Paris, May 3, 1855, ADPEU, 27.

110. Paul to Thouvenel, Richmond, December 19, 1861, CPCEU, 9:291–v.

111. Paul to Drouyn de Lhuys, Richmond, December 23, 1863, CPCEU, 15:87v–88.

112. Lanen to Drouyn de Lhuys, Charleston, October 19, 1863, CPCEU, 14:88.

113. Taylor, *William Henry Seward*, 47; Stuart, *The Department of State*, 129; Van Deusen, *William Henry Seward*, 231; D'Hauterive, "Le prince Napoléon," 256; Hubbard, *The Burden*, 52–53.

114. Scroggins, *Robert Toombs*, 131; Plischke, *U.S. Department of State*, 114.

115. Doyle, *The Cause of All Nations*, 188.

116. Bunch to Russell, Charleston, March 19, 1862, ADPEU, 30:122; Paul to Thouvenel, Richmond, March 23, 1862, CPCEU, 12:26v.

117. Drouyn de Lhuys to Paul, Paris, November 9, 1864, CPCEU, 19:242–v.

118. Lauzac, "Son excellence M. C.-J. Faulkner," 11, 14.

119. Dayton to Thouvenel, Paris, August 13, 1861, ADPEU, 30:63–69v.

120. Méjan to Thouvenel, New Orleans, March 6, 1861, CPCEU, 9:39.

121. Hubbard, *The Burden*, 32.

122. U.S. Army Command, *Diplomats at War*, 23.

123. Meade, "Judah P. Benjamin," 17.

124. Méjan to Thouvenel, New Orleans, February 12, 1861, CPCEU, 9:25v.

125. Thouvenel to Mercier, Paris, July 24, 1862, in Thouvenel, *Le secret de l'Empereur*, 2:247, 349.

126. De Leon, *Secret History*, 96.

127. Sartiges to Thouvenel, The Hague, October 28, 1861, PT, 17:246–47v.

128. Mercier to Thouvenel, New York, September 29, 1861, PT, 13:408.

129. Sears, "A Confederate Diplomat," 256, 263.

130. Dayton to Seward, Paris, March 6, 1863, in Case and Spencer, *The United States and France*, 402.

131. U.S. Army Command, *Diplomats at War*, 105.

132. The Confederate state secretary's office also had a limited budget and struggled to pay its agents abroad. It did not have its space and was housed on the same floor as the offices of the president. Hubbard, *The Burden*, 104–5; Blumenthal, "Confederate Diplomacy," 151.

133. Donald, "Died of Democracy," 79–90.

134. Paul to Walewski, Richmond, December 4, 1859, CPCEU, 7:106–11.

135. *Archives diplomatiques, 1863*, 1:422; Paul to Thouvenel, Richmond, February 27, 1862, CPCEU, 12:17.

136. Karp, *This Vast Southern Empire*, 244.

137. Paul to Drouyn de Lhuys, Richmond, January 15, 1864, CPCEU, 19:174v–75; Paul to Drouyn de Lhuys, Richmond, January 28, 1865, CPCEU, 23:131.

138. Paul to Drouyn de Lhuys, New York, November 18, 1864, CPCEU, 19:247–48.

139. Martin, in *Le Constitutionnel*, January 10, 1861, in Blackburn, *French Newspaper Opinion*, 37; RDDM, 1861 (11/12), 152; RDDM, 1863 (3/4), 369.

140. Prévost-Paradol, in *Le Journal des Débats*, October 4, 1864; RDDM, 1864 (11/12), 800–801.

141. Prévost-Paradol, in *Le Journal des Débats*, September 16, 1864.

142. Prévost-Paradol, in *Le Journal des Débats*, January 13, 1862, and November 27, 1864; Jules Grenier, in *Le Temps*, April 27, 1862.

143. Neely, *The Fate of Liberty*, 115–16.

144. Méjan to Thouvenel, New Orleans, February 12, 1861, CPCEU, 9:27.

145. Paul to Thouvenel, Richmond, March 9, 1861, CPCEU, 9:151, 160.

146. Paul to Thouvenel, Richmond, April 19, 1861, CPCEU, 9:170v.

147. Paul to Thouvenel, Richmond, January 22, 1862, CPCEU, 12:5; Paul to Thouvenel, Richmond, January 22, 1862, CCC Richmond, 5:163.

148. H. Lamarche, in *Le Siècle*, February 8, 1860.

149. Baudrillart, in *Le Journal des Débats*, May 17, 1861; Auguste Léo, in *Le Journal des Débats*, December 14, 1861.

150. A. Hébrard, in *Le Temps*, December 10, 1861.

151. Mercier to Thouvenel, Washington, October 31, 1860, CPEU, 123:356.

152. Méjan to Thouvenel, New Orleans, April 1, 1861, CPCEU, 9:50.

153. Paul to Thouvenel, Richmond, November 2, 1861, CPCEU, 9:253v–54.

154. Souchard to Thouvenel, Boston, February 18, 1862, CPCEU, 12:154; Souchard to Thouvenel, Boston, March 18, 1862, CPCEU, 12:169–v.

155. Boilleau to Drouyn de Lhuys, New York, October 12, 1864, CPCEU, 18:33 (newspaper annexed to the dispatch). The son of a major general, Charles Henri Philippe de Gauldrée Boilleau became first-class consul in Quebec at age thirty-six, in 1859, then consul general in New York in 1863, replacing de Montholon. In 1869 he was sent to Lima as minister plenipotentiary. Papiers du Personnel, 1st ser., no. 1779; Fournier, *Les Français au Québec*, 109–10.

156. Mercier to Thouvenel, Newport, August 14, 1860, and Washington, November 8 and December 17, 1860, CPEU, 123:309–13, 360–64, 403 (annexed to the dispatch).

157. *RDDM*, 1861 (11/12), 151; Jules Grenier, in *Le Temps*, April 27, 1862.

158. Baudrillart, in *Le Journal des Débats*, May 17, 1861; Auguste Léo, in *Le Journal des Débats*, December 14, 1861.

159. *RDDM*, 1861 (11/12), 153–54; Augustin Cochin, in *Le Journal des Débats*, August 9, 1862.

160. A. Hébrard, in *Le Temps*, April 25, 1862.

161. Auguste Léo, in *Le Journal des Débats*, January 20, 1861; F. Camus, in *Le Journal des Débats*, June 27, 1861.

162. McPherson, "Two Irreconcilable Peoples?," 93.

163. Sain de Boislecomte, *De la crise américaine*, 7–8.

164. Souchard to Thouvenel, Boston, March 18, 1862, CPCEU, 12:173–74.

165. Texier, in *Le Siècle*, July 15, 1860; *RDDM*, 1861 (1/2), 152; *RDDM*, 1861 (11/12), 154–55; *RDDM*, 1865 (3/4), 190; Auguste Léo, in *Le Journal des Débats*, July 31, 1861; E. Laboulaye, in *Le Journal des Débats*, August 27, 1862.

166. Paul to Walewski, Richmond, November 10, 1859, CPCEU, 7:91.

167. Méjan to Thouvenel, New Orleans, January 15, 1861, CPCEU, 9:11.

168. Souchard to Thouvenel, Boston, March 18, 1862, CPCEU, 12:172v.

169. Prévost-Paradol, in *Le Journal des Débats*, December 7, 1861.

170. Jules Grenier, in *Le Temps*, July 18, 1861; A. Nefftzer, in *Le Temps*, December 8, 1861; Prévost-Paradol, in *Le Journal des Débats*, April 15, 1863.

171. F. Camus, in *Le Journal des Débats*, February 14, 1861; *RDDM*, 1861 (11/12), 161. *RDDM*, 1862 (5/6), 496; Augustin Cochin, in *Le Journal des Débats*, August 9, 1862.

172. Drouyn de Lhuys to Montholon, Paris, April 28, 1865, CPEU, 133:265. *Le Moniteur* of May 2, 1865, published Drouyn de Lhuys's letter of April 28 to Seward in tribute to Lincoln.

173. Clapp, *Forgotten First Citizen*, 235; Bigelow to Seward, Paris, April 28, 1865, in Gavronsky, *The French Liberal Opposition*, 238.

174. Doyle, *The Cause of All Nations*, 294–96. My thanks to Doyle for drawing my attention to this point.

175. Berenson, *La statue de la Liberté*, 21.

176. A. Nefftzer, in *Le Journal des Débats*, May 3, 1865.

177. Pauli and Ashton, *I Lift My Lamp*, 8.

178. Prévost-Paradol, in *Le Journal des Débats*, April 29, 1865.

179. Dréolle, in *La Patrie*, April 28, 1865; *Le Pays*, April 28, 1865, in Blackburn, *French Newspaper Opinion*, 131–32; Ulysse Cadet, in *Le Temps*, April 29, 1865.

180. Ulysse Cadet, in *Le Temps*, April 29, 1865; *RDDM*, 1865 (5/6), 495; G. Isambert, in *Le Temps*, April 27, 1865; *RDDM*, 1865 (5/6), 476.

1. Doyle, "Slavery or Independence," 113.

2. George Sand, in *La Presse*, December 20, 1852.

3. *RDDM*, 1852 (10/12), 185; Edouard Laboulaye, in *Le Journal des Débats*, February 5, 1856.

4. *RDDM*, 1856 (10/12), 164.

5. Hauteville-House (Guernesey), December 2, 1859; Hugo, *Actes et paroles*, 239.

6. H. Lamarche and Louis Jourdan, in *Le Siècle*, January 2, 3, 12, and 13, 1860; *Le Journal des Débats*, June 16, 1860; *RDDM*, 1860 (11/12), 869–70; *RDDM*, 1861 (1/2), 119.

7. Prévost-Paradol, in *Le Journal des Débats*, December 7, 1861; Auguste Léo, in *Le Journal des Débats*, December 14, 1861; *RDDM*, 1860 (11/12), 690; *RDDM*, 1861 (1/2), 154.

8. Jules Grenier, in *Le Temps*, July 18, 1861.

9. Sanford to Seward, Paris, April 25, 1861, and Bigelow to Seward, Paris, October 31, 1861, in Case and Spencer, *The United States and France*, 40, 182.

10. Dayton to Seward, Paris, November 12, 1862, in Case and Spencer, *The United States and France*, 368.

11. Paul to Walewski, Richmond, January 5, 1857, CPEU, 116:5–9.

12. Méjan to Thouvenel, New Orleans, February 12, 1861, CPCEU, 9:23v.

13. Memo. by General Webb, August 2, 1861, ADPEU, 30:38, 53v–54. In early 1861, *La Revue des Deux Mondes* reported the rumor that the South would like to reestablish the slave trade. *RDDM*, 1861 (1/2), 133–34.

14. Napoléon III, "La traite des nègres," 280.

15. Thouvenel to Treilhard, Paris, February 23, 1860, CPEU, 123:80; Flahaut to Thouvenel, London, June 8, 1862, PT, 8:356v.

16. Helper, *The Impending Crisis of the South*, 420.

17. Report by Montholon, Washington, 1861, ADPEU, 30:85; Souchard to Thouvenel, Boston, March 18, 1862, CPCEU, 12:173–74.

18. Sartiges to Thouvenel, The Hague, December 28, 1861, ADPEU, 30:72v.

19. Paul to Drouyn de Lhuys, Richmond, January 15, 1864, CPCEU, 19:173. *Le Siècle* raised the question of the durability of an economy rendered indolent by servitude. H. Lamarche, in *Le Siècle*, January 12, 1860.

20. Louis Jourdan, in *Le Siècle*, January 13, 1860; E. Scherer, in *Le Temps*, October 19, 1861.

21. Paul to Thouvenel, Richmond, January 9, 1861, CPCEU, 9:145–v.

22. Copy of a dispatch for London and St. Petersburg, Paris, October 30, 1862, CPA, 722: 135; Slidell's memo, in Slidell to Benjamin, Paris, July 25, 1862, *ORN*, 481–87.

23. Geofroy to Drouyn de Lhuys, Washington, November 15, 1864, CPEU, 132:183; Paul to Drouyn de Lhuys, Washington, October 31, 1864, CPCEU, 19:239.

24. Sartiges to Drouyn de Lhuys, Washington, May 6, 1855, CPEU, 112:278.

25. Treilhard to Walewski, Washington, December 4, 1859, CPEU, 122:313.

26. Paul to Thouvenel, Richmond, November 10, 1860, CPCEU, 7:320–22.

27. Montholon to Thouvenel, New York, August 27, 1861, CPCEU, 8:58.

28. For example, Sain de Boislecomte, *De la crise américaine*, 38–42.

29. A. Granier de Cassagnac, in *Le Pays*, January 3, 1861, in West, *Contemporary French Opinion*, 12–13; *Le Pays*, February 9, 15, and 21, 1861; *Le Constitutionnel*, January 10, 24, and

28, 1861, in Blackburn, *French Newspaper Opinion*, 30–31, 63; Auguste Léo, in *Le Journal des Débats*, December 4, 1860.

30. Martin, in *Le Constitutionnel*, November 21, 1860, and January 10, 1862, in Blackburn, *French Newspaper Opinion*, 29, 62.

31. E. Scherer, in *Le Temps*, October 19, 1861; RDDM, 1863 (3/4), 366.

32. RDDM, 1861 (11/12), 152.

33. RDDM, 1863 (3/4), 370–71.

34. Mercier to Thouvenel, Washington, September 23, 1862, PT, 13:502–3; Mercier to Thouvenel, New York, September 30, 1862, CPEU, 128:107.

35. Levasseur to Thouvenel, St. Louis, October 15, 1862, CPCEU, 11:153v.

36. Montholon to Thouvenel, New York, September 23, 1862, CPCEU, 10:196–98; Montholon to Drouyn de Lhuys, New York, January 4, 1863, CPCEU, 13:12v.

37. Auguste Vitu, in *Le Constitutionnel*, October 8, 1862, in West, *Contemporary French Opinion*, 85–86.

38. Melvil, in *Le Pays*, January 9, 1863, in Blackburn, *French Newspaper Opinion*, xi, 63.

39. Léon Plée, in *Le Siècle*, October 12, 1862; Elias Regnault, in *La Presse*, October 8 and 15, 1862, in West, *Contemporary French Opinion*, 85–86.

40. J. J. Weiss, in *Le Journal des Débats*, October 9, 1862, and January 15, 1863; RDDM, 1863 (3/4), 691–722.

41. A. Nefftzer, in *Le Temps*, January 13, 1863.

42. RDDM, 1864 (9/10), 561.

43. Roger to Bastide, New Orleans, October 29, 1848, CPCEU 2:137–38v.

44. Drouyn de Lhuys to T. Ducos, Paris, August 3, 1852, ADPEU, 18:90v.

45. Ducos to Drouyn de Lhuys, Paris, August 21, 1852, ADPEU, 18:92v–93.

46. Théron to Thouvenel, Galveston, July 22, 1862, CPCEU, 11:124. In 1860, after abandoning his wife and children, Benjamin Théron (1807–64) became a consular agent for France and vice-consul for Spain in Galveston. He was previously employed in a tavern and was known for his drinking habits. In 1862 he was the only French consular agent stationed west of the Mississippi. Moreover, after the capture of New Orleans by Federal forces Théron was cut off from his superior, the consul Méjan. Without instructions, he thought he was authorized to take initiatives (see below).

47. Méjan to Thouvenel, La New Orleans, November 28, 1860, CCC New Orleans, 13:250.

48. Mercier to Thouvenel, Washington, January 28, 1862, CPEU, 126:71.

49. Population of the United States in 1860, 270, 452. Slaves accounted for 55 percent of the population in Mississippi and 57 percent in South Carolina.

50. Mercier to Thouvenel, Quebec, September 13, 1861, PT, 13:404v.

51. Mercier to Thouvenel, Washington, January 28, 1862, CPEU, 126:74.

52. France abolished slavery for the first time in 1794.

53. Méjan to Thouvenel, New Orleans, January 31, 1860, CCC New Orleans, 13:200.

54. In French, "petite église abolitionniste dont le fanatisme est en raison de l'infériorité numérique de ses fidèles." Mercier to Thouvenel, Newport, August 14, 1860, and Washington, January 28, 1862, CPEU, 123:310v, 126:71.

55. Mercier to Thouvenel, Washington, April 8, 1862, CPEU, 127:22.

56. Mercier to Thouvenel, Washington, September 30, 1862, PT, 13:510v.

57. Gavronsky, *The French Liberal Opposition*, 71.

58. *Le Journal des Débats*, November 12, 1852; *RDDM*, 1856 (3/4), 274–77.

59. *Le Journal des Débats*, September 17, 1857.

60. Baudrillart, in *Le Journal des Débats*, May 17, 1861; E. Scherer, in *Le Temps*, June 15, 1861.

61. Napoléon III, "La traite des nègres," 465.

62. Drouyn de Lhuys to Bigelow, Paris, January 8, 1866, LJEU, 1866, 96.

63. Montholon to Drouyn de Lhuys, Washington, May 23, 1865, CPEU, 134:85.

64. Montholon to Drouyn de Lhuys, Washington, August 8, 1865, CPEU, 135:17.

65. Saint-André to Drouyn de Lhuys, Charleston, October 26, 1865, CCC Charleston, 7:435–37.

66. Saint-André to Drouyn de Lhuys, Charleston, November 20, 1865, CCC Charleston, 7:443v.

67. Berthémy to Moustier, Washington, August 22, 1867, CPEU, 139:286.

68. Dickey, *Our Man in Charleston*, 42–43.

69. Mercier to Thouvenel, Washington, March 29, 1861, CPEU, 124:122.

70. Ibid.

71. Slidell to Benjamin, Paris, February 11, 1862, *ORN*, 336.

72. The act of February 4, 1794, had abolished slavery in all territories of the French Republic. However, abolition had not taken effect in several colonies, including Réunion and Martinique. The act of May 20, 1802, passed during the Consulate, maintained slavery in these colonies. In territories such as Guadeloupe or Guyana that had chosen to ban slavery, it was reestablished in the following months.

73. Anceau, *Napoléon III*, 73. The emperor's cousin Prince Napoléon, though a strong supporter of the North, used similarly racist vocabulary a few years later. Despite being hostile to slavery, which he described as a hideous canker, he wrote in 1861 in his journal that it was very unpleasant for him to be surrounded by "negroes." D'Hauterive, "Le prince Napoléon," 252, 265.

74. Napoléon III, "La traite des nègres," 461–63.

75. Doyle, *The Cause of All Nations*, 275–77.

76. Mason to Benjamin, London, March 31, 1865, *ORN*, 1270–71; Beringer et al., *Why the South Lost the Civil War*, 388.

77. Doyle, "Slavery or Independence," 112.

78. Plessis, *De la fête impériale au mur des fédérés*, 200–201; Olivesi and Nouschi, *La France de 1848 à 1914*, 100–101. Encrevé, *Le Second Empire*, 105.

79. Karsky, "Les libéraux français," 576. *Le Temps* wrote that the fall of Richmond was a victory for liberal interests worldwide. A. Nefftzer, in *Le Temps*, April 16, 1865.

CHAPTER 6

1. Rouher made this declaration on January 25, 1864. It is possible that the statement was not quite so clear-cut and that Rouher more cautiously said, "Mexico will *perhaps* be considered the reign's grand design." Carteret, *Napoléon III*, 199.

2. Napoléon III to Flahaut, Compiègne, October 1861, CPA, 720:218v.

3. Bruley, *La diplomatie du Sphinx*, 278–79.

4. Barker, "France, Austria and the Mexican Venture," 224–45.

5. Pani, "Juárez vs. Maximiliano," 174.

6. Napoléon III to Forey, Fontainebleau, July 3, 1862, LJM, 1862, 191.

7. Hanna and Hanna, *Napoléon III and Mexico*, 90; Case, "La sécession aux Etats-Unis," 292–93; Willson, *John Slidell*, 204.

8. Chevalier and Rasetti, *La France, le Mexique et les Etats confédérés*, 31.

9. Mercier, *Du Panlatinisme*, 30–31; Chevalier and Rasetti, *La France, le Mexique et les Etats confédérés*, 12.

10. Cullop, *Confederate Propaganda in Europe*, 66–84.

11. Slidell's memo, in Slidell to Benjamin, Paris, July 25, 1862, *ORN*, 481–87; Cleven and Andrew, "The Corwin-Doblado Treaty," 499–506. Thomas Corwin, the U.S. minister to Mexico, and Manuel Doblado, the Mexican minister of foreign affairs, signed the treaty on April 6, 1862. It was designed to allow Mexico to repay its debts to France, the United Kingdom, and Spain, which had landed troops at Vera Cruz in December 1861 and January 1862. The aim was to deprive the European powers of any pretext for continuing their armed intervention. The treaty had the desired effect on the British and Spanish, whose troops reembarked in April, but not on the French, who began their march on Mexico City.

12. Slidell to Thouvenel, Paris, July 21, 1862, ADPEU, 32:57v.

13. Confidential note by Slidell, Paris, July–August 1862, ADPEU, 32:91.

14. Slidell's memo, in Slidell to Benjamin, Paris, October 28, 1862, *ORN*, 574–78.

15. Drouyn de Lhuys to Mercier, Paris, September 13, 1863, LJEU, 1863, 123. Those who suggested a revival of the Republic of Texas have been clearly identified. They were Benjamin Théron, the consular agent in Galveston and René Tabouelle, the chancellor of the French consulate in Richmond. They questioned the Confederate authorities about Slidell's suggestion. Benjamin suspected Napoléon of having given them the idea in order to extend French influence in the territory. Schoonover, "Confederate Diplomacy," 33–39.;Aldis, "Louis Napoléon," 349–50; Hanna, "The Roles of the South," 10. This assumption is questionable. The organization of the diplomatic network made this approach unusual. It was indeed inconceivable that a consular agent or a chancellor of a consulate would have been appointed to sound out the Confederate authorities. So it is more likely that this plan was born in Théron's mind because he wished to play a political role by taking advantage of his isolation. Tabouelle had simply taken up this preposterous idea. Moreover, no French source supports the idea of his government's intention to dismember the Confederacy and establish a protectorate over Texas. The best account of this affair is that of Crook, "Benjamin Théron," 432–34. See also Sim, *La présence diplomatique et consulaire française aux Etats-Unis*, 495–501, and Noirsain, "L'imprudence d'un consul français au Texas," 1–10.

16. In late 1864, reports claimed that Maximilian had ceded the north of Mexico to France. William L. Gwin, a former California senator who was very interested in the riches of these states, had allegedly been made duke of Mexico and viceroy of Napoléon for the new colony, which would include nothing less than Sonora, Sinaloa, Chihuahua, Durango, and Baja California. In November 1864 the rumor was debunked and with it the idea of exploiting Sonora. Crook, *Diplomacy*, 173; Hanna, "The Roles of the South," 15. The following year, the consul in New York reported that Romero, Juarez's envoy to Washington, was speaking of a transfer of several Mexican states to France to repay Mexico's debt. Borg to Drouyn de Lhuys, New York, May 8, 1865, CPCEU, 21:3v–11. Louis André Vincent Jean Borg de Balzan was the vice-consul in New York for over twenty years. He would serve as consul general to Mexico during Maximilian's short reign. Papiers du Personnel, 1st ser., no. 516.

17. Slidell's memo, in Slidell to Benjamin, Paris, June 21, 1863, *ORN*, 812–14. In any case, Paul made no mention of these lights.

18. Paul to Drouyn de Lhuys, Richmond, August 24, 1863, CPCEU, 15:71v–72, and CCC Richmond, 5:303–4.

19. Lanen to Drouyn de Lhuys, Charleston, July 4, 1864, CPCEU, 18:276–77.

20. May, "The Irony of Confederate Diplomacy," 74, 87, 102.

21. Schoonover, "Mexico," 1036–37; Schoonover, "Mexican Cotton," 429–47; Delaney, "Matamoros," 473–79.

22. Mercier to Drouyn de Lhuys, Paris, May 14, 1863, CPEU, 130:76.

23. Avenel, *La campagne du Mexique*, 69; Noirsain, *La Confédération sudiste*, 160–65.

24. Owsley, *King Cotton Diplomacy*, 90–91.

25. Slidell to Thouvenel, Paris, July 21, 1862, ADPEU, 32:57v.

26. Paul to Drouyn de Lhuys, Richmond, December 23, 1863, CPCEU, 15:91–v.

27. Sainlaude, "Los confederados y la expedición francesa en México," 309.

28. Fauconnet to Drouyn de Lhuys, New Orleans, June 17, 1864, CPCEU, 19:90–91v.

29. Boilleau to Drouyn de Lhuys, New York, February 7, 1865, CPCEU, 20:91–v.

30. Geofroy to Drouyn de Lhuys, Washington, January 24, 1865, CPEU, 133:65–67; Montholon to Drouyn de Lhuys, Mexico City, March 10, 1865, CPM, 63:124v–25; Boilleau to Drouyn de Lhuys, New York, February 7 and March 28, 1865, CPCEU, 20:92–v, 202–7; La Tour d'Auvergne to Drouyn de Lhuys, London, February 6, 1865, CPA, 732:70v; La Tour d'Auvergne to Drouyn de Lhuys, London, February 28, 1865, CPA, 732:109–v.

31. Bigelow to Seward, Paris, February 14 and 22, 1865, and Bigelow to Drouyn de Lhuys, Paris, February 23, 1865, in Case and Spencer, *The United States and France*, 563.

32. Drouyn de Lhuys to Geofroy, Paris, March 23 1865, CPEU, 133:176.

33. La Tour d'Auvergne to Drouyn de Lhuys, London, February 27, 1865, CPA, 732:105–6.

34. McCardell, *The Idea of a Southern Nation*, 394; May, *The Southern Dream of a Caribbean Empire*, 286.

35. For example, Boilleau to Walewski, Washington, August 27, 1855, CPEU, 113:85; Sartiges to Walewski, Washington, June 20, 1859, CPEU, 122:103.

36. Sartiges to Walewski, Washington, January 5, 1858, CPEU, 118:26.

37. Boilleau to Walewski, Washington, March 4, 1856, CPEU, 114:195.

38. Sartiges to Walewski, Washington, February 8, 1858, PS, 10.

39. Edouard Laboulaye, in *Le Journal des Débats*, February 5, 1856; *RDDM*, 1856 (3/4), 275–76.

40. Moerenhout to Drouyn de Lhuys, Monterey, January 31, 1854, CPCEU, 4:142v. Jacques-Antoine Moerenhout (1796–1879), a merchant and traveler, was first noticed during the July Monarchy when he facilitated the establishment of the French protectorate over Tahiti. In 1846 he became an honorary consul in Los Angeles, replacing Louis Gasquet. His stay in California gave him the opportunity to report on the gold rush in his dispatches. His file at the Ministry of Foreign Affairs mentions the first name Jacob-Antoine. Papiers du Personnel, 1st ser., no. 2923.

41. Boilleau to Walewski, Washington, September 24, 1855, CPEU, 113:123.

42. Sartiges to Walewski, Washington, February 8, 1858, PS, 10; Sartiges to Walewski, Washington, March 2, 1858, PS, 10.

43. Sartiges to Walewski, Washington, February 15, 1858, PS, 10.

44. Méjan to Thouvenel, New Orleans, January 31, 1860, CCC New Orleans, 13:201–2.

45. Treilhard to Walewski, Washington, January 16, 1860, CPEU, 123:10; Treilhard was unaware of Thouvenel's appointment.

46. Mercier to Thouvenel, Washington, April 6, 1861, CPEU, 124:133.

47. Hahn, *A Nation without Borders*, 235.

48. Sartiges to Drouyn de Lhuys, Washington, April 8, 1855, PS, 8.

49. Sartiges to Walewski, Washington, June 20, 1859, CPEU, 122:103.

50. *Le Moniteur*, January 6, 1858.

51. Sartiges to Walewski, Washington, February 15, 1858, PS, 10.

52. Note from Dubois de Saligny to Thouvenel, Paris, June 7, 1860, CPM, 53:312–20v.

53. Sartiges to Drouyn de Lhuys, Washington, May 2, 1854, PS, 6; Sartiges to Walewski, Washington, April 11, 1858, CPEU, 118:164.

54. Kelly, "The Cat's Paw," 58.

55. May, "The Irony of Confederate Diplomacy," 79, 83.

56. E. Bellot des Minières, "Lettre à M. le ministre des Affaires étrangères sur la question américaine," Paris, May 7, 1861, MDEU, 25:203.

57. Slidell to Thouvenel, Paris, July 21, 1862, ADPEU, 32:56v–57.

58. So as not to overload the text, only the most significant passages are discussed here, but the argument is recurrent.

59. F. Camus, in *Le Journal des Débats*, January 7, 1860.

60. F. Camus, in *Le Journal des Débats*, January 7, 1861.

61. *RDDM*, 1861 (1/2), 149.

62. *RDDM*, 1861 (11/12), 152–53; Auguste Léo, in *Le Journal des Débats*, December 4, 1860.

63. In England also, the federal representative, Charles Francis Adams, urged his son Henry on August 25, 1861, to use the argument of an aggressive Confederacy and a revival of the slave trade in Mexico and Central America. May, *The Southern Dream of a Caribbean Empire*, 240. In April 1861, Seward asked his government's new representative in Madrid, Carl Schurz, to remind the Spaniards that the Southerners had always wanted to conquer Cuba. Cortada, *Spain and the American Civil War*, 53.

64. Memo by General Webb, August 2, 1861, ADPEU, 30:38–40: "I speak advisedly when I say that the program of the leading rebels was, first, to induce the North to consent to them secession and, then, to conquer Mexico and make a great slave Confederacy composed of Mexico, the rebel States and Lower California of which the city of Mexico was to be the capital and the African slave trade to furnish them with laborers citizens fifty dollars per head."

65. Dubois de Saligny to Thouvenel, Mexico City, July 17, 1861, CPM, 55:92.

66. Sartiges to Thouvenel, The Hague, December 28, 1861, ADPEU, 30:72.

67. Sartiges to Thouvenel, The Hague, October 28, 1861, PT, 17:246v–47v.

68. Slidell to Thouvenel, Paris, July 21, 1862, ADPEU, 32:56v–57.

69. Slidell's memo, in Slidell to Benjamin, Paris, June 21, 1863, *ORN*, 812–14.

70. Sain de Boislecomte, *De la crise américaine*, 57.

71. *New York Times*, December 6, 1861. See also *Archives diplomatiques, 1862*, 1:424–*27. Seward to Cowin, April 6, 1861.

72. Telegram, London, April 29, 1862, ADPEU, 30:186.

73. May, "The Irony of Confederate Diplomacy," 73.

74. Sartiges to Thouvenel, The Hague, February 1, 1862, ADPEU, 30:92–96v.

75. Thouvenel to Flahaut, Paris, October 11, 1861, LJM, 1862, 154.

76. Thouvenel to Flahaut, Paris, February 10, 1862, in Thouvenel, *Le secret de l'Empereur*, 236–37.

77. Slidell to Benjamin, Paris, July 25, 1862, *ORN*, 481–87.

78. Paul Becquet du Bellet, in *Le Pays*, September 11 and 17, 1862, in Blackburn, *French Newspaper Opinion*, 95–96.

79. *RDDM*, 1861 (11/12), 146, 150, 161.

80. *RDDM*, 1863 (9/10), 873.

81. *RDDM*, 1863 (3/4), 368–69.

82. *RDDM*, 1861 (1/2), 149.

83. *RDDM*, 1863 (9/10), 875.

84. J. J. Weiss, in *Le Journal des Débats*, September 14 and October 4, 1863; J. J. Weiss.

85. Seward to Corwin, Washington, February 20, 1864, in Blumberg, *The Diplomacy of the Mexican Empire*, 17.

86. Trimpi, *Crimson Confederates*, 243.

87. Slidell to Benjamin, Paris, March 16, 1864, *ORN*, 1063–65.

88. Gouttman, *La guerre du Mexique*, 200.

89. Hubbard, *The Burden*, 163; Hanna, "The Roles of the South," 14–15.

90. Dayton to Seward, Paris, March 11 and 25, 1864, in Case and Spencer, *The United States and France*, 549.

91. Gouttman, *La guerre du Mexique*, 198.

92. Hanna, "The Roles of the South," 18; Harmon, "Confederate Migrations to Mexico," 458–61.

93. The minister of war to Maximilian, Mexico City, June 13, 1865, ADPEU, 39:55v.

94. Dano to Drouyn de Lhuys, Puebla, June 11, 1865, CPM, 63:343v–48.

95. Dano to Drouyn de Lhuys, Puebla, June 11, 1865, CPM, 63:342–43.

96. Karp, *This Vast Southern Empire*, 241.

97. This viewpoint needed qualifying. May, "The Irony of Confederate Diplomacy," 90.

98. Sainlaude, "France's Grand Design and the Confederacy," in *American Civil Wars*, 119.

CHAPTER 7

1. Sain de Boislecomte, *De la crise américaine*, 8.

2. Mercier to Thouvenel, Washington, October 22, 1860, CPEU, 123:352.

3. Mercier to Thouvenel, Washington, November 8, 1860, CPEU, 123:361.

4. Mercier to Thouvenel, Washington, December 7, 1860, CPEU, 123:386v–89.

5. Paul to Thouvenel, Richmond, November 10, 1860, CPCEU, 7:320.

6. Martin, in *Le Constitutionnel*, November 21, 1860, in Blackburn, *French Newspaper Opinion*, 29; Auguste Léo, in *Le Journal des Débats*, December 4, 1860; John Lemoinne, in *Le Journal des Débats*, December 7, 1860; Auguste Léo, in *Le Journal des Débats*, December 30, 1860; *RDDM*, 1860 (11/12), 690.

7. *Le Siècle*, November 24, 1860.

8. Mercier to Thouvenel, Washington, December 31, 1860, CPEU, 123:411.

9. Mercier to Thouvenel, Washington, January 7, 1861, CPEU, 124:8–11.

10. Paul to Thouvenel, Richmond, January 9, 1861, CPCEU, 9:136.

11. Méjan to Thouvenel, New Orleans, January 12, 1861, CPCEU, 9:4.

12. Tooley, *The Peace That Almost Was*, 54.

13. Mercier to Thouvenel, Washington, March 29 and April 26, 1861, CPEU, 124:122, 171.

14. Paul to Thouvenel, Richmond, April 28, 1861, CPCEU, 9:175v; Paul to Thouvenel, Richmond, May 9, 1861, CPCEU, 9:185v.

15. H.-Marie Martin, in *Le Constitutionnel*, January 20, 1861, in West, *Contemporary French Opinion*, 21; J. J. Weiss, in *Le Journal des Débats*, January 10, 1861.

16. Baudrillart, in *Le Journal des Débats*, May 17, 1861; E. Scherer, in *Le Temps*, June 15, 1861; *RDDM*, 1861 (11/12), 140–41, 147.

17. Coquille, in *Le Monde*, January 8 and March 4, 1861, in Blackburn, *French Newspaper Opinion*, 30, 34.

18. *Le Constitutionnel*, February 2, 1861, in Blackburn, *French Newspaper Opinion*, 32; Baudrillart, in *Le Journal des Débats*, May 17, 1861.

19. Thouvenel to Méjan, Paris, November 29, 1860, CPCEU, 7:291; Thouvenel to Paul, Paris, November 29, 1860, CPCEU, 7:325; Thouvenel to Mercier, Paris, January 24, 1861, CPEU, 124:37.

20. Thouvenel to Mercier, Paris, April 25 and May 16, 1861, CPEU, 124:161–63, 216–17.

21. Thouvenel to Mercier, Paris, June 20, 1861, LJEU, 1861, 99.

22. Thouvenel to Mercier, Paris, April 29, 1861, CPEU, 124:161.

23. Faulkner to Cass, Paris, January 2, 1861, and Faulkner to Black, Paris, January 24, 1861, Faulkner to Black, Paris, March 19, 1861, in Wilson, *America's Ambassadors*, 260; Case, "La sécession aux Etats-Unis," 296; Case and Spencer, *The United States and France*, 21–24.

24. Thouvenel to Mercier, Paris, May 16, 1861, CPEU, 124:216–17, and *Archives diplomatiques, 1861*, 1:110.

25. Flahaut to Thouvenel, London, October 14, 1861, PT, 8:191.

26. Dayton to Thouvenel, Paris, August 13, 1861, ADPEU, 30:63–69v.

27. Thouvenel to Mercier, Paris, February 27, 1862, CPEU, 126:188.

28. Rost to Hunter, Madrid, March 21, 1862, *ORN*, 367–70.

29. Souchard to Thouvenel, Boston, March 18, 1862, CPCEU, 12:169–v; Paul to Thouvenel, Richmond, March 23, 1862, CPCEU, 12:39.

30. Paul to Thouvenel, Richmond, April 2, 1862, CPCEU, 12:44; Souchard to Thouvenel, Boston, May 13, 1862, CPCEU, 12:188.

31. Mercier to Thouvenel, Washington, May 12, 1862, PT, 13:452.

32. Mercier to Thouvenel, Washington, June 15, 1862, PT, 13:461.

33. Seward to Dayton, Washington, April 15, 1862, ADPEU, 30:172.

34. Mercier to Thouvenel, Washington, July 19, 1862, PT, 13:471.

35. Montholon to Thouvenel, New York, July 22, 1862, CPCEU, 10:142.

36. Montholon to Thouvenel, New York, August 26, 1862, CPCEU, 10:156.

37. Slidell's memo, in Slidell to Benjamin, Paris, July 25, 1862, *ORN*, 481–87.

38. Thouvenel to Mercier, Paris, July 23, 1862, LJEU, 1862, 136.

39. Thouvenel to Flahaut, Paris, July 21, 1862, ADPEU, 30:215; Thouvenel to Mercier, Paris, July 24, 1862, in Thouvenel, *Le secret de l'Empereur*, 2:348–49.

40. F. Camus, in *Le Journal des Débats*, September 28 and October 25, 1861; E. Scherer, in *Le Temps*, October 19, 1861; *RDDM*, 1861 (11/12), 140–41.

41. Auguste Léo, in *Le Journal des Débats*, October 19, 1861; Prévost-Paradol, in *Le Journal des Débats*, December 7, 1861; L. Legault, in *Le Temps*, November 15, 1862.

42. Mercier to Thouvenel, Washington, September 30, 1862, PT, 13:510–13.

43. Souchard to Drouyn de Lhuys, Boston, February 17, 1863, CPCEU, 15:95v; Montholon to Drouyn de Lhuys, New York, April 14, 1863, CPCEU, 13:32.

44. Slidell to Thouvenel, Paris, July 21, 1862, ADPEU, 32:47v.

45. Mercier to Thouvenel, New York, November 2, 1862, PT, 13:493–95.

46. Thouvenel to Mercier, Paris, April 29, 1861, CPEU, 124:161; Thouvenel to Mercier, Paris, May 11, 1861, CPEU, 124:194.

47. It was in July, in the letter he sent to Thouvenel, that Slidell reiterated the remarks made by the foreign minister on February 7. Slidell to Thouvenel, Paris, July 21, 1862, ADPEU, 32:47–v.

48. Thouvenel to Flahaut, Paris, May 15, 1862, ADPEU, 30:189–90v; Thouvenel to Flahaut, Paris, May 15, 1862, CPA, 721:193v.

49. Thouvenel to Mercier, Paris, October 2, 1862, in Thouvenel, *Le secret de l'Empereur*, 2:414–16.

50. Palmerston to Russell, London, September 14, 1862, in Adams, *Great Britain*, 2:38.

51. Slidell to Thouvenel, Paris, July 21, 1862, ADPEU, 32:47v.

52. D'Hauterive, "Le prince Napoléon," 264.

53. Borg to Drouyn de Lhuys, New York, December 15, 1863, CPCEU, 13:172–76.

54. Paul to Thouvenel, Richmond, December 22, 1860, CPCEU, 7:328–29.

55. Paul to Thouvenel, Richmond, January 9, 1861, CPCEU, 9:136–v.

56. Paul to Drouyn de Lhuys, Richmond, July 5, 1864, CPCEU, 19:222–v.

57. Memo by General Webb, August 2, 1861, ADPEU, 30:40v.

58. Paul to Drouyn de Lhuys, Richmond, January 4, 1863, CPCEU, 15:12–15.

59. Sain de Boislecomte, *De la crise américaine*, 54–55.

60. Edouard Laboulaye, in *Le Journal des Débats*, August 27, 1862; *RDDM*, 1861 (11/12), 151–52.

61. *RDDM*, 1861 (11/12), 151–52; Baudrillart, in *Le Journal des Débats*, May 17, 1861; E. Laboulaye, in *Le Journal des Débats*, August 27, 1862.

62. *RDDM*, 1861 (11/12), 145–46; Jules Grenier, in *Le Temps*, April 27, 1862; E. Laboulaye, in *Le Journal des Débats*, August 27, 1862.

63. F. Camus, in *Le Journal des Débats*, October 25, 1861; J. J. Weiss, in *Le Journal des Débats*, January 25, 1863.

64. Baudrillart, in *Le Journal des Débats*, June 3, 1861; Edouard Laboulaye, in *Le Journal des Débats*, August 27, 1862.

65. *RDDM*, 1864 (11/12), 801.

66. Prévost-Paradol, in *Le Journal des Débats*, December 7, 1861, and April 15, 1863; J. J. Weiss, in *Le Journal des Débats*, January 16, 1863; *RDDM*, 1862 (5/6), 496. See also *New York Times*, April 16, 1861, http//www.query.nytimes.

67. Hubbard, *The Burden*, 140.

68. Mercier to Thouvenel, Washington, May 12, 1861, CPEU, 124:209.

69. Mercier to Thouvenel, Washington, February 24, 1862, PT, 13:434–v.

70. Note for the Minister: Delimitation Plan between the North and the South, Paris, July 4, 1862, ADPEU, 30:199–202v. This seems unrealistic given that the tariff was one of the main things, besides slavery, that divided the two sections.

71. Thouvenel to Flahaut, Paris, August 20, 1862, in Thouvenel, *Le secret de l'Empereur*, 2:364–65.

72. Dayton to Seward, Paris, September 17, 1862, in Case and Spencer, *The United States and France*, 336.

73. Droz, *Histoire diplomatique*, 384–85.

74. Drouyn de Lhuys to Mercier, Paris, January 9, 1863, CPEU, 129:15.

75. *Le Constitutionnel,* January 20, 1863, in West, *Contemporary French Opinion,* 96–97.

76. Souchard to Thouvenel, Boston, March 18, 1862, CPCEU, 12:172.

77. Hahn, *A Nation without Borders,* 268.

CHAPTER 8

1. According to Mercier, cotton accounted for half of the Union's export earnings (or $161,434,923) and contributed nearly a third of national income. Book of Statistics, ADPEU, 30:2–13. These figures are also given by E. Bellot des Minières, "Lettres sur la question américaine," Paris, May 7, 1861, MDEU, 25:192v. In the early 1860s, *Le Temps* exaggerated its assessment of cotton production in the United States, putting it at 4,675,770 bales. L. Legault, in *Le Temps,* November 4, 1861. In fact, cotton production stood at less than 4 million bales in 1860. Owsley, *King Cotton Diplomacy,* 134–35.

2. Karp, "King Cotton, Emperor Slavery," 36, 43.

3. Henderson, "The Cotton Famine," 196.

4. 1,241,346 metric quintals out of a total of 1,392,839. *Direction générale des douanes.* Marzagalli and Marnot, *Guerre et économie,* 288.

5. *Documents statistiques,* 1863.

6. Thouvenel to Mercier, Paris, October 3, 1861, CPEU, 125:108–12v. This figure was also cited by Mercier in an interview with Seward on October 23, 1861. Ferris, *Desperate Diplomacy,* 144.

7. Rouher to Thouvenel, Paris, November 15, 1861, ADPEU, 33:72–v.

8. Rabout, Caen, October 10, November 13, 1861; Millevoye, Rouen, October 12, 1861, in Case, *French Opinion,* 19, no. 29; 23, no. 38; 28, no. 44.

9. De Baillehache, Colmar, October 1861, in Case, *French Opinion,* 20, no. 30.

10. Rouher to Thouvenel, Paris, November 15, 1861, ADPEU, 33:72–v.

11. De Baillehache, Colmar, October 12, 1862, in Case, *French Opinion,* 54–59, no. 70; 86, no. 98.

12. Duveau, *La vie ouvrière sous le Second Empire,* 120.

13. Fohlen, *L'industrie textile au temps du Second Empire,* 267, 284.

14. 126,158,877 francs. *Documents statistiques,* 1863.

15. Millevoye, Rouen, October 12, 1862. Olivier, Caen, April 11, 1863, in Case, *French Opinion,* 96, no. 110; 122, no. 136.

16. Fould to Thouvenel, Paris, 1861, ADPEU, 33:86; Thouvenel to the President of the French Exporters' Federation, Paris, September 4, 1861, ADPEU, 33:51–v; Case and Spencer, *The United States and France,* 179.

17. Bruyère-Ostells, *Napoléon III et le Second Empire,* 55.

18. Case and Spencer, *The United States and France,* 179. These concerns were reported by the Swedish minister to France, Frederik Due to Ludwig Manderström, Paris, October 5, 1861. *Times* (London), October 12, 1861; *New York Times,* October 24 and 26, 1861.

19. Thouvenel to Mercier, Paris, March 13, 1862, in L. Thouvenel, *Le secret de l'Empereur,* 2:248.

20. Fohlen, *L'industrie textile au temps du Second Empire,* 269–73.

21. Auguste Léo, in *Le Journal des Débats,* January 13, 1863; Bedollière, in *Le Siècle,* January 6, 1863, in Blackburn, *French Newspaper Opinion,* 83; A. Nefftzer, in *Le Temps,* January 9, 1863.

22. *Le Journal des Débats* wondered how it was possible that Paris and France gave Norman workers barely one-tenth of what a single English city, such as Liverpool, sent to the workers of Manchester. J. J. Weiss, in *Le Journal des Débats*, January 8, 1863; J. J. Weiss, in *Le Journal des Débats*, January 14, 1863.

23. A. Nefftzer, in *Le Temps*, February 2, 1863.

24. Thouvenel to Mercier, Paris, September 3 and October 3, 1861, CPEU, 125:108–12v.

25. Mercier to Thouvenel, Niagara, September 9, 1861, PT, 13:390–v; Mercier to Thouvenel, Washington, October 22, 1861, CPEU, 125:151.

26. Thouvenel to Mercier, Paris, October 31, 1861, CPA, 720:228v.

27. Thouvenel to Rouher, Paris, November 21, 1861, ADPEU, 33:74–75v.

28. Thouvenel to Mercier, Paris, November 28, 1861, CPCEU, 9:112v–13; Seward to Dayton, Washington, March 26, 1862, ADPEU, 30:129v–32v; Mercier to Thouvenel, Washington, March 31, 1862, LJEU, 1862, 117.

29. Seward to Dayton, Washington, October 30, 1861, in Van Deusen, *William Henry Seward*, 304; Mercier to Thouvenel, Washington, October 22, 1861, CPEU, 125:152; Thouvenel to Mercier, Paris, March 13, 1862, in Thouvenel, *Le secret de l'Empereur*, 2:248.

30. Thouvenel to Flahaut, Paris, January 23, 1863, in Thouvenel, *Le secret de l'Empereur*, 2:231; Thouvenel to Flahaut, Paris, April 14, 1862, CPA, 721:132.

31. Report by Montholon, Washington, 1861, ADPEU, 30:81–82.

32. Mercier to Thouvenel, Washington, February 3, 1862, CPEU, 126:110; Blackett, *Divided Hearts*, 65. Lindsay was one of the negotiators of the commercial treaty between France and Great Britain of January 23, 1860.

33. Slidell's memo, in Slidell to Benjamin, Paris, April 14, 1862, *ORN*, 393–95.

34. Avenel, *La campagne du Mexique*, 39.

35. Thouvenel to Flahaut, Paris, April 14, 1862, CPA, 721:132v–33.

36. Slidell's memo, in Slidell to Benjamin, Paris, April 14 and 18, 1862, *ORN*, 392–96.

37. Hubbard, *The Burden*, 85.

38. Slidell's memo, in Slidell to Benjamin, Paris, July 25, 1862, *ORN*, 481–87.

39. Slidell's memo, in Slidell to Benjamin, Paris, October 28, 1862, *ORN*, 574–78.

40. *La politique impériale*, 385; *Le Journal des Débats*, January 13, 1863.

41. Ferris, *Desperate Diplomacy*, 8, 15–17, 36.

42. Flahaut to Thouvenel, London, February 13, 1862, PT, 8:285–v.

43. This agreement, signed on February 19, 1862, entailed the implicit recognition of the Juárez government since it stated that the Allies did not wish to prejudice the sovereignty of Mexico. It anticipated a British and Spanish departure in April.

44. Case and Spencer, *The United States and France*, 164.

45. See chapter 1.

46. Hubbard, *The Burden*, 82–83.

47. Slidell to Benjamin, Paris, June 1, 1862, *ORN*, 428–29. At the time Wood was secretary of state for India.

48. Thouvenel to Flahaut, Paris, April 14, 1862, CPA, 721:133.

49. Interview with M. Thouvenel, in Slidell to Benjamin, Paris, February 11, 1862, *ORN*, 339–41.

50. Souchard to Thouvenel, Boston, April 29, 1862, CPCEU, 12:184; Flahaut to Thouvenel, London, May 11, 1862, CPA, 721:187; Mercier to Thouvenel, Washington, May 12, 1862, CPEU, 127:134v.

51. Seward to Mercier, Washington, May 5, 1862, LJEU, 1862, 126.

52. Thouvenel to Flahaut, Paris, June 5, 1862, CPA, 721:236.

53. Paul to Thouvenel, Richmond, April 15, 1862, CPCEU, 12:55v.

54. Méjan to Thouvenel, New Orleans, April 29, 1861, and April 20, 1862, CPCEU, 9:60, 11:238; Paul to Thouvenel, Richmond, April 15, 1862, CPCEU, 12:52; Paul to Thouvenel, Richmond, April 15, 1862, CPCEU, 12:55v. Benjamin encouraged his agent in France to put forward this explanation. Benjamin to Slidell, Richmond, December 11, 1862, ADPEU, 32: 137.

55. Drouyn de Lhuys to Chasseloup-Laubat, Paris, April 6, 1863, ADPEU, 45:68v.

56. Paul to Thouvenel, Richmond, November 2, 1861, CPCEU, 9:260–61.

57. Montholon to Thouvenel, New York, June 9, 1862, CPCEU, 10:101–v. See also Fauconnet to Drouyn de Lhuys, New Orleans, August 14, 1863, CPCEU, 14:256–57.

58. Mercier to Thouvenel, Washington, April 28, 1862, CPEU, 127:50–78; Mercier to Thouvenel, Washington, June 15, 1862, PT, 13:461.

59. Slidell's memo, in Slidell to Benjamin, Paris, July 25, 1862, ORN, 481–87; Slidell to Thouvenel, Paris, July 21, 1862, ADPEU, 32:52v.

60. Slidell's memo, in Slidell to Benjamin, Paris, July 25, 1862, ORN, 481–87.

61. Flahaut to Thouvenel, London, September 22, 1861, PT, 8:183v–184; Flahaut to Thouvenel, London, January 25, 1862, PT, 8:278.

62. Seward to Dayton, Washington, April 15, 1862, ADPEU, 30:175–v.

63. Méjan to Thouvenel, New Orleans, December 18, 1861, CPCEU, 9:118–v.

64. Méjan to Thouvenel, New Orleans, May 2, 1862, CPCEU, 11:230v–31.

65. Montholon to Thouvenel, New York, June 9, 1862, CPCEU, 10:101–v.

66. Mercier to Thouvenel, Washington, April 28, 1862, PT, 13:446; Mercier to Thouvenel, Washington, May 6, 1862, *Archives diplomatiques, 1863*, 1:273–74; Mercier to Thouvenel, Washington, May 12, 1862, *Archives diplomatiques, 1863*, 1:277.

67. Mercier to Thouvenel, Washington, June 27, 1862, *Archives diplomatiques, 1863*, 1:281.

68. Mercier to Drouyn de Lhuys, Washington, November 21, 1862, LJEU, 1862, 149.

69. Fauconnet to Drouyn de Lhuys, New Orleans, August 14, 1863, CPCEU, 14:256; Fauconnet to Drouyn de Lhuys, New Orleans, August 14, 1863, CCC New Orleans, 14: 255–59. See also Paul to Drouyn de Lhuys, Richmond, August 24, 1863, CPCEU, 15:66–v.

70. Fauconnet to Drouyn de Lhuys, New Orleans, May 19, 1864, CPCEU, 19:79.

71. Fauconnet to Drouyn de Lhuys, New Orleans, April 22, 1864, CPCEU, 19:74–v.

72. Dayton to Seward, Paris, March 25, 1862, and Sanford to Seward, Paris, April 10, 1862, in Case and Spencer, *The United States and France*, 286–90.

73. Thouvenel to Mercier, Paris, May 21, 1862, CPEU, 127:176–80v.

74. Thouvenel to Paul, Paris, May 23, 1862, CCC Richmond, 5:149v.

75. Drouyn de Lhuys to Mercier, Paris, December 11, 1862, *Archives diplomatiques, 1863*, 1:295–96.

76. Owsley, *King Cotton Diplomacy*, 45–49.

77. Summary of a letter from Bunch to Russell, Charleston, March 19, 1862, ADPEU, 30: 122.

78. Souchard to Thouvenel, Boston, May 13, 1862, CPCEU, 12:188v–89.

79. Paul to Thouvenel, Richmond, May 14, 1862, CPCEU, 12:78–v.

80. Fauconnet to Drouyn de Lhuys, New Orleans, August 14, 1863, CPCEU, 14:256–57.

81. Lanen to Drouyn de Lhuys, Charleston, January 6, 1864, CCC Charleston, 7:334.

82. A. Léo, in *Le Journal des Débats*, October 19, 1861; L. Legault, in *Le Temps*, November 4, 1861.

83. *RDDM*, 1862 (1/2), 183–84.

84. F. Camus, in *Le Journal des Débats*, April 18, 1862; N. Claude, in *Le Temps*, October 2, 1862.

85. J. J. Weiss, in *Le Journal des Débats*, May 15, 1862.

86. Montholon to Drouyn de Lhuys, New York, January 4, 1863, CPCEU, 13:7v–8.

87. Drouyn de Lhuys to Mercier, Paris, May 14, 1863, LJEU, 1863, 119.

88. Baron Erlanger married Matilda, Slidell's daughter. Sexton, *Debtor Diplomacy*, 163.

89. Note for the minister, Paris, February 28, 1863, ADPEU, 34.

90. Sexton, *Debtor Diplomacy*, 165–70.

91. Analysis of a letter from Benjamin to Slidell, Paris, September 1863, ADPEU, 32:159.

92. Paul to Drouyn de Lhuys, New York, February 25, 1864, CPCEU, 19:180v.

93. Fauconnet to Drouyn de Lhuys, New Orleans, October 21, 1864, CPCEU, 19:148; Boilleau to Drouyn de Lhuys, New York, December 23, 1864, CPCEU, 18:171v.

94. Paul to Drouyn de Lhuys, Richmond, January 28, 1865, CPCEU, 23:128–v.

95. In January 1863, *Le Temps* reported that confidence seemed to be recovering in Manchester. L. Legault, in *Le Temps*, January 28, 1863; Valadier (l'Augle), in *Le Courrier du Midi* (Toulouse), April 30, 1863, in Blackburn, *French Newspaper Opinion*, 84.

96. Case, *French Opinion*, 103; 143, no. 165; 147, no. 172; 150–54, no. 176; 155, no. 179; 156, no. 181.

97. In January 1862, the French ambassador to the United Kingdom wrote that the British government was indifferent to the cotton reserves. Flahaut to Thouvenel, London, January 25, 1862, PT, 8:279v.

98. Thouvenel to Mercier, Paris, September 3 and October 3, 1861, CPEU, 125:108–12v.

99. Thouvenel to Flahaut, Paris, October 31, 1861, CPA, 720:226v; Owsley, *King Cotton Diplomacy*, 134–35.

100. Marzagalli and Marnot, *Guerre et économie*, 288.

101. Rouher to Thouvenel, Paris, November 15, 1861, ADPEU, 33:73; Baroche, *Second Empire*, 198; Thouvenel to Flahaut, Paris, April 14, 1862, CPA, 721:132.

102. Ratcliffe, "Cotton Famine," 144–45.

103. *Documents statistiques*, 1863 and 1864.

104. Pomeroy, "French Substitutes for American Cotton," 556–57.

105. Napoléon III to General Forey, Fontainebleau, July 3, 1862, LJM, 1862, 191.

106. Flahaut to Thouvenel, London, January 25, 1862, PT, 8:278; Drouyn de Lhuys to Montholon, Paris, February 12, 1864, CCC Mexico, 8:22v.

107. Marzagalli and Marnot, *Guerre et économie*, 293.

108. In 1865, *La Revue des Deux Mondes* speculated on the importation into Europe of 2.5 million bales, 1.6 million of which would come from India and 300,000 from Egypt. *RDDM*, 1865 (3/4), 201.

109. Slidell to Thouvenel, Paris, July 21, 1862, ADPEU, 32:54.

110. While the decisive backup supply of British cotton enabled an end to the cotton famine, we must not forget that a small part still came from transport by the blockade runners who took advantage of the flaws in the system, though it became increasingly impenetrable.

111. Duveau, *La vie ouvrière sous le Second Empire*, 121.

112. Charle, *Histoire sociale de la France*, 108–9.

113. Barjot, *Histoire économique de la France*, 223. Figures based on the 1866 census of industrial workers. Laroulandie, "Ouvriers," 946. "We had no fewer than 400,000 workers

threatened in their work and in their lives," the wife of Justice Minister Jules Baroche wrote in her memoirs. Baroche, *Second Empire*, 199.

114. Fohlen, "La guerre de Sécession," 265–67.

115. Ratcliffe, "Cotton Famine," 144–45; Ball, *Financial Failure*, 66.

116. Fohlen, *L'industrie textile au temps du Second Empire*, 283.

117. Barjot, *Histoire économique de la France*, 217–18. It was not until 1880 that the big business model was more clearly established, and even then the shift to large-scale industry was not comprehensive.

118. Charle, *Histoire sociale de la France*, 108–9.

119. Laroulandie, "Ouvriers," 946.

120. Fohlen, *L'industrie textile au temps du Second Empire*, 253.

121. Ibid., 274–75.

122. *RDDM*, 1863 (1/2), 211–27; *RDDM*, 1865 (3/4), 201; Delaporte, in *Le Pays*, April 1, 1863, in Blackburn, *French Newspaper Opinion*, 86; J. J. Weiss, in *Le Journal des Débats*, January 8, 1863.

123. Case, *French Opinion*, 61–63, no. 73. The treaty was signed on January 23, 1860.

124. Heffer, *Le port de New York*, 250.

125. Lincoln's first Annual Message. December 3, 1861. See also Seward to Thouvenel, Washington, October 30, 1861, in Van Deusen, *William Henry Seward*, 303–4.

126. Thouvenel to Mercier, Paris, May 16, 1861, LJEU, 1861, 96.

127. *Le Moniteur*, September 16, 1859.

128. Report by Montholon, Washington, 1861, ADPEU, 30:83v.

129. *Documents statistiques*, 1863.

130. Fohlen, "La guerre de Sécession," 261.

131. *Documents statistiques*, 1863.

132. Report by Montholon, Washington, 1861, ADPEU, 30:83v–84v.

133. Paul to Drouyn de Lhuys, New York, February 25, 1864, CPCEU, 19:180v.

134. Report by Montholon, Washington, 1861, ADPEU, 30:83v–84v; Paul to Walewski, Richmond, December 10, 1859, CCC Richmond, 4:171. See also the figures provided by the *Journal des Débats* in 1861 to depict the decline of Virginia. J. J. Weiss, in *Le Journal des Débats*, April 22, 1861.

135. Slidell's memo, in Slidell to Benjamin, Paris, October 28, 1862, and June 21, 1863, *ORN*, 574–78, 812–14.

136. Faulkner to Seward, Paris, April 15, 1861, and Sanford to Seward, Paris, April 25, 1861, in Case and Spencer, *The United States and France*, 26, 133, 164–65.

137. Thouvenel to Mercier, Paris, July 23, 1862, *Archives diplomatiques, 1863*, 1:283–84.

138. Report by Montholon, Washington, 1861, ADPEU, 30:82–v.

139. Sartiges to Thouvenel, The Hague, December 28, 1861, ADPEU, 30:76.

140. Heffer, *Le port de New York*, 33, 36.

141. Report by Montholon, Washington, 1861, ADPEU, 30:83v; Sartiges to Thouvenel, The Hague, December 28, 1861, ADPEU, 30:77.

142. Paul to Walewski, Richmond, March 10, 1858, CCC Richmond, 4:15–23.

143. Boilleau to Drouyn de Lhuys, New York, November 26, 1863, January 16, 1864, March 21, 1864, and December 27, 1864, CPCEU, 13:340–49, 15:17, 118, 18:179v.

144. Paul to Walewski, Richmond, March 10, 1858, CCC Richmond, 4:15–23; Paul to Walewski, Richmond, December 10, 1859, CCC Richmond, 4:171–73.

145. Fohlen, "La guerre de Sécession," 262.

146. Report by Montholon, Washington, 1861, ADPEU, 30:83.

147. Heffer, *Le port de New York*, 61, 64.

148. Mercier to Thouvenel, Washington, November 4, 1861, PT, 13:414–15; Montholon to Thouvenel, New York, November 5, 1861, CPCEU, 8:125.

149. Mercier to Thouvenel, Washington, March 29, 1861, CPEU, 124:124; Mercier to Thouvenel, Washington, February 11, 1862, *Archives diplomatiques, 1863*, 1:261.

150. Thouvenel to Mercier, Paris, May 16, 1861, LJEU, 1861, 96.

151. Gaulot, *Rêve d'Empire*, 92.

152. Gaïffe, in *La Presse*, July 20, 1862, in Blackburn, *French Newspaper Opinion*, 81; Auguste Vitu, in *Le Constitutionnel*, December 13, 1861; Bernard, in *Le Siècle*, August 27, 1862, in West, *Contemporary French Opinion*, 43, 84.

153. Chemin-Dupontès, in *Le Journal des Débats*, February 20, 1861; *RDDM*, 1861 (11/12), 157.

154. Smith, *Starving the South*, 18.

155. Paul to Thouvenel, Richmond, November 2, 1861, CPCEU, 9:260–61.

156. On this subject, *Le Journal des Débats* wrote, "Is it before this imperious warning that we are asked to debase our flag?" Edouard Laboulaye, in *Le Journal des Débats*, August 27, 1862.

157. See chapter 2.

CHAPTER 9

1. The Union states soon totaled twenty-five with the addition of West Virginia and Kansas.

2. Slidell to Thouvenel, Paris, July 21, 1862, ADPEU, 32:49. The ratio adopted by the diplomats was four to one for the Northerners. For the sake of comparison, the population of France at the time outnumbered that of Mexico by about the same proportion.

3. Report by Montholon concerning a document dated October 22, "Note pour le ministre sur les conséquences que pourrait avoir l'intervention de la France dans le conflit anglo-américain," Washington, 1861, ADPEU, 30:83v.

4. Report by Montholon, Washington, 1861, ADPEU, 30:85.

5. Letter from Maury, Richmond, March 15, 1862, ADPEU, 30:114–17v.

6. Analysis of a book of statistics submitted by Mercier, ADPEU, 30:2–13.

7. Ibid.

8. Paul to Thouvenel, Richmond, April 19, 1861, CPCEU, 9:171v–72.

9. Niboyet to Thouvenel, New York, June 11, 1861, CPCEU, 8:32.

10. Letter from Maury, Richmond, March 15, 1862, ADPEU, 30:114–17v. Analysis of a book of statistics submitted by Mercier, ADPEU, 30:2–13. According to Montholon, the tonnage of the South's merchant fleet was one-tenth that of the Union. Report by Montholon, Washington, 1861, ADPEU, 30:82–v.

11. See chapter 8.

12. Bruyère-Ostells, *Napoléon III et le Second Empire*, 75–81; Report by Montholon, Washington, 1861, ADPEU, 30:83v. In fact, the report counted the rail network of the slave states as including four states that remained loyal to the Union. The mileage of railway lines in the North was therefore not twice but two and a half times greater than that in the South. E. B. Long and B. Long, *The Civil War Day by Day*, 723.

13. Sartiges to Thouvenel, The Hague, December 28, 1861, ADPEU, 30:75v.

14. Slidell's memo, in Slidell to Benjamin, Paris, October 28, 1862, and June 21, 1863, *ORN*, 574–78, 812–14.

15. Mercier to Thouvenel, Washington, February 25, 1861, CPEU, 124:79; Méjan to Thouvenel, New Orleans, April 29, 1861, CPCEU, 9:61–v; Paul to Thouvenel, Richmond, April 28, 1861, CPCEU, 9:175v.

16. Mercier to Thouvenel, Washington, April 26, 1861, CPEU, 124:171; Mercier to Thouvenel, Washington, May 12, 1861, CPEU, 124:211; Paul to Drouyn de Lhuys, Richmond, January 4, 1863, CPCEU, 15:4v–6v.

17. For a portrait of Alfred Paul, see Sainlaude, "Alfred Paul," 3–15.

18. Civil registration records of the city of Marseille, Births, year 1817 (419); Papiers d'Agents, Paul, 1st ser., no. 3192.

19. He was the only consul to serve throughout the Civil War, and beyond, as he did not return to Europe until 1866.

20. Paul to Walewski, Richmond, December 4, 1859, CPC 7:106–9; Paul to Thouvenel, Richmond, November 10, 1860, CPCEU, 7:320.

21. Paul to Thouvenel, Richmond, January 9, 1861, CPCEU, 9:136.

22. Paul to Thouvenel, Richmond, December 22, 1860, CPCEU, 7:330v. Paul wrote, "It is not plausible for the split to be accomplished without a civil war."

23. Paul to Thouvenel, Richmond, April 28, 1861, CPCEU, 9:175.

24. Paul to Thouvenel, Richmond, January 4, 1863, CPCEU, 15:11.

25. Paul to Thouvenel, Richmond, April 19, 1861, CPCEU, 9:170v; Méjan in New Orleans had already made a similar remark: "If the attack is strong, the defense will be no less so." Méjan to Thouvenel, New Orleans, April 11, 1861, CPCEU, 9:53v.

26. Paul to Thouvenel, Richmond, April 28, 1861, CPCEU, 9:175v.

27. Paul to Thouvenel, Richmond, July 19, 1861, CPCEU, 9:202v.

28. Paul to Thouvenel, Richmond, April 28, 1861, CPCEU, 9:175v; Paul to Thouvenel, Richmond, July 19, 1861, CPCEU, 9:203v.

29. Paul to Drouyn de Lhuys, Richmond, August 24, 1863, CPCEU, 15:64–64v.

30. Paul to Drouyn de Lhuys, Richmond, May 15, 1863, CPCEU, 15:53.

31. Paul to Drouyn de Lhuys, Richmond, August 24, 1863, CPCEU, 15:64–64v.

32. Paul to Thouvenel, Richmond, December 19, 1861, CPCEU, 9:291–91v.

33. Paul to Drouyn de Lhuys, Richmond, December 23, 1863, CPCEU, 15:87v–88.

34. Paul to Thouvenel, Richmond, April 28, 1861, CPCEU, 9:175v; Paul to Thouvenel, Richmond, November 2, 1861, CPCEU, 9:254v–55.

35. Paul to Thouvenel, Richmond, June 5, 1862, CPCEU, 12:100–v; Keegan, *La guerre de Sécession*, 117.

36. Paul to Drouyn de Lhuys, Richmond, April 12, 1863, CCC Richmond, 5:261–63.

37. Paul to Thouvenel, Richmond, August 14, 1862, CPCEU, 12:125–26. He wrote, "If this inferiority exists, that is."

38. Paul to Thouvenel, Richmond, February 10, 1862, CPCEU, 12:9–v.

39. Paul to Thouvenel, Richmond, November 2, 1861, CPCEU, 9:254v–55.

40. Paul to Thouvenel, Richmond, January 22, 1862, CPCEU, 12:5v–6.

41. Paul to Drouyn de Lhuys, Richmond, March 15, 1863, CCC Richmond, 5:252v–55v; Paul to Drouyn de Lhuys, Richmond, June 23, 1864, CPCEU, 19:216; Souchard to Drouyn de Lhuys, Boston, April 14, 1863, CPCEU, 15:107.

42. Mercier to Thouvenel, Washington, April 28, 1862, CPEU, 127:50.

43. Paul to Thouvenel, Richmond, May 30, 1862, CPCEU, 12:93–94; Paul to Drouyn de Lhuys, Richmond, June 10, 1864, CPCEU, 19:207.

44. Mercier to Thouvenel, Washington, October 22, 1861, CPEU, 125:152.

45. Mercier to Thouvenel, Washington, May 6, 1862, PT, 13:448v; Mercier to Thouvenel, Washington, May 26, 1862, PT, 13:457. Between February and May 1862, besides taking New Orleans, Union forces seized 80,000 square kilometers, secured control of 1,600 kilometers of waterways, conquered the capitals of two Confederate states, and put 30,000 enemies out of action. McPherson, *La guerre de Sécession,* 461.

46. Paul to Thouvenel, Richmond, April 30, 1862, CPCEU, 12:74v–75.

47. Paul to Thouvenel, Richmond, July 7, 1862, CPCEU, 12:122–24.

48. Paul to Drouyn de Lhuys, Richmond, January 4, 1863, CPCEU, 15:4v–6v.

49. Paul to Drouyn de Lhuys, Richmond, January 15, 1864, CPCEU, 19:173–73v.

50. Paul to Drouyn de Lhuys, Richmond, June 10, 1864, CPCEU, 19:207.

51. Paul to Drouyn de Lhuys, Richmond, June 23, 1864, CPCEU, 19:216.

52. Paul to Drouyn de Lhuys, Richmond, September 6, 1864, CPCEU, 19:231-v.

53. Paul to Drouyn de Lhuys, Richmond, January 28, 1865, CPCEU, 23:130v. We can compare Paul's prescience with that of Geofroy, the first secretary of the legation, who wrote in December 1864, in spite of Lincoln's reelection and solid majority in Congress, that the North would be forced to negotiate with the South. Geofroy to Drouyn de Lhuys, Washington, December 5, 1864, CPEU, 132:235. It can also be compared to the feeling of the French ambassador to the United Kingdom that the war would come to nothing for either side. La Tour d'Auvergne to Drouyn de Lhuys, London, February 6, 1865, CPA, 732:70.

54. Thouvenel to Paul, Paris, December 26, 1861, CPCEU, 9:301; Thouvenel to Paul, Paris, January 9, 1862, CPCEU, 12:4. He was referring to Paul's November report.

55. Drouyn de Lhuys to Paul, Paris, February 12, 1863, CPCEU, 15:36; Drouyn de Lhuys to Paul, Paris, May 28, 1863, CPCEU, 15:58-v.

56. Slidell's memo, in Slidell to Benjamin, Paris, October 28, 1862, *ORN,* 574–78.

57. For example, Paul's dispatch, passed on by Thouvenel to Flahaut joined to Mercier's dispatch in Thouvenel to Flahaut, Paris, July 6, 1861, CPA, 720:63. Paul's dispatch shared by Drouyn de Lhuys with Rouher in Drouyn de Lhuys to Rouher, Paris, February 24, 1865, ADPEU, 31:113.

58. Seward, *Reminiscences of a War-Time Statesman and Diplomat,* 183.

59. Borg to Drouyn de Lhuys, New York, November 23, 1863, CPCEU, 13:149v.

60. General Webb's Memo, August 2, 1861, ADPEU, 30:50–56.

61. Seward to Dayton, Washington, March 26, 1862, ADPEU, 30:133; Drouyn de Lhuys to Dayton, Compiègne, November 23, 1862, LJEU, 1862, 147.

62. In 1864, on the night of a ball, Dayton told Eugénie, "Madam, the North will win. It is inevitable." Delamare, *L'Empire oublié,* 75.

63. Thouvenel to Mercier, Paris, May 21, 1862, LJEU, 1862, 128, and *Archives diplomatiques, 1863,* 1:275–77.

64. Slidell's memo, in Slidell to Benjamin, Paris, October 28, 1862, *ORN,* 574–78.

65. Drouyn de Lhuys to Dayton, Compiègne, November 23, 1862, LJEU, 1862, 147.

66. Montholon to Thouvenel, New York, February 11, 1862, CPCEU, 10:16.

67. Saint-André to Drouyn de Lhuys, onboard the *Catinat,* April 7, 1863, CPCEU, 14:32. The *Catinat* was the flagship of Rear-Admiral Reynaud's squadron.

68. Seward, *Reminiscences of a War-Time Statesman and Diplomat,* 183.

69. Drouyn de Lhuys to La Tour d'Auvergne, Paris, July 14, 1864, CPA, 730:317. Captain Pigeard's report: "Aperçu du mouvement maritime aux Etats-Unis depuis le commencement de la guerre," Paris, 1864, MDEU, 25:223.

70. Sheldon-Duplaix, "Un marin du Second Empire au service du renseignement."

71. The French war and navy budgets combined (including 210 million francs for the navy) were fifty times larger than the diplomatic budget. With 400 ships, including 34 ironclads armed with 27 cm and 24 cm guns, the French fleet ranked second in the world. Taillemite, *L'histoire ignorée de la marine française*, 340; Battesti, *La marine de Napoléon III*, 2:788–90.

72. Lieutenant Colonel de Chanal studied the organization of the Union army for eight months. De La Mardière, "La guerre de Sécession," 17–18, 24–25.

73. De Chanal, *L'Armée américaine pendant la guerre de Sécession*, 24, 31, 35, 36, 41, 43, 103, 198–99; Bodelle, *Petite(s) histoire(s) des Français d'Amérique*, 308-9.

74. Coquille, in *Le Monde*, June 9 and 10, 1862; Chantrel, in *Le Monde*, November 15, 1862, in Blackburn, *French Newspaper Opinion*, 58.

75. Lomon, in *Le Pays*, April 19, 1862, in Blackburn, *French Newspaper Opinion*, 58.

76. *La Patrie*, 1863, in Roger, *L'ennemi américain*, 125.

77. Auguste Léo, in *Le Journal des Débats*, July 31, 1861.

78. F. Camus, in *Le Journal des Débats*, April 24, 1862; A. Hébrard, in *Le Temps*, April 25, 1862.

79. Prévost-Paradol, in *Le Journal des Débats*, April 29, 1862; L. Alloury, in *Le Journal des Débats*, February 18, 1863.

80. Victor Mangin, in *Le Phare de la Loire*, November 14, 1862, in Gavronsky, *The French Liberal Opposition*, 153.

81. Prévost-Paradol believed that the weak Yankee command was delaying the South's defeat. *Le Journal des Débats*, November 14, 1862.

82. Guiral, "Prévost-Paradol," 377.

83. F. Camus, in *Le Journal des Débats*, April 16, 1865; A. Nefftzer, in *Le Temps*, April 16, 1865.

84. Paul to Thouvenel, Richmond, January 9, 1861, CPCEU, 9:145–v; Paul to Drouyn de Lhuys, Richmond, January 15, 1864, CPCEU, 19:172–v; Paul to Drouyn de Lhuys, Richmond, January 28, 1865, CPCEU, 23:130v.

85. Borg to Drouyn de Lhuys, New York, December 15, 1863, CPCEU, 13:172–76.

86. Seward to Dayton, Washington, April 15, 1862, ADPEU, 30:175–v; Anonymous dispatch, London, August 2, 1862, CPA, 722:30v.

87. Paul to Drouyn de Lhuys, Richmond, January 4, 1863, CPCEU, 15:6v.

88. Paul to Drouyn de Lhuys, Richmond, January 15, 1864, CPCEU, 19:173–v.

89. De Tocqueville, *De la démocratie en Amérique*, 1:486, 515–16. De Tocqueville's judgment of Jackson was far from accurate, as Jackson never considered granting more rights to the states than to the central government.

90. Mercier to Thouvenel, Washington, February 18, 1861, CPEU, 124:63.

91. Méjan to Thouvenel, New Orleans, April 15, 1861, CCC New Orleans, 13:303.

92. Mercier to Thouvenel, Washington, March 29, 1861, CPEU, 124:122.

93. The document filed under *Affaires Diverses et Politiques* dated August 1861 gives details of the conversation between Faulkner and Thouvenel four months earlier. Dayton to Thouvenel, Paris, August 13, 1861, ADPEU, 30:63–69v; Seward to Dayton, Washington, July 6, 1861, *Archives diplomatiques, 1861*, 3:129.

94. Mercier to Thouvenel, Washington, June 10, 1861, CPEU, 124:301.

95. Vincent, *Lincoln*, 246.

96. Paul to Thouvenel, Richmond, April 28, 1861, CPCEU, 9:175. See also Paul to Thouvenel, Richmond, July 19, 1861, CPCEU, 9:201v.

97. General Webb's Memo, August 2, 1861, ADPEU, 30:55–56.

98. Montholon to Thouvenel, New York, August 27, 1861, CPCEU, 8:59.

99. Flahaut to Thouvenel, London, March 4, 1862, CPA, 721:60v–61.

100. Mercier to Thouvenel, Washington, July 1, 1862, CPEU, 128:5; Souchard to Thouvenel, Boston, August 19, 1862, CPCEU, 12:208–9.

101. Thouvenel to Flahaut, Paris, September 27, 1862, CPA, 722:115.

102. Drouyn de Lhuys to Mercier, Paris, January 23, 1863, *Archives diplomatiques, 1863,* 4:276–77.

103. Seward to Dayton, Washington, February 4, 1863, ADPEU, 31:17v.

104. Gaillardet, in *La Presse*, March 26, 1861; *Le Constitutionnel*, March 4 and 26, 1861, in Blackburn, *French Newspaper Opinion*, 33–34.

105. J. J. Weiss, in *Le Journal des Débats*, March 20, 1861.

106. L. Alloury and Auguste Léo, in *Le Journal des Débats*, April 27 and May 1, 1861; E. Charpentier and de A. Nefftzer, in *Le Temps*, May 1 and 4, 1861.

107. J. J. Weiss, in *Le Journal des Débats*, July 20, 1861; Auguste Léo, in *Le Journal des Débats*, July 31, 1861; A. Grandguillot, in *Le Constitutionnel*, July 7, 1861, in West, *Contemporary French Opinion*, 21.

108. Mercier to Thouvenel, Washington, July 19, 1862, PT, 13:472.

109. Thouvenel to Mercier, Paris, October 2, 1862, in Thouvenel, *Le secret de l'Empereur*, 2:414–15.

110. Drouyn de Lhuys to Souchard, Paris, March 1863, CPCEU, 15:103; Montholon to Drouyn de Lhuys, New York, June 16, 1863, CPCEU, 13:52v–56.

111. Paul to Drouyn de Lhuys, Richmond, July 5, 1864, CPCEU, 19:217–21v.

112. Geofroy to Drouyn de Lhuys, Washington, August 22, 1864, CPEU, 132:16.

113. Taconet, in *Le Monde*, May 21, 1864; Lomon, in *Le Pays*, September 1, 1864, in Blackburn, *French Newspaper Opinion*, 116.

114. Edouard Hervé, in *Le Temps*, October 9, 1864.

115. Excerpt from a New York newspaper annexed to the political dispatch from Boilleau to Drouyn de Lhuys, New York, October 12, 1864, CPCEU, 18:33.

116. Paul to Drouyn de Lhuys, Richmond, September 6, 1864, CPCEU, 19:231–v.

117. Guillaud, in *La Patrie*, October 10, 1864, in Blackburn, *French Newspaper Opinion*, 116; F. Camus, in *Le Journal des Débats*, September 14, 1864; Ulysse Cadet, in *Le Temps*, October 10, 1864.

118. *Le Constitutionnel*, November 21, 1864, in West, *Contemporary French Opinion*, 144; *La Patrie*, November 24, 1864, in Case and Spencer, *The United States and France*, 557.

119. Prévost-Paradol, in *Le Journal des Débats*, November 27, 1864; RDDM, 1864 (11/12), 800–801.

120. Ulysse Cadet, in *Le Temps*, November 22, 1864.

121. Mercier, *Du Panlatinisme*, 11; Du Bellet, *Lettre au corps législatif*, 4.

122. Méjan to Thouvenel, New Orleans, April 11, 1861, CPCEU, 9:54v.

123. Montholon to Thouvenel, New York, February 11, 1862, CPCEU, 10:18v.

124. Levasseur to Drouyn de Lhuys, St. Louis, September 15, 1864, CPCEU, 19:9.

125. Flahaut to Thouvenel, London, March 4, 1862, CPA, 721:61v.

126. Sain de Boislecomte, *De la crise américaine*, 57–58.

127. *Archives diplomatiques, 1863*, 1:266–67.

128. Thouvenel to Mercier, Paris, May 21, 1862, *Archives diplomatiques, 1863*, 1:275–77. For the Quai d'Orsay's plan, see chapter 2.

129. E. Scherer, in *Le Temps*, June 15 and October 19, 1861.

130. F. Camus, in *Le Journal des Débats*, June 27, 1861.

131. F. Camus, in *Le Journal des Débats*, April 24, 1862; *RDDM*, 1863 (9/10), 895–97.

132. Lomon, in *Le Pays*, April 19, 1862; Massoubre (Périgueux), in *L'Echo de Vesone*, November 23, 1862, in Blackburn, *French Newspaper Opinion*, 58, 99. The expression is from Massoubre.

133. Jones, "Wrapping the World in Fire," 35.

134. Mercier reported this plan to Thouvenel. Mercier to Thouvenel, Washington, February 1, 1861, CPEU, 124:39. See also Ferris, *Desperate Diplomacy*, 11; and Mahin, *One War at a Time*, 7.

135. Hubbard, *The Burden*, 55. Was this professed resolve, in fact, a bluff? Glyndon Van Deusen has pointed out that Seward did not like war. Van Deusen, *William Henry Seward*, 231. In any case, he showed no hesitation in using it to subdue the South.

136. Seward to Dayton, Washington, July 10, 1862, ADPEU, 30:207–8.

137. Mercier to Thouvenel, Washington, May 23, 1861, CPEU, 124:225–30.

138. Mercier to Thouvenel, Quebec, September 13, 1861, PT, 13:404v; Mercier to Thouvenel, Washington, October 22, 1861, CPEU, 125:152.

139. Mercier to Thouvenel, Washington, May 6, 1862, PT, 13:449v.

140. Mercier to Thouvenel, Washington, May 12, 1862, PT, 13:453.

141. Mercier to Drouyn de Lhuys, Washington, October 6, 1863, CPEU, 130:207.

142. Thouvenel to Flahaut, Paris, July 21 and 26, 1862, in Thouvenel, *Le secret de l'Empereur*, 2:339–40, 351–55.

143. Auguste Léo, in *Le Journal des Débats*, October 19, 1861; L. Alloury, in *Le Journal des Débats*, December 16, 1861; Bernard, in *Le Siècle*, August 27, 1862, in West, *Contemporary French Opinion*, 84; L. Alloury, in *Le Journal des Débats*, July 22, 1862; L. Legault, in *Le Temps*, November 15, 1862.

144. Edouard Laboulaye, in *Le Journal des Débats*, August 27, 1862; Bernard, in *Le Siècle*, August 27, 1862, in West, *Contemporary French Opinion*, 84.

145. Prévost-Paradol, in *Le Journal des Débats*, November 14, 1862.

146. McPherson, *War on the Waters*, 224.

147. Nean, "Le Canada et la guerre de Sécession," 353.

148. Theis, "Entre besoin de repos et désir de gloire," 600.

149. The expedition was very poorly prepared. The commander in chief, General Forey, did not even have a map of Mexico. Napoléon himself had to give him one!

150. A. Nefftzer, in *Le Temps*, June 15, 1862.

151. Report by Montholon, Washington, 1861, ADPEU, 30:81–82.

152. Thouvenel to Flahaut, Paris, January 23, 1862, in Thouvenel, *Le secret de l'Empereur*, 2:230–31.

153. Thouvenel to Flahaut, Paris, July 21, 1862, in Thouvenel, *Le secret de l'Empereur*, 2:339–40.

154. Flahaut to Thouvenel, London, July 23, 1862, PT, 8:371v–72v.

155. Pradier-Fodère, "M. Drouyn de Lhuys," 14, 20–21. We should not conclude, however, that Drouyn de Lhuys was a pacifist. After Sadowa he wanted a military show of

force against Prussia, which Napoléon III refused. D'Harcourt, *Les quatre ministères*, 336–37, 340. But he preferred to reserve these military engagements for the European arena, where France could most benefit.

156. Theis, "Entre besoin de repos et désir de gloire," 582. Baillou, *Les affaires étrangères*, 1:773.

157. From 1865 onward, he facilitated the troops' departure.

158. Bruley, *Le Quai d'Orsay impérial*, 216–17.

159. Slidell to Benjamin, Paris, June 21, 1863, *ORN*, 811.

160. Drouyn de Lhuys to Chasseloup-Laubat, Paris, April 22, 1864, PR, 8. Drouyn de Lhuys was referring to the recent Senate vote against recognition of Maximilian's empire.

161. Slidell's memo, in Slidell to Benjamin, Paris, October 28, 1862, *ORN*, 574–78.

162. Slidell's memo, in Slidell to Benjamin, Paris, June 21, 1863, *ORN*, 812–14.

163. Slidell to Benjamin, Paris, November 15, 1863, *ORN*, 955–58.

164. Thouvenel to Flahaut, Paris, October 2, 1862, in Thouvenel, *Le secret de l'Empereur*, 2:416. Thouvenel did not resign due to the difference of opinion over the Civil War, as Korolewicz-Carlton suggests. Korolewicz-Carlton, *Napoléon III*, 187. Moreover, he recognized this himself in a letter to Mercier on September 11, 1862: "As important as American affairs may be, our most immediate concerns apply to Italy." Thouvenel, *Le secret de l'Empereur*, 2:388.

165. Slidell's memo, in Slidell to Benjamin, Paris, October 28, 1862, *ORN*, 574–78. In Italy, Garibaldi's march on Rome was stopped in late August by the Piedmontese. In Greece, a revolution had ousted King Otto from the throne.

166. Slidell to Benjamin, Paris, August 5, 1863, *ORN*, 855–56; Slidell to Benjamin, Paris, November 15, 1863, *ORN*, 955–58; Slidell to Benjamin, Paris, December 15, 1863, *ORN*, 976–77.

167. The question of the duchies that began with the death of the Danish king Frederick VII on November 15, 1863, led to a war between Prussia and Denmark, which was won a year later by Prussia. In 1864, the September Convention granted the Holy See the provisional maintenance of French troops in Rome.

168. Mercier to Thouvenel, Washington, May 23, 1861, CPEU, 124:225–27.

169. Renouvin, *La question d'Extrême-Orient*, 56–57.

170. Gros to Drouyn de Lhuys, London, November 26, 1864, CPA, 727:107.

171. Renouvin, *Histoire des relations internationales*, 2:573–74.

172. Napoléon III, *Oeuvres*, 5:227.

173. Drouyn de Lhuys to La Tour d'Auvergne, Paris, December 30, 1864, CPA, 727:240.

174. Callahan, *American Foreign Policy in Mexican Relations*, 287.

CONCLUSION

1. In 1866, the first demographic census reporting data on education was published. Constructed using the signatures on notarial deeds, it revealed that 35 percent of men and 42 percent of women could not read. Furet and Sachs, "La croissance de l'alphabétisation en France," 721. And for the rest of the population, reading was not necessarily a straightforward exercise.

2. Evans, *Memoirs of Dr. Thomas W. Evans*, 118.

3. Exactly 109,870 French were living in the United States, 80 percent of whom remained loyal to the Union and 20 percent of whom remained loyal to the Confederate

states. So the majority was safe and not concerned by the military operations. That explains why the French government had lost interest in the fate of its nationals. U.S. Bureau of the Census, Country of Birth of the Foreign-Born Population, 3:695; Barkan, "Immigrants in American History", 74; Keegan, *The American Civil War*, 21; De La Mardière, "La guerre de Sécession," 45; Bodelle, *Petite(s) histoire(s) des Français d'Amérique*, 299.

4. Camille was the son of the prince de Polignac, former minister of Charles X. Paul to Thouvenel, Richmond, July 20, 1861, CPCEU, 9:210; Paul to Thouvenel, Richmond, November 2, 1861, CPCEU, 9:259. The prince de Joinville was François d'Orléans, grandson of Louis-Philippe, last king of the French. Bodelle, *Petite(s) histoire(s) des Français d'Amérique*, 99, 303, 307.

5. General de Gaulle traveled in Mexico from March 16 to 19, 1964. On September 1, 1966, he was in Cambodia and gave his famous speech at the Phnom Penh sports complex: "That is why, while your country succeeded in safeguarding its body and its soul because it remained its own master, the political and military authority of the United States was seen installed in its turn in South Vietnam and, simultaneously, the war gained new strength there in the form of national resistance."

6. In 1863 he had several bouts of illness. In August 1864 he suffered a heart attack and prolonged hematuria. In 1865 the pain forced him to miss several sessions of the Council of Ministers. He believed his final hour had come. Anceau, *Napoléon III*, 408.

7. Anceau, *L'Empire libéral*, 1:230.

8. Theis, "Entre besoin de repos et désir de gloire," 582.

9. Thouvenel to Flahaut, Paris, April 14, 1862, in Thouvenel, *Le secret de l'Empereur*, 2:277. It was the same for Flahaut, who agreed that these informal relationships complicated his work more than they simplified it. Flahaut to Thouvenel, London, April 16, 1862, PT, 8:324v.

10. Slidell to Benjamin, Paris, May 9, 1862, *ORN*, 414–15.

11. Gros to Drouyn de Lhuys, London, July 1, 1863, CPA, 725:117v.

12. Following the setback at Puebla in 1862, Alfred Paul in Richmond encouraged his government to propose mediation for the sole purpose of delaying the Confederate defeat and allowing time for the French to gain the upper hand. Paul to Drouyn de Lhuys, Richmond, December 19, 1862, CPCEU, 12:139–40v.

13. Geofroy to Drouyn de Lhuys, Washington, December 5, 1864, CPEU, 132:235; Geofroy to Drouyn de Lhuys, Washington, January 16, 1865, CPEU, 133:55. Geofroy declared that "if the Confederacy surrenders, the next day we will have a war with the Americans." Geofroy to Drouyn de Lhuys, Washington, January 30, 1865, CPEU, 133:73.

14. La Tour d'Auvergne to Drouyn de Lhuys, London, April 25, 1865, CPA, 732:266; Boilleau to Drouyn de Lhuys, Washington, May 15, 1865, MDEU, 25:341–v.

15. Bigelow to Drouyn de Lhuys, Paris, May 10, 1865, LJEU, 1866, 83–85, and MDEU, 25: 335–40.

16. Notes to the minister, Paris, May 14 and 15, 1865, MDEU, 25:311v–13, 346v–50v.

17. Drouyn de Lhuys to Bigelow, Paris, May 20, 1865, LJEU, 1866, 85, 87, 95; Drouyn de Lhuys to La Tour d'Auvergne, Paris, April 28, 1865, MDEU, 25:268–v; La Tour d'Auvergne to Drouyn de Lhuys, London, April 30, 1865, MDEU, 25:271; Bigelow to Drouyn de Lhuys, Paris, May 29, 1865, LJEU, 1866, 89.

18. Russell to Cowley, London, May 30, 1865, MDEU, 25:374v. Jefferson Davis was arrested on May 10.

19. Drouyn de Lhuys to Bigelow, Paris, June 8, 1865, MDEU, 25:384.

20. Drouyn de Lhuys to Dano, Paris, May 31, 1865, CPM, 63:322v. On May 8, 1865, Ulysses S. Grant met with Matias Romero, Juárez's representative to the Federal government, and discussed an expedition to Mexico to expel the French. Smith, *Grant*, 415. Seward was opposed to armed action and assured Johnson that peaceful diplomacy and a policy of persuasion would bring the French troops to leave within six months, without incurring any damages. Trefousse, *Andrew Johnson*, 270.

Bibliography

ARCHIVAL MANUSCRIPT SOURCES

All the archival collections used for this book are housed at the
Centre des archives diplomatiques de la Courneuve

Correspondances Politiques (Political Correspondence)

Etats-Unis, vols. 91, 93, 105, 112, 113, 114, 118–39
Angleterre, vols. 715–32
Mexique, vols. 54–65

Correspondances Politiques des Consuls (Political Correspondence of Consuls)

Baltimore, Boston, Charleston, Galveston, New Orleans, Los Angeles, Mobile.
New York: Philadelphia, Richmond, Saint-Louis, San Francisco, volumes 2–4, 7–23

*Correspondances Consulaires et Commerciales
(Consular and Commercial Correspondence)*

Charleston, vols. 6, 7
Mexico, vol. 8
New Orleans (vol. 89), vols. 13, 14
New York, vols. 19–21
Richmond, vols. 4, 5.

Affaires Diverses et Politiques (Political and Other Miscellaneous Business) / United States

Guerre de Sécession, vols. 30–54. Divers (1866–70), 69, 77.

Mémoires et Documents (Memoirs and Documents)

Etats-Unis, vol. 25
Mexique, vol. 10

Papiers d'Agents (Agents' Papers)

Eugène Rouher, vol. 8
Comte Eugène de Sartiges, vols. 8, 10
Edouard Thouvenel, vols. 8, 10, 13, 17

Papiers du Personnel (Staff Papers)

Belligny: 1st series, no. 3635
Borg: 1st series, no. 516
Cintrat (Pierre): 1st series, no. 961
Durant Saint-André: 1st series, no. 1477
Fauconnet: 1st series, no. 1566
Geofroy (de): 1st series, no. 1806
Gauldrée Boilleau: 1st series, no. 1779
Lanen: 1st series, no. 2405
La Forest: 1st series, no. 2276
Mercier de Lostende: 1st series, no. 2848
Méjan: 1st series, no. 1566

Montebello: 1st series, no. 2962
Montholon: 1st series, no. 2980
Niboyet: 1st series, no. 3095
Paul: 1st series, no. 3192
Prévost-Paradol: 1st series, no. 3362
Sain de Boilecomte: 1st series, no. 3667
Sartiges: 1st series, no. 3666
Souchard: 1st series, no. 3793
Treilhard: 1st series, no. 3972
Villefort: 1st series, no. 4116

PUBLISHED PRIMARY SOURCES

Diplomatic Archives

Archives diplomatiques: Recueil de diplomatie et d'histoire, 1861. Vol. 1 (1/3), vol. 2 (4/6), vol. 3 (7/9), vol. 4 (10/12). Paris: Amyot.

Archives diplomatiques: Recueil de diplomatie et d'histoire, 1862. Vol. 1 (1/3), vol. 2 (4/6), vol. 4 (10/12). Paris: Amyot.

Archives diplomatiques: Recueil de diplomatie et d'histoire, 1863. Vol. 1 (1/3), vol. 2 (4/6), vol. 3 (7/9), vol. 4 (10/12). Paris: Amyot.

Archives diplomatiques: Recueil de diplomatie et d'histoire, 1864. Vol. 1 (1/3), vol. 2 (4/6). Paris: Amyot.

Archivo Histórico Diplomático Mexicano, no. 13. Mexico City: Publicaciones de la Secretaría de Relaciones Exteriores, Direccíon General de Prensa y Publicidad, 1961.

Official Records of the Union and Confederate Navies in the War of the Rebellion. Series 2, vol. 3: *Proclamations, Appointments, etc., of President Davis, State Department Correspondence with Diplomatic Agents, etc.* Washington, D.C.: U.S. Government Printing Office, 1922.

Livres Jaunes (Yellow Books)

Livres jaunes Etats-Unis (1861–66)
Livres jaunes Mexique (1862)

Civil War–Era Sources

Chevalier, Michel, and Ernest Rasetti. *La France, le Mexique et les Etats confédérés*. Paris: E. Dentu, 1863.

Clarigny, Cucheval. "La nouvelle élection présidentielle et les partis aux Etats-Unis en 1860." *La Revue des Deux Mondes*, November–December 1860, 650–90.

de Chanal, Victor. *L'Armée américaine pendant la guerre de Sécession*. Paris: Librairie du Dictionnaire des Arts et Manufactures, 1872.

de Leon, Edwin. *La vérité sur les Etats confédérés d'Amérique*. Paris: E. Dentu, 1862.

———. *Secret History of Confederate Diplomacy Abroad*. Edited by William C. Davis. Lawrence: University Press of Kansas, 2005.

de Martens, G. F. "Livre VIII, Chapitre VII: Du rétablissement de la paix." In *Précis du droit des gens moderne de l'Europe*, 2:401–12. Paris: Guillaumin, 1858.

Direction générale des douanes . . . Tableau comparatif des principales marchandises importées. 1853, 1860, 1861, 1863–64.

Discours prononcé Par S. M. l'Empereur à l'ouverture de la Session Législative, Le 12 janvier 1863. Éditeur: Imprimerie impériale. January 1863.

Documents statistiques réunis par l'administration des douanes: commerce de la France, 1863. Paris: A l'administration du Moniteur universel, 1863.

Documents statistiques réunis par l'administration des douanes: commerce de la France, 1864. Paris: A l'administration du Moniteur universel, 1864.

Du Bellet, Paul. *Lettre à l'Empereur: De la reconnaissance des Etats confédérés d'Amérique*. Paris: Schiller Aîné, 1862.

———. *Lettre au corps législatif*. Paris: Tinterlin, 1864.

Duvergier de Hauranne, Ernest. *Les Etats-Unis pendant la guerre de Sécession: Récit d'un journaliste français*. Introduction by Albert Krebds. Paris: Calmann-Lévy, 1990.

Forcade, Eugène. "Chronique de la quinzaine. Histoire politique et littéraire." *La Revue des Deux Mondes*, May–June 1862, 486–97.

Helper, Hinton Rowan. *The Impending Crisis of the South: How to Meet It*. New York: Burdick Brothers, 1857.

Lacouture, Edouard. *La vérité sur la guerre d'Amérique*. Paris: E. Dentu, 1862.

Laugel, Auguste. "Les causes et caractères de la guerre civile aux Etats-Unis." *La Revue des Deux Mondes*, November–December 1861, 140–62.

———. "La guerre civile aux Etats-Unis (1861–1863): Le gouvernement fédéral, les armées et les partis." *La Revue des Deux Mondes*, September–October 1863, 872–97.

———. "Les Etats-Unis pendant la guerre: L'élection présidentielle de 1864." *La Revue des Deux Mondes*, November–December 1864, 777–801.

———. "Le président des Etats-Unis, Abraham Lincoln: Souvenirs personnels." *La Revue des Deux Mondes*, May–June 1865, 476–96.

———. *Les Etats-Unis pendant la guerre, 1861–1865*. Paris: G. Baillière, 1866.

Lauzac, Henry. "Son Excellence M. C.-J. Faulkner." In *Galerie historique et critique du XIXe*, 1–18. Paris: Bureau de la Galerie Historique, 1860.

Lemoinne, John. "Le roman de la vie des Noirs en Amérique: Mme. B. Stowe." *La Revue des Deux Mondes*, October–December 1856, 162–87.

Mercier, Alfred. *Du Panlatinisme: Nécessité d'une alliance entre la France et la Confédération du Sud*. Paris: Librairie Centrale, 1863.

Mercier de Lacombe, H. *Le Mexique et les Etats-Unis*. 2nd ed. Paris: E. Dentu, 1863.

Montégut, Emile. "Le roman abolitionniste en Amérique (*Uncle Tom's Cabin* de Harriett Beecher Stowe)." *La Revue des Deux Mondes*, October–December 1852, 155–87.

———. "La question de l'esclavage et la vie des esclaves aux Etats-Unis." *La Revue des Deux Mondes*, March–April 1856, 269–97.

Musson, Eugène. *Lettre à Napoléon III sur l'esclavage aux Etats du Sud, par un créole de Louisiane*. Paris: E. Dentu, 1862.

Napoléon III. "La traite des nègres." In *Napoléon III, sa vie, ses œuvres et ses opinions*, 280. Paris: Armand Le Chevalier Editeur, 1870.

———. *Oeuvres*. Vol. 5. Paris: Plon, Amyot, 1869.

Périer, Casimir. "Du droit maritime à propos du différend anglo-américain." *La Revue des Deux Mondes*, January–February 1862, 421–43.

La politique impériale exposée par les discours et proclamations de l'Empereur Napoléon III depuis le 10 décembre 1848 jusqu'en février 1868. Paris: Plon, 1868.

Reclus, Elisée. "De l'esclavage aux Etats-Unis: I. Le code noir et les esclaves." *La Revue des Deux Mondes*, November–December 1860, 868–901.

———. "De l'esclavage aux Etats-Unis: II. Les planteurs et les abolitionnistes." *La Revue des Deux Mondes*, January–February 1861, 118–54.

———. "Le coton et la crise américaine." *La Revue des Deux Mondes*, January–February 1862, 176–208.

———. "Les Noirs américains depuis la guerre civile des Etats-Unis: I. Les partisans du Kansas et les Noirs libres de Beaufort." *La Revue des Deux Mondes*, March–April 1863, 364–94.

———. "Deux années de la grande lutte américaine." *La Revue des Deux Mondes*, September–October 1864, 555–624.

Reybaud, Louis. "La guerre d'Amérique et le marché du coton." *La Revue des Deux Mondes*, March–April 1865, 189–208.

Verdeil, F. "La disette du coton en Angleterre et les comités de prévoyance." *La Revue des Deux Mondes*, January–February 1863, 211–27.

Newspapers and Periodicals

Le Constitutionnel
Le Courrier du Midi (Toulouse)
L'Echo de Vesone
Le Journal des Débats
Le Monde
Le Moniteur
New York Times
La Patrie

Le Pays
Le Phare de la Loire
La Presse
La Revue des Deux Mondes
Le Siècle
Le Temps
L'Union

SECONDARY SOURCES

Reference Works

Bely, Lucien, Georges-Henri Soutou, Laurent Theis, and Maurice Vaïsse. *Dictionnaire des ministres des Affaires étrangères, 1589–2004.* Paris: Fayard, 2005.

Blaise, Anik, Serge Cosseron, Pierre-Yves Grasset, and Jean Favier. *Chronique de la France.* Bassillac: Chronique, 1995.

Calvo, Carlos. *Dictionnaire manuel de diplomatie et de droit international public et privé.* Clark, N.J.: Lawbook Exchange, 2009.

Clifton, Daniel. *Chronique de l'Amérique.* Paris: Chronique, 1993.

Current, Richard N., Paul D. Escott, Lawrence N. Powell, James I. Robertson, and Emory M. Thomas. *Encyclopedia of the Confederacy.* Vols. 1–4. New York: Simon & Schuster, 1993.

Diccionario Porrúa de historia, biografía y geografía de México. 4th ed. Vol. 2. Mexico City: Porrúa, 1976.

Dictionary Catalog of the Research Libraries, 1911–1971. Vols. 27 and 28. New York: New York Public Library, Astor, Lenox, Tilden Foundations, 1979.

Echard, William E. *Historical Dictionary of the French Second Empire, 1852–1870.* London: Aldwych, 1985.

Findling, John E. *Dictionary of American Diplomatic History.* 2nd ed. Westport, Conn.: Greenwood, 1989.

Frangulis, A. F. *Dictionnaire diplomatique comprenant les biographies de diplomates du Moyen Age à nos jours constituant un traité d'histoire diplomatique.* Vol. 5. Paris: Académie Diplomatique Internationale, 1954.

Hayt, Franz. *Atlas d'histoire.* 27th ed. Brussels: De Boeck-Wesmael, 1994.

Heidler, David S., and Jeanne T. Heidler. *Encyclopedia of the American Civil War: A Political, Social and Military History.* Vol. 1. Santa Barbara, Calif.: ABC-CLIO, 2000.

Lemarchand, Philippe. *Atlas des Etats-Unis: Les paradoxes de la puissance.* Paris: Atlande, 1997.

Long, E. B., and Barbara Long. *The Civil War Day by Day: An Almanac, 1861–1865.* New York: Da Capo, 1971.

Morris, Richard B. *Encyclopedia of American History.* New York: Harper & Row, 1982.

Neely, Mark E. *The Abraham Lincoln Encyclopedia.* New York: McGraw-Hill, 1982.

Nevins, Allan. *The Ordeal of the Union, 1847–1852: Fruits of Manifest Destiny.* New York: Charles Scribner's Sons, 1947.

———. *The Ordeal of the Union, 1852–1857: A House Dividing.* New York: Charles Scribner's Sons, 1947.

———. *Douglas, Buchanan, and Party Chaos, 1857–1859.* 2 vols. New York: Charles Scribner's Sons, 1950.

———. *The Emergence of Lincoln.* 2 vols. New York: Charles Scribner's Sons, 1950.

———. *The War for the Union.* 3 vols. New York: Charles Scribner's Sons, 1950.

Pancradio, Jean-Paul. *Dictionnaire de la diplomatie.* Paris: Dalloz, 2007.

Population of the United States in 1860, Compiled from the Original Returns of the Eighth Census. Bureau of the Census Library. Washington, D.C.: U.S. Government Printing Office, 1864.

Rousseau, Charles. *Droit international public.* Vol. 3, *Les compétences.* Paris: Sirey, 1977.

Salmon, Frédéric. *Atlas historique des Etats-Unis de 1783 à nos jours.* Paris: Armand Colin, 2008.

Tulard, Jean, ed. *Dictionnaire du Second Empire.* Paris: Fayard, 1995.

———. *Dictionnaire Napoléon.* 2 vols. Paris: Fayard, 1999.

U.S. Bureau of the Census. *Country of Birth of the Foreign-Born Population: Fourteenth Census of the United States: Population, 1920.* Vol. 3. Washington, D.C.: U.S. Government Printing Office, 1928.

Yvert, Benoît. *Dictionnaire des ministres de 1789 à 1989.* Paris: Perrin, 1990.

Bibliographic Collections

Bemis, Samuel Flagg. *Guide to the Diplomatic History of the United States (1775–1921).* Washington, D.C.: U.S. Government Printing Office, 1935.

Bibliographie annuelle de l'Histoire de France, du Ve siècle à 1958. Paris: Editions du CNRS, 1956–2007.

Bourachot, Christophe. *Bibliographie critique des mémoires sur le Second Empire (2 décembre 1852–4 septembre 1870).* Paris: Boutique de l'Histoire, 1994.

Echard, William E. *Foreign Policy of the French Second Empire: A Bibliography.* Bibliographies and Indexes in World History 12. Westport, Conn.: Greenwood, 1988.

Fierro, Albert. *Bibliographie analytique des biographies collectives imprimées de la France contemporaine (1789–1985).* Bibliothèque de l'Ecole des Hautes Etudes, 5th section, Sciences Historiques et Philologiques 300. Geneva: Slatkine, 1986.

Freidel, Frank. *Harvard Guide to American History.* Cambridge, Mass.: Belknap Press of Harvard University Press, 1975.

Hatin, Eugène. *Bibliographie historique et critique de la presse périodique française.* Paris: Anthropos, 1965.

Trask, David F., Michael Meyer, and Roger R. Trask. *A Bibliography of United States–Latin American Relations since 1810.* Lincoln: University of Nebraska Press, 1968.

Research Tools

Astorquia, Madeleine, Ulane Bonnel, and Georges Dethan. *Guide des sources de l'histoire des Etats-Unis dans les archives françaises.* Paris: France Expansion, 1976.

Etat numérique des fonds de la correspondance consulaire et commerciale (1793–1901). Paris: Imprimerie Nationale, 1901.

Etat numérique des fonds des affaires diverses et politiques (1815–1896). Vol. 4. Paris: Imprimerie Nationale, 1896.

Inventaire sommaire des archives du département des Affaires étrangères: Mémoires et documents, fonds divers. Paris: Imprimerie Nationale, 1892.

Inventaire sommaire des archives du département des Affaires étrangères: Mémoires et documents, fonds France et fonds divers, sup. Paris: Imprimerie Nationale, 1896.

Leland, Waldo G. *Guide to Materials for American History in the Libraries and Archives of Paris, Archives of the Ministry of Foreign Affairs.* Vol. 2. Washington, D.C.: Carnegie Institution of Washington, 1943.

Woodworth, Stephen E. *The American Civil War: A Handbook of Literature and Research.* Westport, Conn.: Greenwood, 1996.

Published Books and Chapters

Adams, Ephraïm Douglas. *Great Britain and the American Civil War*. 2 vols. New York: Russell & Russell, 1958.

Aldis, Owen F. "Louis Napoléon and the Southern Confederacy." *North American Review* 129 (October 1879): 342–60.

Allain, Jean-Claude, Françoise Autrand, Lucien Bely, Philippe Contamine, Pierre Guillen, Thierry Lentz, Georges-Henri Soutou, Laurent Theis, and Maurice Vaïsse. *Histoire de la diplomatie française*. Introduction by Dominique de Villepin. Paris: Perrin, 2005.

Alvarez, David. "The Papacy in the Diplomacy of the American Civil War." *Catholic Historical Review* 69 (April 1983): 227–48.

Anceau, Eric. *Napoléon III*. Paris: Tallandier, 2008.

———. *L'Empire libéral*. 2 vols. Paris: SPM, 2017.

Annales du centre régional de documentation. Caen: Institut Pédagogique National, 1969.

Ashley, Evelyn. *The Life and Correspondence of Henry John Temple, Viscount Palmerston*. Vol. 2. London: Richard Bentley and Son, 1879.

Avenel, Jean. *La campagne du Mexique (1862–1867): La fin de l'hégémonie européenne en Amérique du Nord*. Paris: Economica, 1996.

Baillou, Jean. *Les affaires étrangères et le corps diplomatique*. Vol. 1, *De l'Ancien Régime au Second Empire*. Paris: CNRS, 1984.

Balace, Francis. *La Belgique et la guerre de Sécession, 1861–1865: Etude diplomatique*. Vol. 1. Paris: Belles Lettres, 1979.

Ball, Douglas B. *Financial Failure and Confederate Defeat*. Urbana: University of Illinois Press, 1991.

Barjot, Dominique. *Histoire économique de la France au XIXe*. Paris: Nathan, 1995.

Barkan, Elliott R. *Immigrants in American History: Arrival, Adaptation, and Integration*. Santa Barbara: ABC-CLIO, 2013.

Barker, Nancy Nichols. "France, Austria and the Mexican Venture (1861–1864)." *French Historical Studies* 3, no. 2 (1963): 224–45.

———. *Distaff Diplomacy: The Empress Eugénie and the Foreign Policy of the Second Empire*. Austin: University of Texas Press, 1967.

Baroche, Madame Jules. *Second Empire: Notes et souvenirs de 16 années (1855–1871)*. Paris: G. Crès, 1921.

Battesti, Michèle. *La marine de Napoléon III: Une politique navale*. Vol. 2. Chambéry, Université de Savoie; Paris: Laboratoire d'histoire et d'archéologie maritime; Vincennes: Service Historique de la Marine, 1997.

Berenson, Edward. *La statue de la Liberté: Histoire d'une icône franco-américaine*. Paris: Armand Colin, 2012.

Beringer, Richard E., Herman Hattaway, Archer Jones, and William N. Still Jr. *Why the South Lost the Civil War*. Athens: University of Georgia Press, 1986.

Bernardy, Françoise. *Flahaut (1785–1870), fils de Talleyrand, père de Morny*. Paris: Perrin, 1974.

———. *Walewski, le fils polonais de Napoléon*. Paris: Perrin, 1976.

Bernath, Stuart L. *Squall across the Atlantic: American Civil War Prize Cases and Diplomacy*. Berkeley: University of California Press, 1970.

Berwanger, Eugene. *The British Foreign Service and the American Civil War*. Lexington: University Press of Kentucky, 2015.

Bigelow, John. *France and the Confederate Navy, 1862–1868*. London: Sampson Low, Harper and Brothers, 1888.

Bigelow, Paultney. "John Bigelow and Napoleon III." *New York History* 13, no. 2 (April 1932): 154–65.

Binder, Frederick Moore. *James Buchanan and the American Empire*. London: Associated University Press, 1994.

Blackburn, George M. *French Newspaper Opinion on the American Civil War*. Contributions in American History 171. Westport, Conn.: Greenwood, 1997.

Blackett, R. J. M. "African Americans, British Public Opinion, and Civil War Diplomacy." In *The Union, the Confederacy, and the Atlantic Rim*, edited by Robert E. May, 83–114. West Lafayette, Ind.: Purdue University Press, 1995.

———. *Divided Hearts: Britain and the American Civil War*. Baton Rouge: Louisiana State University Press, 2001.

Blanchard, Marcel. *Le Second Empire*. 2nd ed. Paris: Armand Colin, 1956.

Blumberg, Arnold. *The Diplomacy of the Mexican Empire, 1863–1867*. Transactions of the American Philosophical Society. Philadelphia: American Philosophical Society, 1971.

Blumenthal, Henry. *A Reappraisal of Franco-American Relations, 1830–1871*. Chapel Hill: University of North Carolina Press, 1959.

———. "Confederate Diplomacy: Popular Notions and International Realities." *Journal of Southern History* 32, no. 2 (May 1966): 151–71.

———. *France and the United States: Their Diplomatic Relations, 1789–1914*. Chapel Hill: University of North Carolina Press, 1970.

Bodelle, Jacques. *Petite(s) histoire(s) des Français d'Amérique*. Toulouse: Mélibée, 2014.

Bonham, Milledge L. *The French Consuls in the Confederate States*. New York: Columbia University Press, 1914.

Bowen, Wayne H. *Spain and the American Civil War*. Columbia: University of Missouri Press, 2011.

Branaa, Jean-Eric. *La constitution américaine et les institutions*. Paris: Ellipses, 1999.

Brasseaux, Carl A., and Katherine Carmines Mooney, eds. *Ruined by This Miserable War: The Dispatches of Charles Prosper Fauconnet, a French Diplomat in New Orleans, 1863–1868*. Translated by Carl A. Brasseaux. Knoxville: University of Tennessee Press, 2013.

Brauer, Kinley J. "British Mediation and the American Civil War: A Reconsideration." *Journal of Southern History* 38, no. 1 (February 1972): 49–64.

Brogan, Hugh. *Longman History of the United States of America*. 4th ed. London: Guild, 1988.

Brown, David. "Palmerston and Anglo-French Relations, 1846–1865." *Diplomacy and Statecraft* 17, no. 4 (December 2006): 675–92.

Browne, William Hand, and Richard Malcom Johnson. *Life of Alexander H. Stephens*. Philadelphia: J. B. Lippincott, 1878.

Bruley, Yves. "Thouvenel." In *Dictionnaire du Second Empire*, edited by Jean Tulard, 1260. Paris: Fayard, 1995.

———. *Le Quai d'Orsay impérial: Histoire du ministère des Affaires étrangères sous Napoléon III*. Paris: A. Pedone, 2012.

———. "Un spectacle des plus intéressants: Les Etats-Unis vus du Quai d'Orsay impérial." In "Napoléon III et les Amériques." Special issue, *Bulletin de l'Académie du Second Empire*, no. 20 (2013): 21–26.

————. *La diplomatie du Sphinx: Napoléon III et sa politique internationale*. Paris: CLD, 2015.

Bruyère-Ostells, Walter. *Napoléon III et le Second Empire: Instants d'histoire*. Paris: Vuibert, 2004.

Bulloch, James D. *The Secret Service of the Confederate States in Europe; or, How the Confederate Cruisers Were Equipped*. London: Bentley and Son, 1883.

Burnett, Lonnie A. *Henry Hotze, Confederate Propagandist: Selected Writings on Revolution, Recognition, and Race*. Tuscaloosa: University of Alabama Press, 2008.

Bury, Patrick. "La carrière diplomatique au temps du Second Empire." *Revue d'histoire diplomatique*, July–December 1976, 277–98.

Callahan, James Morton. *Cuba and International Relations: A Historical Study in American Diplomacy*. Baltimore: Johns Hopkins University Press, 1899.

————. *The Diplomatic History of the Southern Confederacy*. Baltimore: Johns Hopkins University Press, 1901.

————. *American Foreign Policy in Mexican Relations*. New York: Macmillan, 1932.

Campbell, Duncan Andrew. *English Public Opinion and the American Civil War*. Woodbridge, UK: Boydell Press/Royal Historical Society, 2003.

Carroll, Daniel B. *Henri Mercier and the American Civil War*. Princeton, N.J.: Princeton University Press, 1971.

Carteret, Alain. *Napoléon III: Actes et paroles*. Paris: Table Ronde, 2008.

Case, Lynn M. "La France et l'affaire du Trent." *Revue historique*, July–September 1961, 57–86.

————. "La sécession aux Etats-Unis: Un problème diplomatique français en 1861." *Revue d'histoire diplomatique*, October–December 1963, 290–313.

————. *Edouard Thouvenel et la diplomatie du Second Empire*. Translated by Guillaume de Bertier de Sauvigny. Paris: Pedone, 1976.

————, ed. *French Opinion on the United States and Mexico, 1860–1867: Extracts from the Reports of the Procureurs Généraux*. New York: Rice Institute, D. Appleton-Century, 1963.

Case, Lynn M., and Warren F. Spencer. *The United States and France: Civil War Diplomacy*. Philadelphia: University of Pennsylvania Press, 1970.

Catton, Bruce. *La guerre de Sécession*. Paris: Payot, 2002.

Celozzi Baldelli, Pia G. "The Decisions of the Arbitration Commissions." In *Power Politics, Diplomacy, and the Avoidance of Hostilities between England and the United States in the Wake of the Civil War*, 261. Lewiston, N.Y.: Edwin Mellen, 1998.

Charle, Christophe. *Histoire sociale de la France au XIXe siècle*. Paris: Seuil, 1991.

————. *Le siècle de la presse (1830–1939)*. Paris: Seuil, 2004.

Chassaigne, Philippe. *La Grande-Bretagne et le monde de 1815 à nos jours*. Paris: Armand Colin.

Choisel, Francis. "Drouyn de Lhuys." In *Dictionnaire du Second Empire*, edited by Jean Tulard, 444–45. Paris: Fayard, 1995.

Clapp, Margaret. *Forgotten First Citizen: John Bigelow*. Boston: Little, Brown, 1947.

Clary, Françoise, ed. *La destinée manifeste des Etats-Unis au XIXe siècle: Aspects culturels, géopolitiques et idéologiques de la destinée manifeste*. CETAS, Université de Rouen, 2000.

Cleven, N., and N. Andrew. "The Corwin-Doblado Treaty, April 6, 1862." *Hispanic American Historical Review* 17, no. 4 (November 1937): 499–506.

Commager, Henry Steel. *The Blue and the Grey: The Story of the Civil War Told by Participants.* 2 vols. Indianapolis: Bobbs-Merrill, 1950.

Commager, Henry Steele, and Allan Nevins. *Histoire des Etats-Unis.* 8th ed. Translated by Claude LaFarge. Paris: Economica, 1986.

Cortada, James W. *Spain and the American Civil War: Relations at Mid-Century, 1855–1868.* Transactions of the American Philosophical Society 70. Part 4. Philadelphia: American Philosophical Society, 1980.

Crook, Carland E., "Benjamin Théron and French Designs in Texas during the Civil War." *Southwestern Historical Quarterly* 68 no. 4 (1965): 432–54.

Crook, D. P. *The North, the South and the Powers, 1861–1865.* New York: John Wiley and Sons, 1974.

———. *Diplomacy during the American Civil War.* New York: John Wiley and Sons, 1975.

Cullop, Charles P. *Confederate Propaganda in Europe, 1861–1865.* Coral Gables, Fla.: University of Miami Press, 1969.

Cunningham, Michele. *Mexico and the Foreign Policy of Napoléon III.* New York: Palgrave, 2001.

d'Agreval, B. *Les diplomates français sous Napoléon III.* Paris: E. Dentu, 1872.

Dansette, Adrien. *Louis-Napoléon Bonaparte à la conquête du pouvoir: Histoire du Second Empire.* Paris: Hachette, 1961.

———. *Du 2 décembre au 4 septembre: Le Second Empire.* Paris: Hachette, 1972.

Dargent, Raphaël. *Napoléon III.* Paris: Granger, 2009.

Daridan, Jean. *Abraham Lincoln.* Paris: Julliard, 1983.

Darimon, A. *L'opposition libérale sous l'Empire (1861–1863): Souvenirs de l'ancien député de la Seine.* Paris: E. Dentu, 1886.

d'Arjuzon, Antoine. "Napoléon III et l'Angleterre." In *Napoléon III: L'homme, le politique,* 405–14. Paris: Editions Napoléon III, 2008.

Davis, William C. *The Union That Shaped the Confederacy: Robert Toombs and Alexander H. Stephens.* Lawrence: University Press of Kansas, 2001.

de La Mardière, Gérard. "La guerre de Sécession (1861–1865) vue par les Français." Thesis, Université de Paris IV, 1985.

Delamare, George. *L'Empire oublié: L'aventure mexicaine (1861–1867).* Paris: Hachette, 1935.

Delaney, R. W. "Matamoros, Port of Texas during the Civil War." *Southwestern Historical Quarterly* 58, no. 2 (1955): 473–79.

de Leon, Edwin. *Secret History of Confederate Diplomacy Abroad.* Edited by William C. Davis. Lawrence: University Press of Kansas, 2005.

Dethan, Georges. "La politique italienne d'Edouard Thouvenel." *Revue d'histoire diplomatique,* July–December 1976, 265–79.

de Tocqueville, Alexis. *Souvenirs publiés par le comte de Tocqueville.* Paris: Calmann-Lévy, 1893.

———. *De la démocratie en Amérique.* 2 vols. Preface by François Furet. Paris: Garnier, Flammarion, 1981.

Deusen, Glyndon G. *William Henry Seward.* New York: Oxford University Press, 1967.

de Viel Castel, Horace. *Mémoires sur le règne de Napoléon III (1851–1864).* Paris: Robert Laffont, 2005.

d'Harcourt, Bernard, comte. *Les quatre ministères de Drouyn de Lhuys.* Paris: Plon, 1882.

d'Hauterive, Ernest. "Le prince Napoléon: Voyage aux Etats-Unis I." *La Revue de Paris*, September 15, 1933, 241–72.

d'Hericault, Charles. *Maximilien et le Mexique: Histoire des derniers mois de l'Empire mexicain*. Paris: Garnier Frères, 1869.

Dickey, Christopher. *Our Man in Charleston: Britain's Secret Agent in the Civil War South*. New York: Crown, 2015.

Donald, David Herbert. "Died of Democracy." In *Why the North Won the Civil War*, edited by David Herbert Donald, 79–90. New York: Collier, 1960.

———, ed. *Why the North Won the Civil War: Six Authoritative Views on Economic, Military, Diplomatic, Social, and Political Reasons behind the Confederacy Defeat*. New York: Simon & Schuster, 1996.

Donaldson, Jordan, and Edwin J. Pratt. *Europe and the American Civil War*. Boston: Houghton Mifflin, 1931.

Dorigny, Marcel. *Esclavage, résistance et abolition*. Paris: Editions du CTHS, 1999.

d'Ornano, comte. *La vie passionnante du comte Walewski*. Paris: Comtales, 1953.

Doyle, Don H. "Slavery or Independence: The Confederate Dilemma in Europe." In *The U.S. South and Europe: Transatlantic Relations in the Nineteenth and Twentieth Centuries*, edited by Cornelis A. van Minnen and Manfred Berg, 105–24. Lexington: University Press of Kentucky, 2013.

———. *The Cause of All Nations: An International History of the American Civil War*. New York: Basic Books, 2015.

———, ed. *American Civil Wars: The United States, Latin America, Europe, and the Crisis of the 1860s*. Chapel Hill: University of North Carolina Press, 2017.

Droz, Jacques. *Histoire diplomatique de 1648 à 1919*. Preface by Pierre Milza. Paris: Dalloz, 2005.

Dunning, William Archibald. "The French Consuls in the Confederate States." In *Studies in Southern History and Politics*, 4:83–107. New York: Columbia University Press, 1914.

Duroselle, Jean-Baptiste, and Pierre Renouvin. *Introduction à l'histoire des relations internationales*. Paris: Armand Colin, 1991.

Duveau, Georges. *La vie ouvrière sous le Second Empire*. Paris: Gallimard, NRF, 1946.

Eaton, Clement. *A History of the Old South*. New York: Macmillan, 1966.

———. *Jefferson Davis*. London: Macmillan, 1977.

Eichhorn, Niels. "The Rhine River." In *The Civil War as a Global Conflict: Transnational Meanings of the American Civil War*, edited by David T. Gleeson and Simon Lewis, 146–71. Columbia: University of South Carolina Press, 2014.

Ellison, Mary. *Support for Secession: Lancashire and the American Civil War*. Chicago: University of Chicago Press, 1973.

Emsten, Lewis. "Napoléon III et les préliminaires diplomatiques de la guerre civile aux Etats-Unis." *Revue d'histoire diplomatique*, 1905, 336–48.

Encreve, André. *Le Second Empire*. Paris: PUF, 2004.

Evans, Eliot Arthur Powell. "Napoléon III and the American Civil War." PhD diss., Stanford University, 1941.

Evans, Thomas Wiltberger. *Memoirs of Dr. Thomas W. Evans: The Second French Empire*. New York: Appleton, 1905.

Eymeri-Douzans, Jean-Michel, Xavier Bioy, and Stéphane Mouton. *Le règne des entourages, cabinets et conseillers de l'exécutif*. Paris: Presses de la Fondation Nationale des Sciences Politiques, 2015.

Fenton, Bresler. *Napoleon III: A Life*. London: HarperCollins, 1999.

Ferris, Norman B. *Desperate Diplomacy: William H. Seward's Foreign Policy, 1861*. Knoxville: University of Tennessee Press, 1976.

———. *The Trent Affair: A Diplomatic Crisis*. Knoxville: University of Tennessee Press, 1977.

Feyel, Gilles. *La presse en France, des origines à 1944: Histoire politique et matérielle*. Paris: Ellipses, 1999.

Fogel, Robert William. *The Slavery Debates, 1952–1990: A Retrospective*. Baton Rouge: Louisiana State University Press, 2003.

Fohlen, Claude. *L'industrie textile au temps du Second Empire*. Paris: Plon, 1956.

———. "La guerre de Sécession et le commerce franco-américain." *Revue d'histoire moderne et contemporaine* 8 (October–December 1961): 259–70.

———. "Les historiens devant la politique américaine du Second Empire." *Revue d'histoire moderne et contemporaine* 21 (January–March 1974): 127–34.

Fohlen, Claude, Jean Heffer Jean, and François Weil. *Canada et Etats-Unis depuis 1770*. 3rd ed. Paris: PUF, 1997.

Foreman, Amanda. *A World on Fire: An Epic History of Two Nations Divided*. London: Penguin, 2010.

Fournier, Marcel. *Les Français au Québec, 1765–1865: Un mouvement migratoire méconnu*. Villeneuve d'Ascq: Presses Universitaires du Septentrion, 1995.

Fuller, John Douglas Pitts. *The Movement for the Acquisition of All Mexico (1846–1848)*. Baltimore: Johns Hopkins University Press, 1936.

Furet, François, and Wladimir Sachs. "La croissance de l'alphabétisation en France (XVIIIe–XIXe siècle)." *Annales, économies, sociétés, civilisations* 29, no. 3 (1974): pp. 714–37.

Gaulot, Paul. *Rêve d'Empire: La vérité sur l'expédition du Mexique d'après les documents inédits de Ernest Louet*. Paris: Paul Ollendorff, 1889.

Gavronsky, Serge. *The French Liberal Opposition and the American Civil War*. New York: Humanities, 1968.

Gerstein, Daniel. *Securing America's Future: National Strategy in the Information Age*. Santa Barbara, Calif.: Praeger Security International, 2005.

Gienapp, William E. *Abraham Lincoln and Civil War in America: A Biography*. New York: Oxford University Press, 2002.

Girard, Louis. *Napoléon III*. Paris: Fayard, 1986.

Giraudeau, Fernand. *Napoléon III intime*. Paris: Paul Ollendorff, 1895.

Glantz de Lopez Camara, Margarita. "Le Mexique vu par les Français (1847–1867)." Thesis, Université de la Sorbonne, 1958.

Gleeson, David T., and Simon Lewis, eds. *The Civil War as a Global Conflict: Transnational Meanings of the American Civil War*. Columbia: University of South Carolina Press, 2014.

Gouttman, Alain. *La guerre du Mexique (1862–1867): Le mirage américain de Napoléon III*. Paris: Perrin, 2008.

Graebner, Norman A. "Northern Diplomacy and European Neutrality." In *Why the North Won the Civil War*, edited by David Donald, 55–78. New York: Collier, 1996.

Grant, Susan-Mary. *The War for a Nation: The American Civil War*. New York: Routledge, 2014.

Guillaume-Hofnung, Michèle. *La médiation*. Paris: PUF, 2005.

Guiral, Pierre. "Prévost-Paradol (1829–1870): Pensée et action d'un libéral sous le Second Empire." PhD diss., Faculté de Lettres de Paris, 1955.

Hahn, Steven. *A Nation without Borders: The United States and Its World in an Age of Civil Wars, 1830–1910.* New York: Viking, 2016.

Hamon-Jugney, M., and C. Oudin-Doglioni. *Le Quai d'Orsay.* Paris: Nouvelles Editions Latines, 1999.

Hanna, Alfred Jackson, and Kathryn Abbey Hanna. *Napoléon III and Mexico: American Triumph over Monarchy.* Chapel Hill: University of North Carolina Press, 1971.

Hanna, Kathryn Abbey. "The Roles of the South in the French Intervention in Mexico." *Journal of Southern History* 20, no. 1 (1954): 3–21.

Harmon, George P. "Confederate Migrations to Mexico." *Hispanic American Historical Review* 17, no. 4 (November 1937): 458–87.

Hearn, Chester G. *When the Devil Came Down to Dixie: Ben Butler in New Orleans.* Baton Rouge: Louisiana State University Press, 2000.

Heffer, Jean. *Le port de New York et le commerce extérieur américain, 1860–1900.* Paris: Publications de la Sorbonne, 1986.

Henderson, W. O. "The Cotton Famine on the Continent, 1861–1865." *Economic Historical Review* 4, no. 2 (April 1933): 129–56.

Hendrick, Benton J. *Statesmen of the Lost Cause: Jefferson Davis and His Cabinet.* Boston: Little, Brown, 1939.

Hubbard, Charles M. *The Burden of Confederate Diplomacy.* Knoxville: University of Tennessee Press, 1998.

Hugo, Victor. *Actes et paroles.* Vol. 2, *Pendant l'exil.* Paris: J. Hetzel, A. Quantin, 1883.

Huntley, Stephen McQueen. "Les rapports de la France et de la Confédération pendant la guerre de Sécession." Thesis, Université de Toulouse, 1932.

Husley, Fabian Val. "Napoléon III and the Confederacy: A Reappraisal." PhD diss., Mississippi State University, 1970.

Jenkins, Brian. *Britain and the War for the Union.* Vol. 1. Montreal: McGill-Queens University Press, 1974.

———. *Britain and the War for the Union.* Vol. 2. Montreal, McGill-Queens University Press, 1980.

Jenkins, Brian. *Lord Lyons: A Diplomat in an Age of Nationalism and War.* Montreal: McGill-Queens University Press, 2014.

Johannsen, Robert W. *Lincoln, the South, and Slavery: The Political Dimension.* Baton Rouge: Louisiana State University Press, 1991.

Jones, Howard. *Union in Peril: The Crisis over British Intervention in the Civil War.* Chapel Hill: University of North Carolina Press, 1992.

———. *Abraham Lincoln and a New Birth of Freedom: The Union and Slavery in the Diplomacy of the Civil War.* Lincoln: University of Nebraska Press, 1999.

———. *Blue and Gray Diplomacy: A History of Union and Confederate Foreign Relations.* Chapel Hill: University of North Carolina Press, 2010.

———. "Wrapping the World in Fire." In *American Civil Wars: The United States, Latin America, Europe, and the Crisis of the 1860s,* edited by Don H. Doyle, 34–57. Chapel Hill: University of North Carolina Press, 2017.

Karp, Matthew. "King Cotton, Emperor Slavery." In *The Civil War as a Global Conflict: Transnational Meanings of the American Civil War,* edited by David T. Gleeson and Simon Lewis, 36–55. Columbia: University of South Carolina, 2014.

————. *This Vast Southern Empire: Slaveholders at the Helm of American Foreign Policy.* Cambridge, Mass.: Harvard University Press, 2016.

Karsky, Barbara. "Les libéraux français et l'émancipation des esclaves aux Etats-Unis, 1852–1870." *Revue d'histoire moderne et contemporaine,* October–December 1974, 575–90.

Kaspi, André. *Les Américains: Naissance et essor des Etats-Unis (1607–1945).* Paris: Seuil, 1986.

Keegan, John. *The American Civil War: A Military History.* New York: Vintage, 2010.

————. *La guerre de Sécession.* Paris: Perrin, 2011.

Kelly, Patrick J. "The Cat's Paw: Confederate Ambitions in Latin America." In *American Civil Wars: The United States, Latin America, Europe, and the Crisis of the 1860s,* edited by Don H. Doyle, 58–81. Chapel Hill: University of North Carolina Press, 2017.

Knight, Alan. "La pérfida Albión, la batalla de Puebla y la intervención francesa en México." In *Memorias del Simposio International 5 de Mayo,* 247–67. Puebla, Mexico: Colegio de Puebla, 2013.

Konstam, Angus. *Confederate Blockade Runner, 1861–1865.* Oxford: Osprey, 2004.

Korolewicz-Carlton, Richard. "Napoléon III, Thouvenel et la guerre de Sécession." PhD diss., Université de Paris, 1951.

Lacroix, Jean-Michel. *Histoire des Etats-Unis.* Paris: PUF, 1996.

Lagayette, Pierre. *La «destinée manifeste» des Etats-Unis au XIXe siècle: Aspects politiques et idéologiques.* Paris: Ellipses, 1999.

Lahlou, Raphaël. *Napoléon III ou l'obstination couronnée.* Paris: Bernard Giovanangeli, 2006.

Laroulandie, Fabrice. "Ouvriers." In *Dictionnaire du Second Empire,* edited by Jean Tulard, 945–57. Paris: Fayard, 1995.

Leduc, Edouard. *Louis-Napoléon Bonaparte, le dernier empereur.* Publibook, 2010.

Lesueur, Emile. *Le Prince de la Tour d'Auvergne et le secret de l'Impératrice: Contribution à l'histoire diplomatique du Second Empire.* Paris: Eugène Figuière, 1930.

Mahin, Dean B. *One War at a Time: The International Dimensions of the American Civil War.* Washington, D.C.: Potomac, 1999.

Marzagalli, Silvia, and Brunot Marnot. *Guerre et économie dans l'espace atlantique du XVIe au XXe siècles.* Pessac: Presses universitaires de Bordeaux, 2006.

Maurain, Jean. *La politique ecclésiastique du Second Empire de 1852 à 1869.* Paris: Félix Alcan, 1930.

May, Robert E. "The Irony of Confederate Diplomacy: Visions of Empire, the Monroe Doctrine and the Quest for Nationhood." *Journal of Southern History* 82, no. 1 (February 2017): 70–106.

————. *The Southern Dream of a Caribbean Empire, 1854–1861.* Baton Rouge: Louisiana State University Press, 1973.

————, ed. *The Union, the Confederacy, and the Atlantic Rim.* West Lafayette, Ind.: Purdue University Press, 1995.

McCardell, John. *The Idea of a Southern Nation: Southern Nationalists and Southern Nationalism, 1830–1860.* New York: W. W. Norton, 1979.

McCullough David. *The Greater Journey: Americans in Paris.* New York: Simon & Schuster, 2011.

McPherson, James M. *La guerre de Sécession (1861–1865).* Paris: Robert Laffont, 1991.

————. *War on the Waters: The Union and Confederate Navies, 1861–1865.* Chapel Hill: University of North Carolina Press, 2012.

————. "Two Irreconcilable Peoples?" In *The Civil War as a Global Conflict: Transnational Meanings of the American Civil War*, edited by David T. Gleeson and Simon Lewis, 95–97. Columbia: University of South Carolina Press, 2014.

Meade, Robert Douthat. "Judah P. Benjamin and the American Civil War." PhD diss., University of Chicago, 1944.

Médard, Frédéric. "La visite d'Etat de Victoria en août 1855." In "1855, le voyage de Victoria et l'Exposition universelle." Special issue, *Magazine Napoléon III*, no. 25 (December 2013–January 2014): 8–16.

Merli, Frank J. *Great Britain and the Confederate Navy, 1861–1865*. Bloomington: Indiana University Press, 1970.

Miller, Robert Ryal. *Arms across the Border: United States Aid to Juárez during the French Intervention in Mexico*. Transactions of the American Philosophical Society, n.s., no. 39, pt. 6. Philadelphia: American Philosophical Society, 1973.

Milza, Pierre. *Napoléon III*. Paris: Perrin, 2006.

————, ed. *Napoléon III, l'homme, le politique*, colloquium organized by Fondation Napoléon, Collège de France, May 19–20, 2008. Paris: Editions Napoléon III, 2008.

Monaghan, Jay. *Abraham Lincoln Deals with Foreign Affairs: A Diplomat in Carpet Slippers*. Lincoln: University of Nebraska Press, 1945.

Nacouzi, Salwa. "Les créoles louisianais défendant la cause du Sud à Paris: Latinisme contre anglosaxonisme." *Transatlantica* 1 (2002). http://journals.openedition.org/transatlantica/451.

Nagler, Jörg, Don H. Doyle, and Marcus Gräser, eds. *The Transnational Significance of the American Civil War*. [Cham, Switzerland]: Palgrave Macmillan, 2016.

Nean, Hubert. "Le Canada et la guerre de Sécession, 1860–1865." *Revue d'histoire diplomatique*, October–December 1963, 342–61.

Neely, Mark E. *The Fate of Liberty: Abraham Lincoln and Civil Liberties*. New York: Oxford University Press, 1991.

Néré, Jacques. *La guerre de Sécession*. Paris: PUF, 1975.

Noirsain, Serge. *La flotte européenne de la Confédération sudiste*. Brussells: Editions de la CHAB, 2000.

————. *La Confédération sudiste (1861–1865): Mythes et réalités*. Paris: Economica, 2006.

————. *La naissance du C.S.S. Alabama et sa mort à Cherbourg: La guerre de Sécession sur la côte normande*. Paris: Amis de Serge Noirsain, 2015.

————. *La Nouvelle-Orléans française à la veille et jusqu'à la fin de la guerre de Sécession, 1850–1865*. Paris: Amis de Serge Noirsain, 2017.

————. "L'imprudence d'un consul français au Texas. 1862–1863," 1–10. noirsain.net.

Oates, Stephen B. *Lincoln*. Paris: Fayard, 1977.

Olivesi, Antoine, and André Nouschi. *La France de 1848 à 1914*. Paris: Nathan Université, 1997.

Owsley, Frank Laurence. *King Cotton Diplomacy: Foreign Relations of the Confederate States of America*. 2nd ed. Chicago: University of Chicago Press, 1959.

Owsley, Harriet Chappell. "Henry Shelton Sanford and Federal Surveillance Abroad, 1861–1865." *Mississippi Valley Historical Review* 48 (1961): 211–28.

Paleologue, Maurice. *Les entretiens de l'Impératrice Eugénie*. Paris: Plon et Nourrit, 1928.

Pani, Erika. "Juárez vs. Maximiliano: Mexico's Experiment with Monarchy." In *American Civil Wars: The United States, Latin America, Europe, and the Crisis of the 1860s*, edited by Don H. Doyle, 167–84. Chapel Hill: University of North Carolina Press, 2017.

Paolino, Ernest N. *The Foundations of the American Empire: William Henry Seward and U.S. Foreign Policy*. Ithaca, N.Y.: Cornell University Press, 1973.

Parkes, Henry B. *Histoire du Mexique*. Preface by Jacques Soustelle. Paris: Payot, 1971.

Parton, James. *General Butler in New Orleans: History of the Administration of the Department of the Gulf in the Year 1862: With an Account of the Capture of New Orleans, and a Sketch of the Previous Career of the General, Civil and Military*. New York: Mason Brothers, 1864.

Pauli, Herta, and E. B. Ashton. *I Lift My Lamp: The Way of a Symbol*. New York: Appleton-Century-Crofts, 1948.

Pinkney, David H. "France and the Civil War." In *Heard Round the World: The Impact Abroad of the Civil War*, edited by Harold Hyman, 97–144. New York: Knopf, 1969.

Plessis, Alain. *De la fête impériale au mur des fédérés (1852–1871)*. Paris: Seuil, 1976.

Plischke, Elmer. *U.S. Department of State: A Reference History*. Westport, Conn.: Greenwood, 1999.

Poirson, Philippe. *Walewski, fils de Napoléon*. Paris: Balzac, 1943.

Pomeroy, Earl S. "French Substitutes for American Cotton, 1861–1865." *Journal of Southern History* 9, no. 4 (1943): 555–60.

Pradier-Fodere, Paul. "M. Drouyn de Lhuys." *Le Courrier diplomatique*, September 20 and 21, 1871.

Price, Roger. *The French Second Empire: An Anatomy of Political Power*. New Studies in European History. Cambridge: Cambridge University Press, 2001.

Priestley, Charles. "Mort insolite à Paris: Le cas mystérieux de William L. Dayton." French adaptation by Gérard Hawkins. *CHAB News* 42, no. 2 (2014): 31–49.

Ratcliffe, Barrie M. "Cotton Famine." In *Historical Dictionary of the French Second Empire, 1852–1870*, edited by William E. Echard, 144–45. London: Aldwych Press, 1985.

Rémond, René. *Histoire des Etats-Unis*. 18th ed. Que sais-je? Paris: PUF, 1999.

Renouvin, Pierre. *La politique extérieure du Second Empire*, 1:80. Typescript. Paris: Centre de Documentation Universitaire, Turnier et Constans, 1940.

———. *La question d'Extrême-Orient, 1840–1940*. Paris: Hachette, 1946.

———. *Histoire des relations internationales, de 1789 à 1871*. Vol. 2. Paris: Hachette, 1994.

Risley, Ford. *The Civil War: Primary Documents on Events from 1860 to 1865*. Westport, Conn.: Greenwood, 2004.

Roger, Philippe. *L'ennemi américain: Généalogie de l'antiaméricanisme français*. Paris: Seuil, 2002.

Rolle, Andrew F. *The Lost Cause: The Confederate Exodus to Mexico*. Norman: University of Oklahoma Press, 1965.

Sain de Boislecomte, Charles Joseph Edmond. *De la crise américaine et de celle des nationalités en Europe*. Paris: E. Dentu, 1862.

Sainlaude, Stève. "La politique étrangère de la France à l'égard des Etats-Unis d'Amérique de 1839 à 1867." PhD diss., Université Paris Est, 2009.

———. "Alfred Paul: Un diplomate français dans la guerre de Sécession." *Revue d'histoire diplomatique*, no. 1 (2011): 3–15.

———. *La France et la Confédération sudiste (1861–1865): La question de la reconnaissance diplomatique pendant la guerre de Sécession*. Paris: L'Harmattan, 2011.

———. *Le gouvernement impérial et la guerre de Sécession (1861–1865): L'action diplomatique*. Paris: L'Harmattan, 2011.

———. "L'Empereur et la guerre de Sécession: La tentation sudiste?" In "Napoléon III et les Amériques." Special issue, *Bulletin de l'Académie du Second Empire*, no. 20 (2012): 14–21.

———. "Los confederados y la expedición francesa en México, 1862–1865." In *Memorias del Simposio International 5 de Mayo*, 289–332. Puebla, Mexico: Colegio de Puebla, 2013.

———. "France's Grand Design and the Confederacy." In *American Civil Wars: The United States, Latin America, Europe, and the Crisis of the 1860s*, edited by Don H. Doyle, 107–27. Chapel Hill: University of North Carolina Press, 2017.

Sancton, Thomas A. "The Myth of French Worker Support for the North in the American Civil War." *French Historical Studies* 11, no. 1 (Spring 1979): 58–80.

Schefer, Christian. *La grande pensée de Napoléon III: Les origines de l'expédition du Mexique (1858–1862)*. Paris: Marcel Rivière, 1939.

Schoonover, Thomas David. "Confederate Diplomacy and the Texas-Mexican Border (1861–1865)." *East Texas Historical Journal*, no. 11 (Spring 1973): 33–39.

———. "Mexican Cotton and the American Civil War." *Americas (Academy of American Franciscan History)* 30, no. 4 (April 30, 1974): 429–47.

———. "Mexico." In *Encyclopedia of the Confederacy*, 3:1036–37. New York: Simon & Schuster, 1993.

Scroggins, Mark. *Robert Toombs: The Civil Wars of a United States Senator and Confederate General*. Jefferson, N.C.: McFarland, 2011.

Sears, Louis Martin. "A Confederate Diplomat at the Court of Napoléon III." *American Historical Review* 26, no. 2 (January 1921): 255–81.

Seguin, Philippe. *Louis Napoléon le Grand*. Paris: France Loisirs, 1990.

Sexton, Jay. *Debtor Diplomacy, Finance, and American Foreign Relations in the Civil War Era, 1837–1873*. New York: Oxford University Press, 2005.

Seward, Desmond. *Eugénie: The Empress and Her Empire*. Stroud, UK: Sutton, 2004.

Seward, Frederic W. *Reminiscences of a War-Time Statesman and Diplomat, 1830–1915*. New York: G. P. Putnam's Sons, 1916.

Sheldon-Duplaix, Alexandre. "Un marin du Second Empire au service du renseignement: Le capitaine de vaisseau Pigeard et les programmes navals anglais et américains (1856–1869)." *Vincennes: Revue Historique des Armées*, no. 247 (2007): 6–11.

Sim, Gérald. "La présence diplomatique et consulaire française aux États-Unis (1815–1904). Réseaux, acteurs, pratiques, regards." PhD diss., Université de Nantes, 2017.

Smith, Andrew F. *Starving the South: How the North Won the Civil War*. New York: St. Martin's, 2011.

Smith, H. C. *Napoléon III: Les derniers feux de l'Empire*. Paris: Hachette, 1982.

Smith, Jean Edward. *Grant*. New York: Simon & Schuster, 2001.

Smith, William. "Angleterre." In *Dictionnaire du Second Empire*, edited by Jean Tulard, 63–65. Paris: Fayard, 1995.

Soutou, Georges-Henri. "L'Europe de Napoléon III: Un nouvel équilibre, un nouveau système." In *Napoléon III: L'homme, le politique*, 365–85. Paris: Editions Napoléon III, 2008.

Spencer, Warren F. "Drouyn de Lhuys et les navires confédérés en France: L'affaire des navires d'Arman (1863–1865)." *Revue d'histoire diplomatique*, October–December 1963, 314–41.

———. *The Confederate Navy in Europe*. Montgomery: University of Alabama Press, 1983.

———. "Recognition Question." In *Historical Dictionary of the French Second Empire, 1852–1870*, edited by William E. Echard, 541. London: Aldwych, 1985.

Stuart, Graham H. *The Department of State: A History of Its Organization, Procedure, and Personnel*. New York: Macmillan, 1949.

Sy-Wonyu, Aïssatou. *Les Etats-Unis et le monde au XIXe siècle*. Paris: Armand Colin, 2004.

Taillemite, Etienne. *L'histoire ignorée de la marine française*. Paris: Perrin, 1988.

Taylor, John M. *William Henry Seward: Lincoln's Right Hand*. New York: HarperCollins, 1991.

Theis, Laurent. "Entre besoin de repos et désir de gloire (1815–1870)." In *Histoire de la diplomatie française*, 513–616. Paris: Perrin, 2005.

Thistlethwaite, Frank. *The Anglo-American Connection in the Early Nineteenth Century*. Philadelphia: University of Pennsylvania Press, 1959.

Thomas, Benjamin P. *Abraham Lincoln: A Biography*. New York: Alfred A. Knopf, 1952.

Thomas, Emory M. *The Confederate Nation (1861–1865)*. New York: Harper and Row, 1979.

Thouvenel, Louis. *Le secret de l'Empereur: Correspondance confidentielle et inédite échangée entre M. Thouvenel, le duc de Gramont et le général comte de Flahaut (1860–1863)*. Vols. 1 and 2. Paris: Calmann-Levy, 1889.

Tombs, Robert, and Isabelle Tombs. *La France et le Royaume-Uni: Des ennemis intimes*. Paris: Armand Colin, 2012.

Tooley, Mark. *The Peace That Almost Was: The Forgotten Story of the 1861 Washington Peace Conference and the Final Attempt to Avert the Civil War*. Nashville: Nelson, 2015.

Trefousse, Hans L. *Andrew Johnson: A Biography*. New York: W. W. Norton, 1989.

Trimpi, Helen P. *Crimson Confederates: Harvard Men Who Fought for the South*. Knoxville: University of Tennessee Press, 2010.

Tulloch, Hugh. *The Debate on the American Civil War*. Manchester: Manchester University Press, 1999.

Vagnoux, Isabelle. *Les Etats-Unis et le Mexique: Histoire d'une relation tumultueuse*. Paris: L'Harmattan, 2003.

Van Deusen, Glyndon G. *William Henry Seward*. New York: Oxford University Press, 1967.

Van Minnen, Cornelis A. *The U.S. and Europe: Transatlantic Relations in the Nineteenth and Twentieth Centuries*. Lexington: University Press of Kentucky, 2013.

Verhoeven, Joe. "La reconnaissance internationale dans la pratique contemporaine: Les relations publiques internationales." Special issue, *Revue générale de droit international public*, 1975.

Vincent, Bernard. *Lincoln, l'homme qui sauva les Etats-Unis*. Paris: L'Archipel, 2009.

Warren, Gordon H. *Fountain of Discontent: The Trent Affair and the Freedom of the Seas*. Boston: Northeastern University Press, 1981.

Wehberg, Hans. "La guerre civile et le droit international." In *Recueil des cours*, 1:1–126, Paris: Librairie du Recueil Sirey, 1938.

West, Warren Reed. *Contemporary French Opinion on the American Civil War*. Baltimore: John Hopkins University Press, 1924.

Willson, Beckles. *America's Ambassadors to France (1777–1927): A Narrative of Franco-American Diplomatic Relations*. London: John Murray, 1928.

———. *John Slidell and the Confederates in Paris (1862–1865)*. New York: Minton, Balch, 1932.

Woodworth, Steven E. *Davis and Lee at War*. Modern War Studies. Lawrence: University Press of Kansas, 1995.

Wright, Gordon. "Economic Conditions in the Confederacy as Seen by French Consuls." *Journal of Southern History* 7, no. 2 (May 1941): 195–214.

Zorgbide, Charles. *La guerre civile*. Paris: Presses Universitaires de France, 1975.

SELECTED WEBSITES CONSULTED

academie-française.fr

all-biographies.com

annales.org

archive.bu.univ-nantes.fr (SIM1 and SIM3)

bioguide.congress.gov

bnf.fr

books.google.fr

chass.utoronto.ca

civilwarhome.com

clio.fr

consulfrance-sanfrancisco.org

denistouret.fr

diplomatie.gouv.fr

encyclopediaofarkansas.net

en.wikisource.org

1st-hand-history.com

gallica.bnf.fr

gallica2.bnf.fr

gutenberg.org

historicaltextarchive.com

lablaa.org

millercenter.org

napoleon-series.org

napoleontrois.fr

nationalatlas.gov

nndb.com

noirsain.net

nps.gov

presidency.ucsb.edu

query.nytimes.com

raforum.info

servicehistorique.marine.defense.gouv.fr

sfmuseum.org

sre.gob.mx

state.gov

transatlantica.org

tshaonline.org

tsha.utexas.edu

univ-perp.fr

uselectionatlas.org

wapedia.mobi

whitehouse.gov

yale.com

Index

Page numbers in italics refer to illustrations.

"Flight of the Eagle," 215n7

Florida, CSS, 55–56

Forbes, Charles, 81, 228n13

foreign affairs department, U.S., overview of, 7–8, 208n16

Forey, Elie, 51, 111, 253n149

Fort Sumter, 83, 94–95, 162

Fould, Achille, 54, 80

France, le mexique et les Etats confédérés, La (Chevalier), 111

France et la Confédération sudiste, La (Sainlaude), xiii, 10

Frederick VII, 254n167

freeboots, 18, 23, 115, 117, 118

Fremont, John, 122, 131

French nationals: about, 15, 82–83, 154; as business targets, 88–89; Civil War participation of, 184–85, 254–55n3; consuls and, 8, 15; enlistment of, 89–90, 231n99; neutrality and, 15, 21; slavery and, 104

Gauldrée Boilleau, Charles Henri Philippe de, 173, 233n155

General Rusk (ship), 73

Geneva arbitral tribunal, 66–67, 225n42

Geofroy, François Henri Louis de, 173, 213n78, 213n80, 250n53, 255n13

Georgia, CSS, 56, 58

Gladstone, William, 86, 218n71

Gloire (warship), 63

Gorchakov, Alexander, 209n5

gouvernement impérial et la guerre de Sécession, Le (Sainlaude), xii–xiii, 10

grain crisis, 156

Grand Design: background and overview of, xii, xiii–xiv, 110–13, 188, 236n1; Confederacy charm and sincerity and, 113–16, 237n16; Confederacy expansionism and, 116–22, 124–25, 239nn63–64; neutrality of Maximilian and, 122–24; Union and, 179

Grant, Ulysses S., 50, 81, 166, 256n20

Gros, Jean-Baptiste Louis, 46–49, 50, 220n134, 220n138

Guerra de Reforma, xii

Guizot, François, 4, 62, 69

Gwin, William L., 237n16

habeas corpus suspension, 93, 94

Hammond, James H., 140

Hampton Roads Conference, 40, 116

Helper, Hinton, 101

Hotze, Henry, 81, 82

Hugo, Victor, 2, 100

Hunter, Robert, 91, 213n84

immigration of former Confederates to Mexico, 123–24

Impending Crisis of the South, The (Helper), 101

Index (newspaper), 113

India, 151, 246n108

Isthmus of Tehuantepec, 117, 118

Italy, 6, 71, 181, 254nn164–65

Jackson, Andrew, 215n9, 251n89

Jackson, T. J. "Stonewall," 163, 165, 216n39

Japan, 181–82

Joinville, prince de, 185, 255n4

Journal des Débats, Le (newspaper): about, 88, 210n30; Confederacy and, 49, 94, 95–96, 119, 122; cotton and, 178, 248n156; mediation and, 34, 36, 37–38; neutrality and, 18; Union support of, 87

Juárez, Benito, 51, 72, 113, 115, 116

Kearsarge, USS, 21, 56, 222n192

Kenner, Duncan, 108, 116

"King Cotton" slogan, 140

Laboulaye, Edouard, xv, 88

La Gravière, Edmond Jurien de, 72

Lanen, Louis Charles Arthur, 114, 214n87

Lannes, Auguste Louis Napoléon, 218n94

La Soledad convention, 51, 72, 144

Latin America, 5, 31, 186

La Tour d'Auvergne, Henri de, 68, 74, 210n28, 250n53

Lee, Robert E., 34, 50, 52, 163, 166, 189

Leopold, King, 36, 74

Limayrac, Paulin, 138

Lincoln, Abraham: death of, 97–98; determination of, 171–73; election of, 130–31, 136, 161; Emancipation Proclamation and, 103–4, 108, 139;

French opinion of, 81, 85, 228n16; habeas corpus and, 93; reelection of, 93–94, 95, 173–75; slavery and, 102–3

Lindsay, William Shaw: Britain negotiations and, 244n32; Confederacy recognition and, 42–47, 49–50, 219n114; Union blockade and, 143–44, 145, 244n32

literacy in France, 254n1

Lorencez, Charles de, 51, 179, 199, 200

Lostende, Edouard Henri Mercier de, 209n19

Louisiana, 82–83, 131

Louis-Philippe, King, 60, 62, 68, 194, 224, 255n4

Louis-Philippe government, 29, 215n19, 222n163

Lyons, Richard: about, 19, 211n44; entente cordiale and, 63, 68, 71; neutrality and, 15, 209–10n10, 212n56

Manet, Edouard, 21

manifest destiny, 4, 28

Mann, Ambrose Dudley, 123

maritime affairs: neutrality and, 16, 21–25, 212n59; trade and, 63, 75, 153, 157, 215n9

Martinique, 21, 236n72

Mason, James Murray: about, 18, 219n112; Confederacy recognition and, xiii, 43, 44, 45, 49, 220n128; *Trent* affair and, 69, 70, 211n47

Mason, John Young, 31, 215n16

Matamoros, 114–15, 179

Maximilian of Habsburg, *112*; as emperor of Mexico, 114–15, 123–24, 188, 189, 237n16; selection of as emperor of Mexico, xii, 73, 111

McClellan, George B., 34, 173–75

McLane-Ocampo Treaty, 117–18

mediation attempts, French, 32–42; Britain and, 65–66, 70–71; first, 34–38, 40–42, 218n95, 218n98; Mercier's, 32, 33–34, 40; second, 38–40, 42

Méjan, Eugène, 82, 89, 95, 171, 209n1, 229n39, 249n25

merchant marines, 155

Mercier, Henri: about, 19, 211n44; Confederate expansionism and, 118,

119; Confederate support of, 81, 83–84; Confederate warships and, 55; cotton and, 143, 146, 147; entente cordiale and, 63–64, 68; fear of conflict with North and, 177–78; mediation and, 32, 33–34, 40, 217n49; neutrality and, 20–21, 212n56; power imbalance and, 164, 165, 171, 173; slavery and, 103, 104–5, 107; on Slidell, 92; South's secession and, 130, 131, 132; Union preservation and, 95, 137–38; war outcome and, 133, 134, 176

Mexico: Confederate warships and, 58; cotton and, 150–51; expansionism and, 187–88; fear of conflict with North and, 179–81, 182–83, 189, 253n149; foreign debt of, xii, 72–73; Napoléon III and, 31, 51–52, 186, 222n164, 253n149; neutrality of Maximilian in, 122–24; U.S. war against, 3–4. *See also* Grand Design

military capacity of North, 167–69

minister plenipotentiary, about, 7–8

Ministry of Foreign Affairs, French: about, 6, 7, 208nn16–17; war outcome and, 132–35. *See also specific issues regarding*

Mocquard, Jean-François, 46, 53, 57, 220n132

Moerenhout, Jacques-Antoine, 238n40

Moniteur, Le (newspaper): Confederacy and, 47, 50, 118; mediation and, 37, 38; Seward and, 211n52; trade and, 153

Monroe Doctrine, 5, 110, 115–16, 188

Montalembert, comte de, 81, 228n13

Montholon, Charles de: about, 212n66; mediation and, 37, 42; power imbalance and, 160, 248n10, 248n12; slavery and, 106; Union blockade and, 143; U.S. economy and trade and, 154, 155, 156

Moore, Thomas, 89

Morny, Charles de, 6, 57, 80, 210n18

Napoléon, Prince: divided union and, 135; on Lincoln and Seward, 228n16; Mercier and, 19; power imbalance and, 166–67, 168; racism of, 236n73; Union support of, 87

Napoléon I, 2, 25, 208n2, 208n4, 215n7

Napoléon III: about, 2–3, 5, *30*, 208n2,

208n4, 208n7, 208n14; ambitions of, 1–2;
assassination attempt on, 62, 224n9;
Confederacy recognition and, 9, 42–43,
45, 47, 49–52, 67, 218–19n101, 219n106;
Confederacy support of, 79–80, 109,
133, 227n2; Confederate expansionism
and, 122; Confederate warships and,
52–53, 54–55, 57; Drouyn de Lhuys and
Thouvenel and, 7; entente cordiale and,
61, 62, 64, 70, 74; fear of conflict with
North and, 180; foreign policy making of,
5–6, 175, 187; Grand Design and, xii–xiv,
31, 51–52, 73, 110, 111, 114, 123–24, 222n164;
illnesses of, 186–87, 255n6; Japan and,
182; Latin America and, 5, 31; Lincoln
reelection and, 173–75; mediation and,
32, 34–35, 36–37, 39, 41–42, 215n18;
neutrality and, 17; power imbalance and,
167–68; press and, 184; slavery and, 101,
102, 106, 107–8; trade and, 154, 156; Union
blockade and, 25, 143–45, 214n90; views
of U.S. of, 3–5, 28, 29–31, 186–87. *See also*
Bonaparte, Louis-Napoléon
Napoleonic Code Article 21, 15, 21, 212n59
Napoléonic Wars, 215n9
nationalism, Confederate, 96, 116
navies: Confederate, 52–55; French, 168,
251n71; U.S., 24, 168, 178
neutrality of France, 13–27, 170; background
and overview of, 13–14, 25–27;
belligerency rights and, 14–18; breaches
of, 82; Confederate warships and, 52, 53,
55, 56–58; diplomatic representation and,
18–21, 65; maritime affairs and, 16, 21–25,
212n59
New York port, 155
Niboyet, Paulin Jean Alexandre, 227n2
"Note for the Minister on the Possible
Consequences of a French Intervention
in the Anglo-American Conflict"
(Montholon), 160, 179
Nullification Crisis, 129

Oak Manor Plantation, *80*
Opinion Nationale, L' (newspaper), 54, 55,
82, 87, 88
Oriental Crisis, 61, 63, 223n2

Orizaba, convention of, 72
Orsini, Felice, 62, 224n9
Osaca (corvette), 53, 54
O'Sullivan, John, 4
Overland campaign, 166
Owsley, Frank, Laurence, 220n139, 221n141

Palmerston, Lord: Confederacy difficulties
and, 89–90; Confederacy recognition
and, 44, 45, 47–48; entente cordiale and,
61, 62, 63, 66, 68–69, 73; mediation and,
37; Union blockade and, 144
Pan-Latinism, 83
parallel diplomacy, 187
Paris, comte de, 185
Pastry War of 1838, 51, 221–22n163
Patrie, La (newspaper), 82, 88, 210n30,
229n56
Paul, Alfred: about, 20, 209n20;
Confederacy criticism of, 91, 93–94,
95, 101, 102; Confederacy recognition
and, 50; Confederacy support of,
80, 84, 228–29n37; cotton and, 146,
148; as a diplomat, xiii, xiv, 161, 166,
249n19; divided Union and, 135–36, 171;
enlistment of French nationals and,
89–90; Lincoln's reelection and, 174;
mediation and, 35, 39; Mexico and, 114,
238n17, 255n12; power imbalance and,
162–67, 169, 170, 171–72, 173, 250n53;
South's secession and, 130, 131, 161–62;
trade and, 154, 155; war outcome and,
132–33
Pays, Le (newspaper), 36, 82, 88, 210n30
perpetual struggle, 137, 176
Perry, Matthew C., 181
Persigny, Victor de, 57, 80, 221n146, 222n183,
227n8
Peru, xi, 54
Phare de la Loire, Le (newspaper), 87
Phnom Penh speech (de Gaulle), 186, 255n5
Pickett, John T., 115, 211n49
Pigeard, Charles, 168, 251n69
pirates, 18, 23, 115, 117, 118
Pius IX (pope), 41
Poland, 50, 72, 169, 220n138, 226n92
Polignac, Camille de, 185, 255n4

populations of U.S., 160, 235n49, 248n2
Port Hudson, Louisiana, 50, 165
ports, French: Confederate ship repair at, 55–58, 222n193; shipbuilding at, 53–55
Portz, Nicholas, 209n20
postwar period, 175–77, 186, 189
power imbalance of North and South, 159–75; Confederate need for assistance and, 169–70; French public opinion and, 172–75; military capacity and, 167–69; overview of, 159; Paul's views on, 162–67, 250n53; Union's determination and, 170–72
press, French: Confederacy criticism by, 94–96, 97; Confederacy recognition and, 47, 49–50; Confederate expansionism and, 119, 122; Confederate support of, 85; Confederate warships and, 54, 55; cotton and, 142, 148, 149, 152, 246n95, 248n156; divided Union and, 136–37; entente cordiale and, 67; freedom of, 184; on Lincoln, 97–98, 172, 174–75; Louisiana and, 82–83; mediation and, 34, 37–38, 39; Mexico and, 179; neutrality and, 18, 210n30; postwar and, 176; power imbalance and, 169, 172, 173, 251n81; on slavery, 100, 101, 103–4, 105–6, 117, 234n19, 236n79; South secession and, 131–32; trade and, 153, 156–57; Union and, 87–88, 138, 178; war outcome and, 133–34. *See also specific newspapers*
Preston, William, 123
Prévost-Paradol, Lucien-Anatole, 81, 86, 87, 228n13, 251n81
privateering, 18, 22, 23, 26
propaganda: Southern, 79, 82, 83, 86, 93, 94, 96; Union, 82, 120
protectionism, 84, 87, 152
Prussia, 54, 72, 254n155, 254n167
public opinion: French, 82, 86, 100, 184, 230n73; Northern, 172–75; Southern, 93–94
public works projects, 152, 157
Puebla, Mexico, 51, 52, 114, 179, 221n162

Quai d'Orsay, 6. *See also* Ministry of Foreign Affairs, French

rail networks, 152, 155, 160, 248n12
Rappahannock affair, 55–58, 59
Rémond, René, 186
reparations from France, 29, 215n9
Republicans, xiv, 38, 103, 122, 173, 175
Revolutionary War, American, 3, 39, 186
Revue des Deux Mondes, La (newspaper), 87, 88, 119, 210n30, 234n13, 246n108
Reynaud, Aimé, 24, 213n83
Roebuck, John A., 45–47, 49–50, 52, 220n134
Roebuck affair, 45–50, 52
Romania, 138
Romero, Matias, 237n16, 256n20
Rost, Pierre, 20, 64, 92, 214n88
Rouher, Eugène: Confederate warships and, 53, 54; cotton and, 141, 150; Grand Design and, 110, 236n1; Lincoln and, 97; Union blockade and, 213n79
Russell, John: Confederacy recognition and, 44, 46–49, 220n134, 220n138; entente cordiale and, 63–64, 66, 68, 69, 70, 71; Union blockade and, 25, 144
Russia: French mediation and, 31, 35, 38; Poland and, 72, 169, 220n138, 226n92

Sain de Boislecomte, André Ernest Olivier: about, 229n54; divided Union and, 136, 176; South secession and, 85, 96, 120, 129
Sainte-Croix, Pierre Joseph Belligny de, 213n81, 230n89
Saligny, Dubois de, 118, 120, 221n161
Sand, George, 100
Sanford, Henry Shelton: about, 18–19, 211n35; cotton and, 147–48; support of Union by, 20, 82; trade and, 154
San Francisco (corvette), 53, 54
San Jacinto, USS, 69, 212n60
Sartiges, Eugène de: about, 215–16n25; Civil War prediction of, 102; Confederate expansionism and, 117, 118, 120, 121; entente cordiale and, 63; mediation and, 32; power imbalance and, 160–61; on Slidell, 92; trade and, 155
Schoelcher, Victor, 99
Schoelcher decree, 104, 107
Schurz, Carl, 239n63

secession of South: expansionism and, 118–20, 124; French support of, 84–85; French view of, 129–32, 136–37, 161–62, 249n22; neutrality and, 63–64

Seven Days' Battles, 34, 165

Seward, William: about, 91; Confederacy recognition and, 17, 50, 177, 253n135; entente cordiale and, 73; French mediation and, 32, 33, 34, 40; Mexico and, 120–21, 182–83; neutrality and, 20, 23; *Trent* affair and, 70; war outcome and, 133, 171

Shanghai (corvette), 53, 54

Shenandoah (ship), 67

Sherman, William, 173, *174*

Siècle, Le, 37, 87, 88, 234n19

silk, 84, 153–54, 155

Simplot, Alexander, *141*

slave revolt, fear of, 102, 108

slavery: abolition of (*see* abolition of slavery); as cause of Civil War, 102–3; Confederate expansionism and, 119, 120; French hatred of, 87, 99, 185; as marginal subject, 107–9; weakening of the South from, 100–102

slave trade, 101, 119, 234n13, 239nn63–64

Slidell, John: about, 20, 92, 211n47, 211n50; Confederacy recognition and, 42–44, 45, 48–49, 51, 85–86, 219n103, 219n112, 219n115; Confederate warships and, 52–53, 54, 56–58; cotton and, 145, 146, 149, 151; entente cordiale and, 64, 67, 73; French focus on Europe and, 181; French mediation and, 34–35, 36; French support of Confederacy and, xii, 81, 82; Mexico and Confederate expansionism and, 119, 120, 122, 123; slavery and, 107, 108; *Trent* affair and, 69–70; Union blockade and, 144, 214n88, 214n90; war outcome and, 132, 134, 135

Souchard, Jules Etienne, 167, 226n75

South Carolina, 85, 90, 102, 131, 135, 235n49

Spain, xi, xii, 24, 58, 237n11

Spanish marriages affair, 62, 223–24n3

Spencer, Warren F., xiii, 9–10, 223n1

Sphinx (battleship), 53, 54, 55

states' rights, 85, 135, 137

Statue of Liberty, 97

Stoeckl, Edouard, 209n5

Stone Fleet, 143

Stonewall (battleship), 55

Stowe, Harriet Beecher, 100

Syria, 71

Tabouelle, René, 237

Talleyrand, 210n18

tariffs, 84, 85, 138, 155, 242n70

Temps, Le (newspaper): circulation of, 88; Confederacy and, 49, 94, 221n150; cotton and, 243n1, 246n95; on Lindsay motion, 219n114; mediation and, 34, 36, 38; on Mercier, 211n44; neutrality and, 18; on slavery, 236n79; Union support of, 87

Texas, 3, 113, 237n15

textile industry, 140, 141–42, 149, 150–52, 246–47n113, 247n117

Théron, Benjamin, 235n46, 237n15

Thiers, Adolphe, 61

Thirteenth Amendment, 106

Thouvenel, Edouard: about, 6, 7, 12, 186–87, 208n10; Confederacy criticism of, 87, 89, 91, 92, 101; Confederacy recognition and, 43–44, 178, 219n107–8; Confederate expansionism and, 121–22; cotton and, 142–43, 146, 150; entente cordiale and, 63–65, 66, 67, 68–70, 71, 75; mediation and, 33, 34, 35, 37, 41, 217n49; Mexico and, 179, 181, 254n164; neutrality and, 13, 14–15, 20, 23, 25–27, 82, 212n72; power imbalance and, 160, 167, 172, 173; praise for Paul by, 166; slavery and, 107; South's secession and, 132; trade and, 153, 154, 156; Union blockade and, 145; war outcome and, 133, 134–35, 138–39, 176

Times (London), 49, 216n28

tobacco, 89, 149, 231n93

Toombs, Robert, 91, 115

"Toussaint Louverture" syndrome, 105

trade: Confederate, 114; cotton, 140, 141, 142, 150, 151, 243n1, 246n108; between Europe and America, 22, 23; with the